(*continued on back*)

THE PSYCHOLOGY
OF UNDERACHIEVEMENT

THE PSYCHOLOGY OF UNDERACHIEVEMENT

DIFFERENTIAL DIAGNOSIS AND DIFFERENTIAL TREATMENT

HARVEY P. MANDEL, Ph.D.
SANDER I. MARCUS, Ph.D.

WILEY

A WILEY-INTERSCIENCE PUBLICATION

JOHN WILEY & SONS

New York • Chichester • Brisbane • Toronto • Singapore

This publication is designed to provide accurate and
authoritative information in regard to the subject
matter covered. It is sold with the understanding that
the publisher is not engaged in rendering legal, accounting,
or other professional service. If legal advice or other
expert assistance is required, the services of a competent
professional person should be sought. *From a Declaration
of Principles jointly adopted by a Committee of the
American Bar Association and a Committee of Publishers.*

Library of Congress Cataloging in Publication Data:

Mandel, Harvey P.
  The psychology of underachievement: differential diagnosis and
differential treatment/by Harvey P. Mandel & Sander I. Marcus.
    p. cm.—(Wiley series on personality processes)
    Bibliography: p.
    Includes indexes.
    ISBN 0-471-84855-7
    1. Underachievers—Psychology.   2. Difference (Psychology)
3. Performance.   4. Personality.   I. Marcus. Sander I.   II. Title.
III. Series.
[DNLM: 1. Underachievement.   BF 698.9.A3 M271]
BF697.M24 1988
155.2'3—dc19
DNLM/DLC
for Library of Congress   87-37127
                                                              CIP

Printed in the United States of America

10 9 8 7 6 5 4 3 2

To the memory of
Carole Methot

Series Preface

This series of books is addressed to behavioral scientists interested in the nature of human personality. Its scope should prove pertinent to personality theorists and researchers as well as to clinicians concerned with applying an understanding of personality processes to the amelioration of emotional difficulties in living. To this end, the series provides a scholarly integration of theoretical formulations, empirical data, and practical recommendations.

Six major aspects of studying and learning about human personality can be designated: personality theory, personality structure and dynamics, personality development, personality assessment, personality change, and personality adjustment. In exploring these aspects of personality, the books in the series discuss a number of distinct but related subject areas: the nature and implications of various theories of personality; personality characteristics that account for consistencies and variations in human behavior; the emergence of personality processes in children and adolescents; the use of interviewing and testing procedures to evaluate individual differences in personality; efforts to modify personality styles through psychotherapy, counseling, behavior, therapy, and other methods of influence; and patterns of abnormal personality functioning that impair individual competence.

IRVING B. WEINER

Fairleigh Dickinson University
Rutherford, New Jersey

Preface

This book examines the differences among various personality types of underachievers. Although we focus primarily on academic underachievers in high school and college, the theories, descriptions, research, and therapeutic modalities are applicable to adults in their work lives.

As psychologists, our interest in underachievement extends back to our graduate student days in the late 1960s. Since that time, we have spent the better part of our professional careers diagnosing and counseling underachievers, designing and carrying out research, and training others in education and psychology to help those who underachieve.

Our perspective emphasizes the need for a workable theory, experimental and empirical research, and expert clinical practice. Our goal in this book is to emphasize equally this wide spectrum of concerns. Initially we simply wanted to summarize this perspective in a form useful to professionals in education, psychology, and psychiatry. However, the unwieldy and inconclusive nature of the research literature and the lack of consistent and effective theories and counseling methodologies soon became an additional impetus to expand our objectives. Our new goal was to provide an overall perspective on the relationship between personality and underachievement, while at the same time to address the specific concerns of researchers, theoreticians, clinicians, and educators.

For researchers, we trust that we have provided at least a well-outlined and workable summary of a voluminous and often contradictory literature. In presenting and adapting well-known theories, clarifying less well-known ones, and adding a few modest notions of our own, we hope that we have provided theoretical models which link research and clinical practice.

For the clinician and educator, our models are solidly in the mainstream of diagnostic and therapeutic theory and practice. We have tried to clarify by discussion and example the various personality types of underachievers so that the practitioner will be able to easily recognize each and understand the rationale for differing treatment approaches.

Excluding the Introduction and Part V, Conclusions, our book is divided into four major sections covering research (both others' and our own), theory, and clinical practice. While we are explicit about differential treatment, our major goal has been to examine the process of differential diagnosis, and to provide a model that is consistent with the previous literature, theoretically sound, useful to the practicing clinician, and comprehensive enough to stimulate further research and training.

HARVEY P. MANDEL

SANDER I. MARCUS

Toronto, Ontario, Canada
Chicago, Illinois
March 1988

Acknowledgments

The authors would like to thank the many students and their families who participated in all of the research and clinical work. Without their cooperation and openness, the ideas and insights in this book would not have been possible.

We deeply appreciate the guidance and direction provided by Nancy Colbert, who from the beginning of this project understood the value of our work and encouraged us to fill in the gaps in our thinking.

Carole Methot's expertise in research design and statistics, as well as her excitement about the field of psychology, has contributed to many key studies. Her untimely death robs us all of a knowledgeable, enthusiastic, and committed colleague.

Through her diligence and thoroughness our library research assistant, Barbara Young made it possible for us to spend most of our time organizing and writing the literature review. The difficulties in coauthoring a text by authors living in different countries were largely overcome through the use of two Apple computers. Without the assistance of Hart Hillman of Apple, Canada, we would likely still be typing the manuscript.

The creation of the Institute on Achievement and Motivation of York University, through the generous support of the Counselling Foundation of Canada and its Executive Director, Elizabeth McTavish, makes possible the continuation of counseling, training, and research on underachievement.

The efforts of present and past undergraduate and graduate students and colleagues at York University in Toronto and the Illinois Institute of Technology in Chicago are too numerous to be delineated here. Their many contributions have been substantial.

We would like to give special thanks to Dr. Barry Jackson, Chief Psychologist of the Durham County Board of Education, and the high school principals and teaching staff of the Durham Board for continuing support and their understanding of the value of longitudinal research. A special debt of gratitude is owed Dr. Marjorie Perkins and the North York Board of Education, for their concern about multicultural and racial issues in underachievement, and for their support of our research on such sensitive issues.

Several of our colleagues have contributed through their comments on earlier drafts of the manuscript. In particular, we would like to thank Drs. Morris Eagle and Norman Endler of the Department of Psychology at York

University, and Dr. Howard Marcovitch, psychologist for the Scarborough Board of Education, for their valuable suggestions.

We know we have been fortunate to have John Wiley and Sons as our publisher. Both Herb Reich, Editor, and Judith Overton, Editorial Secretary, have given us expert guidance and support.

Lastly, we deeply appreciate the patience and support of our families, especially Chris, Ellen, and Kathy (in Chicago), and Dorothy (in Toronto), who have put up with our endless research meetings and writing sessions away from home.

H.P.M.

S.I.M.

Contents

THE PSYCHOLOGY
OF UNDERACHIEVEMENT

CHAPTER 1

Introduction: Definition of Underachievement

In the middle 1600s, Anton van Leeuwenhoek used the newly invented microscope to examine some ordinary substances, including a drop of water. We do not know what he expected to see when he closed one eye and peered into that early microscope; perhaps he expected to find some sort of gel-like flow or strands of translucent filaments. More likely, he expected to find nothing at all, but he must have been astounded at what he beheld: a living sea of moving particles and rounded, odd-shaped creatures, seeming miniatures of jellyfish and the most primitive of insects. And with that, what had been considered the ordinary, dull, boring drop of water became instead the teeming, complex world of microorganisms that has intrigued the human mind ever since.

In the same way, the phenomenon this book examines—the relationship between personality and underachievement—is, on the surface, as ordinary as a drop of water before van Leeuwenhoek's discovery. Underachievement, after all, has been common to every educational system throughout history and until this century has been given scant attention. Underachievers were the unmentioned refuse of educational systems until the rise of psychological and educational testing early in this century. Even in the United States, it has only been with the push of some national priority such as the space race in the 1950s and 1960s that the fields of education and psychology, fueled by federal financial and research machinery, have set as a primary goal the examination and remediation of underachievement.

Our first task here is to define underachievement. It does not take long to recognize, however, that one cannot adequately define the opposite of something until one defines that "something." And so, one must ask the question, "What is achievement?"

Dictionary definitions of the term *achievement* include the idea of accomplishment. For example, the *American Heritage Dictionary* defines *achieve* as "to accomplish; do or finish with success. To attain or get with effort, as through exertion, skill, practice, or perseverance" (*American Heritage Dictionary of the English Language,* 1973, pp. 10–11). Chaplin's *Dictionary of Psychology* (1975, pp. 5–6) also stresses the ideas of accomplishment and attainment with effort and adds the idea of a "specified level" of success

1

or attainment, "as evaluated by teachers, by standardized tests, or by a combination of both." Similar definitions can be found in almost any other dictionary.

One notices that each of these definitions explicitly or implicitly embraces the notion of energy expended to conquer difficulties, of effort made to overcome obstacles, or of struggle and perseverance to attain a desired goal. This implies the idea that achievement represents an activity that is "above and beyond the call of duty," not the mundane level of accomplishment that is simply expected in the ordinary course of things. Particularly in the academic world, where the concept of achievement is used most often, achievement is often linked with what is ordinarily expected, what is average. In this sense, the term *accomplishment* is perhaps closer to the term educators, counselors, and psychologists mean when they say *achievement*. Ideally, persons called *achievers* should perhaps be called *accomplishers,* or those who accomplish what is expected, while the term *achievers* should be reserved for that group usually referred to as *high achievers* or *overachievers*.

In the definition of achievement, a second notion is that the level of accomplishment is that "evaluated" by teachers, tests, and so forth. In other words, any but the most idiosyncratic definition of achievement must also depend upon value judgments, opinions, and standards external to the achiever. Achievement, in short, is in the eye of the person beholding the achiever.

It follows, then, that underachievement is likewise a matter of somewhat arbitrary definition. The point at which a certain level of accomplishment changes from being called achievement to underachievement varies from one grade to another, one school system to another, one teacher to another, and even one student to another, and will not only be a matter of widely accepted definition, but will be greatly influenced by the particulars of setting, individuals, and situation. The student from a farm family who sees his future as taking over the farm (which may have little to do with his academic education) or the student whose energy is going into a thriving small business may both be considered as underachievers according to their schools, but in their own minds these students may be achieving in the areas necessary for success in their future careers.

While this relative notion of the concept of underachievement is not new, our intent here is neither to provide a new utopian definition of underachievement nor to launch into a critique of the old, but rather to point out that any definition of underachievement is tied logically to the definition of achievement on which it is based. In fact, definitions of underachievement that have been used specifically in psychology and education have been based on entirely different premises. For example, most of the earlier studies categorized underachievers solely on the basis of the subjective opinions of teachers and others. Another traditional definition of underachievement is based on the difference between past and present academic achievement as measured by grade point averages (GPA). A more recent method is to define underachievement as the discrepancy between two standardized measures:

intellectual capacity (e.g., IQ) and scores on standardized achievement tests (e.g., the Stanford Achievement Tests, the Wide Range Achievement Test, or the Metropolitan Achievement Test). Perhaps the most widely used is the discrepancy between standardized measures of intellectual capacity and academic achievement as measured by GPA. The choice of definition may lead to entirely different categorizations of students, their test results, and interpretations of data. The overall effect is a body of literature which is difficult to integrate. Yet there are problems in accepting any one of these definitions, because each has its own shortcomings.

To define underachievement based on subjective opinion invites the potential for error and abuse based on personal bias. It is also nonstandardized and statistically unreliable. While a comparison of current with previous GPA is an obvious and logical manner of defining who is an underachiever, it does not allow for ability factors. For example, a low-ability student whose grammar school grades are inflated because of his or her pleasant personality will receive lower high school grades, not because of underachieving, but because the high school grades are a more accurate reflection of that student's ability. Discrepancy between two standardized measures (e.g., IQ and an achievement test) as an index of underachievement does not incorporate any direct measure of academic performance (primarily GPA), even though it has the advantage of utilizing reliable and objective measures (Kowitz, 1965). There are also variations in errors of measurement (Morrow, 1970). The differential between ability and performance measures (e.g., IQ and GPA, respectively) would appear to be the most satisfactory definition, but it is subject to the inherent limitations of standardized tests and grading systems (Morrow, 1970).

This last definition has been refined through the use of statistical procedures in which regression models are applied to ability measures and GPA (Banretti-Fuchs, 1972; Farquhar & Payne, 1964; Morrow, 1970). Underachievement is then defined as, for example, a GPA that is one standard error or more below the GPA expected by a regression analysis. The primary advantage of this method is that it combines standardized statistical procedures with ability and performance measures in a manner that allows for individual variability. An underachiever, after all, may be of high, medium, or low ability; mediocre grade point average alone does not necessarily mean that one is underachieving. In spite of the statistical sophistication of this method, it does not eliminate the arbitrary nature of defining underachievement. Why, for example, should underachievement be defined as being one standard deviation (as opposed to 1.5 or 0.7 standard deviations) below the mean GPA?

In a recent study, Dowdall and Colangelo (1982) highlighted the difficulties of classifying underachievers based on the differences in the above definitions. They created a profile of the performance and ability scores of a hypothetical high school gifted underachiever, and utilized varying definitions of underachievement to classify that student. They found that whether the student would be classified as an achiever or as an underachiever depended upon the particular definition used.

The term *overachiever* contains perhaps the greatest logical inconsistency: How can one achieve above one's actual "ceiling" level of ability? How can one incapable of a certain activity nevertheless achieve above his or her actual potential for performing that task? Ordinary common sense tells us that "you cannot do what you cannot do," i.e., you cannot do what, in fact, you are not capable of doing, and yet the term "overachievement" is applied on an everyday basis, and with (we might add) a great deal of face validity.

In examining overachievement and so-called "overachievers," we believe that what we are actually witnessing is not achievement at a level beyond one's actual abilities. Rather, it is achievement up to actual potential when that potential may not have been obvious to the overachiever or to those around him or her, or the overachievement is actually perseverance in tasks where most people do not persevere.

We recognize all of the above questions and inconsistencies when we set out to define underachievement, achievement, and overachievement. We also recognize that our definitions are an amalgam of dictionary definition, scientific and educational usage, common parlance, and our own idiosyncratic connotations. Therefore, the reader should recognize that the definitions used in this book represent a compromise of many points of view and many needs, and may leave many questions unanswered.

Be that as it may, we have decided to utilize the commonly accepted notion of achievement as accomplishment at a level consistent with one's abilities and expected by reasonable and proper internal and external standards. Underachievement can then be defined as "performance which does not measure up to the individual's level of aptitude" (Chaplin, p. 556), or the performance below the "expected level" (*American Heritage Dictionary of the English Language,* p. 1395) indicated by that individual's performance on ability and aptitude tests. Overachievement can be defined as achievement above these standards.

When it comes to the question of why an individual underachieves, we must begin with certain philosophical assumptions. In fact, it is our belief that the theory without philosophical (and therefore scientifically indefensible) assumptions, no matter how rigorous and empirically based that theory, has yet to be formulated. One cannot even collect "hard data" without some a priori assumptions—impossible to validate objectively—of how the concept of "data" is defined.

Our major assumption is based on the medical model: A symptom may have a variety of causes and meanings, and therefore the symptom may not be equivalent to the disease that causes it. A persistent stomachache, for example, may be caused by simple indigestion, muscular strain, ulcer, appendicitis, flu, cancer, or a myriad of other possibilities. One does not think of stomachache as a disease, for that symptom does not automatically indicate whether in any specific case it represents a problem of the musculoskeletal system, the nervous system, the gastrointestinal system, the hormonal system, and so forth.

In general, medical treatment has two points of emphasis: to relieve the symptom and, more importantly, to cure the underlying disease that caused that symptom. An inevitable implication of these simple and self-evident medical goals is that differing underlying diseases or causes require differential treatment. The stomachache caused by cancer will be treated very differently from the stomachache caused by indigestion. In fact, the field of medicine places such a high value on the diagnostic process because there is a direct link to treatment: diagnosis of the symptom's underlying cause determines the choice of treatment. This principle is so embedded in medical thinking that it would scarcely seem to require comment.

In psychology, however, this assumption is far from universal. Problems are often defined by an outstanding symptom (such as alcoholism, anorexia, phobia, and certainly underachievement), and it is then assumed that all people showing this symptom do so for the same reasons. Studies are then performed to uncover the theorized commonalities of all individuals displaying that symptom. Our view, on the other hand, is identical to the medical view that a "symptom," such as underachievement, can be the product of a number of different causes and can represent many different possibilities for interpretation. This is a central point which we will elaborate and further refine throughout this book.

Generally, we view the myriad of reasons for underachievement as falling logically into four major categories: temporary, permanent, internal, and external. As can be seen from Table 1.1, these factors are grouped in pairs that interact. Temporary and permanent factors refer not only to the time element, in that permanent factors last longer than temporary ones, but to the issue of chronicity. Permanent factors are more likely to be those we call chronic or those that cause long-lasting changes in a person's life situation (such as the death of a parent). Internal and external factors, of course, are defined in relation to the underachiever. For example, external factors may include the academic standards in a particular school system, illness of a parent, and the like, while internal factors may include the underachiever's intelligence, presence or absence of specific learning disabilities, and similar factors. Personality factors, which are the focus of this book, fall into the internal category.

These two pairs of factors interact, as shown also in Table 1.1. Temporary factors can be external (e.g., absence of a favorite teacher because of the teacher's short-term illness) or internal (e.g., a student contracts the flu and finds it more difficult to concentrate).

Permanent factors can also be either internal or external. External permanent factors may include, for example, attending a different school because the student's family relocates (which may result in less attention from teachers due to large class size), gang involvement at the new school, and so forth. Permanent internal factors could include such problems as hearing

TABLE 1.1. General Reasons for Underachievement (with Examples)

	Temporary Factors	Permanent Factors
External factors	Teacher absence Parent illness	Change of schools Family breakup Death of family member
Internal factors	Student illness Nutritional imbalance	Learning disability Visual or hearing impairment Personality

or visual difficulties which cannot be improved upon, specific learning disabilities, or a specific personality makeup which may inhibit or interfere with academic performance.

In real life, of course, nothing is quite so easy to categorize. A particular factor may have some temporary and permanent aspects. For example, experimentation with marijuana may result in some decrease in grades if the experimentation is periodic or occasional, but if the usage of marijuana becomes extensive, regular, and continuing, the decrease in performance may become more permanent. Also, some factors may change over time from one category to another. Underachievement may be due also to a combination of internal and external factors, such as a family crisis accompanied by personality factors which affect the student's achievement.

While we will touch on these and other factors and dimensions, our task in this book is to focus on one "cell" in this overall matrix—namely the internal-permanent factor of personality. The questions we address follow from this focus. Yet even here, we see differing personality styles as producing different types of underachievers, a notion we will return to again and again.

Indeed, is there a relationship between personality and underachievement? If so, what is the nature of that relationship? How does one identify the various factors involved? What are the different personality types of underachievers? How do we recognize (or diagnose) these types? What does this process imply in designing effective treatment strategies? These are the basic questions we shall address.

Part One contains two chapters. Chapter 2 provides an overview of research findings on personality, family, peer, school and teacher, and sociological and cultural factors which have been implicated in underachievement. Also, we summarize the attempts to predict underachievement and identify underachievers. Chapter 3 contains a review of treatment studies focused on changing underachievement patterns.

In Part Two, we provide details of a developmental model which forms the basis for our differential diagnosis and differential treatment approach to underachievement. Included here are sections on a specific type of diagnostic interview (Chapter 4), a conceptualization of differential diagnosis of personality of underachievers (Chapter 5), and the Developmental Theory Model, which links normal development both to the development of problems and to a differential conceptualization of treatment (Chapter 6).

In Part Three we summarize approximately 60 research projects in which our model has been used. These cover studies on achievement levels irrespective of personality diagnosis (Chapter 7), research findings of differential diagnostic studies (Chapter 8), and results of differential treatment research (Chapter 9). These studies form the basis for our clinical work with underachievers, as well as assist us in revising the model.

Part Four (Chapters 10–14) contains detailed descriptions of the most frequently seen types of underachievers. Each chapter includes diagnostic criteria for each personality type, background information and typical psychometric testing results, interview characteristics, nature of family, school, and peer relationships, quality and nature of self-perceptions and affect, and perceptions each type of underachiever has about the future. Each chapter concludes with a description of that type of underachiever as an adult.

We conclude the book in Part Five with a brief overview of the links between differential diagnosis and differential treatment of underachievement. The Bibliography contains over 1000 references on the role that personality and motivation play in the underachievement process, covering the years 1927–1987.

It is our hope that as the reader becomes familiar with the intricacies of this topic, a new world of observation—teeming with fascinating complexities—will be opened up, as it has been for us, and that the reader will acquire a new vision, as van Leeuwenhoek did with his ancient microscope.

PART ONE

Research on Underachievement

In Part One, we take a comprehensive look at the standard psychological literature extending back to the mid-1940s. We have divided this material into two chapters, one covering psychological and sociological variables which may influence underachievement (Chapter 2), the other describing treatment variables (Chapter 3). Research findings from the clinical models we have adopted are not included here but will be reviewed in Part Three.

CHAPTER 2

Variables Which Influence the Achievement Process

For decades, the study of academic underachievement has been of continuing concern to educators, psychologists, parents, and students. Spence (1985) has summarized the wide divergence of theories of achievement motivation and the societal, cultural, and generational differences which have given rise to these theories.

As we reviewed and organized the material for this chapter, we became aware of how much this area has undergone periods of relative disinterest as well as periods of frantic and intense activity. Table 2.1 summarizes the frequency of publications on academic underachievement as contained in the Psychological Abstracts of the American Psychological Association (1945–1985). These include publications which focus only on academic underachievement to the exclusion of learning disabilities; i.e., these publications examine personality, motivation, family, peers, school, or cultural variables.

It is clear from Table 2.1 that there was a major increase in the number of publications between 1965 and 1974, years during which the United States was in the midst of the space race and the escalation of the Vietnam War. It is possible that during those years questions of achievement became more important and issues of wasted talent were of greater concern.

From 1975 to 1984 the frequency of published work on underachievement dropped to approximately half that of the decade before ($N = 444$, mid-60s to mid-70s, vs. $N = 204$, mid-70s to mid-80s). During this same period, there was a dramatic increase in the number of publications in the area of learning disabilities (LD), which may account for some of the marked decrease in underachievement publications. It is possible that changes in diagnostic labeling are reflected in the changing publication frequencies. For example, research funding for LD programs increased during the mid-70s and early 80s, and many school boards developed LD special education programs. Many valuable findings have resulted from this relatively new area of study, and many students who in the past had been incorrectly labeled as having a personality or motivational problem were more accurately identified as having a specific LD. In the scientific and educational rush to identify, understand, and remediate specific LDs, however, issues of motivation and

TABLE 2.1.   Frequencies of Professional Publications on
Academic Underachievement (1945–1985)

Year of Publication	Number of Publications
1945–1949	92
1950–1954	63
1955–1959	53
1960–1964	99
1965–1969	193
1970–1974	251
1975–1979	127
1980–1984	77

Note. Marcus (1986).

personality in underachievement appear to have been ignored. Further, many middle-class parents are far more accepting of the LD label than of motivational, personality, family, or other psychological problems.

The following literature review is organized into six major sections: personality, family, peer group, school influences, multifactorial research, and attempts to identify and predict underachievement. This review is not exhaustive, but rather representative of the trends in each area. Even with this restriction, over 500 studies have been incorporated. We now turn to the first research review focus: personality variables.

PERSONALITY VARIABLES AND UNDERACHIEVEMENT

Psychological Test Results

Many researchers who have considered underachievers as an homogeneous group (in terms of personality structure) have utilized clinical observation and various psychological instruments to differentiate underachievers from achievers. Several workers, for example, have assumed that anxiety plays a central role in underachievement and have utilized various anxiety scales to assess differences between achievers and underachievers. However, some have assumed that anxiety fosters achievement, while others have assumed that it fosters underachievement.

Sepie and Keeling (1978), using the General and Test Anxiety Scales for Children and a mathematics anxiety scale, looked specifically at mathematics anxiety in 246 11–12-year-old children. They used regression equations, Otis IQ, and mathematics achievement data to differentiate their sample into underachievers, achievers, and overachievers. They found that the underachievers scored significantly higher on the math anxiety scale but could not be differentiated from the other two groups on the general anxiety measures. Davids, Sidman, and Silverman (1968) gave the Color-Word Test and two anxiety measures (manifest and test anxiety) to high-achieving and underachieving secondary school boys. The underachievers showed more manifest and test anxiety than did the achievers. Smith and Winterbottom (1970) gave interviews, questionnaires, and self-report measures to 49 college students on academic probation. They found not only that those students most likely to get off academic probation had lower anxiety levels than those who were not, but that these students estimated their grades more accurately.

Wittmaier (1976), on the other hand, using the Achievement Anxiety Test on a group of 224 college undergraduates, found that low anxiety correlated with lower levels of achievement. He concluded that underachieving students may not care whether they achieve or not. Rosmarin (1966) gave a perceived stress scale, the Minnesota Multiphasic Personality Inventory (MMPI), a scale of adjustment and values, and an affect adjective checklist to 281 college freshmen males judged as having high ability according to placement test scores. That group was subdivided into achievers and underachievers. Rosmarin focused on anxiety and stress measures on all of the tests he used. He found that underachievers showed less concern for the opinions of others, more indifference in social situations, and more externalization of conflicts and responsibility. He concluded, however, not that underachievers have less anxiety than achievers, but that underachievers dissipate their stress and anxiety by avoidance and denial.

Other researchers have also focused on anxiety as measured by specially constructed and standardized instruments such as the Edwards Personal Preference Schedule, the Cattell Inventory of Personality, the Thematic Apperception Test (TAT), and others. Simons and Bibb (1974) used test anxiety and need for achievement measures on a small group ($N = 68$) of male and female fourth to sixth graders. Fear of failure was found to be closely associated with underachievement. They also found more male than female underachievers in their sample. Propper and Clark (1970) gave a battery of projective and objective personality tests to predominantly Jewish high school senior males. This sample was dichotomized into high and low achievers. They found that anxiety as part of a syndrome of alienation was more characteristic of the underachievers. On the other hand, Ridding (1967) found no correlation of anxiety (as measured on the Cattell High School Personality Questionnaire and a specially designed questionnaire for children) with over- or underachievement in 600 12-year-olds, although extroversion was correlated with overachievement.

The findings of several studies are consistent with the theory that there is an optimum level of anxiety necessary for maximum performance. McKenzie (1964) used anxiety scales on the MMPI and found that both over- and underachievers had higher levels of anxiety than did normal achievers. He also attempted to construct an MMPI underachievement scale and concluded from it that underachievers could be characterized by impulsiveness, absence of long-range goals, dependency upon others for guidance, and hostility. Cohen (1963) used teacher, psychologist, and psychiatrist ratings on a specially devised scale for assessing developmental issues in kindergarten children ($N = 56$ children). He found that excessive anxiety correlated with underachievement in first grade, while moderate levels of anxiety correlated with overachievement. Reiter (1973) found not only higher levels of anxiety among overachievers but also a higher degree of fantasized achievement.

Many have utilized standardized personality tests and specially constructed instruments to delineate various personality traits or characteristics that separate achievers from underachievers. Bachtold (1969) studied bright fifth-grade achievers and underachievers. Using the Children's Personality Questionnaire, she found some sex differences. Female achievers (as compared to female underachievers) tended to exhibit credulity, self-confidence, and self-control, while male achievers (as compared to male underachievers) were characterized by emotional stability, seriousness, and sensitivity. On the basis of the Personal Orientation Inventory (POI), LeMay and Damm (1968) found achievers to be more self-actualized than underachievers. Using the MMPI, McKenzie (1964) found that underachievers (as compared to achievers) tended to be more impulsive, lacking in long-range goals, and dependent on the direction of others.

Other differences between achievers and underachievers have been studied using the Edwards Personality Inventory. Crootof (1963) used the Edwards and the McClelland Picture Story Test to measure self-acceptance and need for achievement (nAch) in bright underachieving, bright achieving, and normal achieving high school boys. Depending on which test he used, he got different results on nAch across the three groups, but there were no differences in acceptance of self. Crootof concluded that while bright and normal achievers have a higher need for achievement than do bright underachievers, the concept of need for achievement needs considerable clarification. Krug (1959) used the Edwards versus achievement tests and high school standing to determine which type of measure had the higher correlation with achievement level in college freshmen. He concluded that these two types of measures were functionally equivalent in correlating with under—or overachievement. Oakland (1967, 1969) found that some scales of the Edwards improved the correlation of Differential Aptitude Test scores with the GPAs of high school over- and underachieving juniors. He concluded that underachievement may result from the lack of certain positive traits (e.g., efficiency, organization, respect for authority and tradition) rather than from the presence of negative traits.

Norfleet (1968) found that several scales of the California Psychological Inventory (CPI), but not the Gough Adjective Check List, differentiated achievers from underachievers. Stoner (1957), using the CPI plus measures of mental ability and achievement with over 1,100 high school students, found five CPI scales in which underachievers scored in a unique manner: Dominance (indifferent, inhibited, silent), Socialization (defensive, demanding, opinionated), Intellectual Efficiency (cautious, confused, easygoing, shallow, unambitious), Psychological Interests (apathetic, considerate, peaceable, unassuming), and Flexibility (insightful, rebellious, touchy, assertive, humorous, informal). Werner (1966) administered the Children's Personality Questionnaire (CPQ) to 87 12-year-olds, some of whom were underachievers and some who were identified as talented. There were some sex differences, in that talented boys tended to resemble artists, writers, and scientists, whereas talented girls tended to indicate more dependency and conformity. Underachieving boys resembled boys with conduct and delinquency problems, whereas underachieving girls appeared more heedless, excitable, and happy-go-lucky.

Studies on achievement motivation, long considered a central concept, have relied on the TAT (McClelland, 1985b; Spence, 1985). Some studies have linked the absence of need achievement to underachievement, as in the studies by Crootof (1963, quoted earlier) and Tamagini (1969). Davids (1966), also using the Edwards, found that achievers not only score higher on the need for achievement measure, but also score higher on measures of self-assurance, dominance, endurance, order, and intraception. Todd, Terrell, and Frank (1962), however, found that need achievement correlated with male but not female underachievers. Shaw (1961b) gave the Edwards, the McClelland Achievement Motivation Test, and the French Need Achievement Scale, but found that none of the need achievement scales differentiated achievers from underachievers except for a few subgroups.

Several studies have pointed to various aspects of psychosocial adjustment (e.g., self-control, socialization skills, independence, and so forth) as differentiating between achievers and underachievers. Horrall (1957) looked at achievement records and the personality test protocols of 94 average ability and 94 bright college students. She found that those students judged as having made the best adjustment to college were high-achieving and bright, whereas those with the poorest adjustment tended to be low-achieving but also bright. Snider and Linton (1964) also found that underachievers were better adjusted, as shown by a comparison of CPI scores and achieving and underachieving 10th and 11th graders. In particular, they found that achievers tend to be more socially and personally responsible. Using MMPI scores, Hoyt and Norman (1954) found that "maladjusted" and "normal" college students differed significantly in the predicted direction in terms of achievement.

Davids and Sidman (1962) compared achieving and underachieving high school boys. They found that the achievers had greater self-control over impulsivity, were more oriented toward the future, were less concerned with immediate gratification and were more concerned with future plans than were the underachievers. Lacher (1971, 1973) also found that college achievers as a group tended to show a greater sense of responsibility and social conscience than did underachievers. Heck (1972), testing underachieving, average, and overachieving elementary school students on the Children's Social Desirability Scale and other measures, found that overachievers tend to have a high need for approval. Morgan (1952) found many aspects of social maladjustment related to underachievement. However, since her sample consisted primarily of institutionalized males, many of whom were delinquent, one might expect to find social adjustment problems among this group. Narayana (1964) used a multiple regression equation on four variables (mental ability, verbal ability, past performance, and recent achievement) to categorize subjects as normal, under-, and overachievers. The measure of responsibility used was whether the students followed through on experimenter requests to keep certain appointments. The overachievers were found to have a greater sense of responsibility than the underachievers and also showed more curiosity. Riggs (1970) found that compared with underachievers, college overachievers showed a higher degree of social conscience (as well as other factors such as motivation for grades and family dependence). One of his concluding recommendations was that, in addition to academic help, schools should assist students in attitudinal, cultural, and social development.

Romine and Crowell (1981) found that college under- and overachievers differed in the predicted direction in persistence, work habits, consistency of effort, seriousness, need to excel academically, and other similar characteristics. Smith and Winterbottom (1970), whose study was also discussed earlier, found that underachievers were unrealistically optimistic in predicting their grades, lacked positive motivation for studying, and blamed their poor grades on academic factors rather than personal factors. Using a modification of the MMPI, Owens and Johnson (1949) found that college underachievers were more socially oriented than achievers. They hypothesized that underachievers may be too socially active to commit their time and energy to the solitary work of academic study. Ringness (1965), studying bright grammar school males, also found that underachievers were more concerned with popularity with peers than were achievers. At the other extreme, Lindgren and Mello (1965) gave the Bell Adjustment Inventory and a sentence-completion test to fourth-grade students in Brazil. The overachievers had significantly more health and emotional-adjustment problems than did underachievers.

Self-Concept

Many studies have attempted to differentiate achievers from underachievers by looking at general or global self-concept. Typically, these studies find that underachievers have a more immature or lower self-concept than do achievers (Paschal, 1968). Bailey (1971) gave various self-ratings to college students. He found that achievers generally had higher self-ratings, smaller discrepancies between perceived and actual academic ability, and smaller discrepancies between perceived and desired levels of academic performance than did the underachievers. Bruck and Bodwin (1962), using the Self-Concept Scale of the Machover Draw-A-Person Test, found that underachievers had a more immature self-concept as compared with achievers. Kanoy, Johnson, and Kanoy (1980) used the Intellectual Achievement Responsibility

Questionnaire and the Piers-Harris Children's Self-Concept Scale with bright fourth graders. Achievers showed higher self-concepts than did underachievers. Shaw, Edson, and Bell (1960) used the impressions of therapeutic counselors to conclude that the most important counseling goal is the underachiever's insight into his or her personality characteristics. Shaw and Alves (1963), based on an adjective checklist, concluded that there is strong evidence for a link between negative self-attitudes and underachievement. Tamagini (1969), using the McClelland and Draw-A-Person tests with grade school children, reached the same conclusion.

While as indicated earlier (Bailey, 1971; Tamagini, 1969), underachievers show a wider gap between expected and actual academic performance, Cress (1975) did not find this to be the case in a group of grade school underachieving males.

Other studies have looked at specific aspects of self-concept. Rogers, Smith, and Coleman (1978) utilized social comparison theory to define self-concept as including the student's academic standing as compared with that of his or her classmates. Using the Piers-Harris Children's Self-Concept Scale, they found that achievement correlated with self-concept only when relative within-classroom achievement standing was taken into consideration. Jhaj and Grewal (1983) found that high school achievers had higher occupational aspirations (as measured by the Occupational Aspirations Scale) than did underachievers.

Bocknek (1959) found in an experimental study that college students who needed external incentives were more likely to become underachievers. Students whose motivation was independent of these outer incentives were more likely to become achievers. Similarly, Haywood (1968) found that 10-year-old overachievers were more likely to be motivated by factors inherent in academic tasks, whereas underachievers were more likely to be motivated by extrinsic factors.

Several studies have utilized self-report measures. Claes and Salame (1975) found that secondary school underachievers' self-evaluations showed cognitive differences from those of achievers. Specifically, underachievers were more self-critical and less accurate in self-evaluations, and they did not internalize high standards of academic performance. Matsunaga (1972) gave several self-report measures (the Self-Concept of Academic Ability, the Importance of Grades Scale, Attitudes Toward Father, Attitudes Toward Mother, Checklist of Trait Names, STS Youth Inventory, and the California Psychological Inventory) to high school students. He found that the achievers had a higher self-concept of ability, a better attitude towards achievement, a more positive image of teacher perceptions, a concern with good relationships, more self-confidence and responsibility, and a greater awareness of the needs of others. Specter (1971) found that high school underachievers rated teachers more negatively, reported greater conflict with their families, and reported greater congruence of values with their peers than did achievers. Likewise, Lauer (1969) found that high school underachievers had a negative attitude toward teachers more often than achievers did. Honor (1971) also found generally negative attitudes among high school under-achievers.

Some studies have not found a strong relationship between self-concept and underachievement. Reisel (1971) gave a 60-item Q-sort to 17 achieving and 17 underachieving high school students. He found that achievers and underachievers could not be differentiated by any particular personality characteristics but hypothesized that achievers' self-concepts tend to be more stable in varied situations. Johnson (1967) found that two measures of self-concept (the Adjective Checklist and the Personal Orientation Inventory) did not generally discriminate between college achievers and under-achievers, but he did conclude that achievers tend to be more free and outgoing, have more drive and resourcefulness, and have a greater degree of self-actualization. Using the Tennessee Self-Concept Scale, Peters (1968) did not find a significant relationship between self-concept and under-achievement. His sample consisted of 164 high school seniors.

In a longitudinal study based on a holistic developmental model, Dullaert (1971) found few differences between the physical and mental growth patterns of 61 college achievers and underachievers. He questioned the legitimacy of the underachievement concept.

Intelligence and Cognitive Style

Generally, few differences in intelligence between achievers and under-achievers have been noted. Kroft, Ratzlaff, and Perks (1986), using the Woodcock-Johnson Achievement Battery, found a full range of intelligence levels among intellectually average, bright, and even superior first-grade students. One might expect, however, that as children become older, fewer low-ability children may be found among superior students. Using the Stanford-Binet Intelligence Test and employing Guilford's Structure of Intellect Model, Holt (1978) found that achievers (ages 8–11) tended to score higher in symbolic content and underachievers higher in semantic content.

A few studies have focused on creativity in underachievers as compared with achievers. Liddicoat (1972) gave female college achievers and under-achievers various tests of creativity, study habits, personality and motivation, and reading skills. He found that the underachievers were not only more creative, but also felt a higher threat of failure, had lower reading comprehension, and were somewhat more emotionally unstable than the achievers. Incidentally, he also found that all students were generally accurate in the grades they expected to get at the end of the semester. Eisenman and Platt (1968), studying high school students, also found that underachievers were more creative than achievers, and cautioned that any random group of underachieving students may contain a larger proportion of high-ability students. In contrast, Edwards (1968) found no differences in creativity between ninth-grade achievers and underachievers but did find that the overachievers tended to be superior to the other two achievement groups in divergent thinking ability. He concluded that teacher evaluations and creativity measures are a more accurate predictor of creativity than are measures of intelligence.

Some studies examining cognitive differences between achievers and underachievers have used standardized mental ability instruments. Bush (1972) and Bush and Mattson (1973) found that the Information subscale was the only Wechsler Intelligence Scale for Children (WISC) subscale to show differences between grade school achievers and underachievers. Similarly, Coleman and Rasof (1963) concluded that WISC subtests in which school-type learning plays a large part (particularly Information) are more likely to differentiate achievers from underachievers.

Using experimental procedures to measure cognitive flexibility and tolerance of ambiguity, Davids (1968) found that high school underachievers were more impulsive in dealing with cognitive tasks and were more rigid and intolerant of ambiguity than were achievers. Murakawa (1968), using Grid, Objective Sorting, and Number Strategy Tests concluded that fifth-, sixth-, and seventh-grade underachievers were low in abstract thinking, solved problems by trial-and-error, and were concrete, personal, and empirical in their conceptualizations, whereas achievers were abstract, impersonal, and general. In a related study, Murakawa and Pierce-Jones (1969) concluded that underachievers were low in deductive and inductive reasoning, numbers, and memory as compared with achievers. Blair (1972) examined reinforcement variables in a size discrimination learning task with 60 third-grade males. He found that achievers learned better under person, performance, and tangible reinforcement, whereas the opposite was true for underachievers. Using a psycholinguistic approach, Davey (1972) concluded that cognitive style (especially hypothesis testing and cue selection) was related to reading underachievement in fourth-grade males. One could conclude from all of these studies that while cognitive style appears to differ between achievers and underachievers, this alone is not sufficient to decide whether these cognitive differences contribute to underachievement or are caused by other factors.

Attention and Distractability

Several studies have tested the assumption that underachievers have problems paying attention to academic material (although not necessarily because of specific attention deficits). Mondani and Tutko (1969) found that on a social responsibility test, junior high school underachievers tended to learn more irrelevant material and therefore may not focus as much attention on the material necessary for academic success. Using the WISC with second graders, Ricks and Mirsky (1974) came to somewhat the same conclusions, noting that the underachievers in their sample were lower in WISC Verbal and Full Scale IQs, but not in Performance IQs. In a related study, Ricks

(1974) argues that distraction by irrelevant stimuli reduces the underachieving student's attention to more academically relevant material and that objective measures of such attention difficulties correlate with teacher reports.

Others have noted that distractability is an important component of underachievement. Baker and Madell (1965) asked a sample of achieving and underachieving college males to work various arithmetic problems under experimental situations in which varied types of distractions were present. Harrison (1976) asked the teachers of 200 grade school underachievers to fill out a classroom behavior checklist. The underachievers were given the WISC and the Wide Range Achievement Test (WRAT). Generally, ratings of distractability varied inversely with achievement scores.

Affective Factors

Of the many possible emotional components of underachievement, hostility has received a great deal of attention. Bresee (1957), for example, utilized semistructured instruments (sentence completion test, a personal essay, and the Rosenzweig Picture-Frustration Test) and structured instruments (the Sims SCI Occupational Rating Scale, the Maslow Security-Insecurity Inventory, the Gordon Personal Profile, and the Study of Values). He found not only that high school underachievers were more hostile and extrapunitive than achievers, but that they also showed less well-defined occupational goals, lower levels of altruism, and other-centeredness.

Shaw and Brown (1957) studied personality differences in bright under- and overachievers. They concluded that underachievement may be related to hostility towards others, particularly authority figures. In a related study, Shaw and Grubb (1958) found that high school underachievers scored higher on measures of hostility than did achievers. However, Shaw and Black (1960) gave the Cook Hostility Scale and the Rosenzweig Picture-Frustration Study to 21 achieving and 21 underachieving males, all with IQs calculated at 113 or higher. They found a somewhat mixed picture in terms of the relationship between hostility and underachievement. Underachievers showed more hostility, but the achievers tended to deny responsibility for inadequate behavior. The underachievers did not deny guilt but did perceive that they were not responsible because of circumstances beyond their control. Shaw and Black suggest that achievers may be more conforming and less creative than underachievers.

Corlis (1963) studied 70 underachieving college freshmen, all of whom were given the MMPI and an individual interview. Among those subjects with the lowest grades, the most common pattern was a generally passive-aggressive hostile style which appeared directed primarily at the parents. Weiner (1971) also noted the passive-aggressive nature of the underachievers' hostility. Brown, Abeles, and Iscoe (1954), looking at attendance records and study habits questionnaires of college underachievers, concluded that they may be unwilling to conform to academic requirements and other expectations. Anikeef (1954) also noted a significant correlation between underachievement and frequency of absence from class. Morrison (1967; 1969) gave 9 TAT cards and a modification of the California Test of Personality to 65 fifth-grade boys. She concluded that underachievement is a passive-aggressive behavior related to a preadolescent conflict based in hostility towards parents and other adults. Capponi (1974) linked depression in underachievers to factors such as hostility, anxiety, unwillingness to give gratification, guilt, and aversion to influence.

Gerolamo (1976) examined restriction of affect (affective inhibition) in fifth- and sixth-grade male underachievers. Using the Bene-Anthony Family Relations Test, he found that underachievers rejected statements of negative affect more than did achievers, suggesting that underachievers may indeed have more affective inhibition.

Rotella (1985), listed a number of personality characteristics of over-achieving and underachieving athletes. Overachieving athletes tend to be perfectionistic and become extremely frustrated with themselves when they don't perform to their high personal standards. Further, they tend to judge themselves and their self-worth on the basis of their athletic performance. Underachievers rarely develop this affective intensity required for athletic achievement.

Studies of Underachievers Only

Many studies have looked at underachieving students without making direct comparisons with achieving students. Dixon (1977), for example, examined mathematics achievement in adolescent women. She found that underachievers were other-directed (rather than inner-directed) and tended to have a more traditional rather than more liberal view of women's roles in society. Sanford (1952) points to a variety of reasons for underachievement: inferiority feelings, insufficient academic stimulation, relationship difficulties at home, unmet economic needs, insufficient intellectual stimulation in class, and physical defects.

Likewise, others stress the role of interpersonal difficulties and role of personality in underachievement. Fliegler (1957) even considers the under-achiever a maladjusted child with parental conflicts and strongly recommends counseling for these students and their families. Sylvester (1949) uses case material to demonstrate personality disturbances. Wilson, Soderquist, Zemke, and Swenson (1967), clinically studying college students, concluded that underachievement is one symptom of an underlying emotional illness.

Some studies have theorized that the underachiever is not simply lazy or lacking in proper academic motivation, but is motivated to underachieve. Dudek and Lester (1968) gave the Rorschach Ink Blot Test to 80 under-achieving and 23 achieving 13–17-year-olds. They found that half of the underachievers (as opposed to 17% of the achievers) exhibited an obsessive-compulsive personality with depressive features. Utilizing a psychoanalytic perspective, Dudek and Lester concluded that underachievers experience anxiety regarding aggressive impulses and that the underachievement and passivity represent a defensive reaction formation.

Grimes and Wesley (1961) contend that a student's personality characteristics combine with the classroom structure to either aid or hinder academic achievement. They studied the development of reading skills in anxious, compulsive, and both anxious and compulsive elementary school students under structured and unstructured teaching conditions. They found significant differences in skill attainment across their groups. High-anxious students performed significantly better under structured teaching conditions, while high-anxious students underachieved in unstructured conditions. Those who were both compulsive and anxious overachieved in structured teaching conditions. Kifer (1975), in a study of students in Grades 2, 4, 6, and 8, reported that previous academic achievement has a strong effect on the emergence of certain personality characteristics, and that these in turn foster continuing achievement. Kifer stressed the key role that family plays in the support of achievement patterns.

On the basis of four case studies, Hollon (1970) asserts that depression is at the root of the underachievement dynamic. Strauss, Lahey, and Jacobsen (1982), on the other hand, found no significant correlations between academic achievement and measures of depression in a sample of 103 7–12-year-olds. It is possible that Hollon's four cases were not representative of the underachieving population. Drawing on theories of the narcissistic personality, Baker (1979) theorizes that underachievement results from a narcissistic process in which the inner grandiose self is protected by avoiding the many failure experiences that come with intense academic work.

Many view the underachiever as highly motivated to fail due to problems in ego development. Anderson (1954) states that the underachiever does not lack motivation, but likely has subconscious negative attitudes which make failure inevitable. In a literature review on underachievement and the gifted student, Cowan (1957) concludes that the underachiever actually withdraws from academic and even social activities because of poor ego controls, lack of clear goals, unsupportive parents, and other related problems. In a more recent review, Newman, Dember, and Krug (1973) discuss problems in ego development as a major contributor to underachievement. Sherman, Zuckerman, and Sostek (1975, 1979) view the underachiever as an antiachiever whose neurosis prevents him or her from accepting the adult world and all of its responsibilities. Westman and Bennett (1985) used specially devised rating scales to study 14 underachieving children, ages 6–15. They discuss the Peter Pan theme: Underachievers may be motivated to fail because failure will perpetuate their infantile dependency on adults.

A few studies look at ethnic and cross-cultural factors. Brown (1973) studied self-esteem and anxiety among Black and non-Black underachievers in open versus stratified classrooms. She found that the Black underachievers in the open classroom setting were more anxious than those in the stratified setting. Hepner (1970) found that Mexican-American underachievers did not have significant problems with self-esteem and suggested that their under-achievement may have more to do with cultural differences.

Summary

Table 2.2 provides a summary of the findings from personality research on underachievers, achievers, and overachievers.

It is clear from Table 2.2 that the list of personality-related characteristics for underachievers is the most heterogeneous and contains seemingly in-congruous combinations. For example, underachievers have been described in some studies as unassuming and easygoing, while at other times they have been described as anxious, depressed, or inhibited affectively.

It is possible that the findings on personality characteristics of under-achievers are confounded by the heterogeneity within that group. For ex-ample, it is possible that one sample of underachievers was predominantly anxious, while another sample predominantly easygoing. This apparent in-congruity is not as evident in either the achiever or overachiever groups, and especially not in the overachiever list. In our research, we have found the overachieving group to be the most homogeneous with regard to per-sonality type, while the underachieving group has been the most heteroge-neous. Thus, the seemingly inconsistent and incongruous findings in the general research literature can be made more understandable through the use of a differential diagnostic model, which we will present in Parts Two and Three.

TABLE 2.2. Personality Research Findings in Comparing Characteristics of Underachievers, Achievers, and Overachievers

Underachievers	Achievers	Overachievers
Submissive	nAch-motivated[a]	Socially Aware
Defensive	Positive self-imaging	Responsible
Easygoing	Serious-minded	Grade-motivated
Considerate	Responsible	Achievement-oriented
Unassuming	Dominant	Family dependent
Rebellious; touchy	Self-confident	Approval-seeking
Extroverted	Disciplined	Internally anxious
Alienated	Future oriented	Very hardworking
Passive-aggressive	Independent	Consistent
Affect-inhibited		Self-starting
Hostile; resentful		Organized
Low-aspiring		
Depressed		
Anxious		
Distrustful		
Pessimistic		

[a]nAch = Need for achievement.

In the next section we will present the research findings on family variables and the achievement process.

FAMILY VARIABLES AND UNDERACHIEVEMENT

A number of studies examine how the family influences and is influenced by children who underachieve. First, we will review studies on sibling variables and achievement: birth order, number of siblings (i.e., family size), and age spacing between siblings. Then we will turn our attention to the relationship between underachievement and child-rearing practices, such as the impact of being raised in a nuclear family versus an extended family. Next we will summarize the findings regarding gender and achievement. This will be followed by an examination of specific parental employment and occupational variables. A major section in this review will also include studies on family relationships. Finally, we will conclude with a brief look at cross-cultural findings and the achievement process.

Sibling Variables

Dunn (1983) reports that in the United States and Great Britain nearly 80% of children grow up with siblings. Therefore, it is important to examine the impact of sibling achievement patterns and the roles siblings may play in the lives of underachievers.

An examination of the research studies on siblings in the first half of the twentieth century reveals a major emphasis on the psychological characteristics of the firstborn. After the early 1960s, researchers began to focus on family size, age spacing between siblings, and the influence of gender. Most of these studies have been correlational. More recent studies have included descriptive and process-oriented material.

Galton (1874) reported that there appeared to be an overrepresentation of firstborn among Fellows of the Royal Society of Britain. His statistics showed that 48 of a total of 99 Fellows were either only-born or firstborn. A number of later studies appeared to confirm that firstborn were superior in their achievement to later-born (Zajonc, Marcus & Marcus, 1979). A great deal of interest in birth order was spurred by Alfred Adler's *Practice and Theory of Individual Psychology* (1951), in which specific effects of birth order were believed to play a pivotal role in the development of certain personality traits.

Gradually, however, research findings began to question the assumption of the intellectual superiority of the only- and firstborn. Altus (1962) looked at the records of 1,878 students who came from two-, three-, and four-child families. Only female firstborn students obtained higher Verbal Aptitude Scores. In a second study, Altus (1965) also found that 55% of over 4,000 freshmen at the University of California were firstborn. He concluded that firstborn were, in fact, overrepresented at the college level. Yet in a study of seventh-grade students, McGillivray (1964) found no relationship between sib position and achievement level.

Lunneborg (1968) improved on the previous research designs by studying a sample in which firstborn were not overrepresented. He found that out of a total sample of 5,401 male and female high school students, male firstborn were superior across all of the 12 tests used and that female firstborn showed a tendency toward superiority. In his conclusions he cautioned against lumping only-born and firstborn into one group, since his results showed that only-borns did not show a tendency toward superiority.

There were a number of studies, however, which reported exactly the opposite results. Steckel (1930) focused on 20,000 typical students from Grades 1 through 12. He found that on four different group intelligence tests, intelligence increased uniformly with birth ordinal number up to and including the eighth-born child. Koch (1954), in a carefully controlled study, focused on 360 5–6-year-olds from Chicago schools and found that second-born outperformed firstborn.

Schacter (1963) examined studies done up to the early 1960s, and concluded that the presence of so many firstborn scholars meant only that more firstborns attended college and university. He found no birth order effects when he looked at 651 high school students in the Minneapolis area. Bayer (1966), controlling for family size and socioeconomic factors, found that children who were born later were as likely to go on to college as were firstborn.

McCall and Johnson (1972) tested 1,430 rural and urban students in Grades 2–12. They did not find any significant relationship between intelligence and birth order or family size. In their review of the literature, they concluded that where studies were properly designed, the correlation between intelligence and birth order was practically zero.

The reader is referred to excellent and comprehensive summaries of the literature on sibship effects, which contain over 2,000 references (Sutton-Smith & Rosenberg, 1970; Wagner, Schubert, & Schubert, 1979). In an article aptly titled, "Birth order effects: Not here, not now!" Schooler (1972) focused on two of the major confounding variables in birth order research: socioeconomic factors (including family size) and long-term population trends in the birth rate. Sutton-Smith (1982) concluded: "Given that birth order effects . . . . have relatively little power in accounting for psychological outcomes, it remains a puzzle that so many thousands of studies have been devoted to such minimal ends" (p.153).

There is also a body of literature which focused on the relationship between birth order and need for achievement (nAch) and locus of control (LOC). The majority of researchers have reported that firstborn do show a greater nAch than do later-born. Sampson and Hancock (1967) studied 251 high school students from two-child families. This study contained all possible combinations of subject's gender, sibling gender ordinal position. It also distinguished between only-born and firstborn. These researchers reported that firstborn had a higher nAch and need for autonomy, and male firstborn subjects exhibited more achievement-related conformity than did second-born.

Adams and Phillips (1972) studied 370 fourth- and fifth-grade students across a range of socioeconomic, racial, and ethnic groupings. Firstborn did score higher than later-born on intelligence, performance, and motivation measures. When the level of motivation was controlled, however, all differences between firstborn and later-born were eliminated. Kanter (1970), in his study on sixth-grade students, also reported no significant birth effects.

Some researchers, however, have found none or at best inconsistent birth order effects in studies on nAch. Wolkon and Levinger (1965) studied three samples: 49 couples, 72 divorce-applicant couples, and 102 male and female hospitalized psychiatric subjects. No birth order differences were found, perhaps because of the unique samples used. Dolph (1966) studied 291 ninth-grade students from three-child families. A total of 36 complete families were involved. In the first part of the study, no significant differences were found in IQ or in achievement scores. Some trends were found, however; more consistent achievement was observed in firstborn than in second-born.

Studies which have focused on the relationships among birth order, self-esteem, and achievement have also shown inconsistent results. Falbo (1981) found undergraduate firstborn scoring higher than undergraduate later-born on measures of self-esteem. In a previous study, Schwab and Lundgren (1978) had found similar results in two undergraduate samples of 164 and 308 students. These researchers also reported gender effects. Yet, Laitman (1975) reported that there were no differences between firstborn and later-born in overall self-esteem.

Regarding the LOC factor, Crandall, Katkovsky, and Crandall (1965) studied 923 elementary and high school students. They did not find significant birth order differences in the younger students, but firstborn in the higher grades showed a more internal LOC than did later-born. These results have been confirmed in separate studies by Falbo (1981) and McDonald (1971).

One of the problems in evaluating findings in this area of research is the wide range and disparate nature of instruments used to study such personality variables as nAch, self-esteem, and LOC. In fact, Sampson and Hancock (1967) used two different measures of nAch, and each instrument produced a different result. Some projective measures have been known to be unstable over time or have problems of reliability, validity, and standardization, and yet the findings from many of these measures are still reported regularly.

It seems logical to assume that the nature of motivation will change as the individual grows. Therefore, it would seem appropriate for future studies to focus on longitudinal approaches and within-family designs so that siblings could be tested when they are at a common age, thus controlling for developmental changes.

Another variable, number of siblings, is often referred to as family size.

Anastasi (1956) reviewed over 100 studies on the relationship between family size and intellectual ability. She concluded that family size does not necessarily limit the intellectual abilities of children, provided that socioeconomic variables are sufficient to permit adequate nurturing, care, and attention for each child. She also found that although there were a number of studies that reported a negative correlation between family size and IQ, the degree of the correlation decreased greatly (in some cases to the point of statistical insignificance) as the socioeconomic status of the family increased. More recent studies support this finding (Cicirelli, 1978; Kennet & Cropley, 1970; Wagner & Schubert, 1977).

Nuttall, Nuttall, Polit, and Hunter (1976) studied a total of 553 male and female students from large and small suburban families. They controlled for IQ and reported that male students from smaller families performed significantly better academically than their large-family male counterparts. Female firstborn students also achieved at significantly higher levels when compared to female students who were not firstborn. Interestingly, crowding was not related to achievement for either male or female students when IQ was controlled. Finally, sibling spacing was found to be significantly related to achievement, but only for male students.

Schacter (1963) studied high school, undergraduate, and graduate students, and found that family size decreased as educational level increased. This finding was also reported by Wagner, Schubert, and Schubert (1979), although it was not confirmed by either McGillivray (1964) or Kunz and Peterson (1977).

Since results also have indicated a relationship between family size and socioeconomic status (SES), one could hypothesize an interrelationship among SES, family size, and academic achievement: As SES decreases, family size increases and academic achievement decreases. In fact, many studies have shown a consistent decline of IQ scores with increasing family size, and this finding has held across a number of different Western countries (Zajonc, Markus, & Markus, 1979).

Zajonc (1983) proposed a Confluence Model to explain the relationships among birth order, family size, and achievement. This model was the first formal behavioral model used in the study of birth order effects. As Rodgers (1984) has stated, the model combined both a psychological theory and a mathematical implementation of that theory. It also assumed that any resulting measurable characteristic (such as IQ) is the result of a number of interactive factors (e.g., birth order, family sibship size, and intellectual ability). Much research has utilized this model, and the question of its validity continues to be studied.

Some have studied the relationships among family size, achievement, and personality traits such as nAch. In two separate and independent studies in which 427 and 367 pairs of boys and their mothers were used, Rosen (1961) found that boys from smaller and medium-size families showed higher nAch than those from larger families. Rosen also reported, however, that the relationship between family size and nAch varied with social class in favor of higher SES. Therefore, SES again was a contributing variable. In a separate study using university students, Masterson (1971) found similar results.

The implications of this particular line of research, involving socioeconomic status, are profound. In discussing society's view of the phenomenon of child abuse, Pelton (1978) notes that while child abuse is typically perceived as being equally common to all segments of society and all cultures, studies on frequency clearly indicate a correlation with poverty and lower socioeconomic status. Pelton concludes that the myth that child abuse is "classless" is convenient for politicians, mental health professionals, and those within the legal system. He argues that the goal of addressing basic economic and social inequities in order to eliminate child abuse is far less popular than perceiving child abuse as a pathology or disease. In the same way, if research continues to point to a significant relationship between lower socioeconomic status and underachievement, the professional and educational community must give serious thought to improving these social problems as at least part of the therapeutic remediation of underachievement. On a case by case basis, this might mean, for example, that the therapist help the student (and perhaps his or her family) to improve vocational, money-management, and job-seeking skills. While the socioeconomic aspect of underachievement is not the focus of this book, it is important in an overall understanding of the underachievement problem and should not be ignored.

Watts (1966), in a study on male high school seniors, found that over-achievers tended to come from large rural families and underachievers from large urban families. This raises the possibility that large family size may have a differential relationship to achievement based on social factors such as rural versus urban family location.

Some studies have examined the impact of sibling age differences on achievement patterns. Apparently, the wider the age difference, the more advantageous for both the older and especially the younger siblings. Koch (1954), in the sample of 384 5–6-year-olds from two-child white families in Chicago, found gender effects but only when children were separated by a 2–4-year age spacing. Wagner, Schubert, and Schubert (1979) also reported that age spacing of less than 18 months is related to lowered abilities in both children. Breland (1974), in a study of 300,000 high school merit scholarship applicants, found that siblings with an age spacing of less than 2 years (from the next youngest) had lower word usage. This did not happen when the age spacing was more than 3 years.

Not all studies have confirmed such results. Schoonover (1959) did not find any significant relationship between age spacing and average differences in IQ and achievement for 38–64 elementary school sibling pairs. Cicirelli (1967) found the same for 80 sixth-grade students from two-child middle-class Detroit families.

One of the difficulties in evaluating this research is that these studies used differing age-spacing groupings, with intervals varying from 18 to 36 months. Additional research is needed to determine exactly at what age differential the effects begin and where they end. Therefore, age spacing, as was the case for birth order and family size, is probably far more complex than was originally thought. For example, some of the studies already cited in this section have reported gender effects (Cicirelli, 1967; Koch, 1954; Schoonover, 1959).

Relatively few studies have focused on the relationship between age spacing and achievement motivation. Hornbostel and McCall (1980) studied 120 university students and found that wider spaced siblings scored higher on nAch than closer spaced siblings. Elliott and Elliott (1970) also reported findings consistent with the above: For those siblings with a wider age differential, when the older sibling is achievement oriented, the younger sibling is more likely to have high achievement aspirations. Schoonover (1959), however, found that age spacing had no relationship to nAch, while Rosen (1961) stresses the effect of a complex interaction involving many variables, such as family size, parental age, ordinal position, and socioeconomic factors.

Tesser (1980), in a study of 313 university students in two-child families, found that when subjects reported that their siblings performed better than themselves on important dimensions, identification between siblings decreased; friction between them increased with closeness in age. When the subjects reported that their siblings performed less well than themselves on important dimensions, however, the degree of identification increased; the degree of friction decreased with closeness in age.

Schacter (1982) studied 383 university students who were asked to judge whether they thought that they were similar to or different from their siblings. Adjacent siblings perceived themselves as being quite different from each other, a finding which held more for the first two siblings in a family than for any of the other sibling pairings.

Overall, research has produced either negative or equivocal results regarding the relationships among birth order, age spacing, and academic achievement. Subtle interactive influences may occur among many variables, but these have not been fully explored. Socioeconomic status has been a confounding variable in many of the studies in this area.

Child-rearing Practices

Shaw (1964) reported the attitudes of parents of 64 achieving and 51 underachieving students, regarding independence training. In general he found that when parents of achievers made demands on their children, these demands tended to be of a specific nature. They also wanted their children to learn to make their own decisions and behave more like adults. Parents of underachievers wanted their children to improve their ability to protect their personal rights.

Davids and Hainsworth (1967) studied maternal attitudes as perceived by adolescent achievers and underachievers. Underachievers tended to perceive their mothers as more controlling. There were no differences between the perceptions of mothers of underachievers and achievers. Further, there were greater differences in perceptions between mothers of underachievers and their children than between mothers of achievers and their children.

Haider (1971) compared the reported child-rearing practices of 33 mothers of gifted achievers, Grades 3–5, with those reported by 24 mothers of gifted underachievers from the same grades. The mothers of achievers reported that they began to defer infant needs earlier than did the mothers of underachievers. The mothers of underachievers were not as effective in their socializing practices. For example, they reported using less praise, less reasoning, and more concrete rewards, whereas the opposite was true for mothers of achievers. Further, Haider found that mothers of achievers reported a willingness to exercise more control of their children than did mothers of underachievers. This increased control was not an authoritarian use of power, but more an authoritative use of control. The mothers of underachievers tended to be more permissive in their practices and appeared less certain in the management and implementation of child-rearing philosophy. This showed itself, for example, in situations where mothers of underachievers would either be lax in rule enforcement or unassertive in punishing in a timely manner.

Other studies have confirmed differences in child-rearing practices between parents of achievers and parents of underachievers. Whiting (1970) reported that parents of achievers had a significantly higher degree of agreement between partners on child-rearing practices than did parents of underachievers.

Rehberg, Sinclair, and Schafer (1970) investigated longitudinal information from over 1,400 male freshmen, in order to study the relationship between adolescent achievement and parental socialization patterns and practices. These researchers found that subjects from middle-class families reported achievement practices which were more conducive to expectations for higher education than did subjects from working-class families. They also found that a father-son relationship based in democratic or participatory principles was more conducive to higher achievement than was a more autocratic parent-child relationship. They concluded that their results supported the concept that certain child-rearing practices were associated with higher achievement patterns.

Finally, Elliott (1967) focused on the differential role that the extended family might play in the achievement process. She compared data from 481 families who had sons in Grades 4 and 5. She reported no significant differences in achievement levels in those students from extended versus nuclear families. Assuming that these results can be duplicated, it appears that whether a child is reared in a nuclear or extended family bears little or no relationship to ultimate achievement, provided certain other variables are held constant.

Overall, Elliott found definite differences in the reported child-rearing practices of parents of achievers and parents of underachievers. There was a lack of agreement between parents of underachievers on standards of expected behavior of the child. Mothers of underachievers were less certain of child-rearing practices than mothers of achieving children, and parents of underachievers were more lax in immediate rule enforcement. Mothers of achievers were found to be more effective socializing agents, in that they used more praise, rational but nonrestrictive control, reasoning, and fewer tangible rewards.

Gender Effects

In a previous section in this chapter, we summarized the differences in male and female achievement patterns that have been reported in the literature. As in other areas of achievement research, many of the earlier studies on gender effects either did not focus on sex differences or simply focused on male subjects to the exclusion of female subjects. This section will focus exclusively on how gender differences affect members of the same family.

Koch (1954) found that children with brothers scored higher on verbal and quantitative measures than children with sisters when there was a 2–4-year age difference. Schoonover (1959) also found that children (of both sexes) with brothers scored higher on IQ and achievement measures than did children with sisters. These findings were confirmed by Altus (1962).

These earlier findings, however, have been questioned in later work by Sutton-Smith and Rosenberg (1970). These researchers found that while firstborn with male siblings scored higher on quantitative measures, children with younger sisters scored higher on language measures. Females tended to be more affected by males than vice versa. Further, Rosenberg and Sutton-Smith (1966) found that for two-child families, females with sisters scored higher than did females with brothers. In three-child families, scores were higher for females with two brothers and for males with both a brother and a sister. In another study, Rosenberg and Sutton-Smith (1969) found that female subjects achieved at higher levels when they had sisters close in age. For males, performance scores were higher when the age differential was greater.

With regard to the effect of gender on personality characteristics, Sampson and Hancock (1967) found that when students had either an older brother or a younger sister, both genders had higher nAch scores. Hornbostel and

McCall (1980) also found that firstborn males and females showed a higher nAch if they had same-sex siblings, and that second-born had a higher nAch if they had opposite-sex siblings. Rosenfeld (1966) reported results which reflect complex interactions among gender, ordinal position, and specific stimulus instrument items.

Granlund and Knowles (1969) investigated the relationship between academic achievement and the degree of sons' identification with their fathers. Using prior academic performance and a measure of intelligence, they classified 48 male students as either achievers or underachievers, and found significant differences between the male achievers and underachievers on the Bell Adjustment Inventory masculinity-femininity scores. Granlund and Knowles concluded that male sex-role identification is related to academic achievement.

In a review article on locus of control (LOC), Bar-Tal (1978) concluded that females tend to report more of an external LOC than do males and also tend to attribute positive outcome to luck. In this sense, males tend to rate their ability higher than females, particularly when it relates to successful situations.

Bank (1972) described some of the personal difficulties that female underachievers experienced in their families. She found that these female students experienced little support for functioning in an achievement-oriented manner in school. These students worried about the impact their achievement might have on their personal sense of security and on their femininity. They appeared to be encouraged to achieve through compliance and conformity rather than through independent self-fulfillment, an expectation which conflicts with normal adolescent strivings for independence. The underachieving role which these students assumed permitted some degree of non-compliance and independence, albeit indirect, from family expectations.

Manley (1977) reviewed the major research findings on the role that parental warmth and hostility have on the achievement patterns of male and female children. In general, she found that a moderate degree of maternal warmth and some slight degree of hostility were related to high achievement patterns in daughters. In contrast, for sons, a high degree of maternal nurturance and affection were related to high achievement patterns.

Not all studies have found significant gender effects. Stockard and Wood (1984) studied the academic histories (Grades 7–12) of 287 male and 283 female graduating high school students. They found no evidence for the widely held belief in psychological and educational professions that due to nonacademic and nonintellective factors, females tend to underachieve more than males through the high school years.

Overall, specific gender differences have been reported in relation to the achievement process. Effects vary depending upon the specific gender constellation within the family, including variables such as older or younger male or female siblings, firstborn male or female and the constellation of younger siblings, and so forth.

Socioeconomic Factors

A great deal of research has been reported about the relation between social class and achievement patterns. Only a small sampling of this work will be presented here.

Douvan (1956) studied the relationship between social class and strivings for success. She concluded that levels of achievement motivation were related to social class. In a more recent study of 60 students in Grades 6 and 7, Broderick and Sewell (1985) found that both lower- and middle-class students attributed future success to similar factors. However, middle-class students were more likely to attribute failure to unstable, external factors. The authors concluded that lower-class students are less prone to attribute failure to external factors. When they do fail, they may suffer greater damage to self-esteem, because they tend to implicate internal factors to a greater extent.

Bazemore and Noblit (1978) reported similar findings using a sample of 241 juvenile delinquents and 284 middle-class high school seniors. They found that social class was strongly related only to academic self-concept.

A number of researchers have focused on the impact of changing social conditions and attitudes toward achievement and education (Larkin, 1980; Levine, 1983). These researchers point to the gradual but definite decline in middle-class student achievement and relate this to economic factors and major changes in the work ethic, including a focus on self and immediate, rather than delayed, gratification.

Many studies have documented the impact of racial factors on academic achievement. Some of these studies will be summarized in the section on teacher and school influences on achievement patterns, later in this chapter. Ruhland and Feld (1977) studied the development of achievement motivation in 197 Black and White elementary school children. They found no significant differences in the levels of autonomous achievement motivation, but Black children did show significantly lower social comparison achievement motivation scores. The authors concluded that the results supported an educational deprivation explanation rather than a cultural deprivation explanation.

Frankel (1964) looked at 29 intellectually matched pairs of high- and low-achieving male students in order to study the relationship of maternal employment to achievement level. In each pair, one student was underachieving and one was achieving. Frankel found that there were significantly fewer working mothers among the 29 achieving students than among the 29 underachieving students. However, McGillivray (1964), in a large survey study ($N = 235$), found no differences in parent occupation or number of outside activities between parents of seventh-grade underachievers and achievers. The relationships among race, socioeconomic status, and achievement will be presented in a later section of this chapter.

Etaugh (1974), in a review of the literature, reported that maternal employment was unrelated to academic achievement levels in daughters, and that for sons, maternal employment was either not related or negatively correlated. Questions have been raised by critics of the research in this area that too often socioeconomic variables were not controlled. Further, conflicting findings have also been reported by a few studies, making solid conclusions even harder to reach. The fact that socioeconomic variables play an important, but not always simple, role in the achievement process and on cognitive development has been pointed out by many researchers (Alwin & Thornton, 1984; Marjoribanks, 1981).

Family Relationships

Campbell (1952) investigated the role of the family environment in achievement. In this study of 100 high school students, Campbell reported that underachievers tended to come from homes that were rated as lower on a home background measure (i.e., the overall environment was considered as less healthy). Many studies have followed, in which more specific questions about the home environment have been raised. Brantley (1969) studied 129 adolescents whose parents had separated and divorced. The students exhibited either conduct problems or anxiety and depression, which hindered their academic performance. With professional assistance many of these students were helped and the impact of the family break-up on academic performance was diminished.

The time at which parents separate and divorce is also crucial for achievement changes in children. Ryker, Rogers, and Beaujard (1971) found that the critical period for negative achievement consequences for children of divorcing families was between 6 and 10 years of age. Levin, Van Loon, and Spitler (1978) found that the impact of the trauma of separation and divorce does diminish over time, so that achievement patterns in children of separating families would be expected to rebound at some point later in their educational history.

A large number of studies were stimulated on the impact of single-parent families on the academic achievement of children. Bales (1955) has criticized the research methodology in this area, citing small and restricted samples of previous studies. His sample consisted of 4,725 children from both rural and smaller towns in the southern United States. He reported that, when socioeconomic factors were controlled, there were no differences in academic and achievement aspirations between two-parent and single-parent families.

Rolick (1965) investigated the relationship between parental interest and involvement in their child's school work and the quality of the marital relationships. He organized data from 4,963 families into one of three groups: marital break-up; intact but unhappy marriage; intact and happy marriage. He found that only for those students whose parents were happily married was there a significant relationship between parent interest/involvement in their child's schoolwork and their child's academic achievement.

Kimball (1953), using the case-study method, reported findings on 20 underachieving gifted male adolescents. She found that these students had poor relationships with their fathers. Tibbetts (1955) found that high school male underachievers and their parents expressed statistically less satisfaction with the relationships in the family than did high achieving males and their parents. Further, fathers and mothers of underachievers showed greater disagreement between them regarding what each expected of their sons. Underachievers were less likely to want to please their parents and were less likely to identify themselves closely with their families.

Sperry, Staver, Reiner, and Ulrich (1958) described the findings from seven underachiever cases in which the family pattern contributed to the underachievement. They concluded that these students maintained dependence on their families through their underachievement. The differences between the images that the families presented outside the home and the types of sacrifices and compromises that they have had to make for family success were implicated in the underachievement of the identified child in each family.

Morrow and Wilson (1961) studied parental relationships in the families of two groups of male high school students: one of achievers and one of underachievers. Both groups were matched for key socioeconomic, age, and intelligence variables. Overall, the results indicated that parents of underachievers shared fewer activities, ideas, or confidences with their underachieving children, and were less approving, affectionate, and encouraging regarding their sons' academic achievement. These findings were confirmed by Shaw and Dutton (1962), who found that parents of underachievers tended to suppress the sexuality of their underachieving children.

In a related finding, Peppin (1963) reported that parents of overachievers showed a greater understanding and acceptance of their children than did parents of underachievers. However, he was not able to confirm Tibbetts' finding regarding degree of similarity; between parents of overachievers. Shaw and White (1965) reported that achieving students identified with the same-sex parent.

Almeida (1968) focused on three levels of achievement in her comparisons of certain family characteristics. One hundred eighty third-grade male students and their families participated in the study. Underachieving boys rated their fathers significantly lower than did either achieving or overachieving boys on a measure of paternal love. Almeida obtained high interparent correlations on the love measure for all of the achievement levels.

Rubin (1968a,1968b) used a projective family drawing technique to explore some of the family dynamics in primary-grade achieving and underachieving students. She concluded that underachieving male students place themselves in the family drawing in a similar manner to the placement of self by emotionally disturbed boys, thus indicating emotional difficulties in the underachievement of males.

Based on group therapy and parent group discussions, Gurman (1970) studied the perceptions high school underachievers had of their parents and vice versa. The students came from a higher socioeconomic background and ranged in intellectual capacity from average to superior, as measured by Otis IQs. They had a variety of personality styles and characteristics, and many had already been in difficulty with the community and with the police. The families reflected three major American religious affiliations.

Gurman summarized major themes which emerged from the group discussions, and although the data were presented in thematic rather than statistical form, they are striking in their clarity and poignancy. Most of the underachieving students and their parents disagreed on the meaning of the term *good grades* and on how much and what type of importance should be placed on grades. Underachieving students perceived their parents to be much more interested in a high grade for its own sake, even when the quality of the education was in question. The parents were quite puzzled by how their sons reached such conclusions, considering that the parents were very concerned about their sons' overall development. Major areas of conflict, distortion, disagreement, and confusion included questions about the students' self-determination, the need for consistent, meaningful adult role models, and the need for greater contact between fathers and sons so that they could get to know each other better and in a more open and trusting fashion.

Whiting (1970) studied the effects of differing parental expectations on achievement levels. In a sample of 52 middle-class families, half with underachieving sons and the other half with achieving sons, Whiting found that parents of achievers began expecting mastery from their sons at a significantly earlier age than did parents of underachieving sons. Also, the parents of underachievers were more involved as a group in their children's homework than were the parents of achievers.

In contrast to the parents of underachieving junior college males, who described their sons in terms of personality and undefined future goals, the parents of matched achieving male students described their sons in terms of scholastic abilities and specific goals (Shore & Lieman, 1965). Through the use of questionnaires and interviews, Buck and Austrin (1971) investigated maternal attitudes of 100 economically disadvantaged Afro-American eighth-grade students. They found that mothers of achieving students rated their children as more competent and were less negative in their ratings than were mothers of underachievers.

Not all studies have confirmed these results. Schmidt (1972) reported no differences in parental aspirations or expectations between underachieving and achieving samples of student families.

In a study on underachieving university students who had had high achievement records in high school, Teicher (1972) found family relationship patterns. These students appeared to be depressed, isolated, and passive-aggressive in dealing with unresolved feelings about their parents. These students reported that their mothers were strong and domineering, while their fathers were passive and distant in their relationships with their sons.

One of the apparent consequences of these perceptions was the attempt to attach themselves to girlfriends as a means of satisfying unmet needs and alleviating unresolved affect. Hendin (1972), in describing three cases of underachievers, presented many of these same family themes, as did Drews and Teahan (1957).

Greenberg and Davidson (1972), in a study of lower-class parental attitudes toward 80 achieving and 80 underachieving fifth-grade Black students, found that parents of underachievers placed less emphasis on education, appeared to be less cognizant of the individual needs of their child, and used a less rational discipline approach. They also reported less structure and sense of order in their homes than did the parents of achieving students. Although the underachievers were mostly in the lower socioeconomic ranges of the overall sample, the presence or absence of a father, whether mother was working or at home, the number of siblings, the number of schools attended, and previous attendance in nursery or kindergarten were not different between the achievers and underachievers.

Baker (1975) delineated at least three major family dynamic factors which may contribute to underachievement. The underachieving child may be serving an important function in a family that cannot tolerate competition, especially competition with the same-sex parent. Underachievement might also be the family's method of maintaining a troubled marital relationship: The child becomes a "problem" in order to keep the parents from focusing directly on conflicts with each other. The child may also be underachieving in order to meet the expectations of a parent who covertly is threatened or made angry by the child's achievement or growing independence. In this situation, the child underachieves in order to prolong and maintain the attachment to the parent and, in this manner, does not threaten the parent with increasing independence.

In studies of underachievers' families, Sperry, Staver, Reiner, and Ulrich (1958) found extensive use of denial; underachievers tended to deny their own feelings about both poor academic performance and problems in family relationships.

In a case-study approach with three families, each of which had an underachieving son, Thiel and Thiel (1977) found that fathers and sons differed markedly on specific cognitive and affective dimensions.

As a group, researchers in underachievement do not appear to have focused as much attention on female as on male underachievers. This may in part be related to societal biases which consider underachievement as a more serious problem in males than in females. Block (1978), for example, found that mothers as well as fathers tend to stress achievement and competition more for their sons than for their daughters. Further, these differential ways of treating male and female children are not always obvious to the parents (Fagot, 1976). In one of the longitudinal studies of the well-known series by the Fels Institute, Hoffman (1972) found that maternal protectiveness was negatively correlated with achievement in daughters, but positively related to achievement in sons. In other words, given the same maternal behavior, there appears to be a differential effect on the achievement patterns of boys and girls. Support for this finding can be found in a study by Crandall, Katkovsky, and Crandall (1965), who found that overprotectiveness in mothers of female students, Grades 2–4, was correlated with decreased academic performance.

Further support has also been published by Nuttall et al. (1976). They found that female students highly motivated to achieve reported that their parents were more accepting of them than did female students who were not high in achievement motivation. Overall, there were differences in the quality of family relationships when comparing achievers and underachievers. Fathers were perceived by underachievers as passive and more distant, while mothers were described as domineering and strong, a pattern which has been reported in the professional literature for other presenting symptoms or psychological problems. Parents of achievers were described as more affectionate, approving, encouraging, and less involved in their children's homework. The families of achievers were depicted as sharing more activities, ideas, and confidences when compared to families of underachievers.

In reviewing these studies, it appears that similar qualities in a parent-child relationship may have a differential impact on achievement depending upon whether the child is male or female.

Cross-Cultural Family Studies

Caudill and De Vos (1956) creatively described how cultural values, in this case of 342 Japanese-American families, impacted on each family regarding the role and value of academic achievement, and how these in turn were expressed through each individual student in his or her personality adjustment and adaptation. The similarity between general American middle-class values and those espoused by Japanese-Americans was also highlighted.

In a study of 87 Mexican-American and 39 Anglo-American families, Evans and Anderson (1973) found that, contrary to previous stereotyping, the Mexican-American families stressed the importance of education and encouraged their children to do well academically. These researchers attributed the lower achievement levels of the Mexican-American students to the impact of poverty, in which students gradually came to doubt their own abilities and developed a present rather than future orientation.

Support for the Evans and Anderson findings has come from later research by McGuigan (1976), who compared Mexican-American and Caucasian students and their families across a number of socioeconomic and value dimensions. He found that there was a relationship between socioeconomic status and achievement, irrespective of the cultural group. For example, when a child's parent was a professional or semiprofessional, the child tended to be an achiever. This held both for the Mexican-American and Caucasian samples. He also reported that the values of the Mexican-American students were more closely aligned with those of their teachers than were the values of the Caucasian students.

Chopra (1967), comparing families of underachievers and achievers in India, found that fathers of achievers were more highly educated, had higher status occupations, and had higher incomes. The achievers had higher occupational aspirations and had already begun formulating higher educational goals and specific occupational plans. They had a greater degree of intellectual stimulation at home than did the underachievers.

Danesino and Layman (1969) investigated 120 Italian and Irish achieving and underachieving college males. They found that the achievers reflected the value system of the family of origin less than did underachievers. No significant difference was found regarding religious ideology.

Yabuki (1971) studied six cases of academic underachievement in Japan. The type of underachiever described generally fit traditional neurotic characteristics in which repression played a major defensive role. Family roles, individual personality structure, and other life history variables were all implicated in the final emergence of underachievement. The need to help the neurotic underachiever shift to a greater reliance on internal rather than external motivation is stressed as a means of facilitating psychological development.

Su (1976) investigated the family perceptions of 252 male and female achieving and underachieving junior high school students in Taiwan. Low achievers perceived their parents to be less loving and respectful rather than rejecting and neglectful; achieving students perceived their parents as making greater use of reward and less use of punishment.

Using the semantic differential technique, Ziv, Rimon, and Doni (1977) investigated the relationship between parental perception and student self-concept in average and gifted eighth-grade underachievers in Israel. One hundred thirty-four students and their parents participated. With the exception of the average achiever sample (in which mothers of achievers rated their child as lower), no significant differences were found among parents in rating their achieving, underachieving average, or gifted children.

Osuala (1981) stressed the mild dysfunction which is usually found in families of underachievers in Africa. The major characteristics seen in underachievers included deficits in motivation, attention, self-concept, and self-esteem. The importance of contact between school and the family was also stressed.

Overall, cross-cultural studies have confirmed many previously presented findings. Socioeconomic factors, including parental occupations and religious affiliation, have been shown to be related to achievement. Specific relationship variables were also confirmed, in that underachievers and achievers have different perceptions of the qualities of parent-child interactions. Certain cultural demands for high achievement affected some students in specific ways, including the development of specific personality defenses to cope with the demands.

In reviewing the research literature on family influences on achievement, it appears that variations in academic achievement are related to a wide range of interacting factors, and that these interactions have differing effects depending upon their exact constellation. Different environments are created for each child through the interaction of these factors. Birth order, family size, age spacing, sibling gender, child-rearing practices, and family relationships may all play some role in influencing intellectual abilities and academic achievement. These variables cannot be considered in isolation. The observed achievements of any given child are dependent upon a complex interaction among these structural factors in combination with other variables such as temperament, personality, cognitive abilities, and wider cultural influences.

We now turn to the findings on peer variables and the achievement process.

PEER GROUP VARIABLES AND UNDERACHIEVEMENT

Considering the extent of peer influence on the lives of latency-age and adolescent students, it is surprising that there have been relatively few studies on peer groups of underachievers and achievers. In one of the earlier reported studies, Keisler (1955) investigated the similarities and differences in peer ratings of 70 male and 54 female high school achievers and underachievers. He reported significant differences in ratings between achiever and underachiever groups, with the underachievers rated as less popular, as liking school less, and as being less persistent.

Morrow and Wilson (1961) studied 98 male high school students divided into matched achiever and underachiever groups. The underachievers were found to associate with peer groups which tended to have more negative attitudes towards school, to oppose authority figures, and to impulsively seek activities which were characterized by high excitement. These characteristics are similar to one of the types of underachievers (the Conduct Disorder type) discussed later in this book, and it is possible that Morrow and Wilson had a predominance of one type of underachiever in their group.

The Department of Special Services of the Champaign Community Unit Schools in Champaign, Illinois (1961), reported that even though there were no significant differences between parental attitudes, self-concept of students, and social maturity measures, overachievers perceived themselves as being much more accepted by their peers than did underachievers.

Powell and Jourard (1963) reported that university achievers self-disclosed to peers, whereas underachievers self-disclosed more to parents. Powell and Jourard interpreted these findings as reflecting a more mature level of development in achievers, a greater involvement with peers, and a greater emancipation from the students' own families.

Teigland, Winkler, Munger, and Kranzler (1966) found that, regardless of sex, fourth-grade achievers were selected by their peers much more frequently than were the matched underachiever group. The underachievers were also more poorly adjusted when compared to the achievers.

Sugarman (1967) studied 540 15-year-old male adolescents and found that the more a teenager was involved with peers, the less favorably he rated school, the lower was his academic achievement, the lower were his delay of gratification scores, and the lower were teacher ratings of his behavior. Pathak (1972) however, found that teens who were rated as popular with their peers were achieving at a higher level when compared with those who had been neglected or rejected by their peers or who were isolated from their peers. Farls (1967), in a study using intellectually average intermediate-grade students, found that there were no significant differences in peer acceptance as friends between achieving and underachieving students. This finding held irrespective of whether the student was male or female.

Seiden (1969) investigated a total of 132 male and 109 female high school students. She found that achievers as a group tended to involve themselves much more in student government than did underachievers. She also found that achievers and underachievers differed significantly from each other in the types of hobbies and interests in which they became involved.

Overall, there have been relatively few studies in the area of peer relationships of achievers and underachievers. There was some agreement about greater peer acceptance of achievers, but not all studies have confirmed this. Further, underachievers tended to participate less in student government activities and were involved in different types of hobbies than achievers.

SCHOOL INFLUENCES AND UNDERACHIEVEMENT

There are many dimensions which have been recognized as contributing to the relationship between teacher variables and student academic achievement. These dimensions include both teacher and student factors. Each of these major contributors will be reviewed in this section.

The original work by Rosenthal and Jacobson (1968) focused attention on the role teacher expectations can have. They introduced the notion of "self-fulfilling prophecy" on the teacher's part as it impacted on the classroom scene. Their results highlighted the role of psychological set on the perceptions by teachers of students.

There have been a number of attempts to reproduce the original Rosenthal and Jacobson results. Brophy and Good (1974) observed the processes by which teachers communicated different academic performance expectations to their students. They utilized classroom-interaction analysis methodology, and their results provided support for the notion of self-fulfilling prophecy.

Kester and Lethworth (1972) also provided research support for this concept. They reported that teachers who had been informed that specific students (actually of average ability) had superior intellectual capacities, were inclined to show increased positive interaction and to spend more time with these designated students. Larsen and Ehly (1978) have emphasized the interactional nature of these self-fulfilling prophesies. They agreed that teacher expectations play an important role, but usually only when there is some confirming evidence.

Good and Brophy (1977) reported that there were a number of teacher behaviors that tended to covary with teachers' academic expectations of students. These include waiting a shorter time to deal with low achievers, praising low achievers less frequently, asking for responses from low achievers less often (thus demanding less from low achievers than from high achievers), and seating low achievers farther from the teacher. Rothburt, Dalfen, and Barrett (1971) reported that teachers were more attentive to students who had high academic expectations. Further, teachers tended to judge those students with lower academic expectations as being less intelligent.

More recent reviews of the concept of self-fulfilling teacher expectations on actual classroom teacher behavior have tended to emphasize the impact of teacher expectations on students (Brophy, 1983; Cooper, 1979; Good, 1980; West & Anderson, 1976). Generally, most reviewers agree that teacher expectations do play a role in student academic performance, but that the extent to which these expectations are a major source of student performance is less than originally suspected.

More recent research literature makes an important distinction between what used to be labeled "teacher expectancy" and what has become known as "teacher bias." Dusek (1975) somewhat facetiously defined "teacher bias" as those self-fulfilling prophecies generated in teachers as a result of deliberately false information supplied to teachers during research on teacher expectations. "Teacher expectancy" referred more to those expectations resulting from teachers' observations of classroom interactions. Dusek believed that there was much less convincing evidence for pervasive "teacher bias" than for "teacher expectancy" effects. Finn, Gaier, Peng, and Banks (1975) concurred with the above conceptualization, and pointed to the situational nature of teacher expectations.

Cooper (1979) and Good, Cooper, and Blakey (1980) highlighted the differences between differing teacher behaviors toward different students which tend to maintain existing student differences, and teacher behaviors which tend to increase or enhance these differences. These authors state that teachers tend to maintain rather than compensate for student differences, but that there is little research evidence to support the notion that teachers routinely increase these student differences.

Teacher expectations play a role in student performance, but there are other factors. Most of the studies cited have used laboratory and experimental rather than observational conditions. Based on naturally occurring classroom situations, Borko, Cone, Russo, and Shavelson (1979) and Brophy and Good (1974) found that most teachers develop fairly accurate perceptions of their students based on classroom interaction, school records, and less formal information (e.g., from previous teachers).

Some studies have shown that there are specific variables which impact on teacher expectations (Brophy & Everston, 1978; Dusek & Joseph, 1983): time of the school year, student attractiveness, cumulative information in the student's school record, race and social class, and sex role behavior. For example, Good, Cooper, and Blakey (1980) found that at the beginning of the school year, teacher-initiated contacts with students were high, while as the year unfolded, there was an increase in student-initiated contacts. It is possible, therefore, that observational data collected earlier in the school year will differ in this respect from observational data collected later. Data collected earlier may reflect teachers' attempts to socialize students and set clear behavioral and academic expectations. Later data may reflect the teachers' self-fulfilling prophecies.

Braun (1976) reported that the more physically attractive the student, the higher the teacher's expectations for that student. Salvia, Algozinne, and Sheare (1977) reported similar results in their study of 84 Caucasian students in Grades 4–6. Dusek and Joseph (1983) also noted that this relationship between physical attractiveness and higher teacher expectations held not only for academic performance expectations but also for social and personality attributes.

Peterson (1966) used an experimental design to determine whether file information about capable underachieving high school students would influence teachers' interest in the students, resulting in a more productive relationship and increased academic performance. A total of 585 high-ability and low-academic-performance high school students were divided into control and experimental groups. Pre- and postmeasures included GPA and self-concept and attitudinal scales. Teachers were given detailed information about underachieving students in the experimental group but no information about those underachievers in the control group. No changes occurred on any of the measures used, indicating the lack of influence of this type of file information on teachers. Peterson concluded that poor academic achievement in capable high school students was probably rooted in more permanent personality structure and dynamics.

Dusek and Joseph (1983), however, reported a significant positive relationship between information contained in a student's school file and teacher expectations for student performance. Further, Willis (1970) had previously found that teachers did not simply extract information from a student's file and accept what the file contained. Teachers were selective, accepting only what they judged to be from a reliable source.

Teacher expectancies have also been shown to be related to socioeconomic and racial variables of students. Wong (1980) found that SES was a basis for elementary school teacher expectancies, but not for high school teacher expectancies. Wong also found that teachers in elementary and high schools tended to expect non-White students to do more poorly than their White student counterparts. This was confirmed by Prieto and Zucker (1980) and Guttman and Bar-Tal (1982). This latter study also found that these differences were diminished when the teachers tended to know the students well.

Benz, Pfeifer, and Newman (1981) examined student gender, grade level, and student achievement in relation to teacher expectation. Teachers tended to classify high-achieving students as "masculine" and "androgynous", while they classified low achievers as "feminine" and "undifferentiated." These results provided support for Bem's (1974) contention that when it comes to issues of academic achievement, teachers perceive androgynous students more positively. It is also consistent with the generally held view that female students produce a gradually diminishing academic performance up to and through high school years. This gradually diminishing female academic performance has been used as a supportive observation for the notion that perhaps females are living up to certain expectations; namely, that because most females would be classified as feminine they would be expected to perform as lower levels. However, a more recent study by McKay (1985) has not found this to be the case.

Other areas which have been studied include a student's name and whether the student had an older sibling who had been taught in the same school by the same teacher. There is some evidence (Harari & McDavid, 1973) that certain names are considered more desirable (e.g., David, Karen), and that other names are considered undesirable (e.g., Elmo, Bertha). Yet the evidence linking this to actual teacher expectations was inconclusive. Seaver (1973) also found that having had an older sibling attend the same school may in the early elementary school years create certain expectations in teachers about the younger student who is just beginning. Again, the degree to which this variable continues to impact on teacher expectation is questionable.

To summarize, a student's physical attractiveness, school file information, SES, racial characteristics, classroom behavior, and academic performance do have an impact on teacher expectations for that student's academic performance. Yet even these may not automatically continue to play a definitive role, especially as the teacher gets to know the student better.

More recent work on student characteristics has examined certain student attributes which may be related to achievement and teacher expectancies. Weiner et al. (1971) have proposed an attributional theory of achievement motivation. They postulated that there were four factors which were related to academic success or failure: the student's ability, the amount of effort the student expends on school work, the role luck plays in the outcome, and difficulty of the academic task. Bar-Tal (1979) and Feshbach (1969) have studied student attributes which tend to attract and repel teachers. Generally, the teachers tended to prefer rigid, conforming, orderly students. The least preferred student group was described as flexible, nonconforming, and untidy. However, it is difficult to generalize because these studies were based only on elementary school female teachers-in-training.

Weiner (1976) found that hardworking students were rewarded more when they did well on school assignments; even when they failed, they had to deal with fewer negative consequences. Weiner also reported that the greatest amount of negative consequencing occurred for those students judged by teachers to have high ability but who did poorly because they expended little effort. This was also found by Prawat, Byers, and Anderson (1983), who noted that teachers were willing to accept responsibility only for negatively affecting a student's motivational level in school, but that they were willing to accept more responsibility and credit for positively affecting motivation. These researchers also found that a teacher's greatest negative reaction was reserved for those students who did not generate any effort but who had succeeded in any case. The greatest teacher pride came from those students who were perceived as having limited ability but who were working hard and were considered highly motivated, especially if the teacher perceived him or herself to be one source of motivation for these hardworking students.

A number of studies have examined teacher characteristics related to student success. Teachers who facilitated the highest student achievement have been found to have effective classroom management skills (Brophy & Everston, 1978), an academic focus, and enthusiasm (Rosenshine, 1970). Shavelson and Stern (1981) and Borko, Cone, Russo, and Shavelson (1979) found that in spite of some differences (e.g., traditional beliefs versus progressive beliefs), all teachers rated basic academic skills as important. Samph (1974) found that indirect (vs. direct) teacher behaviors produced significantly greater positive changes in the development of language skills in sixth-grade underachievers.

Thomas and Chess (1977) have hypothesized that a student's temperament may have the same effect on a student-teacher relationship as a child's temperament has on a parent-child relationship. Gordon and Thomas (1967) found that teachers tended to rate slow-responding students and students who were cautious in approaching new situations as less intelligent than the students actually were. These researchers speculated that such inaccuracies in teacher perceptions based on student temperament may affect a student's performance.

Himmel-Rossi and Merrifield (1977) found that teachers used similar techniques with assertive, tough-minded students and with anxious students. These teachers tended to use directive, monitoring techniques for both types of students but also tended to provide encouragement to the insecure type of student. It appears that teachers do respond differentially to different types of students based on the teachers' perceptions of students' differing needs. Iddiols (1985) has supported this finding, specifically in relation to a student's personality style and characteristics. We will deal with these questions in greater detail in Chapter 4. Sprinthall (1964) studied the relationship between teacher and high school student values. Teachers and overachievers tended to be similar in their values, as were underachievers and nondiscrepant achievers.

In an experimental study, Brandt and Haden (1974) studied the relationship between teacher gender and student achievement. Each of 48 male and female undergraduates was asked to teach a student. For each trial teaching situation, the teacher was told in advance whether the student was an overachiever or an underachiever. Attitudes of the teachers were then analyzed. These researchers found that achievement level defined prior to the teaching trial determined teacher attitudes. Further, they found that male teachers preferred to teach underachievers, and female teachers preferred to teach overachievers. Caution must be exercised here, because of the experimental nature of the research design (i.e., undergraduate teachers working with a student who was role-playing either an over- or underachiever).

A number of studies have attempted to focus on larger, sociocultural factors which impact on the school environment, and therefore on the achievement patterns of students. Schneider, Glasheen, and Hadley (1979) compared a college preparatory high school with three public high schools. They found that the college preparatory school emphasized cognitive achievement, while the public high schools emphasized attendance. The impact that these differences have on student achievement seems self-evident.

Many studies have evaluated the impact of ability grouping and stratification on a student's achievement. Controversy continues regarding not only the basis for such grouping but also the outcome of these educational strategies. Two major sociological principles have been invoked to explain the differential impact of such programs on achievement patterns. The first explanation focuses on the differential impact of peers in different ability groups; the second explanation focuses on the differential impact of instruction on the groups. Rowan and Miracle (1983), in their study of 148 fourth-grade urban students found that initial achievement differences were heightened by ability grouping.

The size of a school or a school district has also been studied in relation to student achievement. Included in these studies were variables related to size, such as fiscal and educational resource availability, and teacher-pupil ratio. An early study from Britain (Lynn, 1959) found that students from larger schools on the whole went on to do better than students from smaller schools. In a more recent study, Bidwell and Kasarda (1975) found that higher teacher-student ratios depress achievement, and that higher teacher qualification standards tend to be related to higher student achievement. It is important to note that school size is usually equated with class size, an assumption which may not always be accurate.

A number of researchers have commented on broader sociological changes in middle-class culture, in which public schools are characterized as catering to the average student, thereby fostering mediocrity (Dodge, 1984; Hogan & Schroeder, 1980; Kozuch & Garrison, 1980; Levine, 1980; Rosenbaum, 1980).

Finally, a unique investigation by Heyneman and Loxley (1983) focused on the relationship between large societal economic factors and degree of achievement and learning. They found that 13- and 14-year-old students from low-income countries learned substantially less than their counterparts from high-income countries. Interestingly, however, they also found that in low-income countries, socioeconomic status had less impact on achievement, while school and teacher variables had a larger impact.

The following list provides a summary of school-related factors which have been implicated in achievement.

1. Teacher self-fulfilling prophecy
2. Teacher expectation versus teacher bias
3. Teacher classroom management style
4. Teacher gender in relation to student gender
5. Previous older sib and teacher expectation
6. Time of year
7. School's social-psychological culture
8. Size of school and school district
9. Ability grouping/educational streaming
10. Teacher-student ratio
11. Student file information
12. Student characteristics: race; socioeconomic; physical attractiveness; gender; temperament; name
13. Larger culture's attitudes and values toward education
14. Level of economic development of larger society

In general, given the above areas of research, the following summary points can be made.

1. Teachers react differently to low- and high-achieving students.
2. Teachers have more positive reactions to students whose academic expectations are higher.
3. Teachers tend to react more positively to those students who are physically attractive.
4. Teachers tend to filter information from the school files on a given student in a selective manner, not accepting all information as equally valid. The teacher's judgment of the reliability of the source of the

information plays a key role in influencing how the information will be accepted.

5. Teachers experience differing reactions to students based on the students' socioeconomic status and racial characteristics, but these differential reactions can be altered as the teachers get to know the students.

6. Students who have androgynous characteristics tend to be judged more positively by teachers.

7. Students who are conforming and orderly are likely to be perceived positively by teachers. Those students who are nonconforming and untidy are more likely to be perceived negatively.

8. Teachers are likely to respond more positively to students who are willing to risk in new situations and who tend to react more quickly. Teachers will tend to respond more negatively to students who are not willing to risk as quickly in new situations and who are slower to react in general.

9. Specific teacher characteristics tend to be associated with increased student achievement. These include enthusiasm and a range of effective classroom management skills.

10. Students who put forth a great deal of effort, irrespective of their ability level, tend to be rewarded more frequently than those who do well in spite of a lack of effort.

All of the above results must be accepted with some caution. First, a number of studies have found inconsistent results when comparing elementary and high school teachers. Second, there were different findings depending upon whether a study was experimental and manipulative or whether it was observational. Third, the time of the school year when any given study was done influenced the results.

MULTIFACTORIAL RESEARCH AND UNDERACHIEVEMENT

Rather than focus on only one dimension, such as personality or family or peer variables and underachievement, a number of researchers have taken a multifactorial approach and studied a number of variables simultaneously. Fransen (1948) emphasized character (personality, motivation, etc.) as a major contributing factor to underachievement, suggesting that less emphasis be placed on intellectual ability. Abrams (1949) and Aguilera (1954) supported Fransen's point of view by emphasizing the multiple causes of underachievement, including psychological, psychodynamic, physical, and school-related variables. A number of multifactorial studies have been reported at the elementary, junior high, high school, and university levels.

Asbury (1974), in summarizing research on preschool achievement, concluded that most studies did not incorporate an interactive concept; i.e., most studies focused on cognitive or noncognitive contributing factors, but not on the interaction between them.

Sutton (1961) studied academic histories, self-reports, personality test measures, behavioral observations, and peer and teacher ratings of fifth graders. She concluded that underachievement was caused by a range of factors, including lack of basic ability, motivation, or positive emotional involvement.

Norman, Clark, and Bessemer (1962) studied bright achieving and underachieving sixth graders. They found that the two groups differed significantly in age, sex, language, and achievement and IQ measures.

Ruckhaber (1967) studied fourth-grade high and low achievers of average ability. He found that the high achievers showed significantly higher scores on need for achievement, involvement with learning, study habits, academic aspirations and expectations, self-concept of ability, and peer acceptance. They were also rated as better adjusted. Using sophisticated statistical analyses, Ruckhaber found patterns associated with either low or high achievement. He concluded that there was much greater homogeneity in the achieving than in the underachieving group and stressed the individual nature of factors related to underachievement.

Helfenbein (1970) used three methods of categorizing 120 male and 99 female students in Grade 5: teacher judgment, test performance on math and reading, and a combination of teacher judgment and test performance discrepancies. He found that the underachievers in his sample were a heterogeneous group of students, that there were significantly more male underachievers than female underachievers, and that if teachers' judgments alone were used, an even higher number of male students would have been labeled underachievers. In general, underachievers scored higher on an anxiety measure, with female underachievers producing the highest anxiety scores. He stated that to alleviate emotional problems in the underachievers would alter the underachievement.

Janes (1971) investigated 168 male and female sixth graders, and focused on teacher, parent, and student perceptions, aspirations, and expectations. He divided his sample into achievers, underachievers, and overachievers, and further subdivided these into low-, average-, and high-ability groups. He found no significant sex differences in student self-perceptions, but underachievers were rated as lower in aspirations, expectations, and motivation than were either average achievers or overachievers. He also found that differences between under- and overachievers were more extensive than were differences between either average achievers and underachievers, or between average achievers and overachievers.

Hirsch and Costello (1970), in case studies of 23 achieving and underachieving male and female children, used projective tests, achievement measures, and academic performance. They concluded that the most important distinguishing factors were self-concept scores and scores on interpersonal ratings by mental-health professionals.

Gordon (1976) examined the role that race and social class play in underachievement. Her subjects were 1,102 Chicago area fifth- and sixth-grade Black and White students, mostly from working- and middle-class families. Controlling for IQ, she found that overachievement and underachievement were related to both race and social class.

Multifactorial investigations have also been carried out with junior high and high school students. Carwise (1968) studied aspirations, attitudes, and achievement of overachieving and underachieving Black junior high school students. He divided each group into low-, average-, and high-ability students. He reported significant attitude differences among the ability levels, with overachievers having the most positive scores. He also found that low socioeconomic Black students have equally high educational aspirations when compared with the dominant American culture. Overachievers tended to have higher academic aspirations and a more positive attitude toward school. This was also true for their parents, although in general a student's attitude toward school played a more powerful role in ultimate academic performance than did parental attitudes.

Abicht (1976) commented on the impact of environmental factors (some subtle) on the Black student. She highlighted achievement motivation, expectations, problems with delay of gratification, language and dialect differences, independence, and discipline concerns as often discussed variables. She pinpointed socioeconomic and racial factors as elements which perpetuate academic difficulties for black children. The use of intelligence tests which were standardized predominantly on White children, the continuing emphasis in the schools on White middle-class values and role models, as well as stereotypic White perceptions of the nature of the "broken" Black family, are examples of how larger socioeconomic factors maintain underachievement in Black students.

Murray and Jackson (1982) postulated the conditioned failure model as a means of understanding Black underachievement. The model consists of five major dimensions:

1. Social inferences (about Black student's ability)
2. Expectations (about Black student's performance)
3. Causal judgments (about actual performance)
4. Sentiment (devaluation of achievement)
5. Behavioral effects (on Black student's performance)

These researchers postulated that since Black students generally were not expected to achieve academically, any such achievement would be perceived by most teachers as being due to factors other than ability. Likewise, poor academic performance by Black students would be attributed to ability levels. When a teacher with these expectations is confronted with an achieving Black student, tension and possible devaluation of the student's achievements may result. It is also possible that Black students may not be rewarded for academic success by this teacher, which may result in student behavior congruent with teacher expectations.

Thornton (1975) examined attitudes of students, teachers, and parents towards 44 achievers and underachievers in seventh grade. He found that underachievers did not show attitudes toward school different from achievers or educable mentally retarded students, but that teachers reported attitudinal differences toward the three groups. Thornton did not find parental differences in their views about school across the three student achievement groups.

In a junior high school study of personality factors, Behrens and Vernon (1978) used aptitude, achievement, and personality measures to differentiate between 292 over- and underachieving Canadian seventh graders. These researchers found substantial correlations between ability and personality factors, including substantial sex differences. They also used multiple correlations (between intelligence and personality variables) as predictors of math and English achievement criteria. They found that the beta weights for personality variables were small and inconsistent.

Using questionnaires, teacher ratings, and an interview, Sontakey (1975) examined study habits, emotional adjustment, self-concept, satisfaction levels, and physical health of achieving and underachieving 11–16-year-old males. Achievers reported more effective study habits and better emotional adjustment, while underachievers had a less clear self-concept and were less satisfied with their progress. Achievers also were rated as more cooperative and sociable, while underachievers had poorer health measures.

Compton (1982), in her article on gifted early adolescents, highlighted many possible causes of underachievement in this age group. She included brain growth, nutrition, peer influences, family difficulties, boredom with curriculum, and burnout.

In one of the earliest multifactorial studies, Ratchick (1953) assumed that underachievement at the high school level was caused by a combination of school, environmental, and personality factors. He used two groups of 26 students, matched for IQ. One group was underachieving, the second was not. Instruments measured reading skills, academic achievement, vocational preferences, and personality characteristics. He found differences between the two groups on a number of instruments, but no single element was consistently related to all of the underachievers. In other words, certain variables distinguish between underachievers and achievers, but even within the underachiever group there is variability.

Kemp (1955) investigated the relationships among 42 environmental and student variables in a sample of 50 junior school students in England. Smaller class size, higher motivational level, higher intelligence, and higher socioeconomic status together were predictive of higher achievement levels.

Reed (1955) attempted to identify traits of matched underachieving, achieving, and overachieving private preparatory high school students. IQs, reading skills, vocational preferences, mental health measures, and student and teacher ratings were used. Reed reported that for the overachievers, the ratio of males to females was 1:2, which was the reverse of the underachieving group. The overachievers were sensitive to psychological pressures and were rated high by teachers on desired school behaviors, while the opposite was true for the underachievers. The achieving group results fell typically between those of the two extreme achievement levels. Sarnoff and Raphael (1955) reported similar findings in their case study of five failing college freshmen. They found that these students had low motivation for their stated expectations, were immature in their attitudes and general outlook on life, and had poor study habits for students at the university level.

Phelps (1957) reported a similar multidimensional study of 200 high school students. He matched two groups (100 students each) for grade level and sex. He found that underachievers came from larger families, participated less in school activities, were absent from school more than achievers, and reported fewer personal problems.

Jackson and Clark (1958) studied a unique sample of 120 underachieving students, comparing them with a normal control group. These 120 underachievers had been caught stealing. Both groups had equal intellectual ability. When compared with the control group, however, the antisocial group had a significantly greater number of underachievers in it. They were more apt to show greater personal maladjustment, tended to come from larger communities, and were more likely to be males than females. This is one of the few early studies which identified a particular behavior (i.e., stealing) and then investigated the characteristics of the underachievers in that group. It is probable that this group of underachievers was more homogeneous when compared with other groups of underachievers reported in the literature.

In his study of 224 achieving and underachieving 10th and 11th graders, Chapman (1959) corroborated some of the previous research findings. He found that underachievers were more likely to be male, to have poor academic achievement histories, to have poorer study habits, to have fewer academic interests, to spend more time on nonacademic hobbies, to participate less in private lessons, and to have parents who were less likely to be professionals or self-employed. Further, achievers' self-ratings of personality characteristics tended to agree more with teacher ratings of student characteristics than was the case for underachievers' and teachers' ratings.

Easton (1959) augmented the above findings in her study of 20 underachieving and 20 matched achieving high school students of superior intellectual ability. She found that underachievers reported less satisfactory relationships with their parents, tended to be more egocentric, and showed less achievement drive.

Frankel (1960) compared 50 high ability male high school achievers and 50 matched underachievers. The families of underachievers were lower in terms of the occupational groups of their parents, and scored lower on math and verbal attitudes. They expressed interest in mechanical and artistic areas, while the achievers were more interested in maths and sciences. Underachievers expressed a more negative attitude toward school and spent more time on athletics and social activities. Similar findings were reported by Carter (1961), who found that in a sample of 725 seventh and eighth graders, achievers were happier in school, exhibited more self-confidence, were more curious intellectually, and had better study habits.

Forrest (1966) tracked the academic history of high school underachievers who went on to college to determine if they dropped out of college at a significantly higher rate when compared to a matched group of high school achievers who attended the same college. A total of 45 males participated. He used high school and college GPAs, ability and occupational measures, and background information from both home and school. He found that students who underachieved in high school did in fact drop out of university after two years in significantly larger numbers than did the matched high school achiever group. This effect was not seen when data were collected after only one, two, or three semesters at the university level, probably indicating that it takes time for the effect to occur. Forrest also found that the high school underachievers continued to underachieve at the university level. Underachievers tended to score significantly higher on one vocational scale (the Real Estate Salesman Scale), and achievers scored significantly higher on the Physical Science Teacher Scale. Size of the high school graduating class differentiated between underachievers and achievers and distinguished between underachievers who remained in college and those who dropped out. The remaining underachievers tended to come from high schools with smaller graduating classes.

De Leon (1970) examined the relationship between underachievement and personal-social difficulties of high school students. She concluded that underachievers do not differ from achievers in the types of adjustment problems, but they do differ in the number of adjustment problems. She also reported that underachievers showed poorer self-concept and more unsatisfactory family and peer relationships; she argued that these were etiological factors in the underachievement process.

Bender and Ruiz (1974) also examined the role of race and social class in relation to underachievement in 176 lower- and middle-class Mexican-American and Anglo-American 11th-grade students. When considering achievement level, academic aspirations, and strength of the students' belief in their ability to effectively control their environment, social class (not racial affiliation) was the determining factor.

Dhaliwal and Saini (1975) concluded that high school overachievers differed from underachievers in study habits, motivations (type and levels), levels of personal adjustment, and feelings of security.

Gadzella and Fournet (1976) examined similarities and differences between achievers and underachievers on in-class learning, study habits and attitudes towards studying, relationships with peers, teacher-student relationships, and physical and emotional student needs. They found significant interaction effects across all five areas.

Schaefer (1977) focused on the often-raised question of low motivation. He emphasized that intrinsic and extrinsic motivational constructs needed to be considered. He concluded that the most effective remedial approaches to underachievement usually incorporate a focus on internal and external motivational factors and usually involve parents, teachers, and the under-achieving student.

Fitzpatrick (1978) studied the academic histories of 43 achieving and underachieving 10th-grade females. The underachievers had begun to show marked decreases in GPA from Grade 6 on. She also found that other-direction and attitudinal factors were related not only to math achievement scores but also to high school grades, and that the achievers differed from the underachievers on these dimensions. For example, the achieving group was less other-directed, exhibiting a greater sense of control over their lives when compared to the underachieving female students.

Agarwal (1977a, 1977b) studied 180 underachieving and 220 overachieving high school students in India, with the sample further subdivided into students from rural and urban areas. Agarwal focused on socioeconomic status, family and personal values, personality factors, and achievement scores. There were significant differences between under- and overachievers on personality and value factors, as well as between socioeconomic status and parental values. Differences were even found between rural and urban students. Saxena (1978) also conducted a study of 530 high school under- and overachievers in India, and found that underachievers overall reported poorer adjustment, as well as a significantly poorer adjustment in home, health, and school areas. Similar findings were also reported in India by Srivastava (1977) who focused on study habits, adjustment, reading, motivation, home and school problems, socioeconomic factors, and recreation variables.

Topol and Reznikoff (1979) focused on fear of success, educational and career goals, and female role conceptualization in 16 underachieving and 16 overachieving female high school students. The female underachievers exhibited significantly lower educational goals, were less contemporary in their career aspirations, and were less committed to realizing these stated career goals.

Pirozzo (1982) focused on the special difficulties that gifted underachievers experience, and summarized the psychological, familial, and cultural characteristics of these bright students. He concluded that underachievement in gifted students is caused primarily by the student's personal adjustment difficulties or by the school's limitation in academic programming for such students. He recommended that remedial programs take both of these etiological sources into account.

There have also been some multifactorial studies at the university level. After reviewing the many futile attempts to predict academic achievement at the university level from intelligence tests, achievement tests, or from high school GPA, Borow (1946a, 1946b) suggested a focus on motivation for school and career. He suggested that time management, study habits, extracurricular activities, employment, and health were more powerful mediators in the achievement process than was intelligence.

Diener (1957) compared 74 overachieving and 64 underachieving university students on aptitude, GPA, reading skill, verbal expression, high school GPA, age, weekly study effort (in hours), extracurricular activities, school attendance, and type of residential accommodations. On almost all of these variables, he found no significant differences between the two groups. The overachievers reported better study habits and were more organized, while underachieving males tended to have more artistically oriented vocational interests.

Nagaraja (1972) reviewed four case histories of college underachievers, and examined social, family, cultural, personal, and intellectual causes for less than predicted academic performance. Nagaraja concluded that rebellion against the family is a major etiological factor.

Lowman and Spuck (1975) investigated nontraditional predictors of academic success in their sample of disadvantaged Mexican-American first-year college students. These researchers found that variables other than SAT scores and high school GPA were better predictors of college success in their sample. Predictors such as family income, difficulty with the English language, high school underachievement, and denial of previous regular college admission were better predictors of college success.

Robyak and Downey (1979) looked at the differences between 27 underachieving and 38 nonunderachieving college students on study skills and personality variables. The nonunderachieving group had a greater awareness of study skills but did not report any greater use of these skills than did the underachieving group. The researchers attributed these findings to differences in personality preferences between the two groups.

Mehdi (1965a and b) listed factors implicated in the etiology of underachievement: environmental, sex, social, and ethnic factors, along with family relationships, personality, and self-concept difficulties. Attwell (1968) added school-related variables such as ability grouping within the school and classroom.

Brower (1967) suggested that underachievement is the result of developmental stages and should not be viewed as psychopathological. These stages include assimilation-recall disparity, test anxiety, intellectualization of failure, breakdown of intellectualization, and ego deflation. Brower recommended that therapists deal with each stage in different ways to break the progression towards underachievement.

In a comprehensive review on the etiological factors in underachievement, Zilli (1971) reported that no one factor has been found to explain underachievement. She summarized those factors implicated in underachievement:

1. Lack of motivation
2. Desire for peer acceptance

3. Excessive authoritarianism by school authorities
4. Poor teaching skills and attitude
5. Personality characteristics of underachiever
6. Overprotectiveness by parents
7. Authoritarianism by parents
8. Overpermissiveness by parents
9. Large families

This list suggests a range of etiological factors, and it has been our clinical and research experience that different types of underachieving students react differently to each of the above conditions. For example, one type of underachieving student may react negatively and intensely to an authoritarian school structure, whereas this may not be true for another type of underachiever. We will describe each type of underachiever in much greater depth in later chapters.

In a review article which was highly critical of the research in this field, Ghosh (1972) discussed nonintellective etiological factors in underachievement: anxiety, neuroticism, need for achievement, intro- versus extraversion, environment, and biographical variables. He outlined the research difficulties in conceptualization, design, and methodology that have plagued this area of inquiry.

Mohan (1974) summarized the most frequently cited etiological factors in underachievement, which were corroborated by Mitchell and Piatkowska (1974a) in their review published the same year. Mohan listed the following etiological factors:

1. Interest
2. Motivation
3. Personality variables
4. Study habits
5. School variables
6. Home and family variables
7. Peer group variables
8. Socioeconomic variables

Lowenstein's (1976a, 1976b) list of etiological factors includes:

1. Overemphasis on competition
2. Inconsistent/conflicting behavioral standards
3. Obsessive-compulsive personality characteristics
4. Negative attitude toward education
5. Impulsivity

6. Lack of follow-through/perseverance
7. Temperamental characteristics

One of the most comprehensive research reviews on the interaction of variables which impact on the learning process was reported in the classic work by Cronbach and Snow (1977). Studies which focused on the interaction among such variables as aptitude, learning rates, type of instruction, content of instruction, personality variables, and cognitive skills, structures, and styles were all conceptually and statistically reviewed and evaluated. Cronbach and Snow's integrative work highlighted the complexity of variable interactions and effects on learning and achievement, and specific recommendations were made for future interaction research in this area.

In their review of research findings and remedial programs for gifted underachievers, Dowdall and Colangelo (1982) criticized the literature's confusion regarding definition, identification, characteristics, and etiology. This confusion has filtered into remedial programs for gifted underachievers. The authors recommend early identification, family involvement, and long-term commitment of programs and fundings.

IDENTIFYING AND PREDICTING UNDERACHIEVEMENT

Several investigators have reviewed the methods by which discrepant achievers (under- and overachievers) have been identified. Farquhar and Payne (1964) concluded that, with few exceptions, there were not only many methods used to identify discrepant achievers, but that there was little congruence among them. They highlighted the inability to generalize from these inconsistent research findings, given such varied and noncomparable identification techniques. They suggested using the Dubois or Farquhar and Payne methods of identifying discrepant achievers, both of which utilize a linear regression prediction model using achievement and aptitude measures. Research updates of their work were reported by Taylor and Farquhar (1966).

Edgington (1964) reviewed the use of regression methods and Goodenough's standard error of estimate to identify discrepant achievers. He extended these methods by suggesting the use of two measures (an obtained deviation of educational achievement and an estimated educational achievement), followed by reference to normal curve tables. He believed that the major advantage over the use of regression in identifying discrepant achievers was that it was a nonparametric approach.

A number of researchers have attempted to construct psychometric instruments to distinguish between underachievers and achievers. The hope was that these scales could predict achievement patterns. McQuarry and Truax (1955) developed the Underachievement Scale, consisting of 24 items derived from the Minnesota Multiphasic Personality Inventory (MMPI), and successfully differentated first-year college underachievers from over-achievers.

De Sena (1964) added a third group, achievers, to the earlier work of McQuarry. He, too, reported significant results in using this scale, although the addition of the achievers group did not produce the same degree of predictive power.

Rather than derive a new underachiever-achiever-overachiever scale from the MMPI, McKenzie (1961) utilized the original validity and clinical MMPI scales in his attempt to distinguish achievement categories. He reported that there were some MMPI validity and clinical scale differences across the achievement levels, but that these differences were often so small as to be meaningless in prediction. When he constituted the achiever group with normal subjects (i.e., nonpathological as defined by the MMPI) and compared them with underachievers, he did find that underachievers scored higher on the psychopathic deviate (#4) and psychasthenia (#7) clinical scales and lower on the L and K validity scales. When he compared his normal achievers with overachievers, he found that overachievers scored higher on the depression (#2), masculinity-femininity (#5), and psychasthenia (#7) scales, and lower on the manic (#9) scale.

McKenzie empirically generated an Underachievement (Ua) scale, but it did not adequately differentiate between underachievers and achievers. He concluded that under- and overachievers were anxious, but that overachievers tended to internalize while underachievers tended to externalize. Underachievers were also depicted as impulsive and as deficient in planning for the future.

Waters (1959, 1964) constructed a forced-choice under- and overachievement scale. The major academic habits variables she examined included concentration, peers, interest areas, level of motivation, family relationships, study habits, and manner of time usage. Using factor analysis, she designed a scale having one general and five group factors (study skills, adjustment, motivation, background, and orientation).

Several researchers have used vocational inventories to predict underachievement. McArthur (1965) used a derivative of the Strong Vocational Interest Blank (SVIB) to design scales which would differentiate achievement categories. He reported success when using data from 1938 and 1960. Underachievers scored significantly higher on social impulsiveness, while achievers and overachievers scored higher on conscientious perseverance. Morgan (1975) utilized a nAch scale derived from the Edwards Personal Preference Schedule (EPPS) to study its capacity to predict academic underachievement. He found that this scale was not able to differentiate significantly.

Duff and Siegel (1960) used the Biographical Inventory for Students (BIS), along with national college entrance scores and GPA, in an attempt to predict achievement levels in 1,454 entering college freshmen. They found that 5 of the 10 biographical subscales on the BIS were significantly correlated with achievement measures. Using a biographical inventory, Reck (1968) differentiated under- and overachievers. He then investigated whether the inventory would be able to predict college achievement. The biographical questionnaire significantly increased the predictability of college grades in 180 male and female second-year students.

Dana and Baker (1961) used the Bell Adjustment Inventory in combination with GPA at the high school level to predict achievement. Using three new Bell scales, they were able to predict low, median, and high achievement.

Flaugher and Rock (1969) utilized a multiple moderator approach to identify over- and underachievers. Their sample consisted of college students. The predictors were high school class ranking and the Scholastic Aptitude Test. The criterion was GPA in the first year of college. The moderator variables consisted of background data, especially family factors. They found that overachievers had only average aptitude but a significantly greater number of fathers who themselves were highly educated. Underachievers, on the other hand, had a number of families who came from small towns, and as a group these underachievers had a greater interest in extracurricular activities.

Riedel, Grossman, and Burger (1971) used the Special Incomplete Sentences Test (SIST), which they had developed for studying underachievers. They validated the SIST on 65 underachieving, 106 achieving, and 33 overachieving high school students, used a factor analysis on the results, and then administered a Personal Reaction Schedule to study the relationships to anxiety measures. The SIST was able to differentiate achievement levels. There were specific differences between achievers and underachievers, but fewer differences between overachievers and achievers.

Felton (1973a, 1973b) constructed the Low Achievement Scale (LAS), an 11-item revision of a previous 24-item scale, which was designed to differentiate college students who performed well in college from a matched group who dropped out. The LAS consists of items focused on drinking habits, introversion tendencies, and personal adjustment. Using the scale, Felton was able to statistically differentiate the two achievement groups ($N = 60$), but sex differences were not significant. Felton stressed the value of early detection of potential underachievement through the use of this scale.

Kahler (1973) used a transactional analytic orientation in constructing the Kahler Transactional Analysis Script Checklist (KTASC). She believed that underachievers have been programmed by their parents and have internalized such scripts as "You're stupid," "Don't succeed," "Don't think for yourself," as well as affective components including feelings of inadequacy and confusion. The KTASC was designed to tap the "stupid" dimension. Her sample consisted of 55 freshmen and 60 senior college males. She also administered the MMPI, given that positive results had been reported by other researchers.

Kahler found that the KTASC was able to statistically identify freshmen underachievers on three criteria and senior underachievers on two criteria, but that the MMPI was not an effective predictor. Kahler constructed two forms for the KTASC, one for freshmen and one for seniors, each of which predicted underachievement. She noted that the new scales, like the original KTASC form, were heterogeneous in item content, which supports the line of research we will review in Chapter 4.

Sinha (1972) used the Nafde Non-Verbal Test of Intelligence, the Taylor Manifest Anxiety Test (MAT), and the Eysenck Personality Inventory (EPI), and successfully differentiated 200 underachievers (age 13) from 200 matched achievers.

Diener and Maroney (1974) warned of the potential errors in using specific standardized tests to identify and categorize minority and racial groups. They compared the scores of Black adolescent underachievers on the Quick Test and the Wechsler Adult Intelligence Scale, and noted differences in degree of agreement between the two tests at the lower end of the IQ range. These differences could result in certain students being labeled as underachievers because of the test differences. Several researchers (Wood, 1984; Yule, 1984) have noted the controversies concerning the use of such tests. In their focus on underachievers from India, Dhaliwal and Sharma (1975) urged caution in generalizing from such results. A parallel concern, although not focused on minority groups, was published by Hale (1979). He concluded that the use of statistical equations derived from group statistics to classify individual students produced dramatic misclassifications in 206 students in Grades 2–11, referred by their teachers because of problems in classroom behavior.

Golicz (1982) assumed that a student's attitudes will determine academic performance. She used the Estes Attitude Scales (EAS) with bright students, and found that a student's attitude toward school subjects was valid in the diagnosis and identification of gifted underachievers.

Researchers have continued to modify and refine their approaches in the hope that a more accurate method of classification of a range of student problems would emerge. For example, McDermott (1980) has developed a computer program to differentially identify students who were mentally re- tarded, under- or overachievers, socially maladjusted, learning disabled, or exhibiting other problems.

In an excellent review of the earlier attempts at prediction of academic performance, Lavin (1965) summarized over 300 published studies. He pointed out that studies used a variety of possible predictors, including personality variables, intellectual functioning, and sociological factors (e.g., socio- economic, demographic, teacher-student relationships, peer relationships, etc.). Lavin clearly delineated the shortcomings of each type of approach to prediction, and stressed the need for research which would combine psychologically based variables (e.g., personality) as they interact with sociologically based variables.

In summary, a variety of approaches have been used to identify under- achievers. Many of the shortcomings of these approaches have been criti- cized by others and reviewed here. Further, there have been a number of studies which have resulted in the construction of instruments and procedures to identify and predict underachievement. These are summarized in Table 2.3.

It is obvious from Table 2.3 that most of the scales are capable of differentiating between underachievers and overachievers (groups which represent polarities on the achievement continuum) but have not been able to differentiate when all three achievement groups are represented. More recently, Lowenstein (1982) has presented evidence regarding the Lowenstein Underachievement Multiphasic Diagnostic Inventory (LUMDI), which combines both type and source of information to differentiate underachievers.

Marcus and Friedland (1987) have developed the Developmental Personality Inventory (DPI) (Friedland & Marcus, 1986a) and a derivative test, the Motivational Analysis Inventory (MAI) (Friedland & Marcus, 1986b). Although both were designed to differentiate various underachiever types based on the *Diagnostic and Statistical Manual,* Third Edition (DSM-III) (American Psychiatric Association, 1980) classification, Marcus and Friedland did not differentially diagnose their sample. They found that MAI scales relating

TABLE 2.3.   Scales Used to Identify and Predict Academic Underachievement

Author/Researcher	Scale Name	Differential Prediction
McQuary & Truax (1955)	UA scale (MMPI)	UA vs. OA
Duff & Siegel (1960)	Biographic inventory	UA vs. OA
Dana & Baker (1961)	Bell Adjustment Inventory	Lo-Med-Hi Ach.
De Sena (1964)	UA scale (MMPI)	UA vs. OA
McKenzie (1961)	MMPI Scales	No prediction
Water (1964)	Academic Habits Checklist (6 factors)	UA vs. OA
McArthur (1965)	SVIB	UA/OA/NDA
Morgan (1975)	EPPS (nAch Scale)	No prediction
Reck (1968)	Biographic inventory	UA vs. OA
Flaugher & Rock (1969)	Multiple Moderators	UA vs. OA
Reidel et al. (1971)	Special Incomplete Sentences Test	UA vs. OA
Felton (1973)	Low Achievement Scale	UA vs. OA
Kahler (1973)	Transactional Analysis Script Checklist	UA vs. NDA
Sinha (1972)	Combination of tests (MAS; EPI; Non-Verbal IQ)	UA vs. AA
McDermott (1980)	Computer combination	UA vs. OA vs. MR vs. LD vs. Soc. Mal. vs. other
Golicz (1982)	Estes Attitude Scale (attitude to school)	UA vs. OA

Note. UA = underachiever; OA = overachiever; MMPI = Minnesota Multiphasic Personality Inventory; SVIB = Strong Vocational Interest Blank; NDA = nondiscrepant achiever; EPPS = Edwards Personal Preference Survey; nAch = need for achievement; MAS = Manifest Anxiety Scale; EPI = Eysenck Personality Inventory; AA = average achiever; MR = mental retardation; LD = learning disability; Soc. Mal. = social maladjustment.

to study skills and work habits had significant correlations with GPA, whereas the MAI scales which related to self-concept, affect, and relationships with others did not correlate with GPA. They concluded that as students mature from the grammar school through the college years, self-esteem and other emotional factors may be less significantly related to achievement than are consistent and effective work habits.

All of the studies that have been presented have attempted to elucidate the nature and contribution of specific variables to the etiology of under-achievement. These included personality, family, peer, school, and broader socioeconomic and cultural variables. In the next chapter we will review the research on attempts to change underachievement patterns.

CHAPTER 3

Treatment Approaches to
Underachievement

We will focus initially on those treatment studies which compared single-treatment approaches with no-treatment controls. Some of these single-treatment approaches are unidimensional, while others contain a number of treatment components, but each focuses on one type of approach only.

In the second section we will present research in which different treatment approaches are compared with each other and with a no-treatment control. For example, a behavioral approach might be compared both with a client-centered approach and a no-treatment control condition.

The third section will summarize findings from a range of miscellaneous approaches, not all of which can be considered treatment in the more traditional sense. This includes approaches in which underachievers were used as therapists or tutors for younger underachievers or in which such diverse methods as summer camp, letters, survival training, human-relations training, lectures, and other approaches were used.

In the fourth section we will summarize studies in which underachievers were treated by parents, teachers, achieving peers, or other older underachievers. In the fifth section we will present the results of remedial study skills or tutoring approaches. In the sixth section we will briefly look at the findings of specific studies in which differential diagnosis of underachievers was linked to their differential treatment. We will conclude with an overview of major trends.

Outcome of Single Treatment Approaches

A number of studies have focused on elementary school underachievers. Silverman (1976) used a behavioral approach with underachieving third to sixth graders. Eight half-hour sessions were held. The results indicate that the majority of the underachieving students benefited from the program.

In a treatment study of 140 elementary school underachievers, Kilmann, Henry, Scarbro, and Laughlin (1979) provided group counseling to 63 underachieving students (Grades 4–6) once per week for 15 weeks. The control group consisted of 77 underachieving fourth to sixth graders. The changes at the end of treatment included significant differences between the control and experimental groups on reading skills and a number of personality dimensions (increased energy, warmheartedness, emotional stability, and willingness to risk in the experimental group members).

Schaefer (1968) studied 288 underachieving elementary school students (Grades 3–7) divided into matched control and treatment groups. The underachieving students from the counseled groups produced significant increases in GPA when compared to the control subjects.

Moulin (1971) used a client-centered approach with 12 of 24 underachieving elementary school students, with the remaining 12 underachievers relegated to the control group. Although the counseled underachievers showed significant increases on several language and nonlanguage intelligence measures, there were no significant increases in GPA for either group.

Harris and Trotta (1962) reported mixed results in a modified group therapy program for preadolescents; some increased their GPA significantly, several showed minor increases, and several showed no change at all.

Thoma (1964) reported the effects of 30 sessions of group psychotherapy with female high school students. Outcome measures included teacher ratings of improvement, self-ratings and group member ratings, and GPAs. All measures produced positive change over the course of therapy, but length of treatment may have contributed to these results.

In a large, well-controlled study, Laxer, Kennedy, Quarter, and Isnor (1966) studied the impact of long-term group counseling on 260 underachieving 4th- to 11th-grade students. They used pre- and postmeasures of anxiety, self-concept, personality traits, and attitudes toward counseling. Control and treatment groups were matched on academic achievement, grade in school, age, and sex. They found no differences between the counseled and noncounseled groups on any of the instruments, nor were there GPA differences.

Rotheram (1982) used social skills training to alter the achievement and behavior patterns of 101 fourth, fifth, and sixth graders who had a variety of presenting problems. Each student was placed into either a social skills training group or a no-treatment control. The groupings included 17 underachievers, 40 behaviorally disruptive students, 29 multiproblem students, and 15 students classified as exceptional. Social skills training took place over 12 1-hour sessions. The underachieving students produced increased social relationship scores, behaviorally disuptive students increased their academic skills, and exceptional students increased social and academic skills.

Several studies have focused on junior high school underachievers. Hawkins and Horowitz (1971) studied differences in body image between 85 achieving and 76 underachieving seventh-grade males. They found that underachievers had lower barrier scores. They then enrolled the underachieving students in an intense therapeutically oriented residential school program, but the barrier scores of the underachievers did not change significantly as a result of treatment.

Drevlow and Krueger (1972) used behavior modification with 24 under-

achieving eighth graders. No significant increase in achievement was reported.

Arulsigamoni (1973) investigated the relationship between self-concept
and academic achievement in 103 seventh- and ninth-grade underachieving
students from a lower socioeconomic school district. Increases in achievement levels and self-concept levels correlated with counseling.

A number of studies have focused on high school underachievers. Finney
and Van Dalsem (1969) studied the impact of group counseling on 154 underachieving high school students over four semesters. The control group
consisted of 85 underachievers, the treatment group, 69 underachievers. At
the end of the treatment period, there were no differences in GPA between
the two groups, although some personality differences were seen between
the two groups on the California Personality Inventory.

Powers (1971) used a particular counseling approach—Vistherapy (strength-
supportive group psychotherapy)—with 48 underachieving ninth graders (24
males and 24 females). The treatment involved 16 specific steps from initi-
ation to termination and consisted of 25 1-hour sessions over one school
year. The counseled group showed significant increases in GPA and attitude
improvement.

Brusnahan (1969) studied 21 control and 21 experimental underachieving
ninth-grade males. The treatment program consisted of 35-minute small group
meetings over a 6-month period. Brusnahan found that the counseling program produced no significant differences in GPA or on most of the instruments used to measure change, the only exception being the Minnesota
Counseling Inventory. He concluded that academic underachievement masks
multidimensional problems.

A study on the effectiveness of individual reinforcement and goal setting
counseling on GPA of 11th-grade underachievers ($N = 100$: 50 in the control
and 50 in the treatment group) was reported by Dinger (1974). She found
significant positive results in the counseled group.

A comprehensive treatment study by Lowenstein (1982) reported a 5–10
year treatment follow-up of 65 9–18-year-old underachievers. In general,
underachievement tended to show itself most markedly between the ages of
11 and 15, with most underachievers scoring between two and three years
below their intellectual age. Those underachievers who had received treatment and who had increased their achievement levels tended to maintain
their gains over the follow-up period. The type of treatment directions included combinations of behavioral and eclectic approaches based on differential diagnoses from the Lowenstein Underachievement Multiphasic Diagnostic Inventory (LUMDI), an instrument structured to provide diagnostic
information about the nature and source of academic underachievement.

A number of researchers have focused on college and university underachievers. Winborn and Schmidt (1962) studied the impact of brief group
counseling on 135 underachieving university freshman. Those who did not
receive treatment produced significant increases in GPA compared to those

who received short-term group counseling. Winborn and Schmidt speculated that even though the counseling process may have had a positive personal effect, it may also have concurrently produced a negative impact on GPA.

Dickenson and Truax (1966) studied the impact of group counseling on 48 college underachievers (24 in the control and 24 in the counseled group). They described these students as essentially neurotic, and found significant increases in GPA in the treatment group. Further, those neurotic students who showed the greatest gains in therapy outcome measures also produced the greatest increases in GPA. This is one of the few studies in the general literature that attempted to describe underachievement in terms of personality characteristics rather than simply as a statistical gap between intellectual potential and academic performance.

Hill and Grieneeks (1966) found no significant differences in GPA pre- and postcounseling in a group of male and female underachievers when compared with a matched control group of underachievers.

Thelen and Harris (1968) reported on three groups of college underachievers ($N = 69$). Thirty-eight did not agree to participate when offered group therapy, 13 did wish to participate in group therapy but were not offered any, 19 agreed to and participated. The treatment group showed significantly greater increases in GPA by the end of the therapy. Even in the group motivated for treatment but who did not receive any, there were no significant increases in GPA. These results were interpreted as highlighting the value of group counseling for underachieving students.

Rand (1970b) used a group approach which combined therapy with a didactic component focused on information about underachievement. Fifty-five underachieving college students received the combined treatment and 69 underachievers did not. The results showed a significant positive effect on GPA for the experimental group both at the end of the treatment semester and in a follow-up one semester after treatment termination. Thommes (1970) also employed a combined treatment program with underachieving college freshman. The majority of experimental group participants ($N = 23$) were males enrolled in both weekly encounter groups and long-term counseling. The control group received neither encounter nor long-term counseling. The results showed that over the course of the semester, the treatment group showed significant increases in GPA and in measures of decisiveness and achievement.

Trotter (1971), however, in a parallel study with college freshmen, reported no significant changes in the treatment group of college underachievers enrolled in group therapy as compared to a no-treatment control group. The group therapy was valuable only in that it produced an improvement in the mood of treatment subjects, but did not appreciably alter their achievement patterns.

Friedman (1971) studied the relationship between achievement motivation and level of academic achievement on outcome in group therapy of 46 college students. Those students reporting higher levels of need achievement (nAch) and actual achievement were predicted as showing more positive therapy outcome. The results, however, did not support the original prediction. Interestingly, she also found that personality factors did not differentiate between the two groups of students.

Rand (1970a) recommended the use of rational-emotive group therapy with underachieving college students. This approach is designed to teach the student techniques of confronting irrational beliefs about course materials, grades, teachers, study habits, and so forth. Group therapy enabled each student to observe the irrational beliefs in fellow group members, which in turn facilitated self-discovery. The focus of the approach was on the "here-and-now."

Werner (1972) investigated the impact of group counseling on attitudes and retention rates of underachieving college freshmen. The group therapy structure was leaderless and focused on growth issues over 10 2-hour sessions. The retention rates of the counseled group were significantly higher than those of the noncounseled control group.

Martin (1952) studied the impact of the interviewing process on the academic performance of underachieving students, and found that while it did not alter academic performance, the interviewing process did increase morale (as evidenced by increased attendance and persistence). Martin also reported that the four most frequently cited reasons for poor grades were low motivation, poor study habits, pressures of outside employment, and poor personal adjustment.

Bhatnagar (1976), who reported on the benefit of individual counseling in altering the achievement patterns of 20 bright underachievers, reached similar conclusions. Major factors which appeared to be related to the etiology of underachievement were motivation, lack of self-confidence, physical problems (eyesight, speech), familial and other socioeconomic issues, and academic study habits.

Several treatment studies have attempted to change underachievement patterns through the involvement of parents, either in family or parent therapy. Southworth (1966) investigated the impact of group counseling with both fathers and mothers of underachievers on GPA, self-concept, and classroom behavior in elementary school students. Fathers attended approximately 40% and mothers 75% of the group sessions. Southworth found no significant differences on any of the change measures following treatment.

Cubbedge and Hall (1964) did find significant standardized achievement test changes in seventh-grade underachievers as a result of concurrent student and parent group counseling. The experimental group consisted of underachievers and their parents who met separately each week over a 14-week period. A matched control group of underachievers and their parents served as the no-treatment control. The results favored the experimental group on the achievement measure but not on GPA changes. There were other personality measure changes favoring the experimental group.

Wechsler (1971) studied the impact of encounter group sessions with

mothers of underachieving fourth- and fifth-grade males. The sessions focused on maternal attitudes. She found significant changes both in maternal
attitudes and in their sons' self-acceptance and maternal-acceptance ratings.
No achievement measures were utilized. Similar findings were reported by
Esterson, Feldman, Krigsman, and Warshaw (1975) in their work with third-
and sixth-grade underachievers and their families.

McGuire and Lyons (1985) reported significant increases in GPA through
the use of a transcontextual family intervention model with 17 families. The
focus of the program was not on motivation of either the underachieving
child or parents, but rather on compliance with the program. The authors
reported significant GPA and classroom behavior changes in more than 80%
of the families.

Several reported studies are based on single cases, with detailed descriptions of several types of underachievers. For example, Margolis, Muhlfelder,
and Brannigan (1977) reported the use of Reality Therapy with an aggressive,
underachieving 15-year-old male. Kintzi (1976) detailed the treatment of a
14-year-old male underachiever with a history of behavior problems. Kintzi's
successful approach combined the efforts of parents, school personnel, and
therapist. Noland, Arnold, and Clement (1980) used self-reinforcement techniques with two Black sixth-grade females who were aggressive underachievers and reported positive but mixed results. Similarly, Salend and Henry
(1981) used a response-cost token system in the classroom for an 8-year-old
second-grade male underachiever. Targeted negative behaviors decreased
significantly. Lowenstein (1983) discussed a 12-year-old underachieving male
student in terms of the expectations of his parents and the school personnel.
She employed a combined treatment approach, including behavioral principles, psychotherapy, and structured environmental changes. Ten years
later, Lowenstein followed up on this case and reported that the subject was
achieving at a level which was commensurate with his intellectual potential
and consistent with his goals.

A number of studies have focused on specific populations of underachievers. For example, Grover and Tessier (1978) described therapy of seven
medical students who were experiencing "Academic Frustration Syndrome": elevated and debilitating anxiety and extreme scores on a locus of
control measure. No differences were found between these troubled students
and 48 other asymptomatic medical students. The therapy approach incorporated attribution therapy and desensitization techniques. Improvement
was reported in six cases.

Morgan (1971) studied the impact of behavior therapy on 84 culturally
disadvantaged underachieving junior high school students. The experimental
group received nine group sessions of behavior therapy, while the control
group received no treatment. Results showed that the experimental procedure had produced significant increases in GPA, study habits, attitudes, and
self-esteem and that these gains were maintained into the following academic
year.

Wittmer and Ferinden (1971) assessed the impact of 12 group counseling sessions on six culturally deprived Black junior high school underachievers compared to a matched control sample of six underachieving Black students. No significant differences were found in GPA or student attitudes. Teacher-attitude ratings toward the students in the experimental group were in the positive direction.

Chadwick and Day (1971) used systematic reinforcement to change the achievement patterns of 25 underachieving Black and Mexican-American students (ages 8–12). Measures included length of time students worked on school subjects, rate of academic productivity, and accuracy of the material. The results showed a positive and significant impact of the behavioral approach, and these gains were maintained except for time at work.

Felton (1972, 1973b) studied the impact of a combination of reading and writing instruction, study skills, problem-solving training, and group therapy on 15 Black male and female college underachievers compared to nine Black underachieving college females who served as the control group. He reported significant gains in IQ for the treatment subjects.

Traditional counseling, tutoring, and mentoring were combined for an experimental group of 150 underachieving and disadvantaged college freshmen (Obler, Francis, & Wishengrad, 1977). The control group contained 150 matched underachieving and culturally disadvantaged students. The experimental group showed superiority across all of the measures, which included GPA, personal growth, and student and teacher ratings.

Few studies have followed underachievers over long periods of time. Most have used treatment measures pretreatment and at termination. Several have done a follow-up, which usually occurs between 3 and 6 months following termination. The following studies attempted to monitor the long-term history of underachievers.

Jackson, Cleveland, and Merenda (1975) investigated the impact of early identification of underachievers and the differential outcome when early psychological intervention was provided. They examined the records of 117 fourth-grade underachievers and followed up six years later. Those in the treatment group, who received psychological intervention which was primarily parent- and teacher-centered during Grades 4–6, were, at high school graduation, significantly higher in class ranking and on standardized achievement testing.

Smith (1971) followed 50 achieving and 50 underachieving bright college males over a 5-year period. He concluded that many bright underachievers would have improved with early academic guidance regarding academic program choices. Fearn (1982) reported on the gifted underachievement treatment program in San Diego, focusing on Grades 6, 8, and 10. When students' programs were aimed at basic skills, achievement levels rose the most.

Valine (1976) followed 54 college freshmen underachievers through their postsecondary education and measured differences between those who graduated and those who dropped out. Those who stayed to their senior year had significantly greater self-concept ratings, reflecting more positive views of self.

In summary, a number of single-treatment studies at the elementary, junior high, high school, and college and university levels have reported an equal number of positive and negative GPA outcomes, with a slight advantage in favor of positive outcomes at the college and university levels. This may have less to do with the treatment than with increasingly narrow client samples, especially in regards to intellectual capacity. However, many of these outcome studies cannot be compared because of the paucity of detailed descriptions of the participants, use of a wide variety of unrelated instruments, and shorter versus longer treatment periods. In addition, the treatment approaches are only briefly described, often in the form of a single statement labeling a general theoretical orientation. It is hard to ascertain whether the professed approach is in fact the approach that was used. Overall, the picture is mixed and inconclusive with regard to single-treatment approaches to underachievement and changes in GPA. Many of the studies reported personality changes in the absence of achievement change.

There have been few longitudinal projects which have tracked underachievers through their academic careers. Those long-term follow-up studies which exist, however, make clear the value of early and varied interventions. The negative long-term effects of early underachievement are clearly documented.

Comparing Different Treatment Approaches

Several researchers have compared differing treatment approaches (including combinations and modifications) to determine which are more effective. The assumption underlying these studies appears to be that one approach (or combination) will emerge as the clear treatment of choice for underachievers. This assumes that underachievers comprise a homogeneous group. Unfortunately, these studies rarely question and often do not even state this assumption.

Rosentover (1974) compared the effectiveness of two treatment approaches for both male and female university underachievers. One hundred eighteen second-, third-, and fourth-year students were assigned to rational-reflective group therapy (10 sessions), a group which focused on career information (10 sessions), or a no-treatment control group. Rosentover found no significant differences in GPA among the groups following treatment.

Hanley (1971) attempted to alter achievement patterns through the use of individual and group counseling with 36 10th- and 11th-grade underachievers. Two counselors were used, and the three research groups were individual counseling, group counseling, and a no-treatment control. Each treatment subject was expected to attend six counseling sessions. Hanley found that neither individual nor group counseling significantly altered the underachievers vocational maturity, self-concept of ability, or GPA. He did find that female underachievers had a higher vocational maturity rating, but they were also lower in mean GPA and mean self-concept of ability ratings when compared to the male underachievers. It is possible that six sessions were simply not sufficient to produce the desired changes.

Chestnut (1965), in a study on underachieving college males, compared two group counseling approaches with a control, and organized his matched groups as follows: counselor structured (CS), group structured (GS), and no-treatment control. The counselor-structured participants showed a significantly higher rate of change in GPA at the termination of counseling, but three months later, there was no longer any difference between the CS and GS groups. These findings imply that the rate of achievement change in college underachievers may be temporally affected in different ways by the type of group structure.

Semke (1968) randomly assigned 163 underachieving college freshmen to a case-study-structured counseling group, an unstructured nondirective counseling group, or a no-treatment control. Group discussions were focused on problem cases of students. No significant changes in GPA occurred due to either of the treatment approaches used, although some positive changes in self-concept were noted.

Hoopes (1969) used a structured goal-oriented group, group counseling, and a no-treatment control. In the goal-structured approach, performance and behavior standards regarding schoolwork were specified. However, 27 underachievers dropped out of the program, creating a nonrandom distribution of subjects who were continuing. It is interesting to note that while attrition from such programs is rarely mentioned as a major research problem, clinicians have been concerned about the problem of keeping underachievers in treatment and research programs.

Sims and Sims (1973) investigated leader-present versus leader-absent group experiences with 48 underachieving eighth-grade males. The students were assigned either to direct (leader-present) group counseling or to indirect (leader-absent) group counseling. The 50-minute sessions were held twice weekly for 12 weeks. In the indirect group, the leader was in communication with the group but not present during sessions. These researchers speculated that it might be easier for insecure underachievers to express themselves when an adult was not present, especially considering these underachievers' supposed negative experiences with parents. The hypothesis appeared to be supported. The indirect group members did talk more about a range of topics, including school.

Some researchers have attempted to alter specific personality characteristics of underachievers. Klein, Quarter, and Laxer (1969) utilized nAch and risk-taking training. They assigned 60 underachieving seventh and eighth graders to one of three groups: nAch training, risk-taking training, or nAch plus risk-taking training. There were no significant group differences in GPA or on other independent measures of change. They concluded that such training did not produce any academic performance changes.

Zani (1969) investigated the differential effects of intensive versus protracted counselor-directed group counseling with 48 underachieving high school students. Students were randomly assigned to intensive small-group counseling, protracted small-group counseling, or a no-treatment control. Intensive treatment involved small-group ($N = 4$) counseling for daily 55-minute sessions over 11 consecutive school days. This approach could be labeled as massed, time-limited treatment. The protracted approach involved small-group ($N = 4$) counseling for weekly 55-minute sessions over 11 weeks. The control groups simply met with teachers.

Zani used various measures to test for change over time, including GPA, teacher ratings of student traits, and the California Personality Inventory. He found significant differences in pre- to postmeasures on personal adjustment, self-reliance, withdrawing tendencies, and school relations for one or both of the experimental treatment groups when compared to the control group findings. Mean differences were highest for the intensive treatment group, in the midrange for the protracted treatment group, and low for the no-treatment control group. Thus intensive, massed treatment produced the greatest change in these underachievers.

Comparisons have also been made between directive and nondirective group counseling. Castelyns (1967) assigned 36 matched underachieving male and female seventh and eighth graders to one of the two approaches Zani used or to a third one-session, motivational, control group. He found no significant differences in GPA or on any other variables tested.

Baymur and Patterson (1960) compared individual versus group counseling of high school underachievers. They assigned their 32 subjects to one of four matched conditions: individual counseling, group counseling, a one-session motivational experience, or a no-treatment control. Significant differences were obtained on GPA and adjustment score change for the first two groups.

Von Klock (1966) compared individual with group counseling seventh- and eighth-grade male underachievers. The treatment group met once per week for two semesters. There were no statistical differences among the two treatment groups and a no-treatment control group on GPA, behavior ratings, or Q-sort measures. However, when von Klock compared the combined treatment groups with the no-treatment control, there were significant GPA changes during treatment and at the follow-up as well. Further, those underachievers who received individual counseling continued to increase their GPA at the follow-up point, which was not true for the group counseling subjects. Von Klock concluded that individual counseling is an effective means of altering GPA in underachieving junior high school students.

Lichter (1966) also compared individual with group counseling, but with underachieving college males ($N = 60$). Each treatment participant received 10 sessions, one per week. The structure of the group and individual therapy was not preset but was adjusted to best meet the needs of the participants. Lichter found that both treatment groups improved their GPA significantly, which was not the case for the no-treatment control group. Interestingly, these students did not show any significant changes in self-concept ratings, pointing to the possibility that personality measures may remain static while achievement behavior changes. Many other studies have reported changes in personality ratings without any parallel change in GPA. One major problem with this type of study is that the details of the therapeutic approach are not clearly delineated, making it difficult to replicate the study.

Comparisons have also been made among individual, group, and a combination (group followed by individual) treatment of underachievers. Goebel (1967) assigned 36 underachieving 10th graders to individual counseling ($N = 8$), group counseling ($N = 8$), group followed by individual counseling ($N = 8$), and a no-treatment control ($N = 12$). Experienced, on-site school counselors provided all of the treatment. The treatment length was only three–four sessions, with the combined treatment group receiving two group sessions followed by two individual sessions. There were no significant differences among all groups on all measures, but this is not surprising given the brief nature of the counseling program.

Variations on this treatment combination theme were reported by Keppers and Caplan (1962). They worked with 28 underachieving 10th-grade males, and created four groupings: underachieving student counseling, parent counseling without students, parents and underachieving sons counseling, and a no-treatment control. The counseling took place once per week for 12 weeks, each session lasting 1 hour. Increases in agreement between self and ideal Q-sorts occurred for underachievers in the second group, i.e., for those students whose parents only had been in counseling. Achievement measures were not used.

Ignas (1969) used the following treatment approaches with 48 underachieving seventh, eighth, and ninth graders: (1) individual counseling, (2) group counseling (students only), (3) group counseling (parents and students), (4) group guidance activities, and (5) a no-treatment control situation. He found that Groups 3 and 4 produced significantly higher GPAs than did any of the others. Further, those students who were in any of the experimental groups produced significant changes on some scales of the High School Personality Questionnaire. Those who were in Groups 2 and 4 showed significantly better school attendance during the course of the program than those in Groups 1 and 3. Taking into account the small cell sizes for each treatment approach and keeping in mind that the focus was on junior high school students, the results of this study do support differential treatment effects on achievement and other measures.

Perkins (1970) and Perkins and Wicas (1971) investigated various counseling structures on 120 matched underachieving ninth-grade males and their mothers. The groups were organized as follows: (1) group counseling (sons only, $N = 6$), (2) group counseling (mothers and sons separately, $N = 6 +$

6), (3) group counseling (mothers only, $N = 6$), and (4) a no-treatment control (mothers and sons, $N = 6 + 6$). Prior to the study, the counselors were given a 40-hour counseling orientation program on the role of empathy, genuineness, warmth in the treatment process, and other basic aspects of counseling. Counseling consisted of 12 1-hour weekly sessions for each group. Both studies reported significant and equivalent GPA increases for all treatment groups. For Groups 2 and 3, there was also a highly significant and equivalent increase in students' self-acceptance ratings. Five months following counseling, the GPA increases continued for those subjects in Group 3.

There have been a number of studies which have used behavioral techniques as one of their treatment approaches. Gourley (1971) compared the impact of individual counseling, group guidance, and verbal reinforcement on the achievement patterns of 48 9th-grade and 48 11th-grade underachievers. The four groups they were placed in were nondirective individual counseling, group guidance, verbal reinforcement, and a control situation. Treatment occurred over an 18-week period. Gourley found no significant GPA differences among any of the groups, including no differences between male and female GPAs. She did find significant sex differences at the 9th-grade level for the study habits measure, and at the 11th-grade level she found significant sex and treatment differences for study habits and attitude measures. She concluded that short-term, nondirective individual counseling, group guidance, or verbal reinforcement do not produce any significant changes in GPA, even though brief individual client-centered therapy does produce study habits and attitude improvement.

Bouchillon (1971) assigned each of 35 college underachievers enrolled in a study skills program to (1) individual client-centered counseling ($N = 6$), (2) group-centered counseling ($N = 6$), (3) individual reinforcement ($N = 6$), (4) group reinforcement ($N = 6$), or (5) a no-treatment control ($N = 11$). Bouchillon did not use pre- and post-GPA, but was more interested in self-concept changes. Groups 1 and 2 showed significant increases in self-concept, while Groups 3 and 4 did not, with the greatest increases in the individual client-centered counseling sample. It is not known what changes, if any, occurred in academic performance.

Andrews (1971) also compared behavioral and client-centered approaches in the treatment of 32 anxious underachieving male high school students. The behavioral approach produced significant decreases in anxiety levels as compared to the client-centered. Neither group showed increases in GPA.

Hussain (1971) studied the outcomes of various behavioral and traditional insight-oriented group therapies on underachievement. Her subjects were fourth- and fifth-grade lower middle-class students who were underachieving significantly below grade level in reading. She assigned eight subjects to each of five groups: noncontingent verbal and token reinforcement, practice in reading, behavior modification (work completion), traditional group therapy, and a no-treatment control. She found no group differences in reading achievement or GPA.

Sawyer (1974) compared a number of treatment approaches to find out what differential impact they might have on both achievement and self-concept of 44 seventh-grade underachievers. She divided her subjects into three groups: (1) control (no-treatment), (2) token reinforcement, and (3) modeling. Subjects in Group 2 received direct reinforcers from teachers and back-up reinforcers (free time and candies) from counselors as part of two academic courses. The subjects in Group 3 were asked to watch 5-minute segments of a film about achievement and to spend about 25 minutes after each segment in group counseling to discuss the film. Again, as in previous research, no significant GPA group differences were found, but there were some self-concept changes in Group 2 (token reinforcement).

Lowe and McLaughlin (1974) compared two behaviorally oriented approaches (verbal reinforcement and a Hawthorne control condition) implemented by high school teacher trainees working with 30 underachieving fourth-grade males. Those students in the verbal-reinforcement group showed significant improvement when compared with those in the Hawthorne control group and a no-treatment control.

Hawkins (1974) studied the impact of several behavioral approaches on inappropriate or problematic classroom behavior of 9-, 10-, and 11-year-old male Conduct Disorder underachievers. Hawkins assigned the students to one of three groups: positive reinforcement, response cost, or baseline (no-treatment). The response cost group showed the most significant positive changes in classroom behavior and academic production, although both behavioral approaches produced significant positive results. This is one of the few studies which controlled for personality characteristics within the underachieving sample, namely by limiting the research to Conduct Disorder underachievers. The findings were significant, both in terms of impact on classroom behavior and academic output.

Mitchell, Hall, and Piatkowska, (1975b) used behaviorally oriented remedial approaches with 94 bright underachieving college males who scored high on test and school anxiety measures but low on study habits and specific academic skills. All participated in a structured small-group program focused on academic and vocational goal-setting. Each of 84 was then assigned to one of the following groups: desensitization, relaxation training, reeducative training, or various control groups. Ninety-three percent of those who received counseling for test and school anxiety and study habits and skills improved from failing to passing grades by the end of the program, and 73% of the original sample had maintained these gains 2 years later.

Cheuvront (1975) assigned each of 80 junior high and high school underachievers a behavior-modification training group, a placebo group (i.e. group sessions without training), or a no-treatment control group. Significant increases in GPA for all occurred for all groups.

McLaughlin (1977) compared two behavioral approaches by assigning each of 80 underachieving sixth to ninth graders to a behavior modification group, a behavior modification plus counseling group, a placebo group in which students were given additional attention, or a no-treatment control group. The teachers and houseparents used as counselors were given 4 hours of training in behavior techniques to increase desired behavior and decrease nondesired behavior. Both treatment approaches produced changes in self-concept and attitudes towards achievement. However, only the combined behavioral and counseling approach produced significant increases in GPA. Further, these changes were still observed at a 5-month follow-up period.

Decker (1978) compared two behavior approaches in the treatment of test anxiety. In the first group, the participants were trained in cue-controlled relaxation (CCR), which they were encouraged to apply to studying and test-taking. They were then assisted in cognitive restructuring (CR) using a specific training procedure. The second group was given a study skills and counseling (SS + C) approach which combined goal setting (including organizational and study habits focus), increasing awareness, decision making, and developing more positive attitudes towards school subjects. A no-treatment control was also used. Both treatment groups showed significant positive change on a number of self-report measures, and these changes were maintained in two subsequent follow-up assessments. The one measure which did not reach significance was GPA.

Another study which compared behavioral approaches to alter underachievement in latency-age children was reported by Cohen (1978). Using only seven subjects, he found that a combination of self-monitoring and token reinforcement techniques produced substantial changes in behavior, but no changes in achievement levels.

Zeeman (1982) investigated socially alienated and underachieving high school students under different treatment conditions: (1) psychology course (Personality and Human Development), (2) tutorial project (teaching elementary students), (3) a combination of Groups 1 and 2, and (4) a no-treatment control. He reported that all of the treatment groups showed significant increases in self-concept scores, with the largest increases in Group 1. Group 2 participants showed more academic increases than did those in the control group, while Group 3 students showed general improvement in their school behavior. The author concluded by emphasizing the differential contributions of each approach.

Comparisons have also been reported between encounter group and related group counseling approaches with underachievers. Myrick and Haight (1972) placed each of 429 male and female high school underachievers (ratio 3:1, male:female) into growth group counseling, individual counseling, or a no-treatment control. The growth group counseling focused on school-related topics such as satisfaction with school and teachers and concerns about the future. Counseling sessions were held twice a week for 4 weeks. No major differences were reported in GPA among the three groups, although teacher ratings showed significant improvement for the two treatment samples.

Stone (1972) attempted to organize a study skills group of underachieving college freshmen but had a great deal of difficulty in recruiting underachieving students because of their negativity to counseling. Finally, she found enough interested students. She subdivided the males and females into (1) group counseling and (2) an encounter group marathon. Group 1 consisted of six 2-hour group counseling sessions. Group 2, the encounter group, met for one 6-hour session and chose not to meet again. A third group served as the no-treatment control. No significant group differences in GPA were found, although those in the counseled group did increase their self-concept ratings significantly. The encounter group treatment time was half that of the group therapy experience but the value of a longer encounter group experience, or one that is spread out over a greater number of sessions, remains to be explored.

Another area of comparison research has been to look for differential effects between counseling (i.e., internal focus) and environmental manipulation (i.e., external focus). Eller (1971) identified 42 underachieving high school students and assigned them randomly to a counseled group, an environmental manipulation group, or a no-treatment control. The students were then tested to assure that they were comparable on achievement, socioeconomic, and self-concept measures. The counseled group participated in weekly nondirective group sessions which lasted one academic term. Students in the environmental manipulation group were assigned specific environmental solutions based on a Self-Solution Underachievement Checklist which they had completed. These environmental manipulations included being assigned to special reading class, individual tutoring, conferences with teachers, changing timetables and class schedules, study habit remediation, and parent involvement. Eller found no significant differences among the three groups in GPA changes, although the counseled group did show a significant increase in self-concept measures.

Using a variety of counseling approaches and reading instruction (each lasting approximately 14 hours), Teigland, Winkler, Munger, and Kranzler (1965) reported no significant changes in the GPAs of 121 elementary school underachievers.

Eckhardt (1975) structured her study of elementary school students in upper grades to take into account the time between treatment of underachievers and any observable changes in GPA or self-concept. Her groups were (1) group counseling for 64 sessions, (2) a no-treatment control, and (3) a learning-disabled group. She found no significant increases in GPA in Groups 1 or 3, but the control group means had in fact increased significantly. Within three months, however, the group means showed no differences across all three groups. No self-concept differences were obtained at any point in the study.

Barcai, Umbarger, Thomas, and Chamberlain (1973) assigned each of 62 underachieving fourth and fifth graders from lower socioeconomic strata to group counseling, group remediation, or art activity. They found differential effects (including changes in achievement) related to classroom environmental factors and to treatment approach. These results were later reported by Barcai and Dreman (1976).

Doyle (1978) compared small-group counseling with teacher-consultation intervention to see the changes in achievement levels of 66 underachieving ninth graders. The small-group counseling group met for 30 sessions, each lasting about 50 minutes. The counseling orientation was nonstructured, focusing on the present concerns of the students. The teacher-consultation group participated in 150 sessions which were similar to the first group, except that this group was led by a teacher. Both treatment groups showed significant increases in GPA as well as on self-esteem measures, and students from both groups graduated from ninth grade at a significantly higher rate than did the students in a no-treatment control group.

Valine (1974) utilized videotape with first-year college underachievers, each assigned to one of four groups: counseling with immediate video feedback, counseling with delayed video feedback, counseling with no video feedback, and a no-treatment control. Approximately two-thirds reported that videotape feedback was helpful in stimulating group discussion. No academic performance measures were used.

Sharma (1975) tested the effectiveness of a rational-emotive group approach with 84 anxious high school underachievers assigned to rational-emotive group counseling, a teaching of rational ideas group, a study skills instruction, or a no-treatment control. The assumption was that high-anxious underachievers uncritically accept irrational beliefs about themselves and school, beliefs which interfere with effective academic performance. As predicted, those anxious underachievers from the rational counseling sample reported a significant decrease in their "irrational" beliefs. At a 5-month follow-up, these same students showed a significantly greater GPA improvement. Thus, identifying a specific type of underachiever (in this case the high-anxious underachiever) and using an approach which addresses some of this student's personal needs and characteristics, results in significant changes in personality characteristics and achievement. We will present strikingly similar findings from our own research in Chapter 9.

Rodick and Henggeler (1980) treated 56 low-achieving, inner-city seventh-grade Black students. The approaches used were a motivation reading technique, home environment restructuring with parents, a standard reading approach, and a no-treatment control. Students from the first two groups showed significant increases in academic skills and achievement motivation.

Most of the studies cited have attempted to produce changes in achievement levels through intervention. One study investigated what happens to problem-solving skills of underachievers and overachievers under conditions of low and high stress. Rollins and Calder (1975) studied 12 underachieving and 10 overachieving tenth-grade males. They assigned each and his parents to either a success or a failure stress lab situation. When the level of stress was increased, underachievers tended to decrease their problem-solving flexibility, whereas overachievers tended to increase these abilities. According to Rollins and Calder, differences in self-perceptions of personal adequacy accounted for these findings, with the underachievers feeling significantly less adequate personally.

Gerler, Kenney, and Anderson (1985) used the multimodal approach in group counseling with third- and fourth-grade underachievers. The multimodal approach combines individual and group treatment and stresses the importance of behavioral, affective, sensory, cognitive, and interpersonal dimensions. Twenty-four underachievers underwent this multimodal approach, while 24 matched underachievers served as a no-treatment control. Students' GPAs and perceptions of classroom behavior increased significantly in the multimodal group. It is conceivable that each component of the multimodal approach differential impacts on different types of underachieving students.

The reader will note that no one treatment of choice has emerged from the studies reviewed in this section.

Outcome from Miscellaneous Approaches

Some studies report attempts to alter achievement patterns by the use of nontraditional approaches. For example, Nemecek (1972) used a human potential seminar focused on themes of self-actualization and achievement as a means of changing achievement patterns in 39 university underachievers, but no changes in GPA were found. Stimpson and Pedersen (1970) used survival training to enhance self-esteem in underachieving high school students. They reported significant changes in self-evaluation and evaluation of parents and peers by eight students. GPA was not used in this study.

Using an achievement motivation course, Biggs and Felton (1973) attempted to alter anxiety patterns in 79 male and female underachieving college students. No achievement measures were used. The female students produced significantly lowered anxiety scores at the conclusion of the course, while the male underachievers did not. Furthermore, the reduction of anxiety was marked among the high-anxious underachievers, but not among the low-anxious underachievers.

McCurdy, Ciucevich, and Walker (1977) reported using a human-relations training program with 12 underachieving seventh graders with behavior problems. Only nine completed the training, but they showed positive changes in self-esteem. GPA was not used. Rocks (1985) reported that interpersonal skills training for 30 teachers and 60 underachieving high school students produced no significant changes in GPA, nor did it alter student attendance or attitudes. Duclos (1976) also employed a systematic human relations training model with 36 underachieving first-year college women. No changes in GPA were found as a result of the program. Thirty hours of structured socialization were used with 28 underachieving male Canadian high school students (Claes, 1976). Positive increases in self-evaluation were reported in the experimental group, as well as the attribution to an increase in the willingness of the students to plan their personal goals realistically. No GPA measures were used.

Rawson (1973) organized a summer camp educational experience (including academic remediation) with 24 underachieving and behavior problem students. The program was run by teachers. Emphasis was placed on group-dependent activities in which cooperation by all members was a requisite for successful completion of the activity. Significant gains were reported in GPA and in attitudes towards peers and teachers. Academic encouragement of underachievers has also been used at the college level (McGuire & Noble, 1973). No differences were found between the experimental and control groups on pre- and post-GPAs.

Darrell and Wheeler (1984) reported that art therapy was an effective method of altering attitudes and self-perceptions of 12 underachieving seventh graders.

Single session counselling has also been used in an attempt to alter achievement patterns (Long, 1967). This session included feedback regarding the student's ability level in relation to academic achievement, identification of specific problems, discussion of the potential effect of such personal difficulties on academic performance, and referral to relevant information sources. No significant results were reported, and longer term counseling was recommended.

Thompson, Griebstein, and Kuhlenschmidt (1980) used EMG biofeedback and relaxation training with 19 underachieving, anxious, first-year college women. Positive changes in GPA were reported for the experimental group, suggesting the value of such an approach with a specific type of academic underachiever.

In summary, a wide range of nontraditional approaches have been used with underachievers. These include human-potential seminars, survival training, motivation courses and encouragement, human relations training, summer camp, art therapy, single session counseling, and biofeedback and relaxation training. The results are difficult to assess in that the age groups varied, too few studies using each approach have been reported, not all studies utilized actual achievement (GPA) as a change measure, and instruments used varied widely. In general, the results are as inconclusive for these nontraditional methods as for the more traditional methods.

Teachers/Parents/Peers/Underachievers as Therapists

Some have asked teachers, parents, and peers to change the achievement patterns of underachievers. Birr (1969) used parents and teachers of 60 junior high school underachievers. In seven group meetings, parents of 30 underachievers were provided with methods designed to enhance the self-concept of their children's abilities. Fifty teachers were asked to facilitate the self-concept of ability of a second group of 30 underachievers. The control group consisted of another 30 underachievers who received neither parental training nor teacher input. No significant GPA differences were reported at the end of treatment.

Horowitz (1967) studied 36 underachieving and behavior problem male elementary school students (Grades 2–4) and trained their parents in a behaviorally oriented treatment approach. The parent-therapists produced had a positive impact on their hyperactive and withdrawn children, but the underachievers who did not exhibit behavior problems did better without parental intervention. Enzer (1975) reported a similar use of parents as therapists in a behavioral approach with two underachieving children.

A number of studies have utilized peer counseling. Vriend (1969) found that peer study groups significantly improved the grades, social skills, and raised expectations of 48 inner-city 11th-grade underachievers. Bridges (1972), however, did not find changes in GPA as a result of a peer-facilitated small-group approach with 52 underachieving college freshmen. Similar work in the use of peers as models was reported by Pigott, Fantuzzo, Heggie, and Clement (1984), who used a group-oriented contingency program administered by students. These researchers reported a significant increase in underachievers' math achievement, but follow-up data were less encouraging. The academic achievement scores in math remained above the original baselines, but they did not continue to improve. Bost (1984) also reported significant increases in GPA of 67 college freshmen underachievers as a result of participation in time-management peer counseling. Wolfe, Fantuzzo, and Wolter (1984) reported the successful use of reciprocal peer management and group contingencies on arithmetic scores of 15 underachieving fifth and sixth graders.

A number of researchers have used underachievers as helpers of other underachievers. Erickson and Cromack (1972) used 12 underachieving seventh-grade males to tutor the same number of underachieving third-grade males, and the changes were compared to matched classmates. Significant academic gains were reported for both the tutored and tutor groups. Strikingly similar findings were reported by Allen and Feldman (1973) in their work with 10 fifth-grade underachievers' tutors. Bar-Eli and Raviv (1982) organized 15 male underachieving fifth and sixth graders who were poor in math as tutors for 15 second-grade underachievers who were also doing poorly in math. Both groups showed significant academic gains in math after a 4-month period, and the fifth- and sixth-grade tutors also showed a significant overall academic improvement.

Other researchers have studied the impact of underachievers on younger students who had been identified as struggling with mental-health and behavior problems. McWilliams and Finkel (1973) used 15 underachieving high school students to help 23 problem students enrolled in grades 1–3. They reported positive results for the elementary school students. Tefft and Kloba

(1981) carried out a similar study with 16 underachieving high school students who were matched with 20 elementary school acting-out or shy problem children. They reported positive results.

In summary, it appears that counseling programs or approaches staffed by nonprofessional therapists can produce increases in academic performance in underachieving students, although not all studies have confirmed this conclusion. Fewer reports of the use of parents or teachers as change agents have appeared in the literature, and the results are equivocal.

Tutoring or Study Skills Training

Olsen (1969) studied changes in self-concept, achievement, and intelligence in 60 underachieving second- to fourth-grade elementary school students in an enrichment tutoring program. Thirty students participated, while 30 other students were designated as a no-treatment control group. Measures included the Coopersmith Self-Esteem Inventory, the California Achievement Test, and the California Short-Form Test of Mental Maturity. All instruments were administered prior to and following the tutoring program. Overall, Olsen found that the program produced no differences in student self-concept, no changes in achievement scores, and no changes in intelligence scores between the experimental study skills group and the no-treatment control group. Olsen did report some significant differences in favor of the experimental group at specific grade levels. For example, the fourth graders in the experimental group exhibited higher social self-concept than did those in the control group, while at the second-grade level the tutored group exhibited significantly greater language achievement scores. Third-grade experimental group members scored significantly higher on arithmetic achievement than did the nontutored control group members. Further, teachers rated tutored students as exhibiting more positive self-confidence, self-attitudes, and self-worth than the control group students, as well as having improved study habits, improved academic performance, and improved reading.

Shaver and Nuhn (1971) studied the effect of tutoring on reading and writing of 4th-, 7th-, and 10th-grade underachievers. Underachievement was statistically defined through the use of the Sequential Tests of Educational Progress (STEP) and the California Test of Mental Maturity. Not only did tutoring produce significant increases compared to the control group across all three grade levels, but these gains held for 7th- and 10th-grade tutored students at a 2-year follow-up.

Treatment comparisons using underachievers as tutors for younger students were reported by Haggerty (1971). She studied 10th- and 11th-grade male high school underachievers and assigned each to one of three groups: group counseling, tutoring, or a no-treatment control. The counseled group met weekly, and the focus included school, friends, future goals, or problems with teachers, parents, and others. The tutoring group met twice each week.

The underachieving high school students who acted as tutors to the elementary school students showed the greatest improvement, with significant increases in GPA and self-concept measures. The counseled group produced significant increases in self-acceptance, but not in self-concept measures or in GPA. Further, their attitude toward school worsened during treatment.

Pigott, Fantuzzo, and Clement (1986) studied the effects of peer tutoring combined with group reinforcement contingencies on arithmetic performance of 12 underachieving fifth-grade students. At the end of the program, the tutored students' arithmetic scores were equal to those of the nontutored classmates of the underachievers. These academic gains were sustained at a follow-up 12 weeks later. Further, by the end of the program, the tutored students reported that they had increased their degree of affiliation with other tutored peers.

These studies support the notion that tutoring of underachievers and/or tutoring by underachievers can have a positive effect on academic performance and on certain social characteristics, and that these changes can last beyond the tutoring period. These studies, however, have not explored which types of underachievers tend to gain most from such an approach and which types tend to sustain these gains.

A number of researchers have examined study skills training and academic underachievement. Foreman (1969) used Robinson's SQ3R (Survey, Question, Read, Recite, and Review) study skills system with 45 bright underachieving college students (identified by the Quick Word Test and GPA). She found that a combined study skills and self-reinforcing program produced the greatest increase in outcome measures, which included the Nelson-Denny Reading Test, the Survey of Study Habits and Attitudes, the Test of Information About the Library, and the Study Habits Checklist. Those underachievers who received only the study skills program also showed gains, but these were less than the combined program participants. The no-treatment control underachievers showed no changes over time. Foreman speculated that her positive results, including significant GPA increases, were probably due both to the combination treatment and to the apparent higher motivational levels of her sample, since her results were more positive than previous research reports.

McQuaid (1971) developed and evaluated a study skills program with 108 underachieving eighth graders. These students were identified through the use of the Otis Quick-Scoring Mental Ability Test (Beta), and the Iowa Tests of Basic Skills. Pre- and postmeasures included the Sequential Tests of Educational Progress, Listening Test, Differential Aptitude Tests, Clerical Speed and Accuracy Test, and an achievement test constructed especially for the study. In addition, teacher and student evaluations were collected. Two matched groups of 54 underachievers were formed, one designated the study skills treatment group, and the other the no-treatment control. Findings included positive increases in the ability to use graphic aids, newspaper, reading, and library skills for the experimental group. Smaller increases were noted in listening skills, with no differences in alphabetizing skills. Again, no differentiation was made within each of the underachieving groups.

Through the use of group reinforcement counseling techniques, Altmann, Conklin, and Hughes (1972) offered study skills training to ninth-grade underachievers. Of the original 74 students contacted, 44 volunteered for the study while 30 did not. Achievement tests clearly indicated that the program was effective for those underachieving students who had volunteered. Those nonvolunteer underachievers who received a study guide instead of the study skills counseling also showed increases in achievement. It is highly probable that these results are confounded by the differences in motivational levels of the two groups of subjects.

Elder (1974) studied two groups of underachieving college freshman ($N = 391$) identified by SAT scores and GPA. The treatment group ($N = 50$) consisted of those who enrolled in and completed a remedial reading and study methods course, while the control group consisted of 315 underachieving students who had not received any special treatment. Those in the experimental group achieved significantly higher GPAs than predicted when compared with the control group. Elder made no differentiation within each group.

Robin, Martello, Foxx, and Archable (1977) used a systematic behavioral procedure to enhance the note-taking skills of college underachievers. Twelve underachievers, divided into two treatment groups, received identical note-taking enhancement training, while six underachievers were assigned to a no-treatment control. The treatment included "modeling, discrimination training, practice, prompting, shaping, fading, and positive feedback" (Robin, Martello, Foxx, and Archable, 1977). The treatment subjects showed significant increases in note-taking ability.

Crittenden, Kaplan, and Heim (1984) used a study and written language skills course to enhance the academic performance of 16 underachieving students in the sixth through ninth grades. Instruments included the Cornell Learning and Study Skills Inventory, Piers-Harris Children's Self-Concept Scale, the Picture Story Language Test, and questionnaires pertaining to demographic and intellectual information. There was a noted improvement in those specific skills which were taught, but no increases were observed in nontaught skills. Overall, males gained more from the program, females improved more in written and study skills, and younger subjects produced the most rapid rate of increase in skills. As in so many of these studies in the general literature, no information was presented regarding potential intragroup differences.

It appears that programs to enhance the study skills of underachieving students have produced positive results, particularly when combined with other approaches. Yet, none of the studies cited looked carefully at the similarities and differences among the underachievers, nor have they examined the potential impact of different study skills training on different types of underachievers.

Differential Diagnosis and Treatment of Underachievement

Few studies have assumed that underachievers comprise a heterogeneous group in need of differential diagnosis and differential treatment. Further, only a few investigators who had begun with a homogeneous concept of underachievement have modified their views based on findings which obviously suggest heterogeneity of the sample as a possible explanation. These studies will be summarized here.

Gilbreath (1967) reported a comparative group counseling design in examining the issue of dependence in college underachievers. He organized the two types of groups: authority leader-structured (LS) and group-structured (GS). Ninety-six male underachievers were divided between these two group counseling approaches. The underachievers were categorized on the basis of degree of dependence versus independence. Gilbreath reported significant GPA changes for the LS group when the underachievers were high-dependent. Conversely, with the high-independent underachieving group, he found that the GS group format resulted in significant increases in GPA. In other words, by differentiating within the underachieving sample, Gilbreath was able to show differential effectiveness related to different treatment approaches.

Chestnut and Gilbreath (1969), reporting a 3-year follow-up of 80 of these same underachievers, found no differences in GPA across the LS, GS, and control groups. Interestingly, these researchers did find one subgroup with continuing significant GPA differences; namely, even after three years, those high-dependent underachievers who received LS counseling continued to show higher GPAs than matched high-dependent underachievers who received GS counseling. These researchers also replicated their research, which confirmed the earlier findings (Gilbreath, 1968).

Gilbreath (1971) compared a group of motivated male college underachievers with a comparable group who did not respond when offered counseling. He reported that even without counseling, the motivated group significantly increased their GPA, and that this increase held over a 2-semester period of time, highlighting the role of motivation in the underachievement and change processes.

Allen (1975) constructed a Student Behavior Inventory (SBI) to examine various behavior categories which might differentiate types of underachievers. In the initial stages of his research, teachers rated the behaviors of 518 underachievers using the SBI. Factor analysis revealed four behavioral factors which differentiated within the underachieving sample. He then refined the SBI by administering it to 4,089 public school students in Grades 4 through 8 and found four refined differentiating factors: aggression, alienation, anxiety, and activity. Allen analyzed these factors and determined that they represented distinct and different behaviors. The mean scores of each factor gradually increased from Grades 4 through 8, except for a significant decrease in all factor means at Grade 6. Underachievers as a group scored higher on all four factors. Gender did not affect the mean scores in Grades 4 and 5, but did in Grades 6–8 for both underachievers and achievers. The best overall single predictor of underachievement was the alienation factor. Allen's four factors appear related to four of the DSM-III differential diagnoses of underachievers which we will describe in detail in chapters 10 through 14.

Krouse and Krouse (1981) proposed a multimodal theory of academic underachievement. They recommended that underachievement be viewed as the result of a complex interaction among three major contributing factors: academic skill deficiencies (poor self-discipline, self-control), self-monitoring skills (which would affect time management), and emotional factors (including personality characteristics and makeup) which interfere with achievement. Although not using the identical model, Ludwig (1981) also recommended a differential explanation and treatment for underachievement.

One unique study at the junior high school level examined the relationship between underachievement and depression. Seagull and Weinshank (1984) asked teachers to identify depressed underachievers through the use of a rating scale. Sixteen identified depressed underachievers were matched with a control group. The researchers found that depressed underachievers were absent from school and were late for school significantly more often than were achievers. The depressed underachievers were rated by teachers as more task avoidant, more anxious, and more introverted than those in the control group. The parents of these depressed underachievers rated them as less socially competent when compared with the ratings of parents of achieving students. Clinicians rated the depressed underachievers as lower in overall affect when compared to the achieving students. The parents of depressed underachievers also had fewer years of formal education, and were more likely to use corporal punishment in their child-rearing practices.

Over the past two decades, several review articles have appeared which summarize major findings and trends in the treatment of academic underachievement. Gurman (1969) concluded that more studies needed to be conducted using behaviorally oriented approaches such as cognitive therapy, goal-directed treatment, and problem-solving. He urged that these be compared with the more traditionally oriented insight therapies. He would be pleased that his suggestions have been followed and that positive reports of behavioral and cognitive approaches now exist in the professional literature.

Gurman also tentatively concluded that leader-structured group treatment was effective in altering underachievement patterns. He cited specific counselor variables as affecting achievement change, although he criticized research in underachievement as not addressing these variables adequately. Gurman also concluded that short-term counseling appeared to be ineffective in producing achievement change in underachievers. Further, he criticized the lack of adequate outcome comparisons between individual and group therapies, as well as the wide range of methods of defining underachievement which further confound the findings.

Bednar and Weinberg (1970) focused on treatment outcome studies at the college level. They concluded that the most effective therapeutic approaches were those that were structured, longer term, and both academically and dynamically focused therapies in which a high level of empathy, warmth, and genuineness existed. They also found that to be maximally effective, they needed to adapt these techniques to the specific needs of the 23 underachievers they counseled.

Mitchell and Piatkowska (1974a, 1974b) also reviewed treatment outcome at the university level ($N = 31$), specifically focusing on group therapy. They attempted to isolate specific variables which were related to increases in GPA, such as the experience of the counselor, the type of counseling provided, the length and structure of treatment, outcome targets, and levels of client motivation for treatment and change. In general, they found few positive outcome reports and few clear relationships between specific variables and positive change in GPA.

Lowenstein (1979, 1983a) concluded that successful programs for underachievers tended to combine several approaches, often provided concurrently. She recommended the early identification and evaluation of underachievers, the application of systematic intervention, the involvement of parents in counseling, the addition of individual tutoring to any treatment approach, and the training of teachers to maintain a positive rapport with underachieving students.

Wilson (1986) reviewed 19 research studies in order to evaluate the impact of counselor intervention on GPA for underachieving elementary, junior high, and high school students. She found, as had Gurman, that directive and behaviorally oriented group programs of a longer term and voluntary nature tended to be associated with the largest GPA changes.

UNDERACHIEVEMENT: A CRITIQUE OF THE LITERATURE

To summarize, in reviewing the professional literature, major difficulties exist in reaching definitive conclusions based on the following:

1. Range of definitions of underachievement
2. Range of methods of identifying and categorizing underachievers
3. Use of widely divergent range of concepts to understand and instruments to measure personality characteristics of underachievers, thus making comparisons difficult
4. Overemphasis (until recently) on male underachievers

5. Lack of differentiation across underachievers, achievers, and over-achievers

6. Overemphasis on the mother-son dyad in family relationship studies, especially in research conducted in the 1960s and 1970s

7. Ignoring age differences in underachievement research; i.e., developmental differences from elementary to junior high, to high school, to college and university samples

8. Major unquestioned assumption by most researchers about the homogeneous nature of the underachiever group

9. Confounding nature of socioeconomic variables and achievement behavior

10. Lack of clarity and detail about specific approaches used in some treatment studies

11. Lack of consistent positive changes in GPA as a result of counseling

12. Evidence of personality change in the absence of any changes in achievement behavior

Still, with all of these difficulties, major trends have emerged in the literature. Research consistent with the model we hypothesize—which assumes that there is no single underachieving personality type—provides one way to explain and integrate many of the seemingly inconsistent findings that have been reviewed. The reader will find that, with a full understanding of this book, particularly the line of theory and research presented in Parts Two and Three, a rereading of Part One will yield new ways of accounting for these widely divergent findings.

PART TWO

The Model of Differential Diagnosis

This section provides the reader with the conceptual and practical series of assumptions, theories, and rationales which together form the research and clinical models we have adopted. Since the research and clinical accuracy of these models depends on the properly conducted diagnostic interview, we begin with the discussion of the interview procedure and its rationale in Chapter 4. Chapter 5 provides a framework for understanding the differential diagnostic method. Chapter 6 summarizes one clinical model, The Developmental Theory Model, which links specific diagnostic categories with stages of normal personality development and differing treatment methods.

The reader is alerted to the authors' having included in this section background material on the issues discussed in order to establish the groundwork for a thorough understanding of interviewing, diagnosis, and model development.

CHAPTER 4

The Diagnostic Interview

The theories, philosophies, concepts, and techniques of diagnostic interviewing form a voluminous and detailed literature extending back to the beginnings of psychological treatment and across to the procedures of virtually every psychotherapeutic approach. Our purpose in this chapter is neither to provide a comprehensive overview nor to present an approach that is radically different from the mainstream of diagnostic interviewing techniques. However, there are certain aspects of the fundamental techniques of interviewing which require special clarification.

The diagnostic interview recommended here is semistructured and tape-recorded (always with the consent of the student). The value of having a taped record is primarily so that other clinicians can independently make a diagnostic judgment. This is especially important if the resulting diagnosis is going to be used for research purposes or to make some educational or clinical decision involving the student. Depending upon the situation and the purpose of the interview, the time can range from 20 minutes up to an hour or more. Generally, we have found that 30 to 45 minutes is sufficient. Extra time should always be given if it is necessary either to get a somewhat more complete picture of the student or for other clinical reasons.

The data of an interview come from several sources. One is certainly the information provided by the student, although this is sometimes undependable, either because the student's information simply is not accurate enough or because the student is intentionally withholding or distorting facts. It is our view that the role of the interviewer is not to pass judgment on the truth or falsehood of the information elicited, at least for purposes of diagnostic interviewing. In fact, if certain information the student gives is found later to be false, rather than focusing on how the updated information changes the overall picture, perhaps more attention should be given to why the student would want to distort that particular piece of information and what this might imply diagnostically about the student.

Even more than in eliciting information, however, the diagnostic interviewer is interested in the student's *perceptions* of self, family, school, friendships, and the future. These perceptions, whether information contained in them is later found to be true or false, form an accurate and complete picture of what the student is willing to tell the interviewer. These perceptions can then be interpreted in a variety of ways. They can represent, for example, the way the student perceives his or her life situation. They can also represent, however, not the actual way the student perceives the world, but rather how he or she wants the interviewer to perceive that world.

A third important source of interview data comes from the interviewer's observations about the relationship processes going on during the interview. Many interviewers assess an interviewee's interpersonal style and major interpersonal issues from the reports that the interviewee gives concerning relationships outside of the interview. We believe that the single most powerful piece of data that an interviewer possesses is what goes on in the interview itself. The relationship between the interviewer and the interviewee, which is not always obvious but can often be inferred from a detailed review of the interview through tapes and discussions, is assumed to begin from the moment the two enter the same room and continue at least until the interview is over and the interviewee leaves.

The question arises, how can such a time-limited, apparently superficial, formalized procedure be considered a relationship in the same sense as a long-standing family, peer, or work relationship? There is, after all, no interpersonal history between the two people, perhaps very little in the way of common interests, and often no visible reason why at least one of the parties (the student) would even want to enter into a relationship. We can answer this question in several ways.

Many treatises on and guides to the art of interviewing discuss the need to form a relationship with the interviewee. Usually, it is assumed that this is accomplished by a certain attitude on the part of the interviewer (willingness to listen, acceptance of the interviewee as a person, and so forth). The implication of this kind of view seems to be that if the interviewer does not present him or herself in a particular way, then a relationship with the interviewee will not be formed. If all that the interviewer wanted was factual information from the interviewee, then this might make some sense. The interviewer, however, is trying to assess the nature of the relationship characteristics of the interviewee in his or her personal life.

With deference to the skills and insights of the countless clinicians who have advocated the need to form a relationship with the interviewee, we believe this view is one-sided in the sense that it ignores the fact that the *interviewee* may also (and, in our view, does also) approach the relationship hoping and expecting to form a relationship. Just because one of the parties is a mental health professional does not mean that he or she defines the presence or absence of a relationship or even the total nature of that relationship. In fact, the diagnostic aspect of the interview is precisely the assessment of those expectations, needs, and interpersonal pushes and pulls which the interviewee brings into the interview. We believe that the student enters the interview already expecting a particular kind of relationship and acting as if it already exists. To assume that this does not happen without the interviewer's allowing it to happen reflects a somewhat grandiose and unrealistic picture of the interview process, and indeed of any human relationship. What the interviewer can do, however, is to offer a relationship which does not "get in the way" of the interpersonal needs of the interviewee, so that in the interpersonal mix of the two individuals, those needs are likely to become more obvious to the interviewer.

We also need to consider the assumptions made in sampling statistics. Most of the time, statistics are used on small samples in order to make inferences about the larger populations from which they come. The experimental study in which laboratory rats are trained to complete a maze in a certain manner makes the assumption that consistent and unequivocal results on this small sample are generalizable to the entire population of laboratory rats and perhaps to other living things as well. The survey of randomly selected middle-class homes as to their television viewing preferences or political beliefs makes the assumption that the statistical procedures involved in random sampling allow a conclusion about the entire population of middle-class people. Even in physiology, such as an experiment in which a part of a monkey's brain is ablated and certain behavior is observed as a result, it is assumed that the results are generalizable to all other monkeys of that species. One does not conclude that the experiment is meaningless because one has not performed the same surgery on every monkey brain in existence.

In the statistical model, the whole is inferred by studying a part, in much the same way that a person who is given a piece of apple pie on a plate makes the likely inference that the whole pie this piece came from is made of the same stuff, is formed in a round shape (as inferred from the curved nature of the crust at the edge of the piece), and that any other piece is likely to look the same as this piece. This is a kind of thinking we take for granted every day without recognizing it as the basis on which a procedure such as sampling statistics makes sense. In fact, the very reason for sampling statistics in the first place is that it is not even *possible* to directly assess the entire population.

No matter how tenuous, fleeting, superficial, or time limited, the interview is in fact a relationship and is subject to the same interpersonal needs and interactional factors as any other relationship, albeit on a more limited basis. The authors believe that interpersonal needs and personality styles of interaction are always present, and not simply absent now and then because the interaction is not formally defined as a relationship. The interview is, indeed, a statistical sample of the larger population of the student's (and interviewer's) interpersonal interactions with others. From this sample inferences can be made about other interactions and the basic structure of the personality.

Now the question arises as to how any interviewer can be so positive as to make a diagnostic judgment on the limited basis of a half-hour or even an hour interview. The answer is that a diagnosis is not an unchangeable piece of reality that is written in stone. It is no more (and no less) than a working hypothesis, subject to change if warranted by new data. Those who argue that one can make no diagnostic judgments until a voluminous amount of data has been amassed make the erroneous and naive assumption that diagnosis comes *after* data collection. In fact, data collection is determined by diagnostic scheme; otherwise, how would one know what data to collect? In a diagnostic interview or any other diagnostic process, the diagnostician is making tentative hypotheses (or, if you will, diagnoses) from the first bit of data, testing each to see if it is confirmed, and eliminating or adding diagnostic judgments as the data are collected. It is no different in medical diagnosis nor in the most objective of laboratory experiments in physics or chemistry. In the diagnostic process we have adopted in this book, any diagnostic judgment about any particular student is open to question at any time in the light of new data or new insights into old data. We make no exceptions to this rule.

The interviewer, then, makes inferences about the student's characteristic style of relating to others by examining the brief here-and-now interaction in the interview. Based on the interview interaction, the interviewer should be able to reach some tentative conclusions about how dependent or independent the student is in seeking adult approval, or what kind of anxiety the student experiences in an interpersonal situation, or whether the student appears to have an internal or external locus of evaluation. How guarded is the student about his or her emotions? What is the nature of the thought processes this student has? Does the student evidence a sense of guilt or lack of guilt? Is the student introspective or not? These and countless other related questions are certainly possible to approach in an interview. The better the quality and meaningfulness of the information and perceptions elicited, and the greater the attention the interviewer gives to the interaction, the more likely these questions will result in a meaningful working hypothesis in the form of a diagnostic judgment.

If these are the interviewer's objectives, however, it is most important that an objective, friendly, nonjudgmental, low-keyed atmosphere be created. Without being confrontive or threatening, the interviewer must be able to utilize approaches which can rapidly probe the student's life and perceptions about that life. If such an attitude could be put into words, it might read as follows:

I am not here to judge you, evaluate you, do therapy with you, criticize you, praise you, confront you, or make any decision about you or for you. I am not here to force you to answer any questions you do not want to answer or that would make you overly uncomfortable. I am not here to change you. I am here to clarify my understanding of who you are, how you came to be who you are, and what your life experiences have been. I am interested and curious as to what your perceptions are of yourself, your family, your teachers, your friends, your present situation, your goals, your future, and how you plan to reach those goals and that future. I am interested—even intrigued—by what you have to say, and I hope that you will be able to enlighten my understanding of you. To understand you and your situation is all that I am here to do: simply to learn, clarify, and understand. I appreciate your giving me this opportunity to share who you are with me.

What is required here is what we would call *perceptual empathy*. Perceptual empathy is empathy not only for the range of emotions and affects which the interviewee has, but also for the interviewee's point of view: the way in which he or she perceives self and others, family and friends, opportunities and setbacks, past and future, choices and constraints, puzzlement and meaningfulness. It means a willingness to see the world through the eyes of the interviewee, to understand, *from the point of view of the interviewee,* the reasoning and logic that supports the interviewee's decisions, actions, and rationales. Perceptual empathy requires not evaluating or judging the perceptual world of the interviewee, but rather clarifying and understanding it. Diagnostically, it is most significant not only to catalogue the various symptom patterns, but to use perceptual empathy to define the world through the eyes of the interviewee. This is as important to a complete diagnostic picture as any other aspect of the process, and perhaps even more important.

We hope that the reader will understand that this philosophy of interviewing is embedded in our approach and that of our colleagues who have been trained in this model and who have taken the initiative to do research and report their findings in the many studies reviewed in this book. It is our belief that each interviewee, no matter how problematic his or her behavior, is a human being with unique perceptions, values, feelings, experiences, and goals, and that it would be presumptuous for any interviewer to be certain of understanding the totality of another's life based on only one interview hour. In fact, we advocate this same caution even with psychological test batteries, teacher and family reports, life history data, and other independent sources of information, all of which should be utilized routinely in any diagnostic assessment.

More than a humanistic philosophy of interviewing, it is our belief that only when the interviewer presents a low-keyed, nonprovocative, facilitative relationship, that the personality structure of the interviewee stands out most clearly in and on its own terms. The interviewer who asks threatening questions or utilizes a threatening or confrontive manner of approach may appear dynamic and able to ''get to the real feelings,'' but one can never be sure whether the interviewee's reaction is a typical part of his or her style or is a response to an unusually provocative interpersonal stimulus. Provocation and confrontation, in short, cloud the diagnostic picture. The low-keyed and positive approach advocated here will make the task of reaching a clearer understanding of the interviewee much easier, and is likely to make the diagnostic judgment more accurate.

The diagnostic interview is semistructured in the sense that while there are definite areas of focus, these are not necessarily in any particular order of presentation or importance, and it is not always necessary to gain specific information in all of these areas. Sometimes, for example, if a subject such as the opposite sex is mentioned by the interviewer, and the interviewee is determined to avoid that topic, it is enough, diagnostically, to know that the person is avoiding that area. Thus certain questions may or may not be answered in an interview. In addition, if the interviewee volunteers information in a given category, it is possible that the interviewer may not need to ask anything in that area.

A technical point about interviewing is that the interviewer is well advised to avoid a pattern of only asking questions. If this happens, the interview is likely to degenerate into a question-and-answer format rather than foster the kind of interpersonal rapport that will result in more substantive diagnostic data. When possible, the interviewer should consider statements rather than questions. For example, the question "How would you describe yourself?" could also be phrased, "Tell me something about yourself." Reflective statements could also be used instead of questions. For example, in place of "How do you feel about the grades you got this semester?" one could say, "I wonder how you feel about these grades." It is a small thing to rephrase in this manner, but it does avoid the interpersonal singsong effect of a question-and-answer format.

One should think of the interview process in much the same way as a projective test, such as the Rorschach ink blot test. The examiner asks only what the subject sees in the amorphous shapes. To answer, the subject must impose a structure not inherent in the design, and it is that structure—the personal perceptions and reactions, the structure of the person's psychic world—that the examiner attempts to assess in the person's responses.

Similarly, to answer a nonspecific question in a diagnostic interview, the interviewee must decide from the world of possibilities the context of the stimulus and must then structure a meaning and a response. If the interviewer says, "Tell me something about yourself," it is diagnostically significant whether the person answers by saying, "I'm five-foot-nine and I like sports," or "What is it you want to know?" or some other response. The interviewer's questions and comments are not the focus: the interviewee's responses are. From the way the person expresses him or herself, the diagnostician infers a world of affect, perception, style of interaction, way of thinking, and motivation. The interviewer's questions and comments should be thought of as evoking rather than provoking a response, similar to the hypnotic concept of evoking reactions, emotions, ideas, and behavior by use of hypnotic techniques (Erickson, Rossi, & Rossi, 1976).

There are five major areas or issues to which the interviewer will want the interviewee to respond. They are:

1. The nature of school performance and related issues, especially if they are problem areas
2. The nature of family relationships
3. The nature of social relationships (peers, the opposite sex, etc.)

4. The nature of the student's self-perceptions and affect
5. The student's perceptions of and plans for the future

We will now consider the relevant questions, issues, and factors possible to focus on in each of these areas.

1. *The nature of school performance and related issues, especially if they are problem areas*

This is the area where some specific information may be helpful, but the interviewer will also want to elicit attitudes, perceptions, expectations, rationales and other reasoning, and emotional reactions related to the educational situation: school subjects taken, performance in each subject (including grades, tests, papers, class performance, labs, etc.), attitudes toward each subject and the teachers, methods of study (memorization, test preparation, time management, etc.), problem areas, and so forth. If the interviewee is an adult, the interviewer can focus on similar issues related to career and vocation. As with other areas of focus, the interviewer should elicit as much detail as possible. Some typical questions and content areas are listed below. We will alternate questions, evocative statements, and reflective comments to give an example of the variety of linguistic possibilities available to the interviewer. These can, of course, be modified on the basis of the flow of the interview, the particular style of the interviewer, and the nature of the interviewee responses.

A. How are you doing in school this semester (or term)?
B. Specifically, which courses are you taking now?
C. Tell me how you're doing in each one. What is your grade in this particular course? Why did you receive that particular grade?
D. To what do you attribute your grade in each subject (i.e., for both those subjects that the student is doing poorly and well in)?
E. What are the marks based on in that particular course?
F. Did you expect to get the grade you did? I wonder why (or why not).
G. Are you satisfied with your grades? Why (or why not)? Are these the grades you really want? Why (or why not)?
H. If you're not getting the grades you really want, I wonder if you have some idea of why that is. What have you tried to do about it? What happened?
I. How much time do you spend on homework or study each day? Give me an example: How much did you study yesterday? And how much

did you accomplish in that time? Now tell me about the day before that. And before that.

J. Do you want to get better grades than the ones you are getting now? Why (or why not)?

K. Do you think you could be doing better? What can you do that you are not doing now? I wonder what's kept you from doing these things before.

L. Do you like school? Why (or why not)? Tell me the things you like about it and the things you don't like about it.

M. I wonder if you believe, as many people do, that school is important. Why (or why not)?

N. What would you change about school if you could?

O. How far do you plan to go in school? Why (or why not)?

P. Do you look forward to graduation? I wonder what you plan on doing after graduation.

Q. Have you performed at this level throughout your school career? (Ask for details.)

This list is neither exhaustive nor inviolate. The reader may well be able to generate a number of equally revealing questions, but this list should give a good idea of the range of focal areas possible within the question of school or vocation.

2. *The nature of family relationships*

In this portion of the interview, the focus can be on family composition, activities the family does separately and together, the frequency and importance of such activities, the interviewee's opinion of the perceptions of other family members regarding a particular issue (particularly the student's performance in school), questions about family conflicts, and so forth. In particular, the interviewer wants to assess the student's closeness to each family member, sense of affiliation, identity with a particular parent, relationships with siblings, the nature of any sibling's performance in school, what role the student feels he or she plays in the family, and related issues.

Overall, the interviewer wants to get a sense of the importance of family life to the student and his or her perception of roles in the family. Does the student seem to have a small or large investment in his or her family? How independent, rebellious, or happy does this student appear to be in relation to the family? How are family feelings expressed? How are family problems addressed and solved? In particular, how does the family react to the student's academic performance, and what is the student's reaction to that family perception? These and related questions should be the focus of inquiry, no matter what the wording of the interviewer's questions and comments.

Here are some suggested questions:

A. What is the composition of your family? (Mother and father living at home, siblings, grandparents, cousins, uncles and aunts, etc.)
B. How do your mother and father feel about your school performance? How do you feel about their reaction? How do you handle this?
C. How are your brothers and sisters doing in school?
D. Who in the family do you get along with best? Least? Why (or why not)?
E. Which of your parents do you feel closest to?
F. Which of your parents are you more alike?
G. When you and your parents have differences, how do you usually settle them?
H. Tell me about how are things decided in your family.
I. What does your family expect of you?
J. At what age do you feel you will be ready to leave home and get out on your own?

3. *The nature of social relationships (peers, the opposite sex, etc.)*

In general, questions in this area should elicit not only the nature of the student's relationships with his or her peers, but also the importance of those relationships in the student's interpersonal world. Questions should include the types, frequency, intensity, and range of peer relationships, and should make a distinction between same-sex and opposite-sex relationships. For opposite-sex relationships, especially when interviewing young adolescents, the interviewer should ask questions that will help assess whether these relationships reflect a growing sense of sexual or romantic awareness on an adolescent level or whether they are same-sex peer relationships only.

The types of activities and attitudes toward these should also be assessed. The student's opinions of how he or she is perceived by peers should also be explored. The interviewer can focus on the interviewee's reasons for affiliating with certain peers and not with others. Finally, one can ask questions regarding hobbies, interests, and social activities which the interviewee may have in common with peers.

Sample questions are as follows:

A. Do you have friends? How many? Male? Female? I wonder how important these friendships are to you.
B. Tell me about your really close friends. How many? For how long have they been close friends? What would you say it is about these friendships that makes them so close?
C. What is it about those friends that attracts you to them?

hopes will happen? Is the future an issue the student is intensely involved in or actually avoids even thinking about? Does the student perceive his or her future in optimistic or pessimistic terms?

Some recommended questions are as follows:

A. What do you see yourself doing ten years from now (vocationally and otherwise)? What do you need to do in order to get there? How much have you done so far to get there?
B. What do you think your chances are of getting there? Why or why not? What are you going to do about it? And how come you haven't done these things up to now?
C. Do you think about the future a lot or just a little bit? Why? In what ways?
D. How do you think your parents and friends would react to your plans? What do you think of their reaction?
E. Generally, are you looking forward to your future? Why or why not?
F. Do you want to leave home and get out on your own? When and under what circumstances do you see yourself doing that?
G. Do you want to get married? When and under what circumstances do you see yourself doing that? What kind of person would you consider marrying? How do you feel that you and your spouse would deal with money, decision making, career choices, children, etc.?
H. Would you want to have children when you got older?

Follow-up Questions in the Interview

If the interviewer would like the interviewee to expand upon or further clarify a comment or response, we would recommend the following.

Do not push the student to explore an area or topic if it is clear that the student does not want to do so because the area is threatening, embarrassing, or otherwise uncomfortable. It may be diagnostically important simply to recognize that a particular area is one that the student would rather avoid. In fact, if somehow an area extremely uncomfortable or anxiety-arousing is tapped and the student for some reason has trouble avoiding it, we would recommend that the interviewer simply and matter-of-factly change the subject, even if the discussion is in midstream. This is, after all, a diagnostic interview, not a therapy or counseling interview, and the goal is neither to change the person nor to confront difficult areas, but rather to clarify and assess.

Unless there is need for a specific kind of answer in a specific area, it is usually a good idea to keep questions as open-ended as possible, especially during follow-up questions. Providing specific questions which can be answered by "yes" or "no" does not give an opportunity for the interviewee to expand upon or really clarify a response. Likewise, multiple-choice questions (e.g., "Was it because of this, or that?") give the interviewee an opportunity to avoid expanding upon a response by simply indicating one of the choices. An interview in which the interviewer ends up doing all the talking and the interviewee simply agrees or disagrees is rarely the kind of diagnostic interview from which a meaningful diagnostic judgment will result.

Traditionally, expert interviewer responses include statements such as "Tell me more about that," or "What do you mean?" or "I wonder what that has to do with." These kinds of interviewer responses allow for an expansion of the interviewee's statements without predetermining the nature of the interviewee's responses. Notice how nonspecific and low-keyed these statements are; they reflect the phraseology of normal conversation, which is a good model to approach in a diagnostic interview.

Sometimes an interviewee will appear to answer a question, but the interviewer will notice that the response is in the form of a generalized cliche that seems logical on the surface but has little specific meaning. For example, in response to a question on how much the student studies, he or she might respond, "Well, I try to do as much as I can each week." This may seem to answer the question, but it doesn't. To "try" may imply that the student works very hard and studies long hours, or it may mean that the student intends to study but does not.

If the interviewer detects these pat answers or in fact any other sort of generalization, it is usually a good idea to attempt to get more of the specifics. Perhaps the best general interviewer follow-up is, "Can you give me an example of that?" Related questions are also valuable: "What do you mean?" or "What do you actually do or say?"

If the interviewer believes that the interviewee's statement is not well considered or even intentionally misleading, it is better, instead of confronting the person, to present an attitude of not fully understanding his or her response. Ask for further clarification, much like the fictional television detective Lieutenant Colombo, who continues to ask probing questions in the guise of merely trying to understand something for himself. This technique allows for exploration without confrontation.

In considering areas for follow-up, the interviewer would do well to choose areas that are not only of interest to the interviewer, but which seem of crucial importance or concern to the student. The interviewer looks for clues as to which areas these might be for each interviewee. One clue might be how much energy, intensity, or focus the student uses in describing something. Another might be the range of emotion expressed around a given topic. The amount of time spent on a particular area is another good clue.

Because of the short-term nature of the diagnostic interview, the interviewer can feel free to "shift gears," or change topics. This can allow for the avoidance of areas of extreme anxiety to the interviewee, the expansion of topic areas of diagnostic significance, and the most efficient use of time.

Concluding the interview

At the conclusion of the interview, the interviewer should ask matter-of-factly, "Do you have any questions you'd like to ask me?" and wait for a response. There are some variations in the types of questions that students from differing personality styles are likely to ask. Some students wish to know if they have given the interviewer the kind of information they think was sought. Others may want to know how the information will be used. Others are genuinely grateful for the opportunity to talk about such a wide range of issues and wonder if they can continue the process. Still others have no questions at all and simply wish to leave the interview room. Often these questions will provide additional diagnostic clues.

Any questions should be answered as openly, honestly, and as matter-of-factly as possible. It is unlikely that the interviewer will have all the answers to the questions asked, but appropriate referral can be made to other resources (for example, other school personnel), or a simple "I don't know as yet" can be offered. Waiting for the student's response is most important; it tells the interviewer whether the interviewee indeed has questions, and it sends a message that the interview is in many ways a "two-way street" and that the interviewee's questions and concerns are legitimately respected.

Flow of Questions During the Diagnostic Interview

The nature of the semistructured diagnostic interview advocated here is such that the actual sequence of questions and the specific questions asked will depend upon each student's reactions to the interview situation. There is an art to effective, nonjudgmental, interpersonal information-gathering. Nevertheless, whatever the sequence of questions, it is assumed that each interview will elicit enough information across the various topic areas to permit making judgments about the type of academic underachievement and related personality factors. Thus the method and ordering of questions will vary dramatically from interview to interview, but the overall range of information should be comparable across all of the interviews.

Computerized and other structured assessments, for all their scientific and clinical advantages (which are, we believe, considerable), simply cannot replace the rich diagnostic data available when one human being interacts with another. It is this aspect of the diagnostic process that is the greatest strength of the interview format.

CHAPTER 5

Concepts of Differential Diagnosis

Armed with interview skills, the diagnostician must now have a clear notion of the diagnostic process. It is not simply the "slapping on" of a label to some easily identifiable set of symptoms. Differential diagnosis requires a careful and well-considered series of perceptual and mental operations. We begin this discussion with an attempt to define differential diagnosis.

J. P. Chaplin's *Dictionary of Psychology* (p. 142) defines differential diagnosis as "the process of distinguishing between two similar diseases or abnormalities by discovering a critical symptom which is present in one but not in the other." This definition implies (but does not state directly) that a different diagnosis will dictate a different course of treatment specific to that problem. Indeed, what other practical purpose could a different diagnosis serve? Before we consider this concept in detail, however, we must examine the nature of the diagnostic process itself.

One could consider the necessity for a psychological diagnostic judgment as fulfilling three distinct objectives: as providing the orderly understanding of psychological problems and their interrelationships, as communicating that understanding in a standardized way to others (via jargon, terminology, concepts, etc.), and as providing a guide to treatment. The first of these, an orderly understanding of psychological problems and their interrelationships, is more in the nature of scientific examination and academic understanding simply for the purpose of increasing our knowledge. In this it is akin to what is known as *pure research* in the so-called hard sciences. Pure research is that which has no immediate practical use. Often, however, important applications of such research are eventually found, sometimes in surprising ways. The early theories and experiments relating to atomic research, for example, had no immediate practical application, even though awesome visions of peaceful and destructive applications of atomic power were glimpsed by a few of the scientists involved. Other examples may include research and theorizing in certain areas of astronomy, work which may have little current practical value beyond increasing our understanding of the universe in which we live.

The second of these objectives of the diagnostic process is the communicating of this understanding to others, especially other professionals within the same discipline. Imagine the laborious, time-consuming, and even dangerous situation in which a patient is having an appendicitis attack, but his physician has no orderly jargon or other abbreviated terminology for explaining this to the surgeon and so must give a detailed explanation of the anatomical and physiological processes involved. The patient will have died before the explanation is half finished. Jargon and technical terminology are often criticized as being incomprehensible to outsiders, as fostering a professional elite, and as providing a wall of gibberish behind which incompetents can hide. Yet professional jargon serves a specific and useful purpose: it provides a kind of conceptual shorthand which professionals can use to save time and energy when they communicate with each other. Thus the physician in the above example need tell the surgeon only that the patient has appendicitis, and the surgeon has an immediate and complete understanding of the essential picture.

Too often in psychology and psychiatry, diagnoses are considered as labels rather than as this kind of mental shorthand. Imagine the chaos of not having such labels available to tell a clinician that one is dealing with a phobic person or a paranoid person or, for that matter, a drug addict or alcoholic. If a diagnostic judgment is no more than a label, especially one that has some sort of moral connotation (as, in ordinary conversation, has become attached to the term *neurotic*), then indeed we are not discussing diagnosis but rather labeling, and this is indefensible from almost any point of view. If, however, diagnostic judgments allow mental health professionals to communicate with each other rapidly and efficiently, so that when the term *neurosis* is used there is an immediate understanding of a theory, a set of symptoms, and a course of treatment involved, then this is a legitimate and efficient means of communication of what would otherwise be complex, lengthy, repetitive, and impractical discussions.

The third objective of diagnosis—providing a guide to treatment—is perhaps the most important from the point of view of clinical practice. After all, why formulate a diagnosis that will not be put to use in a treatment scheme? More specifically, different diagnoses will dictate different forms of treatment. This, in a nutshell, is the central definition of differential diagnosis, and it is this concept with which we will concern ourselves in the remainder of this section, since it is in this area that there seems to be the most significant gap: the gap between psychological diagnosis and the related psychological treatment. Let us first consider general concepts of diagnosis.

The term *diagnosis* is defined by the *American Heritage Dictionary of the English Language* (p. 363) as: "1.a. the act or process of identifying or determining the nature of a disease through examination. b. The opinion derived from such an examination. 2.a. An analysis of the nature of something. b. The conclusion reached by such analysis." There is an additional definition relating specifically to biology: "A precise and detailed description of the characteristics of an organism for taxonomic classification." Similarly, *Webster's Deluxe Unabridged Dictionary* (1983, p. 502) offers a three-pronged definition of *diagnosis:* "1. the act or process of deciding the nature of a diseased condition by examination. 2. a careful investigation of the facts to determine the nature of a thing. 3. the decision or opinion resulting from such examination or investigation.''

What is interesting about these and similar general definitions of diagnosis is that while they fulfill the first two objectives of diagnosis (understanding and communication), there is little stated connection between the assessment of a disease and its treatment. Whether the description of the nature of the disease has any usefulness for treatment purposes is not only unstated but barely implied. Certainly there is little need to link diagnosis to treatment if our purpose is to diagnose in order to gain an intellectual understanding of the world in which we live, a goal which is reasonable and appropriate to many academic and scientific disciplines. If the goal, however, is clinical usefulness, then there needs to be some link between diagnosis and treatment.

Surprisingly, many of the medical definitions of diagnosis offer little help in this regard. ''Webster's Medical Dictionary'' (*Webster's Encyclopedia of Dictionaries*, 1978, p. 597) defines diagnosis simply as ''determination of a patient's disease.'' Similarly, one can find definitions such as ''the process of determining the nature of a disorder'' by considering various signs, symptoms, and the results of medical tests (*Bantam Medical Dictionary*, 1982, p. 115).

Even in psychological and psychiatric definitions of diagnosis, treatment considerations are hardly mentioned. Chaplin's *Dictionary of Psychology* (p. 141) defines diagnosis as ''1. the determination of the nature of an abnormality or disease. 2. the classification of an individual on the basis of a disease or abnormality.'' Freedman, Kaplan, and Sadock (1976, p. 42–43) discuss psychiatric diagnosis within the context of general systems theory. They stress the need to link each process identified to the ''structure'' that carries it out, the elucidation of input and output factors in the system, and the need to recognize a given set of ''critical subsystems'' in all living systems. These definitions fulfill well the objectives of understanding and communication, but at no point is even the slightest statement offered as to the need to diagnose in such a way that an effective course of treatment is illuminated.

Indeed, it appears from all of these examples that whether it be medicine in general, psychiatry in particular, or the practice of clinical psychology, diagnosis is considered a process independent and almost unrelated to treatment. On the other hand, clinical medicine in practice makes a definite and obvious connection between diagnosis and treatment; every physician suggests a treatment plan in connection with a specific diagnosis of the patient's medical condition. The logic of this paradigm seems so elementary and self-evident, that it hardly seems necessary to include it in any of the standard definitions of the diagnostic process.

However, by failing to include treatment considerations in these definitions of diagnosis, the danger is that diagnosis can become something wholly descriptive and not necessarily related to treatment whatsoever. Without the necessity of providing a rationale for treatment, any diagnostic scheme, no matter how complete, internally consistent, and all-encompassing, can be so unrelated to treatment that it is virtually useless in helping the practicing clinician deal with real people in real-life situations. One would end up with elaborate systems of diagnoses that have intellectual, philosophical, and perhaps literary significance but are of no practical use in helping people solve problems of living, coping, and growing.

What saves clinical medicine from this situation is the necessity for practical results. Questions of pure research aside, the practicing physician has little time for elaborate theories which do not translate directly into treatment plans. Patients require direct relief from their ills, and the physician's sole objective is to arrive at the most effective, direct, rapid, and safe means for providing this relief.

Let us now consider a definition that does include a link to treatment. Taber (1983) defines diagnosis as "the use of scientific and skillful methods to establish the nature and cause of a sick person's disease. The value of establishing a diagnosis is to provide a logical basis for treatment and prognosis." Here we have the recognition of a rationale for diagnosis other than increased understanding, classification of the phenomena of nature, etc.: the purpose of a diagnosis is to determine the direction of treatment. The implication of this definition, in contrast to most others, is that diagnosis is not some isolated endeavor unrelated to treatment; it has the direct purpose of determining the nature of that treatment. This implies that diagnosis must itself have an inherent and logical connection to treatment. In fact, a medical diagnosis unrelated to medical treatment is unthinkable.

Consider this example: A person develops a headache which will not disappear no matter how many ordinary remedies are applied. The person visits a physician, who, after listening to the person's story, begins a long monologue of the general nature of the human condition in the twentieth century (the impact of conflicts between economic systems and countries, the events leading up to various wars, the pressures of contemporary global conflicts on the ordinary individual, and so forth) and how this relates to basic physiovascular processes in the brain. The monologue, although long and tedious, provides a complete and compelling rationale for the origin of the headache and its resistance to treatment.

The person (who by now is called the patient) replies, "Yes, Doctor, I understand all that, but what are you going to do about my headache?"

"Take two aspirin and call me in the morning," says the physician, now slightly annoyed that his explanation has apparently fallen on deaf ears.

"I do not understand," says the patient, "why you couldn't just tell me that when I came in?"

"Because," replies the physician, "I needed to make a diagnosis."

The patient understands intuitively that in the midst of suffering and pain, the physician has spent an inordinate amount of time creating a diagnosis totally unrelated to the reasons for the visit, and the patient immediately seeks the services of another doctor. The physician, on the other hand, judges the patient to be resistant to treatment and to lack the intelligence to understand the nature of the disease.

This sort of ridiculous scenario, unthinkable in medicine, happens all of the time in the clinical mental health fields. Practitioners are prepared with one basic diagnostic scheme to which they are committed (whether that be learning theory, psychoanalysis, psychopharmacology, cognitive psychology, family systems theory, etc.) and go through elaborate diagnostic processes in order to rationalize the particulars of the patient's situation into that scheme. Both of the present authors can testify from professional experience in a variety of clinics and mental health settings that practitioners concoct elaborate and lengthy diagnostic judgments, only to end with the prescription that "psychotherapy is recommended for the patient." Diagnoses should not be judged by their length, but by the degree to which they meaningfully guide treatment.

Back to our original example, the physician offered the headache patient an elaborate diagnosis which may have been of tremendous meaning but which was entirely unrelated to the treatment needs of the patient's problem. On the contrary, from a clinician's point of view, a diagnosis must provide a rationale for treatment. The physician takes this concept for granted; the mental health professional may not. Yet there is the same need in clinical mental health practice for diagnoses that point the way to treatment, and it is this requirement of diagnosis that we believe should be equated in importance with the objectives of understanding and communication.

However, this still does not clarify the relationship between diagnosis—particularly differential diagnosis—and treatment. Recall that Taber's definition specified "nature and cause." These terms refer loosely to two separate aspects of diagnosis: *Nature* is linked to the currently observable pattern of symptoms and behaviors, while *cause* is less observable and is inferred, usually having a time element in that the cause precedes the effect.

In medicine, nature and cause often appear fused into one distinct process in which the symptoms of a disease and its biological etiology are considered as one observable process. In this context, the use of jargon and concise diagnostic terminology clouds what are essentially two entirely different aspects of the diagnostic process: the process of observation and the process of theorizing. Let us take, for example, our headache patient mentioned previously. The headache itself—the subjective pain, the behavioral symptoms of distress, the patient's verbalizations of pain—is current and is observable by any independent examiner. Thus the headache, using Taber's definition, can be considered the nature of the disease. The cause, however, is an entirely different matter. Depending upon one's training and theoretical point of view, the cause could be seen as muscular tension, changes in the vascular system, psychological stress, hereditary predisposition, brain tumor, eyestrain, or some combination of these and other factors. Because we have agreed that the patient is suffering from headache does not mean that we will agree on the cause. It is readily apparent that the observable symptom pattern, the nature of the disease, is easier for independent examiners to verify and agree upon. The cause, however, is more of an abstraction; it is inferred from the observable data and thus cannot be verified or validated in the same way.

Because of this difference, it is important that these two aspects of the diagnostic process be recognized as separate and in many ways as contrasting or conflicting. This raises two questions: (1) Is a diagnosis made primarily on the basis of the symptoms or of the cause of a disease? (2) Does the "basis for treatment" depend upon the nature of the disease, the cause of the disease, or both?

One answer to the first question is to allow two different diagnostic processes, instead of trying to make a choice between using symptoms or causes as a basis for a diagnostic judgment. In fact, workers such as Small (1979) argue for three distinct types of psychological diagnoses: that based on description (the *clinical* diagnosis), that based on underlying psychodynamics (the *dynamic* diagnosis), and that based on etiological factors (the *genetic* diagnosis). Indeed, DSM-III-R (APA, 1987) makes a similar distinction in that it presents essentially what Small would call a clinical diagnostic scheme, relying primarily on observed behavior and interaction and leaving the question of underlying causes to the practitioner or social scientist. However, accepting a model such as Small's still leaves the question of the relation to treatment unanswered. On which of the three diagnostic processes is a recommendation for treatment made?

We would like to propose a model of differential diagnosis which involves four distinct diagnostic steps, each conceptually, logically, and indeed philosophically different from the other three. We call these the Observational Diagnosis, the Dynamic Diagnosis, the Treatment Diagnosis, and the Practical Diagnosis. If treatment is a goal of the diagnostic process, then all four diagnostic judgments are necessary in any given case. If scientific observation, intellectual understanding, or other related research is the goal, then the Treatment and Practical Diagnoses are unnecessary.

THE OBSERVATIONAL DIAGNOSIS

The Observational Diagnosis consists of the observations of current behavior and interaction that comprise the current or presenting problem. This diagnostic judgment is determined by the examiner's actual observations of the patient's behavior and interactions, clinical tests, reports by others of the patient's behavior and interactions, and the patient's own statements of the objective and subjective factors involved in his or her situation. The Observational Diagnosis is more objective than subjective and can be confirmed by independent observation. This corresponds to Taber's notion of the nature of an illness and what Small (1979) calls the clinical diagnosis and is very much the kind of diagnostic judgment attempted by DSM-III-R, in that it is purely descriptive.

THE DYNAMIC DIAGNOSIS

The Dynamic Diagnosis, in contrast to the Observational Diagnosis, is neither directly observable nor is it subject to independent confirmation. It is the underlying "cause" (in Taber's terminology), an abstract concept of the underlying reasons, and is inferred from the Observational Diagnosis (that is, from observed behavior and interaction). This is why it cannot be verified by independent observation. It corresponds to both the dynamic and genetic diagnoses in Small's terminology. Incidentally, it includes a prognosis. The process of arriving at a Dynamic Diagnosis is not observational, even though it is based on the Observational Diagnosis, but rather depends upon the logical inferences, theoretical point of view, and particular training and experience of the diagnostician.

THE TREATMENT DIAGNOSIS

The Treatment Diagnosis charts a course of treatment based on the particulars of the Dynamic Diagnosis, not on the basis of the Observational Diagnosis. The Treatment Diagnosis is arrived at through a deductive process: If Dynamic Diagnosis "A" is made, then Treatment Diagnosis "X" is indicated; if Dynamic Diagnosis "B" is made, then Treatment Diagnosis "Y" is indicated.

Table 5.1 summarizes the essential distinctions among these first three diagnoses: observational, dynamic and treatment.

THE PRACTICAL DIAGNOSIS

In this book we concern ourselves with these first three diagnostic realms, the goal of which (for the practitioner) is to arrive at the treatment diagnosis.

TABLE 5.1.   Distinctions Between Observational, Dynamic, and Treatment Diagnoses

	Observational	Dynamic	Treatment
Method	Observation Testing	Inductive reasoning Theorizing	Deductive reasoning
Focus	Current behavior and interaction Test results	Theoretical notion based on Observational Diagosis	Prescribed treatment modes based on Dynamic Diagnosis

Yet the treatment diagnosis leads to a fourth diagnostic process, one which the working clinician must come to in order to begin to actually help a real client or patient. This diagnosis we refer to as the *Practical Diagnosis,* and it is the actual blueprint for action in any specific case. This diagnosis is made up of the following:

1. The first three diagnostic processes we have outlined
2. The client's idiosyncratic perceptions, motivations, emotions, and goals
3. Situational factors such as the particular school environment, family involvement, teacher and counselor considerations, cultural variables, and so forth
4. The actual realistic goals and agreements among examiner, client or patient, family, school, physician, and others

In other words, the Practical Diagnosis will make the treatment goals specific to the particular client and the situation. It may be, for example, that an underachieving student with intense obsessive-compulsive personality characteristics could actually benefit from 5 years of psychoanalysis (or, if one prefers, 6 months of behavior therapy or 1 year of family therapy). To the school psychologist, this may be an impractical goal which is far removed from the presenting problem of the student's underachievement. Under these circumstances, the school psychologist might recommend such longer term treatment focused on the personality style, but this could not be considered a Practical Diagnosis since it does not take into account the situational features of the case. A Practical Diagnosis might be, for example, to utilize the obsessive features of the student's personality and briefly counsel the student in such a way that the student is encouraged to turn that obsessiveness toward more productive academic ends, such as memorization or completion of schoolwork. While this may seem like a band-aid on a gaping wound, in real-life situations such approaches help the student improve his or her academic standing. This, in turn, aids the beleaguered ego by increasing mastery of the situation, reduces anxiety, leads to better coping skills, and perhaps provides therapeutic rapport so that at some later date the student will feel comfortable with the idea of more intensive therapy. Thus the Practical Diagnosis is the final working plan for counseling.

The Practical Diagnosis should be the last step in the diagnostic process, whereas it is the first step for many diagnosticians, counselors, and others. If a student is underachieving, for example, someone might say "Let's give him some math tutoring and see if that helps." Making the practical diagnosis first is comparable to a surgeon deciding what kind of incision to make without first considering what surgery is to be performed and on what part of the body. A practical diagnosis alone, without considering the context provided by the other diagnostic processes we have discussed, is often a meaningless "shot-in-the-dark." Sometimes, of course, what appears to be only a practical diagnosis does have an implied and unrecognized rationale behind it. The teacher who senses a student's math problems may suggest math tutoring because of the knowledge that this particular student has a specific problem with math, is likely to be helped by tutoring, is usually cooperative in such ventures, and probably does not have some other interfering problem. This rationale may or may not be well articulated or even accurate, but our point here is that it is often nonetheless well considered.

We believe that especially in medicine and certain psychological models (such as behavioral), the Dynamic Diagnosis in particular is likely to be viewed as unscientific, arbitrary, and subjective, and for that reason it is avoided or minimized. However, to the extent that this model reflects the reality of the diagnostic process, all four diagnoses are always present and are equally important, especially if the goal is treatment.

Let us return to our suffering headache patient as an example. The Observational Diagnosis (from both the physician's and the patient's points of view) is headache. There is no doubt that this diagnosis would be agreed to by other physicians, psychologists, psychiatrists, nutrition experts, faith healers, and so forth. However, because of theoretical orientation, scientific training, and mission as a medical healer, our physician concludes that the patient is suffering from a so-called tension headache and that the goal here is simply relief of pain. This entire body of inferences (which would not necessarily be made by another physician, psychologist, faith healer, nutritionist, etc.) constitutes the Dynamic Diagnosis. In medicine, however, the Dynamic Diagnosis is so standardized and taken for granted that it is not recognized as a separate step in the diagnostic process. The treatment for tension headache, as the physician has learned it, consists of certain medications. This is the deductive reasoning that comprises the Treatment Diagnosis, and it follows from and depends upon the Dynamic Diagnosis, not the Observational Diagnosis. That is to say, the physician concludes that the patient needs tension-relieving medication not because the patient is observed to have a headache, but because the physician is trained to believe that physiological tension is the cause and must be treated accordingly. A nutritionist or psychoanalyst may well arrive at entirely different Dynamic, Treatment, and Practical Diagnoses while agreeing essentially on the Observational Diagnosis.

Let us say that our headache patient is being seen by a behavioral psychologist. The psychologist arrives at the same Observational Diagnosis— headache—but different Dynamic, Treatment, and Practical Diagnoses. This behaviorist's Dynamic Diagnosis may well agree with the physician's only in that the headache is caused by tension, but the behaviorist is likely to see the source of that tension in learned modes of thinking and reactions to stress that result in muscular contractions causing the headache. This Dynamic Diagnosis suggests the Treatment Diagnosis: training the patient in muscular relaxation and teaching the patient, perhaps through a series of behavioral reinforcements, to think about stress-related situations in a different way.

The particular choice of specific behavioral treatment would constitute the Practical Diagnosis.

Our view is that Differential Diagnosis is a function of the Dynamic Diagnosis, not the initial observational step. It is in the Dynamic Diagnosis that differential judgments are made concerning origin of the problem, etiology, causative factors, and prognosis. These determine the course of treatment.

To return to our presenting problem of underachievement, we would consider underachievement the Observational Diagnosis, one which could yield a variety of Dynamic, Treatment, and Practical Diagnoses, depending upon the particulars of each individual case. It is for this reason that we believe that research which has simply combined all individuals with the same presenting problem (whether that be underachievement, headache, phobia, alcoholism, etc.) in the same group and assumed that an examination of that group will yield the identical Dynamic Diagnosis is doomed to fail.

Therefore, our amended definition of Differential Diagnosis would read as follows:

Differential Diagnosis is: (1) the process of determining the range of possible Dynamic Diagnoses (and their resulting Treatment and Practical Diagnoses) for each Observational Diagnosis; or (2) for a given individual with a given Observational Diagnosis, the process of determining the most reasonable Dynamic Diagnosis that will yield an effective treatment and practical diagnostic plan; or (3) a delineation of the particular signs that will distinguish one Observational Diagnosis from another, one Dynamic Diagnosis from another, and so forth.

MAJOR UNDERACHIEVER CATEGORIES

We will be using the standard psychiatric diagnostic scheme of psychopathology found in the *Diagnostic and Statistical Manual of Mental Disorders, Third Edition–Revised* (DSM-III-R)(APA, 1987), as a basis for a description of different personality styles or types of underachievers. In fact, we do not necessarily assume psychopathology or abnormality, as would usually be assumed in every case by using the DSM-III-R labels. We do assume, however, that the labels reflect differences in personality structure, and our interest in their use is toward a better understanding of personality styles in underachievement rather than as a means of detecting psychopathology.

For example, if we describe an individual underachiever as having the characteristics of Overanxious Disorder, we are using the conventional psychiatric scheme but are not implying that this student is abnormal. We are merely using the label in an attempt to capture a personality style with its various characteristics. Unfortunately, the most universally accepted and understood language with which to accomplish this is the lexicon of psychopathology.

We classify the diagnostic scheme of DSM-III-R as an observational diagnostic system: It is behaviorally and observationally oriented, its various syndrome patterns can be confirmed by independent observers, and it allows for a variety of alternate underlying rationales which could explain each syndrome. We limit our review only to those DSM-III-R categories which are consistent with personality styles found in the majority of underachievers. In ordinary everyday life, severely disturbed individuals rarely function well enough that underachievement is seen as their major problem. The student who is actively hallucinating or who is acutely depressed is rarely treated for underachievement or even considered an underachiever, but rather a person in need of medical or psychological attention. In these kinds of situations, it would be inappropriate to consider underachievement as the major problem requiring immediate attention.

With less intense mental health problems or with problems which do not severely interfere with daily functioning, the person may very well be perceived primarily as an underachiever. These are problems likely to be classified by DSM-III-R, Axis IV (Severity of Psychosocial Stressors) as Code 1 (None), 2 (Mild), or 3 (Moderate). On Axis V (Global Assessment of Functioning Scale), they are likely to be judged as falling somewhere between 90 (absent or minimal symptoms) and 60 (moderate symptoms). The reader is referred to DSM-III-R for a detailed discussion of this multiaxial classification system.

In our clinical experience and (as can be seen in Parts One and Three of this book) in clinical research, it appears that certain personality types are found in large percentages among any randomly selected group of underachieving students. These personality types are consistent with certain DSM-III-R diagnostic categories within Axes I and II. In this section, we will briefly review these particular categories, but the reader who wants a comprehensive overview of concepts and categories is referred to DSM-III-R. The reader might also refer to the numerous books, monographs, and other publications which further clarify and expand the DSM-III-R model.

We will look briefly at four DSM-III-R categories likely to include the majority of underachieving students: the Overanxious Disorder (313.00), the Academic Problem (V62.30), the Identity Disorder (313.82), and the Conduct Disorders (312.00, 312.2, and 312.90). We will also look briefly at one other disorder which is seen less frequently in clinical practice, the Oppositional Defiant Disorder (313.81).

The Overanxious Disorder (313.00)

This category is listed within those disorders affecting infants, children, and adolescents. However, its analog can be found among adults. The outstanding feature of this person is excessive and chronic worry and anxiety not attributable to psychosocial stressors. This anxiety can focus itself on any aspect of the person's daily life: worry about future events, psychsomatic concerns, acceptance by others, and so forth. Often these individuals display obsessive and compulsive features and are greatly worried about being approved of by others. Consequently there is a constant state of tension related to a need for reassurance. Adults with this pattern may be diagnosed as having a Generalized Anxiety Disorder.

The Conduct Disorders (312.00, 312.2, and 312.90)

DSM-III-R defines these categories as having in common "a persistent pattern of conduct in which the basic rights of others and major age-appropriate societal norms or rules are violated. The behavior pattern typically is present in the home, at school, with peers, and in the community" (p. 53). Other common characteristics may include a repetitive and persistent pattern of aggressive behavior, lack of guilt or remorse, or paucity of meaningful relationships with others.

There is a significant similarity and overlap between these conduct disorder categories of adolescence and the adult category labeled Antisocial Personality Disorder (301.70).

The Academic Problem (V62.30)

DSM-III-R's only comment and discussion regarding this category is as follows:

> This category can be used when a focus of attention or treatment is an academic problem that is apparently not due to a mental disorder. An example is a pattern of failing grades or of significant underachievement in an individual with adequate intellectual capacity, in the absence of a Specific Developmental Disorder or any other mental disorder to account for the problem (p. 359).

This problem is the only DSM-III-R category analogous to the Nonachievement Syndrome (Roth & Meyersburg, 1963), to be discussed in more detail in Chapters 8, 9 and 12.

The Identity Disorder (313.82)

This is an individual not suffering from another mental disorder, who nevertheless may be depressed, anxious, or preoccupied with inner rather than external issues. The predominant focus is ". . . severe subjective distress regarding inability to reconcile aspects of the self into a relatively coherent and acceptable sense of self" (DSM-III-R, p. 89). The person may be so impaired in social or occupational decision making because of confusion and uncertainty over the nature of the self that it is difficult to make commitments.

Other pathological characteristics (e.g., borderline or affective disorder symptoms) aside, DSM-III-R considers this problem as representing a normal conflict associated with maturation, particularly during adolescence and the so-called midlife crisis (p. 90).

The Oppositional Defiant Disorder (313.81)

This individual is characterized by a pattern of active, open, and persistent rebellion against authority figures. The person is continually disobedient, negativistic, and provocative in opposition to authority figures and parents. Examples include argumentativeness, active defiance and refusal to adhere to adult authority, and a deliberate attempt to annoy others, even in the face of negative personal consequences for the individual. All of these problematic behaviors occur ". . . without the more serious violations of the basic rights of others that are seen in Conduct Disorder" (DSM-III-R, 1987, p. 56).

All of these preceding categories can be studied in greater detail by referring to DSM-III-R and related publications. Our thumbnail sketches here are to give the reader the essential descriptive characteristics—the Observational Diagnosis—of these types of individuals. We will be referring to and expanding on all of these categories throughout this book, detailing prevalence, etiology, family factors, and, in particular, differential diagnostic and differential treatment considerations.

CHAPTER 6

The Developmental Theory Model

THE NATURE AND FUNCTION OF THEORIES

Our concept of differential diagnosis is based on a diagnostic scheme called the Developmental Theory Model (Roth, Berenbaum, & Hershenson, 1967). This scheme is based on an assumed relationship between diagnostic category and level of psychosocial development. It represents a dynamic diagnostic model which is used to explain the observational diagnostic model of the DSM-III-R categories we have already discussed. In this chapter, we will delineate and expand on this model, which considers the relationships among stages of normal personality development, types of psychopathology, and modes of psychotherapy.

The original Developmental Theory Model (Roth et al., 1967) was an outgrowth of the clinical experience, research, and numerous discussions of those in charge of a counseling program for underachievers at the Illinois Institute of Technology (IIT) in the 1960s. It was used as a theoretical model for clinical training, research, and teaching at IIT in those years, and was further discussed in several subsequent publications (Berenbaum, 1969; Goodstein, 1969, 1980; Hartley, 1985; Kearney, 1971; Mandel, 1969; Mandel, Marcus, Roth, & Berenbaum, 1971; Mandel, Roth, & Berenbaum, 1968; Marcus, 1969; Noy, 1969; Roth, 1970). The present authors have been involved in the research, clinical, and educational uses of this model since the late 1960s as part of their working theoretical hypotheses. The following discussion represents a modification of the original theory combined with our present level of understanding and insight into this model. We do not claim that it explains everything or that it is infallible, but in our experience it has provided a consistent framework that lends itself admirably to teaching, training, and generating meaningful clinical research.

First, however, we need to look at the typical process of clinical theory-building. Many famous theories of psychopathology and psychotherapy were originally generated by first identifying a particular behavioral pattern considered abnormal or problematic. All individuals identified as having the problem would then be studied *as a group* in order to find commonalities of behavior, affect, personality, background, and other factors. To Freud and his colleagues, for example, all those exhibiting phobias and other hysterical symptoms were classified as belonging to one group—hysterical neurotics. Individuals in the group were observed and studied, and common characteristics were then elucidated. The psychoanalysts made the reasonable assumption that the etiology of neurotic phobias or other hysterical symptoms must be the same, since the symptoms are the same.

Other pathological groups have been similarly studied: those exhibiting delusions, hallucinations, and other psychotic symptoms; those exhibiting antisocial behaviors; substance-abusers, such as alcoholics and drug addicts; and sexual deviates, to name just a few. In our own time, we have seen labels applied to hijackers, terrorists, gambling addicts, smokers, chocolate eaters, spouse abusers, heart-attack candidates, and indeed underachievers. That within each of these groups similarities can be found is not surprising. There certainly are common factors within each group.

Traditionally, the next step has been to construct a theory which explains those commonalities. The theory is complete with corollaries, constructs, and intervening variables, all of which fit the particular problem as applied to that particular population. The theory is usually constructed and rationalized with particular clarity and specificity, often made more vivid by the introduction of new terminology which reflects the concepts involved.

We now come to a step which fills the function of a kind of secular leap of faith: Namely, the theory (and all of its related terminology and concepts) is now assumed to be "real," to represent an actual, real thing in the real world. Instead of being considered a useful or valuable way of explaining reality, it becomes reality itself. Individuals and their behavior are now explained as examples of that theory, and researchers and clinicians learn that theory and use it to explain and understand the phenomena of human psychology. More often than not, the adherents to the theory become embroiled in bitter arguments with the adherents of other theories, each assuming that its own concepts represent reality. We are not suggesting that theoretical disputes are always arguments among proponents of various models. Some theoretical disagreements serve the genuine function of refining and testing various points of view.

We might point out that this process is almost totally opposite to the development of scientific theory, in which a theory is accepted only to the extent that it provides the best explanation of all of the relevant data in a given area. When there are data which cannot be explained by the theory, or when a better theory (one that explains more data more completely) comes along, the original theory is relegated to history or is accepted as having limited utility (such as Newtonian mechanics in the age of Einstein). No true scientist is so wedded to a theory that he or she would not be willing to discard it if a better explanation of data comes along.

Nevertheless, theorists in clinical psychology tend to assume that their theories embody living truths and therefore are applicable to everyone. Recall that a theory is originally formulated by observing a specific group having certain deviant, abnormal, or at the very least unhealthy characteristics. The theory constructed to apply specifically to that group—that theory now being considered as truth—is then applied to all of humanity. Since for some strange reason it doesn't quite fit, corollaries are added, concepts are defined in slightly different ways, new intervening constructs are created so that the theory can be made flexible enough to incorporate the widest range of human behavior. Unfortunately, in the process the theory loses its sense of specificity and applicability to the original group.

The above scenario, although admittedly exaggerated, does indeed reflect the current state of clinical theory. It also explains why there are so many different clinical theories that appear to have little relation to one another: Freudian, Rogerian, and so forth. The Developmental Theory Model asserts that these theories are different because the originators of these theories were in fact observing *different groups of people*. Freud, for example, was studying predominantly Victorian era females with a specific set of presenting problems: hysterical symptoms of various kinds. The description of psychopathology, theory of personality, and method of treatment which Freud devised are all appropriate to and effective with that population. Freud then assumed that since his theory fit that population, it could be generalized to everyone else. Likewise, the client-centered movement was built on clinical experience with another specific group: American college students. The theory (self-concept) and treatment approach which fit this group were then generalized to every person in every kind of situation requiring psychological treatment.

If one accepts the notion that theories are neither real nor carry the weight of absolute truth, then it becomes possible to explain why one person working with a certain population is likely to arrive at an entirely different set of conclusions and effective treatment methods from another person working with a different population. It becomes possible to see psychological theory in a more flexible and relative way. It is this that the Developmental Theory Model assumes: that a theory is not real, but is only a best explanation for some set of clinical and experiential data. If the explanation does not fit the data, then one finds a better explanation.

This, in turn, makes it possible to have many theoretical models at one's disposal, each having its own validity with a specific population. Freudian theory and treatment is ideal for a neurotic population, Rogerian theory and treatment for an adolescent population. This means that it is not enough for the clinician to learn only one system of thought; the clinician must be well versed in many of them and be ready to apply them differentially where indicated or to know when to refer to therapists trained in other systems. The Developmental Theory Model provides one such flexible framework.

THE NATURE OF THE DEVELOPMENTAL THEORY MODEL

The Developmental Theory Model, unlike the standard paradigm summarized above, assumes that the same behavior in two different individuals (or even two different instances in the same individual) can have different meanings, different motivations, and a different place within the personality. For example, a pattern of underachievement in one individual can result from an entirely different motivational process than the same pattern in another individual. Therefore, to theorize a one-to-one correspondence between a particular behavior and the underlying motivation or personality causation leads to a categorization on the basis of a similarity of behavior. In spite of its being a dominant trend in psychology, this can be misleading because it may blur the motivational distinctions between different types of individuals.

Conversely, different behaviors in different individuals can arise from the same motivation in individuals who have similarities in personality type. The differences in behavior may not be the result of differences in personality, but of differences in background and experience which lead the similar motivational factors to express themselves in different ways.

If the preceding is true, then the clinician may not be on firm ground in categorizing according to behavioral differences. In fact, the Developmental Theory Model assumes that the clinician's role is primarily perceptual rather than behavioral.

> The function of psychotherapy is to offer the client a significant human relationship. To do this the therapist needs a set of applicable constructs. Since any bit of behavior may stem from a variety of psychodynamic sources, it is unreasonable to systematize behavior. However, personality constructs, the content of the therapist's conceptual system, have long been used as material for systematization. The significant activity of the therapist, then, involves formulating the "set," not the techniques, with which he interacts with the client (Roth et al., 1967, p. 2).

To take this principle a step further, we assert that the most important clinical tool a therapist has is perception of the problem, the individual, oneself as a therapist and as a person, and the nature of the interaction with the client. Standard therapeutic techniques (interpretation, behavioral interventions, reflection, hypnosis, etc.) are useless without some purpose or plan for the particular problem and the appropriateness of those techniques in dealing with that problem. Simply applying a learned therapeutic technique makes as little sense in psychotherapy as it would, for example, in medicine.

Another tenet of the Developmental Theory Model is that a theory does not exist simply for the purpose of satisfying some sort of intellectual curiosity. The purposes of clinical theories, presumably, are to aid in treatment: to provide rationales and guides for the remediation of psychological problems. While theories which exist only to explain and understand (rather than to change anything) are perfectly legitimate as intellectual and scientific activities, such theories are useless to the psychotherapist, who needs a theory that will lead to treatment. The Developmental Theory Model attempts to link theory to treatment in a direct and straightforward manner.

A cardinal concept in this model is the concept of *personality structure*. The term *structure* has been used in classic psychoanalytic literature to categorize the structural elements of the personality (such as the id, ego, and superego). Concepts such as motivation have been considered a function of personality dynamics rather than structure. However, the Developmental Theory Model defines personality structure as an organized theory of an individual's motivation. This definition has several implications. First, the term *organized* implies not a collection of isolated traits or a syndrome of behaviors, but rather personality as a meaningful and interrelated organization of concepts. In other words, the various aspects of the personality structure of each individual are meaningfully interrelated rather than separated into isolated compartments which do not interact.

Second, the personality structure concept is indeed a theory, meaning that it is conceptual; it is a construct. Furthermore, this construct, or theory, is derived from observable data. Thus the theory is never observed directly, but rather is inferred in the same way that a statistic infers from a small sample a fact about a population. The fact is inferred but never observed directly. This is a perfectly acceptable process in statistics (which is considered a scientific procedure); therefore, the same conceptual process ought to be considered equally scientific when it comes to clinical theory. If this is true, however, then it means that the theory can never really be proven; it is never an eternal truth, but rather a working hypothesis.

Third, stating that personality structure is an organized theory of an individual's motivation defines motivation rather than behavior as the key element. A central assumption in this model is that behavior is motivated; people do things for reasons, not because of some meaningless sequences of neurological activity. If there are primarily neurological or other extra-motivational factors driving the personality, then these factors are legitimately not part of the personality structure and the personality of the individual, but rather fall into one of the other areas of psychological or psychiatric study (e.g., neurological, hormonal, etc.). The psychotherapeutic clinician is constantly asking, "Why does this person do such-and-such?" If the answer is neurological, then the patient ought to be referred to a specialist in that area. If the question, on the other hand, is how a person is to cope with a neurological problem, then the role of the psychotherapist is appropriate and it is important for the therapist to understand enough about the neurological problem to know what can be attributable to the personality structure and what cannot.

Another implication of this definition of personality structure is the idea that if the individual's motivation is central to that structure, then people indeed behave with a purpose.

> The individual interacts with his world and has a major role in determining the kinds of experiences he ultimately integrates. The environment provides an array of experiences from which to choose. The individual will select those

that are meaningful, and will create situations that produce these kinds of experiences. Further, the greater the individual's maturity, the more this selection process is determined by his decisions (Roth et al., 1967, p. 1).

The Developmental Theory itself is a theory of normal development, motivation, psychopathology, and psychotherapy organized around a succession of core issues typical of the normal stages of the development of the personality structure. This definition has several aspects and implications which require some explanation and elaboration.

The model assumes that the personality structure is not only organized, but *meaningfully* organized with a core set of issues or needs at its center. This means that for any individual, personality factors are arranged in an interactive matrix with certain core issues which define the central motivating factors. Certain peripheral factors at any stage do not disappear, but they become expressions of the core issues and as such are not invested with as much psychic energy or given as high priority. For example, one can discuss the issue of the self-concept in the 18-year-old, the 10-year-old, and the infant, but for the infant it is likely to be a less significant issue than for the other two individuals.

Different core issues are associated with different stages of normal personality development. In fact, each stage of normal personality development is defined in terms of the core issues of the personality structure expected at that chronological stage of development. At each successive stage of development, the core issues of the personality structure are replaced by a different set of core issues, which changes the entire matrix of all of the issues in the personality structure, not just the core issues. In addition, the core issues often involve strong conflicts or ambivalences which are necessary for the individual to resolve or come to terms with in order for the personality structure to mature.

The Developmental Theory Model states that the chronological stages of normal personality development from birth through the mid-20s are organized along a continuum from dependence to independence. Each new stage of development within this age range marks a new qualitative step along the road toward psychological independence. From the mid-20s on, psychological independence is no longer as significant an issue, and questions of personal meaning become paramount.

Growth is assumed to be stepwise: Either a person is or is not at a certain stage. Certainly, aspects of several stages can be seen in any individual, but the core issues are seen as clustering in such a way as to result in only one stage of development at a time. In addition, a stage may be minimized or passed through with relative ease, but never omitted.

It is assumed that the core issues at the hub of the personality structure all involve human relationships; that is, they all have to do with interpersonal transactions and represent transactional needs. With growth into a new development level and its particular personality structure, core issues, and personality matrix, there is a corresponding change in relationship needs. Therefore, the type of meaningful relationship needed for personality growth will be different depending on whether the individual is an infant, toddler, preadolescent, and so forth. Personality growth from one stage to the next occurs if and only if the individual has a significant human relationship to meet the needs of the core issues at that particular stage. Incidentally, under normal circumstances, true personality regression is not recognized as a valid psychological concept in this model.

There are, of course, a variety of ways to define *need*. For example, there are the ''needs'' that may be voiced by an individual, which, if met, would satisfy their wishes but which would not necessarily result in psychological growth. A 5- or 6-year-old child may express the need to stay up late, when he or she actually needs to get to bed at a reasonable hour. In the Developmental Theory Model, psychological or interpersonal needs are assumed to be those related to psychological growth.

An additional concern is whether in clinical practice a therapist or counselor should be expected to meet the full range of a client's psychological needs. Indeed, is meeting all of a client's needs even therapeutic? For example, should the therapist attempt to meet the overwhelming dependency needs of, say, a patient with Borderline Personality Disorder? Although the Developmental Theory Model does not directly address these issues, we believe that determining the advisability of meeting or not meeting certain client needs in any individual case should be a function of the Practical Diagnosis.

If for whatever reason the relationship needs of a particular stage are not met, the person's central interpersonal motivation engages in a continuous search for a relationship that will meet those needs. In psychoanalytic terms, this is referred to as fixation. In the Developmental Theory Model, the presence of fixation defines the pathology. For example, for a 5-year-old child to be seeking parental approval is expected; for a 40-year-old to be seeking, as a major psychological priority, the same kind of parental approval is indicative of immaturity of the personality structure. Thus the psychopathology here, probably defined as one of the neuroses, is based not on abnormal behavior or motivation, but rather upon an immaturity of the personality structure. The determining factor is the difference between the person's chronological age and the core issues of the earlier stage of development. This concept of psychopathology is consistent with classic psychoanalytic theory.

To the extent that this hypothesis is true, one must then define psychotherapy not as problem solving, but as a relationship process meeting the needs of the core issues at which that person is fixated. It is with the experience of this kind of relationship that growth and change will occur. Certainly, there is problem solving in any meaningful therapeutic process, but the Developmental Theory Model asserts that the curative agent is the depth of the relationship itself. This concept of psychotherapy is not radically different from many of the psychodynamic therapeutic models (psychoanalytic, client centered, and so forth). However, the *kind* of relationship that will be therapeutic will differ depending on the person's stage of development. (The specifics of differential diagnosis and differential treatment relating to needs and stages of development are discussed more fully in the remainder of this chapter and in Part Four).

The therapist, then, does not simply offer the same relationship to every client or patient, but gears the approach to the particular relationship needs of the client. These are determined by the developmental level of the personality structure. Further, to decide which type of relationship is appropriate to the client, the therapist must make a differential diagnosis by assessing the personality structure of the client. Being trained only in one theory or model and applying only one therapeutic approach simply is not sufficient.

The Developmental Theory Model asserts that the famous personality and psychotherapy theorists (Freud, Rogers, Sullivan, etc.) each dealt with a specific client sample, most of whom within that sample being fixated at the same stage of development. Each theorist then created a theory which described the personality structure at that stage, defined the psychopathology resulting from fixation of the personality structure at that stage, and formulated a treatment approach specific for that type of person. Each then generalized his or her model to apply to other people and other stages of development. Thus in the Developmental Theory Model the theories of Freud are appropriate when describing the Oedipal stage of development (roughly, ages 5 to 7) and the treatment of those whose personality structures continue to revolve around Oedipal issues (the range of the classic neuroses). In Rogers' theory, the crucial stage of development is more likely late adolescence, where issues of self-concept and psychological independence are paramount. Here the client-centered approach is likely to be more effective clinically than a psychoanalytically oriented model.

What follows is a brief discussion of each stage of normal development, including personality factors, related psychopathology, and appropriate treatment. The discussion of each stage is considered neither exhaustive nor necessarily valid. In fact, one of the strengths of a model such as this one is its open-ended nature: Stages of development can be split into two if warranted, eliminated, or replaced at another point in the chronological continuum.

For each stage, the following points will be discussed:

1. Approximate chronological correlates of normal development
2. Relevant psychological concepts, constructs, or theories
3. The personality structure: core issues, central motivation, central conflicts and ambivalences
4. The kind of relationship needed in order for psychological growth

5. The related psychopathologies if fixation occurs
6. Related DSM-III-R diagnoses
7. The appropriate type of psychotherapeutic relationship or school of psychotherapy
8. Prominent theorists whose concepts have relevance for this particular stage

These stages, in chronological order, are now presented, utilizing the above outline for each stage.

Stage 1: Early Infancy

1. Approximate chronological correlates of normal development

Early infancy lasts from birth to approximately 6 months of age.

2. Relevant psychological concepts, constructs, or theories

The concepts relating to this developmental stage include orality, the need for sensory stimulation and the related problem of sensory deprivation, the concept of "psychic energy," the "feeding" relationship paradigm, and the establishment of basic trust.

3. The personality structure: core issues, central motivation, central conflicts and ambivalences

Crucial here is a secure, ongoing parent-child relationship, based on meeting the infant's overwhelming physical needs—"feeding" of sustenance and sensory experience.

More than any other animal, man is born into helplessness. The newborn is dependent upon the surroundings for its very maintenance. In the physiology of early infancy this kind of maintenance is a real problem; food provides the necessary energy, yet the baby, unable to store it in large quantities, lives from meal to meal. In addition, there is the need for energy from sensory input across all receptors in the form of sensory stimulation, the mouth being one receptor (Mandel, Marcus, Roth, & Berenbaum, 1971, p. 115).

It is only with the satisfaction of physiological needs that there is an investment of psychological energy into the psychic system. This model views other theories of development which assume a rich inner fantasy life at this stage as not reflecting the basically physical nature of the young infant.

4. The kind of relationship needed in order for psychological growth

The predominant relationship between the parent and early infant is through the medium of physical contact initiated by the parent. One does not communicate with a young infant through the medium of verbal interchange.

Normally, in the first four to six months, parents do not let their child "be." There is such extensive involvement with the child's alimentary canal, from one end to the other, that this takes practically all of the parents' time (Mandel et al., 1971, p. 115).

These physiological and sensory needs are met via a feeding prototype. The parents' physical actions and physical communication with the infant, not only in feeding it but in all of the concomitant physical contact (stroking, holding, cooing, smiling, kissing, etc.), literally feed sensory experiences which infant needs in order to grow and develop.

5. The related psychopathologies if fixation occurs

If these relationship needs via the physical feeding paradigm are not met, the infant is in a state of constantly seeking this kind of relationship— virtually a situation of significant sensory deprivation—and it can become a matter of survival. Certainly, cases of failure to thrive and hospitalism can be seen as logically falling into this category. Sensory withdrawal from the infant during the crucial first few months of life may contribute to this pathology.

6. Related DSM-III-R diagnoses

Seen here is Reactive Attachment Disorder of Infancy (313.89).

7. The appropriate type of psychotherapeutic relationship or school of psychotherapy

Obviously, successful approaches to this problem will all have in common the sensory stimulation or physical feeding interactions with the infant. Also, these approaches do not assume or rely on a rich inner psychic life of the child, but approach the child in a more direct and usually more physical manner. This, in terms of the Development Theory Model, is most likely to meet the child's needs and therefore more likely to be therapeutic.

8. Prominent theorists whose concepts have relevance for this particular stage

Theorists to consider here are those who focus on the effects of sensory restriction or deprivation on newborns and young infants in particular. This list would certainly include the experimental work of Harlow and Harlow (1962) and the studies of hospitalism by Spitz (1972) and Bowlby (1969, 1973).

Stage 2: Infancy, or Oral Phase

1. Approximate chronological correlates of normal development

This stage can be considered as lasting from approximately 6 months to 2 years of age.

2. Relevant psychological concepts, constructs, or theories

In this stage we talk about the concept of orality in its usual psychoanalytic meaning. Other concepts related to needs at this stage include: ego development (particularly the impulsive nature of the personality, as in the psychoanalytic concept of the id); Erikson's (1963) concept of basic trust; the need to learn reality testing or the roughly equivalent Sullivanian concept of concensual validation (Sullivan, 1954); the series of family systems factors that produce a true double bind (Bateson, Jackson, Haley, & Weakland, 1956); and other related issues.

3. The personality structure: core issues, central motivation, central conflicts and ambivalences

The primary needs at this stage are for impulse fulfillment and a sense of basic security or trust. At this point, the infant has a primitive but growing ego and an unsophisticated differentiation of feelings and affects. As Erikson has pointed out, there is an ambivalence over the issue of trust. The infant needs to learn when and who to trust, as well as when and who *not* to trust. The trust needed here is total and all-encompassing, and ego boundaries (or similar concepts of an early sense of identity) are weak. This stage ends with the development of speech (Marcus, 1969).

> Ego techniques are minimal, archaic, and can be characterized as a "management of impulses," with emphasis on impulse fulfillment. Early developmental tasks include the identification of impulses and communication of them to the outside world (as in crying when hungry) (Roth et al., 1967, p. 3).

4. The kind of relationship needed in order for psychological growth

Although parents must provide a secure relationship and the establishment of basic trust during this critical period, the infant has limited ability to communicate specific needs and wants. Therefore, parents do not wait for the infant to state its needs clearly but first empathize with the infant so that the needs can be sensed and identified. The parents then communicate these needs to the child by fulfilling them. It is this process that builds trust.

Note that the kind of empathy, attention, and fulfilling of needs required on the part of parents requires a symbiotic relationship that, on a phenomenological basis, involves "becoming one with the infant" in order to understand, communicate, and meet the infant's critical needs. This symbiosis permits the psychological individuation of the infant (Mahler, 1974).

While the nature of this relationship on the part of a parent is often labeled maternal, this is purely descriptive, since either parent can offer this kind of relationship to an infant. Symbiotic mothering is a more fitting and vivid metaphor for this kind of relationship, but it would be sexist, illogical, and psychologically naive to assume that only females can offer it.

5. The related psychopathologies if fixation occurs

In the original formulation of the Developmental Theory Model, lack of a trust-building relationship at this point would result in a personality whose core issues were continually fixated at this stage. This was thought to include the entire range of the schizophrenias and psychoses, except for related conditions with proven physiological causes. In the years since the Developmental Theory Model was formulated, there has been mounting evidence that many of the psychoses have genetic and/or biochemical bases. At this point it appears that there may be a small number of schizoidlike conditions relating to this level of development which are psychogenic and which exhibit significant conflicts regarding trust.

6. Related DSM-III-R diagnoses

Included here are the Paranoid Disorder (297.10) and the Schizoid (301.20) and Schizotypal (301.22) Personality Disorders.

7. The appropriate type of psychotherapeutic relationship or school of psychotherapy

The Developmental Theory Model asserts that whatever the *mode* of psychotherapy, a successful outcome will depend upon the development of a trusting relationship between the client and the therapist which will allow for the acceptance of the client's primitive emotional needs. In general, effective psychotherapies for this group of pathologies involve a relationship approaching a consistent, basic trust-building therapeutic role.

8. Prominent theorists whose concepts have relevance for this particular stage

It is not our place here to provide a comprehensive review of the extensive and controversial literature in this area, but among well-known theorists,

Sullivan (1954) has emphasized interpersonal security and trust issues, Arieti (1974) has focused on the thought process dysfunctions, Laing (1965) has looked at the phenomenological world of the client, and Haley (1969) has emphasized an interpersonal interactive model.

Stage 3: Toddler

1. Approximate chronological correlates of normal development

Generally, this stage can be thought of as coexisting with the "terrible twos" and the achievement of toilet training, approximately ages 2–3½ years.

2. Relevant psychological concepts, constructs, or theories

The concepts appropriate here all revolve around issues of impulsivity: id, impulse expression and impulse control, growing ego strength (particularly around the control issue).

3. The personality structure: core issues, central motivation, central conflicts and ambivalences

At this stage, the person has gained enough ego or intrapsychic strength so that the personality exhibits a sense of coherence and direction. However, the essential nature of the person at this stage is still impulsive, so that the core motivation of the person centers on impulsivity. If the impulsive nature of the individual at Stage 2 (Infancy) can be thought of as a number of vectors extending in many directions simultaneously, then the impulsive nature of the individual at the Toddler stage can be considered the coalescing of these vectors into a single direction. This results in an individual of single-minded purpose with the capacity to act behaviorally on that purpose.

The central task at this stage involves learning appropriate impulse expression on the one hand and impulse control on the other. This is the age at which the child often uses a one-word vocabulary—"No!"—and seeks, often unreasonably, the immediate gratification of impulses. At this age, children will usually push the most reasonable and permissive of parents to exercise behavioral controls, limit setting, and discipline, and will alternate between fighting these limits with all of their will and gratefully accepting the limits as expressions of love from the parents. These contradictory reactions, often puzzling to parents, represent the child's ambivalence between the needs for impulse gratification versus the security that comes from someone stronger than the child not only setting but exercising reasonable limits.

In learning self-control, the child experiences an important mastery over self and a crucial sense of safety in knowing that inner impulsivity will not be allowed to destroy his or her interpersonal world. In fact, the child's acting-out is often a plea for parental intervention.

4. The kind of relationship needed in order for psychological growth

The appropriate parental response shifts at this point from the symbiotic role of the previous stage to a concern for dealing with the child's new-found impulsive nature. The parent lends ego strength to the child, in the sense of helping the child to learn self-control by exercising that control from the outside. In other words, the child achieves the inner controls by having reasonable, consistent, and behavioral limits set by the parents.

Interestingly, many parents perceive that their child needs to learn discipline in the sense of learning right from wrong, whereas it is more often an issue of learning self-control rather than morality. Therefore, the parents must reinterpret the problem as a need to learn self-controls rather than as a need for punishment for bad behavior.

5. The related psychopathologies if fixation occurs

In terms of normal development, certain personality styles can be seen as resulting from a failure to transcend this stage. The predominant normal correlate of this stage is the so-called "spoiled child," forever testing the limits of others and demanding immediate and total impulse fulfillment. Such a person continually provokes others into punitive, rejecting, or controlling responses, which is a disguised plea for help with impulse control and affect.

6. Related DSM-III-R diagnoses

Included here is the Borderline Personality Disorder (301.83).

7. The appropriate type of psychotherapeutic relationship or school of psychotherapy

Parents of terrible-twos children often interpret their children's behavior as bad or wrong. They may also misperceive the impulsive behavior as aimed personally at them, as if the child were purposefully singling them out for attack. They might well consider interpreting to the child that he or she needs to learn self-control and that the parental interventions are not punishments, but rather the means of helping the child to learn this important task. It is sometimes humorous to observe parents saying how much they are helping as they physically restrain a screaming and kicking child.

Psychotherapeutic interventions parallel the parental role of helping the person gain impulse control. In fact, for this group, impulse and affect control are the major therapeutic issues. Whether the therapist wishes to focus on these or some other issues, the impulse conflicts in these people are so overwhelming and dominant that there is no way for the therapist either to avoid them or to meaningfully deal with other issues until these are dealt with. Therapists working with these types of people report countertransference reactions that parallel parental reactions.

It is generally helpful for the therapist to interpret to this person that the problem is one of self-control, and to offer behavioral or psychological help that assists the person in achieving this goal. Adopting a nondirective or emotionally exploratory approach is often counterproductive here (although not, as we shall see, with other types of problems) because it discourages mastery of impulses and fosters a continual impulse-ridden relationship. It also fosters client fantasies about the availability of the therapist to provide an all-encompassing parental relationship in which the client becomes the center of the therapist's life. In contrast, the therapist should consider setting reasonable limits in positive ways so that the experience of the relationship allows the client to develop needed internal impulse and affective controls.

8. Prominent theorists whose concepts have relevance for this particular stage

While there are few psychotherapists known primarily for an exclusive focus on this type of problem, those who discuss the need for helping with impulse control and affect belong here. In terms of normal development, workers who discuss various aspects of rearing a child at this stage of development, particularly in matters of discipline and reasonable supportive limits, are of special importance. This would include theorists such as Anthony and Benedek (1970), Rutter (1980), Thomas and Chess (1980), and Winnicott (1951, 1957).

Stage 4: Preschool Phase

1. Approximate chronological correlates of normal development

This stage of development lasts approximately from the end of the terrible twos until age 5.

2. Relevant psychological concepts, constructs, or theories

The Developmental Theory Model asserts that the most appropriate theoretical orientation that fits the child's dynamics at this stage is the psychoanalytic scheme *in toto*. This includes the classic analytic notions of the id-ego-superego personality structure and the clash of psychic forces within this system, with particular emphasis on superego development.

3. The personality structure: core issues, central motivation, central conflicts and ambivalences

It is at this stage that the external struggle over impulses of the previous stage moves to an internal arena. The child internalizes the demands for impulse control, and this new-found mastery over self represents another step along the road toward ego development and psychological independence. Also, along with this internalized impulse control comes real personal autonomy.

However, the method of impulse control here consists of the still fairly primitive mechanism of obsessive compulsive techniques. It is at this stage that the child begins to invest a great deal of time and energy in repetitive play and other repetitive experiences. For example, the child wants the same routine every day or wants to watch the same videotaped program many times a day without getting tired or bored. The inner impulsiveness, now more or less coalesced around feelings of love (with a strong childhood sexual element) and hostility toward the parents (feelings which are still threatening and overwhelming to the child) is controlled by being bound up in these obsessive compulsive rituals and routines.

4. The kind of relationship needed in order for psychological growth

The parental role is still one of sanctioning the child's behavior and ideas, but whereas in the previous stage this sanctioning requires an almost behavioral intervention, at the Preschool stage the sanctioning has moved much more to the psychological realm and consists of issues of approval, morality, shame, and the like. The parental role here requires a combination of providing models and standards in an evaluating sense, while at the same time balancing that with a basic approval of the child's inner impulsive nature.

5. The related psychopathologies if fixation occurs

To use a rapidly aging lexicon, the Developmental Theory Model asserts that the predominant psychopathology here is Obsessive Compulsive Neurosis. Like the child at this stage of development, the Obsessive Compulsive individual is utilizing this style to deny inner feelings of hostility and to a lesser extent sexualized love toward parental figures. In psychoanalytic terms, the personality structure revolves around issues of anality.

6. Related DSM-III-R diagnoses

The predominant classifications here are an anxiety disorder (Obsessive Compulsive Disorder or Obsessive Compulsive Neurosis, 300.30) and a personality disorder (Obsessive Compulsive Personality Disorder, 301.40).

7. The appropriate type of psychotherapeutic relationship or school of psychotherapy

Traditionally, the most appropriate therapeutic systems for this type of problem all have a psychoanalytic base, particularly those systems which focus on the analysis of the negative transference. This is an approach which within the analytic model was taken to its extreme by Wilhelm Reich, particularly in his early work on the analysis of what he called the character armor (Reich, 1945). In recent years, the work of Milton Erickson (1980) has gained increased attention for his creative paradoxical approaches to obsessive compulsive individuals, but Erickson was careful to point out the psychoanalytic theoretical roots from which he worked. Also, there are an increasing number of published reports of successful treatment of obsessive compulsive symptoms through the use of behavioral therapies.

8. Prominent theorists whose concepts have relevance for this particular stage

As has already been mentioned, the predominant theorists here include Freud and his followers (particularly when they focused on therapeutic problems associated with the negative transference), Wilhelm Reich, and Milton Erickson. It should be noted that, with the passage of time, Milton Erickson is being given more and more credit as the spur toward the use of paradoxical psychotherapeutic approaches.

Stage 5: Oedipal Phase

1. Approximate chronological correlates of normal development

The Oedipal stage lasts roughly from age 5 to age 7.

2. Relevant psychological concepts, constructs, or theories

Once again, it is appropriate to apply the entire range of psychoanalytic concepts and models to this stage of development, particularly the processes involved in id-ego-superego differentiation.

3. The personality structure: core issues, central motivation, central conflicts and ambivalences

The central task at this stage is to work out a series of interpersonal relationships in the family via a differentiation of feelings, particularly love, sexuality, and hostility. More than any other stage thus far, various affects and impulses (love, sexuality, hostility, anxiety, etc.) begin to emerge and are experienced as clearly defined and separate emotional entities. The child struggles with the expression of these, and the development of ego strength (in purely psychoanalytic terms) is crucial.

This is accomplished via the intrapsychic process described by classical analytic theory.

The child sees one parent as an unattainable sexual object, due to the threat of the more potent parent of the same sex, and so decides that the only way out of the dilemma is to become as much like the parent of the same sex as is possible. In other words, the child needs identification in order to deal with the impossible dynamic interaction among id, ego, and superego, and the family situation (Roth et al., 1967, p. 4).

4. The kind of relationship needed in order for psychological growth

Basically, parents help the child through this stage by acceptance of the Oedipal sexual and aggressive impulsivity directed toward them. The parents may not approve of the appropriateness of some of this expression but do approve of the child as a person and help the child to differentiate feelings. This means that the parents must accept the child's impulsiveness without being themselves overwhelmed or threatened by it. This acceptance helps the child to achieve a healthy identification with the parents. It also enables the child to develop ego strength, to work out a more mutually satisfactory role in the family, and, through the identification process, to begin preparing for social roles outside the home.

5. The related psychopathologies if fixation occurs

Parental rejection of the child's impulsive feelings (especially love, sexuality, and aggressiveness) fosters the child's own rejection of these feelings. This forces the child to restrict an open expression of these feelings, which in turn can lead the child to deny that these feelings even exist. This process, briefly stated, is what the psychoanalysts refer to when they talk about repression. This situation creates ongoing anxiety and inner turmoil which the child is consistently overwhelmed by. The personality structure, not yet fully formed, is too unsophisticated to handle these intrapsychic conflicts, and the result is a series of defenses which are only partially successful.

In psychoanalytic terminology, this type of dynamic forms the classic picture of the neurotic, which is considered the predominant psychopathology associated with this stage of the development. This is a concept with a literature so vast that we believe only this capsule summary has been necessary here.

6. Related DSM-III-R diagnoses

The primary diagnoses in this category are the Generalized Anxiety Disorder (300.02), Overanxious Disorder (313.00), Somatoform Disorders (300.81,11,70), Dissociative Disorders (300.12–14, 60), and certain disorders from other categories which in years past would have been considered one of the neuroses (e.g., Histrionic Personality Disorder (301.50).

7. The appropriate type of psychotherapeutic relationship or school of psychotherapy

One of the most appropriate therapeutic models here is obviously psychoanalysis, not in terms of its classical rituals (the couch, dream analysis, free association), but in terms of the therapist's focus upon the transference relationship and related issues as of primary concern to the patient and crucial in a successful outcome. The variants of the psychoanalytic school are numerous and well documented, and it is not our purpose to provide an overview of them, but to indicate that they apply.

More recently, there has also been increasing support for the use of rational-emotive (Ellis & Grieger, 1977), cognitively oriented therapies (Beck, Emery, & Greenberg, 1985), cognitive-behavioral (Michelson & Ascher, 1987), and behavioral therapies (Wolpe & Lazarus, 1966; Wolpe & Reyna, 1976).

8. Prominent theorists whose concepts have relevance for this particular stage

Obviously, the most prominent theorist of the Oedipal stage is Freud, followed by a host of his followers who stayed primarily within his framework.

Stage 6: Early Latency

1. Approximate chronological correlates of normal development

Early Latency occurs between the ages of 7 and 9, approximately.

2. Relevant psychological concepts, constructs, or theories

At this point, the value of psychoanalytic concepts begins to diminish in favor of peer relationships, social (vs. familial) roles, and the beginnings of mature self-concept. It should be emphasized that these issues are present from an early age, but at this stage they begin to assume greater importance.

This "self" is a concept widely treated in the literature: it is the perceived self, the person as he sees himself operating in various situations, a kind of "perceived ego." It develops out of quite adequate and sophisticated ego defense systems, and, in effect, represents the individual's ability to "step outside" of himself, observe his ability to cope with other people, and then modify his behavior on the basis of these observations (Roth et al., 1967, p. 5).

3. The personality structure: core issues, central motivation, central conflicts and ambivalences

At this stage, the child's central need is to become more independent of the family via the development of social roles outside the home (peers, school, etc.). The child begins to put his or her energies into these nonfamily relationships and roles and needs a growing body of social skills to do so.

> Early latency, occurring between the ages of six and nine, represents a coming to terms with the Oedipal conflict by a deinvestment of energy in the family and the beginnings of a focus on social development outside of the home. In this period, too, are the beginnings of self and an increasing importance of peer relationships (Marcus, 1969).

To the extent that the Developmental Theory Model is valid, this would explain why children at this particular age are ready for school: They are no longer so psychologically tied to the family that the school experience would become too traumatic.

4. The kind of relationship needed in order for psychological growth

At this point the child needs a parental relationship in which the parent is not so much a family figure as a representative of society. The parent becomes a role model for how the child should behave in the world outside of the family, as well as being a guide and teacher, a reasonable and stable social authority model.

5. The related psychopathologies if fixation occurs

The Developmental Theory Model asserts that the core issues at this stage of development are also the core issues for persons with character disorders—sociopaths and psychopaths.

> Character disorders . . . . are people struggling with the transition from impulse-controlling ego-techniques of the Oedipal period to self expression in a confusing world. This transition requires the cataloging of self images that are "tested out" on peers and authority adults. Channels for acceptable expression are thus found (Roth et al., 1967, p. 9).

In contrast to the person with Overanxious Disorder, who has attempted to repress the impulses in favor of a controlling and punitive superego, the character-disordered individual has done the opposite: repressed an overwhelmingly punitive superego and allowed the impulses somewhat free rein. Therefore, there is no self-controlling factor to allow the child to experience the consequences of his or her behavior. The superego, traditionally thought to be absent in people with character disorders (i.e., they have no "conscience") can be seen in the typically self-disparaging comments they often make and in their sometimes rigid adherence to codes of conduct, even though those codes of conduct are usually socially deviant. The punitive superego can also be seen in the depression and self-disparagement typical when psychotherapeutic intervention is successful. Because people with character disorders deny superego demands, they do not conform to the moral and ethical standards of society at large or of the agents of that society.

In their relationships with others, these individuals are extremely manipulative and exploitive, the purpose of which is to avoid the kinds of intimacy and genuineness that are the fabric of meaningful relationships. Basically, the interpersonal manipulation occurs in such a way that the other person must react either punitively or as a deviant cohort. For example, a character-disordered student will tell the counselor of some planned antisocial act, such as cutting a class the next period. The counselor is then placed in the position of either: (1) telling the student that this would be improper behavior, in which case the student can view the counselor as inappropriate for a relationship because he or she is a punitive authority figure; or (2) agreeing with the plan in the hope of maintaining the relationship, in which case the counselor has become an accessory before the fact. He or she has entered into an elaborate "game" with the character-disordered student which makes genuine intimacy impossible and manipulation of the counselor an accepted fact. It should be noted that this way of relating to others shows considerable sophistication in terms of ego strength, and therefore is somewhat contradictory to those theories which see character disorder as essentially a variation of a less developed personality structure.

The Developmental Theory Model makes a distinction between psychopaths and sociopaths. The psychopath rejects internalized societal ethics and is basically a loner. The sociopath, on the other hand, allows the superego expression in that he or she adheres strictly to and identifies with the rules of a subcultural group, but the group is deviant to the culture at large. A typical gang member, for example, would be considered sociopathic rather than psychopathic.

The Developmental Theory Model's view of psychopathy and sociopathy as related to Early Latency issues is another concept that appears at variance with traditional thought in this area, particularly the notion that the character disorder displays no conscience and perhaps represents a much lower level of personality organization than theorized here. Once again, our goal here is neither to fully elaborate this controversy nor resolve it.

6. Related DSM-III-R diagnoses

Included are the Conduct Disorders (312.20; 312.00; 312.90), the Antisocial Personality Disorder (301.70), and the Antisocial Behavior Disorders—Adult (V71.01) or Childhood and Adolescent (V71.02).

7. The appropriate type of psychotherapeutic relationship or school of
   psychotherapy

Group therapy is often appropriate for this category, especially when the focus is on the social and interpersonal manipulations. In any case, the therapist, paralleling the role of the parent, is an authority figure who teaches the person with character disorder better ways to meet impulsive needs.

Although a traditional therapeutic view has been that psychotherapy is not effective with character-disordered individuals, many successful cases and approaches have been reported in the literature (Greenwald, 1967; Lindner, 1944; Reid, Dorr, Walker, & Bonner, 1986).

8. Prominent theorists whose concepts have relevance for this particular stage

The Developmental Theory Model holds that theoretical models appropriate to this pathology include game theory (Berne, 1964, 1966), ego psychology (Hartmann, 1958), group social work approaches (Redl & Wineman, 1951), and countermanipulative approaches (such as Greenwald).

Stage 7: Preadolescent Latency

1. Approximate chronological correlates of normal development

Preadolescent Latency lasts approximately from age 9 through age 12 (or the onset of puberty).

2. Relevant psychological concepts, constructs, or theories

At this point, theories of the self and self-concept become dominant. Also, the individual's concept of his or her future becomes an important factor; the psychoanalytic assumption that the past determines the present gives way to the importance of the future in determining present choices. In addition, the peer group continues to increase in its importance. In other words, the concept of causality gives way to the concept of teleology.

3. The personality structure: core issues, central motivation, central conflicts and ambivalences

During this stage, the child has moved through the Oedipal issues and has achieved a kind of social autonomy from the family. The self-structure begins to emerge, but the child is still young and dependent. At this age, the child begins to recognize that the future (in terms of psychological and social growth and change) is not some far-off concept, but is "right around the corner." The child recognizes that other children just a few years older are going through tremendous changes, physically and socially, that lead to independence from the family, more personal responsibility, and greater involvement with the opposite sex. But the 10-year-old has simply not lived enough years to have the kind of maturity to deal with these impending changes. They are, in fact, extremely threatening.

Whereas in earlier stages of development the future was a relatively non-threatening issue, at this stage it becomes so overwhelming that the child must make a massive attempt to deny its inevitability. But to do this, the child must deny areas involving vocational and psychosexual development that would lead to increased maturity.

> Although the integration of differentiated self concepts is occurring, areas of self such as sex, vocation, and scholastic development are not integrated or even owned, since they carry with them the "threat" of independence and the beginning of the end of one's role in the family. Thus, dependence is preserved in being projected from the family onto peer relations. Through these peer relations, independence experiences can be accumulated in the form of self concept structures that carry little threat (e.g., athletics, boys clubs) while those that are threatening (e.g., sex, vocational choice) can be denied (Roth et al., 1967, pp. 5–6).

This would explain why children at this age are extremely dependent upon the opinions of their same-sex peers, tend to avoid areas of increasing personal responsibility (such as household chores and homework), and occasionally will even talk about not wanting to grow up. Academically, this is the age range (roughly Grades 4 through 6) when a substantial demand is made for a new level of personal responsibility in the form of increased homework, and many children find this adjustment difficult. This emphasis on the future is why this stage is more properly referred to as Preadolescent Latency and is qualitatively different from the earlier latency period.

The mechanism by which the child deals with the threatening issues is to deny them by finding certain behavioral patterns and thought processes which will both avoid the new areas and repress the decision-making process. For example, the child who does not do homework because he or she "forgot to bring it home" accomplishes in one deft mental process the avoidance of achievement and the denial of responsibility. Forgetting, after all, can happen to anyone; it is not a choice; it is beyond one's control.

4. The kind of relationship needed in order for psychological growth

The parent here becomes neither an agent of approval nor a social role model, but rather one who intervenes in the child's attempts to avoid responsibility and at the same time one who encourages the child to deal with his or her expanding role in the outside world. The parent must also do this without making that world too threatening or overdemanding for the child's readiness to cope. Still, the parent must intervene and not let the child retreat to a "Peter Pan" style of life.

5. The related psychopathologies if fixation occurs

Traditionally, this pathology, the Behavior Disorder (as opposed to the character disorders of the Early Latency period), has been described by what it is *not,* rather than what it is. A chronic underachiever, for example, who shows no medical problems, no learning disabilities, no neuroses or other psychopathologies, and no other mental abnormalities, but who continues to comfortably underachieve is likely to have been placed in this often puzzling group. The Behavior Disorders are characterized by normal functioning in most areas of life except one—the "disordered behavior"—which accomplishes the functions of avoiding the future, the integration of self-concept, the achievement of psychological independence, and the working out of one's adult psychosexual role.

One such disorder, the Non-Achievement Syndrome (or NAS), includes individuals for whom everything seems to be normal except for a persistent pattern of mediocre achievement, primarily academically but also noticeable upon a careful examination of other areas of life such as hobbies and household responsibilities. Individuals are characterized by low anxiety and absence of any identifiable mental disorder or abnormal behavior. However, they show little initiative in their daily lives and support mediocre academic performance or other lack of achievements with seemingly endless rationalizations or excuses. For example, a Non-Achievement Syndrome underachiever might support a pattern of low achievement by statements such as "I keep forgetting my homework," or "I studied the wrong material for the test," or "I guess I'm not good in math." These kinds of statements are made as a way of denying that one has made any sort of choice to underachieve, and that the low level of productivity is something beyond the control of the student.

> Such people get along well, function, have friends, work and do reasonably well in life, except they flunk out of school. If one discusses this with them, or asks them how things are, they will respond by saying that everything is fine. When it is pointed out that things cannot be fine if they are flunking out of school, they usually reply: "Yeh, everything is fine but that." They have an enormous series of rationalizations concerning why they did not do well in school at a particular time. They know all about football, baseball, cars, or a variety of other activities, and they do rather well in them. Only in terms of academic achievement do they fail. This behavior is specifically designed to prevent the completion of college, the achievement of maturity, and the acceptance of the kinds of demands that come with these things. The NAS individual, in effect, knows precisely the demands from which he is protecting himself, and is well aware of what he is doing. He is dealing with the anticipation of the independence-dependence bind by electing to remain dependent (Roth et al., 1967, p. 11).

What has made it difficult for mental health professionals, educational specialists, and indeed parents to fully understand and successfully cope with these students is that rather than being unmotivated, they are highly motivated (albeit unconsciously) to underachieve. Rather than being solely caused by early childhood events, this motivation to underachieve stems from their perceptions of a personal future they would rather avoid.

6. Related DSM-III-R diagnoses

In terms of underachievers, the Academic Problem (DSM-III-R classification V62.30) is the most relevant here. The brief definition of this problem in DSM-III-R is as follows:

> This category can be used when a focus of attention or treatment is an academic problem that is apparently not due to a mental disorder. An example is a pattern of failing grades or significant underachievement in an individual with adequate intellectual capacity, in the absence of a Specific Developmental Disorder or any other mental disorder to account for the problem (p. 359).

The reader may notice that the problem, as defined by DSM-III-R, is consistent with the historical definition of this category of problem according to what it is *not* (i.e., *not* an intellectual problem, *not* a mental disorder, etc.).

Occasionally, Behavior Disorders can appear within other DSM-III-R categories, such as Occupational Problem (V62.20), and Adjustment Disorder with Work (or Academic) Inhibition (309.23). This does not mean that every person in each of these categories has the kind of personality structure identified as Behavior Disorder by this model. It does mean, however, that one would expect to find large proportions of behavior-disordered individuals within these various DSM-III-R groups.

7. The appropriate type of psychotherapeutic relationship or school of psychotherapy

One of the problems in dealing with Behavior Disorders is that traditional forms of treatment do not seem to be effective. NAS, for example, does not respond to psychoanalytically oriented psychotherapy, client-centered therapy, behavior therapy, traditional educational guidance and counseling, or a variety of other approaches.

The Developmental Theory Model advocates a particular type of approach initially labeled *intervention* (Roth et al., 1967, p. 20) and later conceptualized as cognitively oriented confrontation (Mandel & Marcus, 1984a). The emphasis here is on how the specific disordered behavior (in this case, underachievement) allows the person to deny the future, to delay the development of psychological independence, and to avoid the definition of self. The therapist must constructively confront each excuse the NAS student offers. This point will be discussed in detail in Chapter 12.

8. Prominent theorists whose concepts have relevance for this particular stage

While theorists, such as Eric Berne (1964), who advocate game theory are appropriate here, there are few who have focused specifically on this category. Roth and his colleagues in the 1960s specialized in this area, and many (such as the present authors) trained in the Developmental Theory Model continue to expand and develop the theory and practice of treating this group, particularly the NAS (Mandel & Marcus, 1984a).

Stage 8: Early Adolescence

1. Approximate chronological correlates of normal development

In the original Developmental Theory Model, the stage of Adolescence was seen as extending approximately from puberty to age 21. In our current formulation, we believe a case can be made for distinct qualitative and psychodynamic differences between younger and older adolescents. The stage of Early Adolescence can be seen as existing approximately from age 12 through age 17.

2. Relevant psychological concepts, constructs, or theories

The four important psychodynamic concepts here are the developing self-concept, the independence-dependence conflict, peer relationships, and the adolescent rebellion.

3. The personality structure: core issues, central motivation, central conflicts and ambivalences

Freud saw the adolescent period as a reworking of the Oedipal drama. Others have seen it as related to the psychosexual elements of puberty, the rites of passage into the adult world, and so forth. The Developmental Theory Model sees this stage as the integration of isolated self perceptions into a new sense of self-concept. At this age, however, the individual is still quite immature, inexperienced, and frightened of future growth. Young adolescents are still too dependent and unprepared for independent existence, and yet their new-found self-concept demands that they achieve instant independence from the role of child in the family.

The solution to this independence-dependence bind is the utilization of peer support in a rebellion against the role in the family. Peer support meets the need for dependence, while rebellion against authority meets the need for independence. Thus the independence-dependence conflict is externalized, in that independence is defined as how one is treated by others rather than by what one chooses and commits oneself to through action. A person at this stage can be independent only if doing the opposite from what is expected by parents and other adults in positions of significant authority. This rebellion, aided by peer support, helps the person to maintain a sense of self-esteem and to deny the still-present dependency needs, while avoiding the considerable burden of true independence.

4. The kind of relationship needed in order for psychological growth

Parents typically report extreme frustration in dealing with children at this stage. The child balks at the slightest parental demands or even mild suggestions, yet in the next breath also claims that the parents "don't care." These two types of reactions reflect the young adolescent's inner conflictual needs for independence as opposed to maintaining dependence upon the family. Parents must tread a thin line between providing support for the child's expanding needs to make his or her own independent decisions, coupled with enough strength to stand up to the rebellion and set reasonable limits. This parental stability in the face of the young adolescent's rebellion is necessary in order to give the adolescent a safe relationship within which independence and new areas of self-concept can be tested out.

Peer relationships are often more impactful at this stage than relationships with parents. The adolescent needs the support of the peer group, and yet many parents see clearly the danger of a likeminded peer group whose dominant group psychology is based on a rebellion against the values of authority or "the system."

5. The related psychopathologies if fixation occurs

People whose central personality structure never moves from the needs of this stage are often not seen as pathological. They are, however, seen as unhappy people, constantly opposing "the system," supposedly repressive authority figures, and anyone who even hints at having expectations of them—in short, perpetually rebelling. They often become angry easily and are sensitive to the mildest of directives from friends, family, and co-workers. They often blame their unhappiness on being treated poorly and feel that if they received the independence and respect they deserve, they could do their work, become happier, succeed, etc.

Having considerable ego strength and personality development, such individuals can be quite effective in their rebellion, and are often found railing against social injustices and unfair aspects of "the system." This is not to say that these individuals are always wrong in their evaluations or actions regarding social injustices, or that anyone who rebels against social injustice has this personality structure. However, persons fixated at this stage are in a continual state of rebellion which touches every aspect of their lives. Like the peer relationships among 13- or 14-year-olds, every relationship becomes dominated by the need to rebel against authority figures or social systems perceived as unjust.

6. Related DSM-III-R diagnoses

The predominant DSM-III-R diagnosis appropriate here is the Oppositional Defiant Disorder (313.81).

7. The appropriate type of psychotherapeutic relationship or school of psychotherapy

While there is no particular school identified with dealing with this stage, those that are more directive and focus on power relationships are appropriate. Family therapy often helps the family to accept and yet set reasonable limits on the emerging independence of the adolescent.

8. Prominent theorists whose concepts have relevance for this particular stage

In our opinion the fields of psychology and human development have subsumed the issues of this stage under general theories covering the entire spectrum of adolescent development. Therefore, although much has been written about adolescent rebellion, few well-known theorists have recognized early adolescence as a distinct developmental stage with its own unique psychological issues. Conceptually, issues here revolve around what the adolescent is *against,* and it is often difficult for parents and teachers to ascertain what the adolescent is *for*.

Stage 9: Late Adolescence

1. Approximate chronological correlates of normal development

Psychosocially, adolescence is usually seen as ending at age 20 or 21. The Developmental Theory Model, however, views the psychological issues of adolescence *as core issues* which extend into the early 20s. Specifically, Late Adolescence occurs approximately between ages 17 and 22.

2. Relevant psychological concepts, constructs, or theories

The predominant psychological concept appropriate here is the self-concept, as well as all of those theories which consider it the cardinal explanatory psychological principle.

3. The personality structure: core issues, central motivation, central conflicts and ambivalences

The central issues at this stage include the adult definition of self and the establishment of genuine psychological independence. This is often accomplished via an intense and often painful and confusing introspective look at the self. Self questions such as "Who am I?" are common.

> The working through of these issues involves, to a great extent, a major investment in openness to oneself and experience, which carries with it threats of dealing with one's own inadequacies (Marcus, 1969, p. 25).

People at this stage are intensely preoccupied with questions of self. All of their energy seems to go into this introspective process; every experience and interaction becomes an object of intensive self-reflection as to its implication for the meaning of self.

4. The kind of relationship needed in order for psychological growth

The predominant interpersonal need of the person at this stage of personality development is an accepting and trusting individual who is willing to listen but not offer advice, direction, or expectations. What is also required is nondirective support for the adolescent's emerging struggles in making his or her own life decisions. This kind of relationship allows the adolescent to work through or "hash out the issues" (Shaw, 1970), and is more likely to be fulfilled by peers. No longer are parental and authority figures significant, except as nondirective mentors willing to listen and respect the self-directed needs of the adolescent.

5. The related psychopathologies if fixation occurs

Although there is no specific name for this category, an individual for whom these issues are paramount can best be described as psychologically independent and mentally healthy, but otherwise depressed, confused, and introspective, with all energies bent on the intense exploration of self. The Developmental Theory Model originally identified this as the Adolescent Reaction.

6. Related DSM-III-R diagnoses

DSM-III-R conceptualizes this as the Identity Disorder (313.82).

7. The appropriate type of psychotherapeutic relationship or school of psychotherapy

The type of psychotherapeutic relationship needed here parallels the accepting, listening nature of the peer relationship outlined above. To be effective, the therapist is neither directive nor focused on problem solving.

There is instead a role of empathically listening, following, clarifying, reflecting, and accepting the adolescent's ideas, emotions, and decisions. This kind of therapeutic relationship is the hallmark of the client-centered model and its derivatives.

8. Prominent theorists whose concepts have relevance for this particular stage

Obviously, the theorists most closely associated with this approach are Carl Rogers (1951) and those who have followed his model. Theorists who stress the importance of the self-concept also belong in this category.

Stage 10: Early Adulthood

1. Approximate chronological correlates of normal development.

This stage can be considered as lasting approximately from the early to late 20s.

2. Relevant psychological concepts, constructs, or theories

Relevant concepts here are less psychological than sociological: the establishment of an adult role, the achievement of vocational adequacy, an adult commitment to an intimate relationship, and similiar concepts.

3. The personality structure: core issues, central motivation, central conflicts and ambivalences

The predominant need here is to accomplish and achieve a life direction, interpersonally as well as vocationally. The self-concept here is concerned with achieving specific roles in society (spouse, employee, professional person, wage earner, member of the adult community, etc.). Energy goes into actively building one's life and career; this is a stage of doing, not pondering.

4. The kind of relationship needed in order for psychological growth

The primary relationship needed here is built on intimacy and on shared action-oriented goals—the building of family and career—with a significant other person, usually the spouse or other intimate partner.

5. The related psychopathologies if fixation occurs

Problems at this stage are not defined as pathology, but rather as a sense of failure and loss of adequacy in fulfilling the life direction.

6. Related DSM-III-R diagnoses

The most likely diagnoses for someone having difficulty at this stage of life are the Phase of Life Problem or Other Life Circumstance Problem (V62.89) Other Interpersonal Problem (V62.81), and Marital Problem (V61.10).

7. The appropriate type of psychotherapeutic relationship or school of psychotherapy

The predominant therapeutic relationship here is one of a mature and experienced peer who is willing to help the individual derive personal and behavioral techniques for solving problems in the real world. This may include advice and guidance, skills training (e.g., study skills, job-interviewing skills, etc.), direction for personal improvement (e.g., assertiveness training), or guidance in dealing with a spouse. Without real problem-solving help, the person stuck at this stage will continually experience a sense of failure, inadequacy, and impotence in fulfilling his or her needs, no matter how much self-understanding is gained.

8. Prominant theorists whose concepts have relevance for this particular stage

Although there is no single theorist for this stage of personality development, the self-help movement can be seen as having some relevance here.

Adulthood Stages

The area of adult stages was foreshadowed by Erik Erikson (1963) and has received increasing attention in the last two decades. Books and articles on "midlife crisis" and on later life stages now appear on a regular basis, giving needed attention to important aspects of life usually overlooked by theorists. However, when the Developmental Theory Model begins to discuss adult stages of development, we find that our 8-item outline for each stage loses some of its utility. The issues and problems of adulthood are more diffusely defined and do not lend themselves as easily to categorization as the childhood and adolescent stages. Therefore, we have arbitrarily chosen to present Early Adulthood as the last stage before we conclude our discussion of the Developmental Theory Model. We certainly acknowledge the work of Levinson (1978) and others who have researched the stages of adulthood, but we believe that these are less related to the problem of underachievement.

Conclusions

The Developmental Theory Model concludes:

> With such a system, the therapist is armed with a vast, organized body of
> constructs from which to evaluate and treat patients. Of course, patients do
> not move from their pathology to maturity in one jump, but rather move from
> one level of fixation to the next. The therapist must be able to shift his con-
> ceptual system and therapeutic approach so as to be consistent with the move-
> ment of the patient. Ideally, all therapies should yield people who ultimately
> resolve existential crises, having moved through the other levels of develop-
> ment between their present pathology and the existential crisis, albeit taking
> with them their characterological remnants (Roth et al., 1967, p. 21).

Table 6.1 summarizes the essential characteristics of each stage in the
developmental continuum as outlined in this chapter.

We would like to remind the reader that the Developmental Theory Model
represents the diagnostic scheme which we classify as Dynamic Diagnosis.
In addition, for each dynamic diagnostic category in the Developmental
Theory Model there is the related Treatment Diagnosis. However, this does
not complete the picture. In each individual case, one must finally arrive at
the Practical Diagnosis, including factors which we have not emphasized in
this chapter.

It is critical to include the unique characteristics of each individual's
personality makeup. For example, each person has a certain range of intellectual capacity, a certain degree of ego strength, a typical level of memory
practiced or used, a specific quality of reality testing, certain strengths and
weaknesses in cognitive processing, and so forth. It is the amalgam of all
of these, in combination with the core developmental issues, that constitute
the individual's personality.

Factors That Interact with Personality Structure

There are, of course, factors other than internal personality structure that
play a significant role in underachievement. These include physical factors
(such as learning disabilities or illness) and environmental or situational
factors (such as family issues or a change of school). While these may or
may not be directly related to the type of Dynamic Diagnosis outlined in the
Developmental Theory Model (or for that matter in psychoanalytic, cognitive, and other models), they may have a strong impact on the Practical
Diagnosis. For example, two students diagnosed as Identity Disorder underachievers may receive differing treatments because one has an identified
learning disability and the other's parents are going through a divorce. Again,
we refer the reader to the excellent book by Cronbach and Snow (1977), on
the interaction of factors in the learning process.

TABLE 6.1. Summary of Developmental Stages

Stage	Age Range	Core Concepts	Relationship Needs	DSM-III Psychopathology	Relevant Theories/Theorists
1. Early Infancy	0 to 6 mos.	Physical sustenance Sensory stimulation Orality	Physical care "Feeding" of sensory and motor experiences	Reactive Attachment Dis. of Infancy (313.89)	Sensory stimulation in therapeutic relationship (Spitz)
2. Infancy	6 mos. to 2 yrs.	Impulse fulfillment Basic trust/mistrust Orality	Security of predictable caring parenting	Paranoid Dis. (297.10) Schizoid Pers. Dis. (301.20) Schizotypal Pers. Dis. (301.22)	Trust issue (Arieti, Sullivan)
3. Toddler	2 yrs. to 3½ yrs.	Impulse expression and control Ego development "Terrible twos"	Reasonable external behavioral controls by parents	Borderline Pers. Dis. (301.83)	Winnicott Anthony Rutter
4. Preschool	3½ yrs. to 5 yrs.	Beginning autonomy Internalization Developing mastery	Approval for limit adherence Shame for limit/control violation	Obsessive Compulsive Dis. (300.30) Compulsive Personality Dis. (301.40)	Alleviation of symptom—behavioral approach Insight into symptom—analytically oriented
5. Oedipal	5 yrs. to 7 yrs.	Identification Family relationships	Accept/understand aggressive impulses, allowing development of reasonable superego	Overanxious Dis. (313.00) Generalized Anxiety Dis. (300.02) Somatoform Dis. (300.81,11,70) Dissociative Dis. (300.12-14, 60)	Behavioral (Wolpe) Cognitive (Beck) Analytically oriented Rational-emotive (Ellis)
6. Early Latency	7 yrs. to 9 yrs.	Self-development through peers/school Beginning responsibilities	Reasonable social role model	Conduct Dis. (312) Antisocial Pers. Dis. (301.70) Antisocial Behavior Dis. (V71.01,02)	Reality-oriented, confrontational therapy Ego psychology theory

Stage	Age		Therapeutic Focus	DSM Diagnosis	Therapy
7. Preadolescent Latency	9 yrs. to 12 yrs.	Self-concept Future School/home responsibilities (e.g., homework, chores)	Confrontation re. new responsibilities	Academic Problem (V62.30) Occupational Problem (V62.20) Adjustment Dis. (309.23)	Cognitive-behavioral theory, Confrontational therapy
8. Early Adolescence	12 yrs. to 17 yrs.	Externalized independence/dependence conflict (against authority) Self-development	Testing out new independence Challenging values of authority	Oppositional Defiant Dis. (313.81)	Reality therapy
9. Late Adolescence	17 yrs. to 22 yrs.	Internalized independence/dependence conflict Self-definition Identity/introspection Values for self	Acceptance of self-direction Respect for self-definition	Identity Dis. (313.82)	Nondirective therapy (Rogers)
10. Early Adulthood	22 yrs. to 30 yrs.	Adult role Definition of life direction Vocational commitment/adequacy Intimacy Doing/action	Intimacy Shared commitments Mentor Action-oriented goals	Phase of Life Problem (V62.89) Other Interpersonal Problem (V62.81) Marital Problem (V61.10)	Career counseling Problem-solving skills Marital counseling
11. Catch "30"	30 yrs. to 40 yrs.	Increasing importance of personal "meaning" Fulfillment of initial dreams/commitments Questioning of outcomes	Options for life-direction changes	Phase of Life Problem (V62.89) Other Interpersonal Problem (V62.81) Marital Problem (V61.10)	Supportive counseling
12. Midlife Crisis	40 yrs. to 50 yrs.	Existential crisis—mate, children, vocation	Existential empathy	Identity Dis. (313.82)	Existential therapies (Frankl, May)

TABLE 6.2.   Factors That May Interact with Personality to Produce Underachievement

Factors	Examples
Physical	Medical illness (mononucleosis, thyroid imbalance, ulcer, asthma)
	Neurological deficits (brain damage, seizure)
	Perceptual-motor deficits (learning disabilities, developmental lags)
	Physcial disabilities
Environmental and situational	Family issues (separation, divorce, birth, death, parent-child relationship, sibling relationship)
	Peer relationships
	School (teacher, curriculum)
	Culture (ethnicity, religion)
	Socioeconomics
	Race (stereotyping)
	Change (school, job, friendships)
	Trauma (accident, crime, natural disaster)

Table 6.2 lists some of these additional factors.

Not only should these factors be taken into account along with the Dynamic Diagnosis, but there are situations where these factors may be more significant than diagnostic category in producing underachievement. A child diagnosed as an Overanxious Disorder underachiever may be underachieving not because of the anxious personality, but because one of these other factors has pushed the level of anxiety to a point where that child has become dysfunctional in the classroom. Another example comes from our clinical experience: Conduct Disorder underachievers from higher socioeconomic families are less likely than those from lower socioeconomic families to suffer immediately from the legal consequences of their antisocial behavior. Their families have the resources to provide competent legal and professional support.

In Part Three we will present the results of approximately 60 research projects on underachievement by our colleagues and ourselves which utilized the Developmental Theory Model and the concepts of differential diagnosis and differential treatment. The findings of these studies have resulted in a number of modifications to the model and form the cornerstone for current and planned research.

PART THREE

Research on the Differential Diagnostic Model

The theoretical point of view of this book has its origin in a 1963 article called "The Non-Achievement Syndrome" by Roth and Meyersburg, which reported work done at the Hampton Institute in West Virginia. In the late 1960s and early 1970s, a group of related studies were done at the Illinois Institute of Technology in Chicago. These attempted to validate and further study the Non-Achievement Syndrome and to expand the original concept so that it would incorporate the whole area of psychosocial development.

From the middle 1970s to the present, further research at York University in Toronto, Canada has included more detailed studies of demographics (age of onset, sex ratio, and family and cultural dynamics) related not only to the Non-Achievement Syndrome but to underachievement in general, and to other underachiever types in particular. In Part Three, we review the relevant findings of these studies, particularly as they relate to differential diagnosis and differential treatment. Overall, data on approximately 1,000 males and 300 female students form the basis for the findings.

In Chapter 7, we summarize the research findings from studies in which levels of achievement were the major focus, and in which differential diagnosis was not part of the design. Chapter 8 provides striking support for our differential diagnostic model. Chapter 9 examines the research findings on the efficacy of differential treatment of underachievers, based on the principles of differential diagnosis.

CHAPTER 7

Nondifferential Diagnostic Research

Some of our own research and that of our colleagues has been devoted to the phenomenon of underachievement irrespective of differential personality diagnosis. In this chapter we focus on the results of these studies of achievement patterns to the exclusion of personality factors.

Developmental Difficulties

Mandel (1984) studied 200 volunteer Grades 9–10 achieving, underachieving, and overachieving high school students. He found that less than 7% of the entire sample reported developmental difficulties in their histories, and that most of the reported difficulties were of a minor self-correcting nature. If this finding were confirmed by further studies, it would suggest that personality, motivation, and other nonphysically based factors play a major role in the genesis of underachievement.

Birth Order

In this same study, Mandel found no significant differences among the underachieving, achieving, and overachieving groups regarding birth order.

Intellectual Factors and the Role of Learning Disabilities

One question raised often has been whether learning disorders (even if mild and undetected) play a role in the genesis of underachievement. Freeman (1984) studied 16-year-old high school students ($N = 15$) diagnosed as having Non-Achievement Syndrome (NAS). She analyzed their Wechsler Intelligence Scale for Children-Revised (WISC-R) profiles. No significant differences between their scores and normative data were found. The mean verbal IQ of this NAS group was 101.6 ($SD = 14.45$) and the performance IQ 101.7 ($SD = 12.12$). Scatter within each of these scales was also within normal ranges. One subject did exhibit a significant discrepancy between verbal and performance IQs, and with further diagnostic testing was found to have an identifiable moderate learning disability.

Freeman also calculated the Bannantyne categories for learning disabilities and found that the NAS group pattern was, "Conceptual greater than

Spatial greater than Sequential.'' This pattern was not comparable with the literature reports on learning-disabled subjects, who tended to produce a "Spatial greater than Conceptual greater than Sequential" pattern (Rugel, 1974; Smith, Coleman, Dokecki, & Davis, 1977). Although more research needs to be done to replicate this study using a much larger sample, it appears that approximately 7% of NAS students may also exhibit an identifable learning disability. The data from this study appear to suggest that learning disabilities in an NAS high school sample do not play a major contributing role.

Race, Demographics, and Family Stability

Gale (1974) studied the relationships among race (primarily between Blacks and Whites), achievement level (GPA), self-concept (the Brownfain Self Rating Inventory), study habits and attitudes (the Brown and Holtzman Survey of Study Habits), socioeconomic status, and the presence or absence of a father figure in the homes of junior college students. Gale found that Black and White students differed in some self-concept and socioeconomic measures but not in the study skills measure. GPA groups differed in the study skills measure but not in the others. No other variables showed significance. Gale concluded that only the study orientation scale had some ability to predict achievement level.

Lawrence (1985) looked at the relationship between family stability and achievement level in 200 volunteer high school students. All achievement groups were matched for intelligence and socioeconomic status. He found that family size, socioeconomic status, and frequency of domicile change were not significantly related to grade point average. He also found, however, that there was a significant statistical relationship between marital disruption and academic achievement in the predicted direction. One must recognize, however, that marital and other family disruption can be a major contributor to many childhood and adolescent problems. A large-scale research project by the Ontario Ministry of Community and Social Services (1986) found that the factor most related to the disorders they examined was family dysfunction.

Further, Lawrence found a significant relationship between extent and type of religious affiliation and grade point average. There was a high proportion of Catholics in the achieving and overachieving high school sample. He also found that the importance of religion to each family was related to academic achievement. It would be valuable to continue to study the manner in which religion impacts on the achievement process. Perhaps certain family and cultural (including academic achievement expectations) are related to the importance of religion.

Finally, Lawrence found that negative life change events appeared to contribute to the underachievement process. A greater proportion of families of underachievers reported negative life events changes when compared to families of achievers or overachievers. Lawrence's study, therefore, strongly implicated marital disruption and other negative life events as factors related to underachievement.

Parents' Educational History

In a study looking at the relationship between parents as educational role models and high school students' academic performance (controlling for socioeconomic status), Dennis (1985) found that when the parents' elementary school achievement level had been poor to moderate, there were more of their children who were average achievers (46%) than either under- or overachievers. When the parents' achievement levels had been good or excellent, there was a higher incidence (50%) of overachievement than either underachievement or average achievement in their children. When the results were analyzed by achievement category of the students, 75% of the underachievers had parents who had performed in the good-to-excellent category. These results suggest that while parental school achievement level may have an impact on children's achievement level, the presence of an underachieving student does not automatically mean that that student's parents had underachievement or mediocre achievement in their school histories.

Dennis also attempted to control statistically for socioeconomic status, expectation levels, and intelligence, and found that the proportion of the variance predicting ninth-grade GPA was as follows:

 7%—Father's overall educational performance
 NS—Mother's overall educational performance
28%—The student's own academic expectation
 8%—The student's intelligence
 0—Parental expectation as perceived by the student
 NS—Socioeconomic status

These results suggested that the predominant contributing factor was the student's own expectation for academic performance. How such expectations are normally generated needs to be more fully explored.

Parental Employment, Occupation, and Sex of Student

Hartley (1985) reported that there was a significant relationship between age at which the student's mother became employed outside the home and the sex of the student. She found that "mothers with sons began to work when sons were significantly older, whereas 50% of mothers with daughters began working before their daughters started school" (p. 144). This relationship is shown in Table 7.1.

TABLE 7.1.   Frequency of Employment for Mothers of Male and Female Students

| Sex | N | Student Age at Mother's Return to Work | | |
		0–5	6–11	12–16
Male	33	8	13	12
Female	40	20	27	3
Total	73	28	40	15

Note. From Hartley (1985). By permission of the author.
*Chi Square = 10.50 (df = 2; p = .01).

Further, Hartley had hypothesized that there would be significant relationships between 13 maternal employment measures and female students' achievement levels, but none of the measures showed a significant relationship. She did find, however, that mothers with underachieving sons "had a 72%–28% split between [being] employed outside the home and homemaker. The reverse was found for mothers with overachieving sons; 38% were employed outside the home and 62% were homemakers" (p. 150).

In other words, mothers of underachieving sons tended to be employed outside the home, while mothers of overachieving sons tended to be homemakers. The exact nature of the influence of maternal employment on the achievement patterns of children needs a great deal more clarification. Many factors play a role in the final achievement outcome in relation to maternal employment, including socioeconomic factors, as well as subtle attitudinal factors.

Further study is needed regarding both paternal and maternal variables which impinge on the achievement categories of children. Hartley found that although maternal occupation was not related to achievement categories of either male or female children, paternal occupation was significantly related to male achievement category. "When under- and average achievers were combined and compared to overachievers it was found that overachieving males had a greater proportion of fathers in professional occupations" (p. 152).

Parental Expectations of Child's Academic Performance

Mukherjee (1972) examined self-concepts and socioeconomic values and attitudes among parents of high-achieving and low-achieving adolescent males (N = 30; age range, 16–18). Instruments used were the Study of Values, the California Psychological Inventory, and the Attitude Towards Current Social and Community Issues (constructed by Mukherjee for this study). Predicting that parental values would in part determine the achievement level parents expect of their children, Mukherjee found that parents of high achievers were more oriented towards theoretical, economic, and political values than were parents of low achievers. Parents of low achievers, on the other hand, were more oriented towards aesthetic, social, and religious values. In addition, parents of high achievers tended to view themselves as dominant, tolerant, responsible, intellectually efficient, self-accepting, and self-controlled. They also placed a high value on status and achievement (as opposed to conformity and independence). Parents of high achievers were more involved in social and community issues, whereas parents of low achievers tended to want others to solve problems in these areas. Mukherjee interpreted these findings as reflecting the relatively high expectations for independent responsibility and academic achievement among parents of high-achieving students, and the contrasting expectations of relative passive dependency among parents of low-achieving students.

Mukherjee also hypothesized that high and low achievers would have values and self-concepts similar to those of their respective parents, but this hypothesis was only partially supported. For example, high achievers favored aesthetic and social values, while their fathers favored theoretical and economic values, and their mothers favored economic and responsibility values. Low achievers favored political values, whereas their fathers and mothers favored religious values. Mukherjee concluded that underachievers may actually try to fulfill parental expectations by underachieving.

In a predominantly middle-class, White, Anglo-Saxon, Protestant sample, Hartley (1985) found that fathers expected their sons, but not their daughters, to complete postsecondary education. This finding held within all achievement categories: underachievers, achievers, and overachievers. She reported also that fathers tended to label their daughters' academic performance as "average" significantly more often than their sons' academic performance. That is, fathers tended to discount a daughter's academic achievements more than they did a son's. Thus, paternal expectations for their children varied according to the sex of the child. If this finding were found to be widespread, it would suggest that girls have less family support for high academic achievement than boys.

Student Attitudes Toward School

Mandel (1984) used regression analysis to categorize 200 volunteer high school students by achievement category (underachievers, achievers, and overachievers). Of the entire sample 82% expected to complete postsecondary education, and most rated their parents as expecting the same; 84% rated school as important or very important. These results can be interpreted as reflecting broad cultural norms regarding the positive value of education.

In attitude toward school, underachievers tended to be more negative, indicating that they felt that school was not as important, and achievers' and overachievers' attitudes were more neutral. These results are predictable if one hypothesizes that a generally negative attitude toward school will be found in underachievement for any reason having to do with personality and motivation, although this does not necessarily imply cause and effect. It could as easily be interpreted as a consequence of poor academic achievement.

Sib Achievement Patterns

In a study on achievement patterns of the siblings of students in varying achievement categories, Leverett (1985) found significant differences between the mean GPAs of siblings of overachievers and average achievers and between the mean GPAs of siblings of underachievers and overachievers. Although some caution is warranted here because of small sample size, Leverett concluded that siblings of overachievers tended to perform at levels comparable to their brothers and sisters. This same relationship tended to hold for siblings of achievers and siblings of underachievers, despite the small sample size.

The siblings of the original volunteer high school sample ranged across elementary and high school years. It is not known whether the siblings' actual achievement would have resulted in their being classified in the same achievement categories (underachiever, average achiever, or overachiever) as their brothers and sisters, because only actual GPA was used for sibling performance. It is possible, however, that some larger family variables affect the overall achievement patterns of all children in a family.

Relationship Among Sex, Age, and Achievement

McKay (1985) studied GPAs from Grades 1 through 10 of 200 students, including underachievers, achievers, and overachievers. She found an overall 0.5 correlation between GPA and ability as measured by the Otis-Lennon School Ability Test (O-LSAT). Thus, approximately 25% of the variance in academic performance throughout elementary and high school years can be accounted for by intellectual capacity, while about 75% must be accounted for by factors other than intellectual capacity. These would include personality, family and school, peer group, cultural, and other factors.

McKay found no statistically significant sex differences in her entire study. There was no significant difference between males and females in the correlation between ability and performance at any age and no significant sex difference in achievement from Grades 1 through 10.

Family Relationships

Hilliard and Roth (1969) used a mother-child questionnaire to study the relationship between mother-child interaction and academic achievement. He reported significantly greater acceptance by mothers of achievers, but no difference between maternal attitudes perceived by achieving and underachieving students. This study did not look at father-child interaction.

McRoberts (1985) used the Inventory of Family Feelings (Lowman, 1981) to study the affective relationships between 99 high school students and their families, particularly affective child-parent relationships, parental personality, and the achievement categories of the students.

In general, the families with underachieving children (as opposed to those with achieving children) showed significantly less positive affective dyads (child-mother, child-father, mother-father), greater discrepancies in the dyadic members' perceptions of the affective relationships, and larger discrepancies in how the students felt towards their mothers (vs. their fathers). This suggests that while an open and caring relationship between children and parents may not result directly in an achieving student, the relative absence of this kind of relationship may have a negative impact on the child's achievement motivation.

Among the relationship dyads studied, McRoberts found that the most distant and conflictual were between underachievers and their cross-sex parents. In addition, the parents in these dyads tended to have a more positive perception of the relationship than did their cross-sex underachieving sons or daughters. This finding has many possible interpretations, and more intensive family research in this area is needed.

McRoberts also found that as male students' achievement level increased, their fathers tended to describe themselves as more extroverted, assertive, dominant, competitive, and bossy. The reverse pattern was found for female students. To the extent that fathers of high achievers may have this kind of personality, their children (whether male or female) may simply be attempting to meet the expectations of a strong and domineering parent. The difference may be that such a father may expect his son to be an achiever but his daughter not to be.

These relationships are graphically depicted in Figure 7.1. McRoberts had 12 female and 12 male underachievers, 17 female and 15 male achievers, and 21 female and 22 male overachievers participate in her study, for a total of 99 10th-grade high school students.

Personality Differences Among Achievement Levels

Using the Developmental Theory Model as a theoretical base, Friedland (1972) examined whether the measurement of certain personality factors (anxiety and self-concept) could be utilized to predict achievement level. Three hundred thirteen male and 36 female college students were given the Taylor Manifest Anxiety Scale and a true-false Self-Ideal Q-Sort. Friedland hypothesized a curvilinear relationship to achievement. Extremely high or low scores on a measure of anxiety or self-concept would correlate with poor achievement, while midrange levels would result in an optimum level of achievement. A curvilinear relationship was in fact found for males, but a linear relationship was found for females. Friedland concluded that 93%

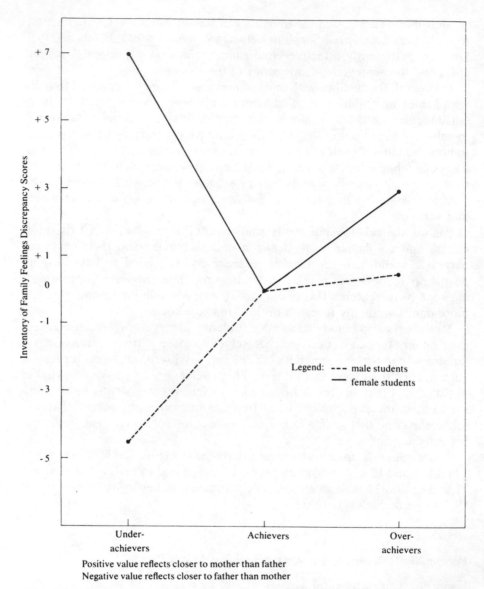

Positive value reflects closer to mother than father
Negative value reflects closer to father than mother

Figure 7.1. Interaction effects of sex × achievement. Discrepancy between students' feelings toward their mothers versus their fathers. From McRoberts (1986). By permission of the author.

of his sample fell into one of three categories: high anxiety, low self-concept; low anxiety, high self-concept; and normal ranges on both scores.

Roth and Puri (1967), in a nondiagnostic study of elementary and high school students, looked at the relationship between underachievement and the direction of aggression hypothesized for the NAS student. The Rosenzweig Picture Frustration Test was given to matched groups of achieving and underachieving males and females in Grades 3, 6, 9, and 12. Roth and Puri found that male achievers and male underachievers differed significantly in the direction of their aggression: Male achievers were more extrapunitive; male underachievers were more intropunitive and impunitive across all grade levels studied. The female underachievers differed from the female achievers in their direction of aggression only at the Grade 6 level: Like males, female achievers were more extrapunitive; female underachievers were more impunitive and intropunitive.

Exner (1974) has used the Roth and Puri study (and others) in arguing for a passive-aggressive dynamic as the major dynamic factor in underachievement; i.e., underachievement is considered an indirect acting-out of hostile impulses, an interpretation in line with classical psychoanalytic theory.

Hartley (1985) found statistical differences between all male and all female underachievers on eight High School Personality Questionnaire (HSPQ) fac-

TABLE 7.2. Summary of Research Using a
Multifactorial Model in Studying Underachievers,
Achievers, and Overachievers

Research variable	Reference
Affective family relationships	McRoberts (1985)
Aggression	Roth & Purl (1967)
Anxiety	Friedland (1972)
Birth order	Mandel (1984)
Developmental difficulties	Mandel (1984)
Family demographics	Lawrence (1985)
Learning disabilities	Freeman (1984)
Marital stability	Lawrence (1985)
Parent and student expectations	Dennis (1985)
	Hartley (1985)
	Mukherjee (1972)
Parent and student values	Mukherjee (1972)
Parent educational history	Dennis (1985)
Parent employment/occupation	Hartley (1985)
Racial factors	Gale (1974)
Religion	Lawrence (1985)
Self-concept	Friedland (1972)
Sibling achievement	Leverett (1985)
Student academic history	McKay (1985)
Student attitude toward school	Mandel (1984)

tors. When students were grouped only on the basis of achievement category and sex, these differences on the HSPQ emerged.

The Roth and Puri and Hartley studies support the notion of personality differences between achievers and underachievers and between male underachievers and female underachievers. Whether these assumed personality differences create achievement or underachievement (or whether they are the result) cannot be definitively stated.

Summary

We have reviewed a number of studies pertaining to the development of underachievement and have found that developmental difficulties and learning disabilities were not major contributors to the achievement process. This is not surprising, in that most of these studies had screened out such factors in order to focus on the role of personality. Neither birth order nor parental educational history appear related to achievement category.

Certain environmental variables, however, appear to be related to achievement: religion, marital stability, life events, parental employment status, parental values and expectations for child achievement, student attitude toward school, and (for certain variables) sex of the child. On the other hand, one study on racial factors found no significant relationship between race and underachievement. None of these studies examined the school environment in any detail. Some personality variables (anxiety, aggression, and self-concept) appear generally related to underachievement. A summary of the range of studies is presented in Table 7.2.

In the next chapter we will summarize research findings on the role of personality variables in the achievement process, especially the studies that highlight the importance of differential diagnosis.

CHAPTER 8

Differential Diagnostic Research

Roth and Meyersburg (1963) identified a pattern of personality characteristics in certain underachieving students and called this the Non-Achievement Syndrome (NAS). Their article, based on clinical experience, includes a description of the syndrome, a recommended counseling approach, and speculations as to etiology. Their article has continued to stimulate clinical insights, but it does not include a formalized, statistical attempt to validate the syndrome, differentiate it from other types of problems, or place it in a diagnostic or developmental context with other syndromes.

The original article by Roth and Meyersburg began with a series of constructs about the NAS student:

1. "The student's poor achievement does not arise from an incapacity to achieve" (p. 535).

These students have the intellectual capacity to achieve good grades, and many have done so in their earlier years. Roth and Meyersburg assumed that current GPAs did not reflect actual abilities in NAS students.

2. "Poor achievement is an expression of the student's choice" (p. 535).

Although unaware of their own underlying motivation, NAS students actively choose to do poorly or to just "get by" academically. Should NAS students be confronted with this interpretation, they would probably deny it.

3. "The student's choice for poor achievement operates in the preparation he makes for achievement" (p. 535).

These students do not consistently or adequately make a commitment to academic tasks such as term papers, homework assignments, or preparation for exams. NAS students avoid regular studying and even evaluate the need for study in terms of how much time it may take away from being with friends, watching television, and other such activities.

4. "Poor achievement is a function of the preparation for achievement which a student makes" (p. 536).

As the logical consequence of their lack of preparation, NAS students earn mediocre or unexpectedly low grades. Most do not focus on grades as a logical sequence of events that begins with little consistent effort and ends with poor grades.

5. "Poor academic skills are related to poor achievement and are an outgrowth of previous choices for poor achievement" (p. 536).

Many NAS students do not develop or consistently utilize effective learning skills. They are able to formulate effective study strategies, but they do not implement these strategies consistently or often enough to improve.

6. "The choice for poor achievement may be expressed as overall limited achievement or as achievement in deviant channels" (p. 536).

NAS students perform in a mediocre fashion, far below their capacity of achievement. Some do commit energy and perform at higher levels in nonacademic areas but, when asked about plans for achievement in athletics or music or auto mechanics, they are just as vague and noncommital as they are in academic areas. They avoid making the commitment to do what is necessary to achieve in academic and nonacademic areas.

7. "The patterns of choice for poor achievement are enduring and do not undergo spontaneous change" (p. 536).

Without someone else's intervention, NAS students do not change this pattern. Meaningful intervention can come from a wide variety of sources—parents, teachers, school counselors, or mental health practitioners—yet these adults usually do not intervene successfully, partly because they lack an understanding of the underlying motivation of NAS students.

8. "Achievement patterns, like other enduring behavior patterns, can be considered to be related to 'personality organization' " (p. 536).

Non-Achievement Syndrome students are remarkably consistent (some would say resistant). Their stable and predictable pattern of underachievement is a central part of their personalities, not a "tacked on" trait, such as achievement motivation. Roth and Meyersburg specified the major characteristics of the NAS student as "poor academic achievement; general self-depreciation; lack of recognition of pleasure at 'being'; no clear system of personal goals or values; vulnerability to disparagement by others; immature relations with parents; frequent depressions; lack of insight about self and others; and free-floating anxiety" (p. 538).

The depression was conceptualized as a mild but persistent depression, more like a sense of dissatisfaction with the present situation than a deep, incapacitating clinical depression. Similarly, anxiety levels tend to be mild and tied to specific precipitating causes only, such as exams and the issuance of report cards.

Roth and Meyersburg believed that the etiology of the NAS could be found in family dynamics: subtle devaluations of the child by the parents or the focusing by the parents on the child's failures rather than on successes. Such experiences were thought to lead the child to feelings of self-denigration and unexpressed hostility that slowed the development of autonomy and other aspects of the self-concept.

9. "The counseling relationship can serve as the impetus to change the achievement patterns" (p. 536).

Roth and Meyersburg did outline what, in their clinical experience, was an effective treatment for this problem:

1. Encourage the NAS student to present all complaints about his or her current academic situation, as well as general complaints in other significant life areas (financial, relationship, family, etc.).
2. Discuss in detail the ways in which the student prepares for each course.
3. Verbalize to the student how the obvious deficits in frequency, intensity, and duration of academic preparation predict academic failure or poor academic showing.
4. Present the inescapable conclusion that since such behavioral patterns will inevitably lead to poor academic performance, the student must want this outcome to occur.
5. Point out how such behavior patterns are evident in other areas of the student's life (e.g., not doing accepted chores at home, etc.).
6. Ask if the student would like to change such patterns. (Almost all NAS students will say yes.)
7. Ask which behaviors need to change, and also ask the student to present a remedial plan of action and make a commitment to the plan.
8. Ask the NAS student to predict what may interfere with these planned changes in the problematic behavior and discuss safeguards against these potential roadblocks.
9. When the student has begun to use successful achievement strategies, help the student expand understanding of the ways such behavior patterns show up in nonacademic areas.

Gradually, such discussions begin to generate an increasingly positive self-image by the student, including a clearer self-understanding and an increased willingness to assume personal responsibility in academic and nonacademic areas (e.g., peer relationships and relationships with family members). At this point also, achievement levels begin to rise, and counseling is then terminated.

Reliability and Validity of the Diagnostic Procedures

Because so many of the studies using the diagnostic scheme in this book are dependent upon the accuracy of the diagnostic process, it is important to consider the attempts at assessing the reliability and validity of the differential diagnostic procedures used.

Garfield (1967) found that three trained clinical psychologists were able to independently agree on 80% of their diagnoses of 37 tape-recorded subjects. Pomp (1971) found that his trained clinical judges agreed in 90% of 79 tape-recorded diagnostic interviews. In a more recent study (Mandel & Marcus, 1984b), trained clinical judges independently agreed in their diagnoses of 24 out of 28 tape-recorded diagnostic interviews. Hartley (1985) reported that two trained clinical judges independently agreed on 56 of 68 taped interviews (81%). Fraser (1987) found an agreement rate of 80% between two trained Caucasian clinical judges, and an agreement rate of 90% between one trained Caucasian clinical judge and a trained West Indian clinical judge. Thus, the diagnostic interview procedures used in much of this specialized clinical research appear to have been reliable, even across cultures.

A question can be raised about the validity of the diagnostic process in these studies: Do clinical judges trained in the Developmental Theory Model have such high rates of agreement because the model is so clinically accurate that any clinician trained in it will become an unerringly accurate diagnostician, or are these results an artifact resulting from a model that may be internally consistent but unrelated to real clinical issues? Three studies have attempted to address this question directly.

Berenbaum (1969) asked clinical judges to diagnose each individual in his sample based not only on the interview tapes, but on blind test protocols (primarily group Rorschach and group TAT tests). His clinical judges included three trained in the Developmental Theory Model and three who were at least equivalent in professional experience but who were unfamiliar with the Developmental Theory Model and were trained in differing theories and techniques. The clinicians trained in the Developmental Theory Model were asked simply to make a diagnostic judgment. They were able to accurately diagnose the major groups represented (NAS, Neurotic, and Adolescent Reaction). The clinicians untrained in the model were given the 16-item, 7-point rating scale presented in Table 8.1.

Statistical analyses showed that the ratings by the clinicians untrained in the Developmental Theory Model produced different group profiles which fit into the diagnostic categories predicted by the Developmental Theory Model and which were consistent with the ratings by the clinicians trained in it. In other words, clinicians untrained in the Developmental Theory Model

TABLE 8.1. Rating Scale Used by Untrained Clinical Judges

Instructions: Please rate this individual on the basis of dynamic characteristics evidenced in the test protocols supplied for this person. The 16-item rating scales are to be treated as equal interval scales in terms of the characteristics described:

Subject #: _____

1. Self-effacing	1	2	3	4	5	6	7	Self-enhancing
2. Negative value for self	1	2	3	4	5	6	7	Positive value for self
3. Introjected goals	1	2	3	4	5	6	7	Chosen goals
4. Introjected values	1	2	3	4	5	6	7	Chosen values
5. Internally consistent value system	1	2	3	4	5	6	7	Internally inconsistent system
6. Little ego strength	1	2	3	4	5	6	7	Considerable ego strength
7. Permeable ego boundaries	1	2	3	4	5	6	7	Evaluative ego boundaries
8. Dependent on parents	1	2	3	4	5	6	7	Nondependent on parents
9. Frequent depression	1	2	3	4	5	6	7	Infrequent depression
10. Defensive perception of self	1	2	3	4	5	6	7	Realistic perception of self
11. Self-centered	1	2	3	4	5	6	7	Other-centered
12. Unaware of motives	1	2	3	4	5	6	7	Aware of motives
13. Free-floating anxiety	1	2	3	4	5	6	7	Bound anxiety
14. Little anxiety	1	2	3	4	5	6	7	Intense anxiety
15. Frequent anxiety attacks	1	2	3	4	5	6	7	Infrequent anxiety attacks
16. Attitude of despair	1	2	3	4	5	6	7	Attitude of promise

Note. From Berenbaum (1969). By permission of the author.

could differentiate personality types on the basis of the diagnostic categories predicted by this model, even though those judges were unaware of the particular categories. This is even more important when one considers that Berenbaum also found that all clinical judges, trained and untrained, were unable to differentiate the test protocols of achievers from those of under-achievers to any degree of statistical significance.

With regard to the NAS, Berenbaum concluded that "the results of this study support the view that the Non-Achievement Syndrome represents a consistent pattern of personality characteristics differentiating this particular group of underachieving students from others" (p. 1502-B). These results have even larger implications, however, in that they suggest that a theory such as the Developmental Theory Model taps a common clinical experience and perception in seasoned professional diagnosticians and therapists.

Marcus (1969) followed a similar procedure. He gave clinical protocols (group Rorschachs and group TATs) of alcoholics and achieving college students to clinical judges trained and untrained in the Developmental Theory Model. The alcoholics had previously been diagnosed by personality category on the basis of taped diagnostic interviews. All clinical judges were asked whether each protocol was that of an alcoholic or a nonalcoholic. The judges trained in the Developmental Theory Model were asked simply to reach a diagnostic judgment. The judges untrained in the model were asked to rate the protocols using a clinical rating scale identical to the one used by Berenbaum (1969) and presented in Table 8.1. As with the Berenbaum study, clinical judges were better able to differentiate by personality diagnosis (consistent with the Developmental Theory Model) than by the presence or absence of a particular behavioral pattern. Specifically, all of the judges had difficulty accurately deciding whether a protocol was that of an alcoholic or a nonalcoholic. The judges trained in the Developmental Theory Model, however, were able to diagnose the personality structure reliably and accurately.

On the basis of the 16-item, 7-point rating scale, the judges untrained in the model were also able to accurately diagnose the categories predicted by the model in a manner consistent with their trained colleagues. For example, on the basis of the rating scales, Neurotics (or in our terminology, Overanxious Disorders) differed from the control group in that they had significantly greater anxiety and depression. These are the characteristics predicted by the Developmental Theory Model. In the diagnostic category labeled Behavior Disorder, the category in which the NAS personality fits (according to the Developmental Theory Model), the rating scales listed the following characteristics as differing significantly from the control group: an attitude of despair, a defensive perception of the self, an apparent lack of awareness of motives, permeable ego boundaries, dependency on parents, self-centeredness, negative value for self, self-effacing attitude, and no internally consistent value system. Many of these characteristics are consistent with the classic theoretical and clinical description of the NAS.

Although not all of the personality categories predicted by the Developmental Theory were tested in his study, Marcus (1969) concluded that: (1) None of the clinical judges were able to correctly assess the alcoholic behavior; (2) Two out of the three trained judges were able to correctly diagnose; and (3) Analysis of the untrained judges' rating scales fell within the lines predicted by the Developmental Theory Model. All these factors appear to indicate that "the theory provides a more meaningful, more consistent, and more clinically valid approach to the problem of alcoholism than does any descriptive summary of alcoholic behavior" (p. 69). While this conclusion may or may not prove to have an impact on current diagnostic notions of alcoholism, its importance here is in the reliability of the clinicians' rating process and in its sensitivity to real clinical issues.

Mandel (1969) utilized a similar procedure but added another group: underachieving students. His findings confirmed what Marcus (1969) had reported. Five of the six clinical judges were unable to significantly differentiate the samples according to behavioral symptom (i.e., underachievement vs. alcoholism). Yet, two of the three trained clinical judges were able to reliably diagnose personality patterns across presenting behavioral symptom, and the untrained clinical judges were able to produce differential diagnoses using the 16-item, 7-point rating scale (see Table 8.1). More specifically, Behavior Disorder alcoholics and Behavior Disorder underachievers (i.e., NAS) were statistically similar to each other's profiles on 10 of the rating scales. Further, when compared to the ratings of the control group, both the Behavior Disorder alcoholics and Behavior Disorder underachievers differed from the control group on eight of the original ten scales. In comparison to the control group, the Behavior Disorder subjects (alcoholics or underachievers) were rated by untrained clinical judges as being more self-effacing, more dependent upon parents, and more defensive in their self-perceptions. They were rated as having a less internally consistent value system, as well as a more negative value for self. They showed no differences in comparison to the control group in the degree of free-floating anxiety or frequency of anxiety attacks.

The untrained clinical judges consistently rated both the neurotic alcoholics and the neurotic underachievers as exhibiting statistically more depression than the control group. Finally, the untrained judges rated the neurotic alcoholics as showing more self-enhancement, more positive value for self, more evaluative ego boundaries, and a more internally consistent value system than the individuals with Behavior Disorders (combined for presenting problem). The neurotic underachievers, on the other hand, showed more free and intense anxiety and were rated as exhibiting more frequent anxiety attacks than those persons with Behavior Disorders (also combined for presenting problem).

The personality profiles generated by the untrained clinical judges closely matched the dynamic personality descriptions derived from the Developmental Theory. Thus, the results from the Berenbaum (1969), Mandel (1969), and Marcus (1969) studies provided validation for some aspects of the theory, the model of differential diagnosis, and (even more importantly here) consistent evidence of the reliability of clinical diagnoses.

The issue of interjudge reliability was also addressed by Fraser (1987), Hartley (1985), and Phillips (1987). Hartley studied 200 high school students, about one third of whom were classified as underachievers, one third as achievers, and one third as overachievers. She employed a regression equation in which ability and performance were included. These students were also given individual tape-recorded diagnostic interviews, and two clinical judges trained in the Developmental Theory Model were asked independently to rate each.

The clinical judges agreed on 183 of the 200 subjects, an interjudge reliability of 91% and both consistently agreed in spite of differing achievement levels of the students. Interjudge agreement rates varied from 83% (underachieving females) to 97% (overachieving males).

Fraser (1986), in a cross-cultural study, examined the interrater reliability of clinical judges from different cultural and racial backgrounds. His student subjects were also from differing cultural and racial backgrounds ($N = 65$): 36 Canadians of West Indian descent, 17 Caucasian Canadians born in Canada, and 12 from a mixed immigrant group (mostly from Europe, Asia, and South America). All students agreed to individual tape-recorded diagnostic interviews.

Fraser used three trained clinical judges: two male Caucasian clinical psychologists (Judges 1 and 2), and one Black senior clinical psychology graduate student of West Indian descent (Judge 3). Interrater reliabilities between Judges 1 and 2 and between Judges 2 and 3 were both 90%. These pairs of judges were able to agree on 9 of 10 diagnoses from interviews. The agreement rate between Judges 2 and 3 was 88%. These latter two judges were able to agree on 57 of the 65 independently rated diagnostic interviews. Judges 1 and 3 were unable to diagnose 4 of the 65 subjects, because of either poor quality audio reproduction or paucity of information elicited in those interviews. They disagreed only on 5 of the remaining 61 subjects. Therefore, the interrater reliability that Fraser reported is a conservative figure. Fraser also found that high interrater reliabilities held across the student samples, ranging from a low of 83% to a high of 94%. Therefore, even with the cultural differences in the students and the clinical judges, Fraser found that clinical judges trained in the Developmental Theory Model could reliably reach diagnostic decisions from semistructured diagnostic interviews.

Fraser found not only that the clinical judges showed high interrater reliability, but that their diagnoses of personality style were better predictors of academic achievement (as measured by scores obtained in English) than were intellectual ability (as measured by the Matrix Analogies Test, a nonverbal measure), academic level (i.e., general vs. advanced curriculum), and ethnic group (West Indian, mixed immigrant, Canadian). The multiple regression correlation among these variables (R) was 0.2979 ($F = 3.56; p < 0.01$), and diagnosis was the only significant predictor. In fact, the square of the correlation when diagnosis alone was the only predictor variable was 0.2089 ($F = 12.15; p < 0.01$).

Using Cohen's Kappa test for interrater agreement, Phillips (1987) recalculated the reliability rate for the 200 independent diagnostic judgments originally done in the Hartley (1985) study. (Cohen's Kappa is a more conservative measure.) Phillips found that based on the original diagnostic categorizations by two clinical judges, the Kappa value was 0.863. Here again, even using a more conservative reliability measure, results support the reliability of the clinical diagnostic model.

All of the above studies point to a high degree of clinical raters' consistency in diagnosing based on the tape-recorded interview. Other studies have focused on the validity of the differential personality model of underachievement, and thus far these studies (reported below) have produced positive results also.

Psychometric Personality Assessment and Differential Diagnosis

Pomp (1968) used the Self-Ideal Q-Sort technique to examine the relationships among self-concept, achievement level, and diagnostic category in male university students. A total of 64 male underachievers from the IIT Counseling Center's underachievement program participated, as well as a control group of 28 achieving IIT male students. Pomp employed the basic diagnostic interview technique and clinical judges (trained in the Developmental Theory Model) to assign each subject to one of four diagnostic groups: Neurotic (i.e., Overanxious Disorder), Behavior Disorder (i.e., NAS or Academic Problem), Adolescent Reaction (i.e., Identity Disorder), and Healthy Adolescent.

Pomp found significant self-ideal discrepancy score differences between achievers as a group and underachievers as a group (underachievers produced greater self-ideal discrepancy scores). The achievers' concepts of who they were and who ideally they would like to be were not as discrepant as the comparable underachievers' concepts of themselves. This finding was consistent with previous reports in the professional literature regarding differences in self-ideal scores between achievers and underachievers. Pomp did not find significant differences in the discrepancy scores within diagnostic category between achievers and underachievers.

In the other major finding from Pomp's study (1968), the achieving Overanxious Disorder students described themselves as busy, successful, studious, worthy, helpful, and considerate; Overanxious Disorder underachievers described themselves as democratic, kind, and friendly; achieving Healthy Adolescents described themselves as accurate, competent, dependable, and friendly; and underachieving Identity Disorder students described themselves as helpful, considerate, and inefficient. Finally, Pomp reported that in comparison with Overanxious Disorder achievers, achieving Healthy Adolescents described themselves as alert, friendly, purposeful, and tactful, but not intellectual. Thus Pomp found differences in self-perception related both to achievement level and to personality diagnosis.

In another study, Pomp (1971) used a high school sample to study the relationship between psychodiagnosis and level of psychosexual development in adolescents. Seventy-three male high school students participated in individual tape-recorded diagnostic interviews. None of these students had been in psychotherapy, none had any severe psychopathology as identified by teachers, and none had ever been hospitalized for mental health problems.

Three clinical judges trained in the Developmental Theory Model of psychotherapy rated the tape-recorded interviews. As we have reviewed in Chapter 6, this model postulates that specific diagnostic categories are fixated at specific psychosexual stages of development. The clinical judges were asked to independently diagnose the tape-recorded interviews as to whether students exhibited Oedipal personality dynamics, post-Oedipal latency dynamics, preadolescent latency dynamics, or adolescent personality dynamics. The diagnostic breakdown from the trained clinical judges reported by Pomp (1971) is presented in Table 8.2.

The post-Oedipal latency group (i.e., Conduct Disorder) was not used in the statistical analysis because of small group size. The frequency distribution in Table 8.2 is consistent with other research results, in that approx-

TABLE 8.2.   Diagnostic Judgment Frequencies from Interviews

Category	Frequency	%
Oedipal (i.e., Neurotic)	16	21.9
Preadolescent latency (Non-Achievement Syndrome)	42	57.5
Post-Oedipal latency (Conduct Disorder)	2	2.8
Adolescent Reaction (Identity Disorder)	13	17.8
Total	73	100.0

Note: Data from Pomp (1971).

imately 50–60% of high school and university samples fit NAS personality characteristics, while approximately 15–20% each fit Overanxious Disorder and Identity Disorder characteristics. It is likely that in a nonvolunteer sample these distributions might change somewhat, including percentages for the Conduct Disorder category and other diagnostic categories (e.g., Schizoid Disorder of Adolescence) that had been eliminated by the selection criteria.

Using a standardized, objectively scored personality inventory, the California Personality Inventory (CPI), Pomp measured differences across the diagnostic categories. He reported significant differences between the Adolescent Reaction and NAS students, with the Adolescent students producing a significantly higher mean CPI score. Adolescent Reaction students generally perceived themselves as dominant, tolerant, achievement-oriented via independence, intellectual, efficient, and flexible. In other words, they perceived themselves as possessing leadership ability, persistence, self-reliance, and independence. They rated themselves as being able to exert self-control, and considered themselves mature, insightful, confident, idealistic, assertive, and rebellious. These CPI characteristics match the developmental theory description of the Healthy Adolescent.

Pomp also found that those in the Oedipal group (i.e., Overanxious Disorder) perceived themselves as creating a favorable impression and as concerned about how others would react to them. They tended to rate themselves as cooperative, enterprising, sociable, and warm. These descriptions are similar to the discussion of the Neurotic, or Oedipally fixated, individual in the Roth, Hershenson, and Berenbaum paper (1967) outlining the original Developmental Theory Model.

The preadolescent group (i.e., NAS students) scored significantly lower in comparison with the Oedipal group on the Good Impression trait of the CPI; they perceived themselves as more self-centered and less concerned with the needs and wants of others. This also fits the description of the NAS derived from the Developmental Theory Model. These preadolescent latency NAS students also were significantly lower on Intellectual Efficiency and on Achievement via Independence traits in comparison to the Adolescent group; that is, the NAS students perceived themselves as less independent, less self-reliant and less mature than the Adolescent students. This finding is congruent with Developmental Theory Model descriptions of the NAS.

The Adolescent group was the only group that considered someone other than their parents when asked to specify a favorite person. They appeared to be less tied to family members when compared to either NAS or Overanxious Disorder students, who rated themselves as more tied to their families and less well established as independent teenagers.

All of the above descriptions parallel those of the diagnostic personality groupings at specific levels of psychosexual development and support a differential diagnostic model in the area of academic underachievement.

Kearney (1971) used the Self-Ideal Q-Sort technique, an Area Concern Magnitude Estimation (ACME) methodology, and a Multidimensional Scaling Analysis (MDSA) to study the relationship between self-concept in male underachieving college students and Erikson's (1963) scheme of levels of psychosexual development. The assumption was that students at each level of psychosexual development would perceive and organize themes differently from subjects at other levels of development. The multidimensional scaling approach required that each subject rate how similar his concern was across 10 predetermined areas. These areas were chosen for their appropriateness for the university age male sample, and they included independence, authority, identity, sex, values, parents, future, school, commitment, and intimacy. "The multidimensional successive intervals scaling analysis integrated these similarity-dissimilarity judgements so that it was possible to reconstruct the 'psychological map' used by the various groups" (Kearney, 1971, p. 109).

Eighty-seven Caucasian male underachievers from the IIT Counseling Center achievement program participated. They ranged in age from 17 to 24 years. Tape-recorded diagnostic interviews were conducted, and clinical judges provided their diagnostic impressions. Thirty-eight underachievers were diagnosed Neurotic (i.e., Overanxious Disorder), 32 NAS, and 17 Adolescent Reaction (i.e., Identity Disorder).

Overanxious Disorder students were assumed to be fixated at Erikson's Stage III (initiative vs. guilt), NAS students at Stage IV (industry vs. inferiority), and Identity Disorder students at Stage V (identity vs. identity diffusion). The resulting frequency distributions within the diagnostic groupings differed somewhat from those typically found in previous and subsequent studies. Kearney reported a greater percentage of Overanxious Disorder than NAS students, whereas the reverse is usually the case. It is possible that Kearney's method of obtaining research subjects differed somewhat from that in other studies. His focus, however, was on how each of these diagnostic groups perceived major life issues, rather than on their distribution frequencies.

Kearney found that the Q-sort did not differentiate among the Neurotic, NAS, and Adolescent Reaction groups. In other words, all three diagnostic groups shared a common set of attitudes about the self. On the test of self-concept areas, however, he did find significant differences in variability: The Neurotic group had a narrow variability, while the NAS and Adolescent Reaction groups had a wider variability. This could be interpreted in terms of the high needs for approval of Overanxious Disorder students, making their performance on instruments such as the ACME demonstrations of stereotyped notions of what they think is expected.

Kearney also found that the magnitude estimation technique produced reliable and valid results as a measure of self-concept concerns. He concluded that it was an error to construct self-concept scales unidimensionally rather than multidimensionally. The multidimensional scaling technique produced different self-concept structuring for each of the diagnostic categories. Kearney noted that in terms of specific scales, the three diagnostic groups differed in areas such as the relationship of self to school, future, parents, and authority. This should be expected (given the divergent place each of these issues occupies in the personality structure of these three diagnostic groups) and is consistent with descriptions of the personality dynamics based on the Developmental Theory Model (Roth et al., 1967).

However, Kearney unexpectedly found that the three groups were most similar in the way they dealt with the areas of commitment, identity, and independence. He interpreted these similarities as resulting from the same threat to all subjects: being dropped from school for academic failure if their grades did not significantly improve over the semester during which they participated in this study. Kearney hypothesized that this situation may have determined a similar ego content for all three diagnostic groups.

The Kearney and Pomp studies suggest that the magnitude of self-ideal correlation is not necessarily associated with psychosexual level of development. To the extent that the Developmental Theory is correct, however, it would predict that self-concept is a multidimensional construct, and that the manner in which it was measured in the Kearney and Pomp studies may have produced results which were meaningful primarily for an adolescent population (which is struggling psychologically with issues of identity). Therefore, the use of instruments (such as the Q-sort) attuned to self-concept would be most issue-appropriate to the diagnostic category most sensitive to that dimension (i.e., the Identity Disorder underachiever). Future research could examine the specific use of a differential diagnostic series of psychological tests, each issue-appropriate for only one psychosexual level of development and hence for only one diagnostic category.

Nixon (1972) investigated whether a statistically significant dependency hierarchy could be uncovered among three types of differentially diagnosed underachieving male students. The existence of such a hierarchy would provide further validation for the Developmental Theory (Roth et al. 1967) and support the use of a developmental framework within which to conceptualize various diagnostic categories of underachievers.

Nixon studied 46 underachieving male high school students. Tape-recorded diagnostic interviews were administered, along with a Dependency Proneness Scale (Flanders, Anderson, & Amidon, 1961), and two Internal-

External Scales (Crandall, Katkovsky, & Crandall, 1965; Rotter, 1966). Clinical judges rated each interview and provided diagnostic judgments. Because of the small sample size of the Adolescent Reaction group, Nixon was able to compare measures of psychological dependency and locus of control only between Neurotic and NAS underachievers.

She found that the Overanxious Disorder group scored significantly higher than the NAS group on a measure of dependency. The two groups did not differ, however, on locus of control measures. Why Overanxious Disorder students would score higher on a dependency measure is predictable. They have overwhelming needs for approval and are dependent on a particular kind of relationship in which interpersonal acceptance, constant reassurance, and parallel emotional issues are paramount. This is the kind of dependency likely to be reflected in dependency measures of almost any kind. While the NAS is also theorized as dependent, it is not the same kind of dependency as that of Overanxious Disorder. NAS underachievers do not need or want the kind of emotionally intense and dependent type of relationship with their parents or other authority figures that Overanxious Disorder underachievers constantly need.

Some projective findings highlighted the differences in dependency issues between the NAS and Overanxious Disorder underachieving students. On the following three items on the Dependency Proneness Scale, significantly more Overanxious Disorder students than NAS students disagreed. In other words, significantly more Overanxious Disorder underachievers rated the following statements as being atypical of them. These items were:

Item 3:   "It's fun to try out ideas that others think are crazy."

Item 8:   "My folks usually have to ask me twice to do something."

Item 12: "I often disagree with my parents."

Additionally, on Item 39, "I like to follow instructions and do what is expected of me," 90% of the Overanxious Disorder students agreed, whereas only 55% of the NAS students agreed. These results highlighted the increased interpersonal dependency on significant authority figures typical of the Overanxious Disorder underachieving student.

Theoretically, NAS students are not dependent upon a *relationship,* but upon a *social role:* namely, that of a child of about 10 years of age. At this age, the person is dependent in terms of personal responsibility (preparing meals, laundering clothes, paying the bills, etc.), but not dependent upon a relationship in which the issue is one of approval. Therefore, the NAS students would not be expected to score high on dependency measures which focused on interpersonal particulars. In fact, the items on the Dependency Proneness Scale on which the NAS students differed from the Neurotics were, for example, "It's fun to try out ideas that others think are crazy," or "I often disagree with my parents." A Neurotic would not be expected to agree with these statements, but a NAS student might very well.

But why would Overanxious Disorder underachievers and NAS students both produce similar scores on a measure of locus of control? Perhaps the Overanxious Disorder and NAS students produced similar scores but for different reasons. People with an external locus of control would tend to blame external factors (chance, luck, or significant others) for events that happened to them. Such individuals would not be likely to accept responsibility for their own actions and would seek reinforcement from significant others. Internally oriented people, on the other hand, would accept responsibility for their actions and would view themselves as the controlling factor in what happened. Such people would be expected to obtain reinforcement from within themselves. Perhaps for the Overanxious Disorder underachievers, the external locus of control is driven by classical psychoanalytic transference issues, insecurity, or other related dependency needs. For the NAS student, the external locus of control simply provides a means of shifting personal responsibility outside the self so that the self-concept is not threatened by having to make choices. In either case, the result would appear to be an external locus of control.

Here again, as in some of the previous research by Pomp (1968; 1971) and Kearney (1971), instruments which were constructed based on unidimensional conceptualizations (e.g., self-concept; internal-external locus of control) may have been used to measure multidimensional concepts. In any case, Nixon's study (1972) supports the hypothesis that Overanxious Disorder underachievers are more dependent than their underachieving NAS classmates.

Tirman (1971) attempted to generate three separate MMPI scales that would differentially identify three frequently reported underachieving types. Eighty-three male underachieving university students from the IIT Counseling Center underachievement program received tape-recorded diagnostic interviews, and clinical judges were asked for diagnostic impressions. These independent diagnoses were 38 Neurotic (i.e., Overanxious Disorder), 30 NAS, and 15 Adolescent Reaction (i.e., Identity Disorder) students. Subjects were also administered the MMPI.

Tirman then performed an item analysis to determine which items correlated significantly with each diagnostic category. MMPI items that were consistently answered either true or false by subjects from one diagnostic category were chosen as representing that category. Tirman used further statistical procedures to generate three derivative MMPI scales: the Neurotic scale (71 MMPI items), the NAS scale (17 items), and the Adolescent Reaction scale (28 items). Using a multiple discriminant analysis, he found that these newly developed scales agreed with the original clinical diagnostic judgments in 69 of the 83 cases (83%).

If Adolescent Reaction students were excluded from the sample, a 116-item instrument derived statistically from the MMPI could differentiate Neurotics from NAS students. Once again we see the ease of distinguishing between NAS and Overanxious Disorder students and the difficulty of differentiating Overanxious Disorder from Identity Disorder underachieving students. Tirman concluded, however, that the most reliable method for differentially diagnosing underachievers remained the clinical interview.

The use of a much researched diagnostic instrument such as the MMPI has yielded some differentiating factors. Barger and Hall (1964) concluded that MMPI profiles of underachievers were likely to have elevated Psychopathic-Deviate (*Pd*) and Manic (*Ma*) scales. This has been partially confirmed by our clinical experience, in that NAS students in particular have produced either no MMPI scale elevations or moderate elevations in the *Pd* and/or *Ma* scales. The elevated *Ma* scale may have little to do with the underachievement process, since many college-age individuals have this as the one elevated scale, presumably an index of available psychic energy at that age level. The *Pd* scale, however, suggests a problem more traditionally related to that of the Conduct Disorder. This may be partially accurate, if one considers that for the NAS, the original Developmental Theory Model (Roth et al., 1967) assertion is that the problem lies in preadolescent latency and the Conduct Disorder problem lies in post-Oedipal latency, one developmental stage earlier. Therefore, these two personality categories would be closely related developmentally and should have similar patterns.

Kaminska (1984) continued some of the earlier MMPI research, but rather than attempt to generate new MMPI scales as Tirman (1971) had done, she simply had each of 15 diagnosed NAS underachieving high school students complete the MMPI. Kaminska scored the 7 male and 8 female MMPI protocols according to the traditional validity and clinical scales, using adolescent norms. The students ranged in age from 15 to 17 years, with a mean age of 16.13 years and had been underachieving for approximately 2 years. The sample was suburban, Caucasian, and middle class. Kaminska had predicted that NAS subjects would not exhibit gross psychopathology on the MMPI scales and that the variability in subscales scores would also be low.

Group means for the scales were as follows:

Clinical Scales		Validity Scales
Hypochondriasis (*Hs*) = 56.5		*L* = 40.6
Depression (*D*) = 51.0		*F* = 54.8
Hysteria (*Hy*) = 53.7		*K* = 43.5
Psychopathic Deviate (*Pd*) = 59.8		
Masculinity-Feminity (*Mf*) = 41.8 (F)		
60.3 (M)		
Paranoia (*Pa*) = 53.8		
Psychasthenia (*Pt*) = 60.1		
Schizophrenia (*Sc*) = 59.2		
Hypomania (*Ma*) = 66.8		
Social Introversion (*Si*) = 44.8		

The subjects simply did not show pathology across the MMPI scales. Further, Kaminska did find low variability across subjects on specific scales (*Hs*, *Hy*, and *Si*). Standard Deviations ranged from 5.7 to 16.3. The majority of the NAS students scored within the nonpathological range on 6 of 13 MMPI scales (*L*, *F*, *Hs*, *D*, *Hy*, and *Pa*). A majority of NAS students also scored within or below the normal nonpathological range on 3 of 13 MMPI scales (*K*, *Pd*, and *Si*). A majority of NAS students scored within the normal or slightly elevated range on 3 of the MMPI scales (*Pt*, *Sc*, and *Ma*). There was an even distribution of scores across the *Mf* scale, probably reflecting a range of concerns in this sample regarding masculinity-femininity. A few subjects had single scale scores above 70, which occurred on scales *Hs*, *Hy*, *Pd*, *Pt*, *Sc*, *Ma*, and *Si*. None appeared to be in the extreme range. Interestingly, Kaminska was unable to find the previously reported typical MMPI underachiever profile (Barger & Hall, 1964). A probable reason for this is that the original underachiever profile was most likely generated from a heterogenous sample of underachievers. Kaminska's study focused only on the NAS underachiever.

These results support the hypothesis that the NAS student has a relatively normal profile. Either the NAS student is not emotionally disturbed or pathological in the usual sense of the term, or, although virtually pathological in terms of motivation, the NAS student has a highly developed personality structure which can cope internally and externally with a variety of normal conflicts, pressures, perceptions, and emotions.

Perhaps the most dramatic validation of the clinical diagnostic interview procedure is provided by Phillips (1987). Using 200 high school students, he performed a discriminant function analysis comparing diagnoses based on psychometric tests, demographic data, and teacher ratings with diagnoses based on clinical judgments of tape-recorded interviews. Using ratings of English teachers, he found an agreement rate of approximately 97%. Using ratings of science teachers, the agreement rate was 92%. This suggests that it may be possible to devise an accurate, valid, reliable diagnostic procedure independent of the clinical interview.

Intellectual Functioning, Differential Diagnosis, and Academic Performance

Looking at the question of abilities and the present underachievement model, Freeman (1984) gave the WISC-R to 15 underachieving NAS 10th-grade students (mean age 16.8; 7 males and 8 females). All were from middle-class suburban families, 93% of which were intact. The mean verbal IQ was 101.6 (Range, 90–140; Standard Deviation, 14.45), and the mean performance IQ was 101.7 (Range, 82–124; Standard Deviation, 12.12), clearly indicating no significant group differences from the norms.

The scatter of subtest scores was also within normal ranges, and deviation quotients and discrepancies were not significantly different from the standard sample. For the Bannatyne factors, the overall NAS pattern was "Conceptual greater than Spatial greater than Sequential," which is not comparable to the professional literature reports for learning-disabled subjects. Spatial, conceptual, sequential processing were all within the normal range. In the course of this research, one of the NAS subjects was diagnosed as having a demonstrable learning disability which previously had gone undetected. It is possible that for a small percentage of NAS students (in this case 6.6%), identifiable learning disabilities coexist with the expected personality characteristics.

McKay (1985) studied Overanxious Disorder and NAS students and (among other factors) looked at intellectual functioning within these diagnostic categories. Individual tape-recorded diagnostic interviews (with 205 volunteer suburban high school students) were rated by trained clinical judges, and 176 subjects were selected because they formed large enough diagnostic groups for statistical analyses. A group of students who had been diagnosed as healthy by these same judges was included among the 176 students. Mean Otis-Lennon School Abilities Test (O-LSAT) scores for each group were statistically compared using a one-way analysis of variance.

In this sample, the significantly lower O-LSAT scores for the NAS group may have contributed to their lower academic performance. However, the NAS students did not differ in their O-LSAT scores from the Normal Adolescent students, and yet this Normal Adolescent group was performing academically at a significantly higher level, equal to the academic performance of the Overanxious Disorder students. It is possible, therefore, that intellectual factors play a more significant role in the final academic performance profile for certain diagnostic groups and less so for others. This speculation is supported by McKay's results. The correlation between ability (as measured by the O-LSAT) and GPA was stronger at every grade level for the Normal Adolescent group than for the NAS and Overanxious Disorder groups.

Clinically, this is logical, since Normal Adolescents would be expected to have the least internal conflict inhibiting the fulfillment of their academic potential. Theoretically, both the NAS and Overanxious students invest some energy toward their own particular achievement conflicts, with a resulting decrease in the correlation between intellectual capacity and academic performance. This prediction was dramatically supported by the results shown in Figure 8.1.

Hartley (1985) studied achievement levels and diagnostic categories of female high school students. One hundred and two subjects were given the High School Personality Questionnaire (HSPQ, an objective measure of personality) and individual tape-recorded interviews which were rated independently by clinical judges. She found that although there were significant personality differences on the HSPQ across various diagnostic categories, there were no significant differences among the diagnostic groups on Factor B (Intelligence, or concrete vs. abstract reasoning ability). That is, no differences were found among Overanxious Disorder, NAS, Conduct Disorder,

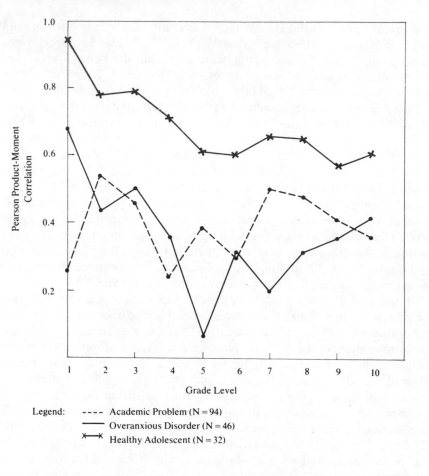

Figure 8.1. Correlations between mean O-LSAT scores and mean grade point averages for different diagnostic categories. From McKay (1986). By permission of the author.

or Identity Disorder female underachievers on the HSPQ measure of intelligence.

Cohen (1986) studied whether differences in intellectual functioning could account for achievement differences within a group of NAS students. Based on diagnostic interviews with 205 high school students, 96 NAS suburban high school students were chosen to be administered the O-LSAT. A regression formula was then used to classify these 96 NAS students into underachievers, achievers, and overachievers. Those whose GPA was one standard error of estimate below the regression line predictor were classified as underachievers; those whose GPA was within one standard error of estimate below or above the regression line predictor were classified as achievers; and those whose GPA was one standard error of estimate above the regres-

TABLE 8.3. ANOVA for O-LSAT by Achievement
for NAS High School Students

Achievement category	N	Mean O-LSAT
Underachieving NAS students	41	106.9
Achieving NAS students	36	104.3
Overachieving NAS students	19	103.7
Total	96	104.9

Note. From Cohen (1986). By permission of the author.
$*F = 0.91$ (*NS*); $df = 2$.

sion line predictor were classified as overachievers. The results of Cohen's analysis of variance are presented in Table 8.3.

From Table 8.3 it is clear that the differences in achievement level of these NAS high school students could not be attributed to differences in intellectual functioning. The underachieving, achieving, and overachieving NAS students were intellectually equivalent. Again, this highlights the role that nonintellective factors play in producing differences in achievement level, especially considering that basic personality characteristics were controlled for by using a diagnostically homogeneous group.

Incidentally, it is interesting that the NAS style of functioning produced a range of achievement—from those performing below their intellectual level to those functioning above. It is important to remember that these students were enrolled in a range of high school programs: some in the basic, most in the general, and some in the advanced academic levels.

Phillips (1987) studied the relationships among intellectual capacity (as measured by the O-LSAT), diagnostic category (using the scheme presented in this book), and academic performance (as measured by GPA). His sample consisted of 200 tenth-grade high school students, predominantly Caucasian and Protestant. There were 92 males and 108 females in the sample, all of whom were differentially diagnosed from individual, tape-recorded interviews. Subjects were grouped by diagnostic category irrespective of their GPA.

Phillips found that the relationship between intelligence and academic performance varied, depending upon diagnostic category. For example, as can be seen in Table 8.4, even though Identity Disorder and Overanxious Disorder students had identical O-LSAT group means, they differed significantly in mean GPA. On the other hand, although Academic Problem and Conduct Disorder students had similar O-LSAT means, they had dramatically different mean GPAs. The Overanxious Disorder students and those diagnosed as Normal Adolescents had the highest mean GPAs.

These results support the general notion that achievement is not dependent solely upon ability but is mediated by personality factors. More specifically, the Normal Adolescents (by virtue of their relatively conflict-free personality) and Overanxious Disorder students (by virtue of their anxiety-

TABLE 8.4.   Mean O-LSAT and Mean Grade 9 GPAs of 200
Differentially Diagnosed High School Students

Diagnostic category	N	Mean O-LSAT	Mean GPA[a]
Overanxious Disorder	46	113.00	76.09
Conduct Disorder	11	102.09	46.64
Academic Problem	96	105.32	60.46
Identity Disorder	8	113.37	60.50
Normal Adolescent	34	110.68	75.62

Note. From Phillips (1987). By permission of the author.
[a]Mean GPAs are presented in mean percentages.

driven need to achieve) are the two diagnostic groups one would expect to
have the higher achievement levels. Conduct Disorders, given their behavioral and antisocial style, are likely to have the lower achievement level.
The Identity Disorder and Academic Problem students would be expected
to fall somewhere in between these achievement extremes. These theoretical
predictions are supported by Phillips' study.

Sex Differences and Differential Diagnosis

Hartley (1985) compared 102 female with 98 male high school students according to achievement category, diagnostic category, and O-LSAT scores.
Using a regression equation on the discrepancy between actual GPA and
predicted GPA, she classified each student into one of three achievement
categories (underachiever, achiever, or overachiever). Individual diagnostic
interviews were tape-recorded, and clinical judges' diagnostic ratings classified students into one of a number of personality categories. As an added
measure, the HSPQ was administered to provide an objectively scored personality inventory. Hartley predicted that there would be specific differences
within the various achievement and personality categories. She also predicted that within diagnostic category, female and male students would exhibit significant differences with regard to some HSPQ personality factors.

   Hartley found that four HSPQ factors differentiated between Overanxious
Disorder and NAS female underachievers. These two groups differed on
Factors O (Guilt-proneness) and Q4 (Free-floating anxiety), with the Overanxious Disorder female underachievers scoring in the low range and the
NAS students in the middle ranges. This may reflect Overanxious Disorder
students' need to perceive (or report) themselves as less anxious. These two
groups also differed on Factor C (Ego strength) and on a second-order Factor
of Anxiety-adjustment. The Overanxious Disorder female underachievers
scored in the high range on ego strength, and the NAS female underachievers
scored in the midrange. Those female underachievers who had been diagnosed as Normal Adolescents also scored in the low range on Factor C and
differed from the NAS female underachievers. The Overanxious Disorder

female underachievers also scored in the very low range on Anxiety-adjustment, while the NAS female underachievers scored in the midrange. The Overanxious Disorder female underachievers perceived themselves as showing better adjustment than the NAS female underachievers. Note that none of these female underachievers had sought professional help for their academic difficulties. It is possible that the responses to the poor academic performance by the Overanxious Disorder and NAS female underachieving groups were different. It is also possible, however, that the Overanxious Disorder female underachievers had a greater investment in portraying themselves as capable than had the NAS female underachievers. Finally, the NAS female underachievers consistently produced HSPQ ratings in the midrange; that is, they consistently reported themselves as typical rather than exceptional.

When comparing male and female underachievers within diagnostic categories, Hartley found significant sex differences for the NAS group for Factors C (Ego strength), E (Dominance: Accommodating vs. stubborn), O (Guilt-proneness), and Anxiety-adjustment. These differences, although statistically significant, resulted from male and female NAS mean scaled scores that were within the midrange. Again, even when differences were found, the NAS underachiever (male or female) tended to produce scores in the average range.

For the Overanxious Disorder underachievers, males and females differed only on Factor I (emotional sensitivity: tough-minded vs. dependent and sensitive). Males scored toward the high end of the scale (dependency and sensitivity), female students at the low end (tough-mindedness). Conclusions were limited, however, because of small sample size.

Factor I also differentiated between Conduct Disorder female and male underachievers, but in the exact opposite direction from the Overanxious Disorder underachievers. The male Conduct Disorder underachiever tended to perceive himself as being tough-minded, while the female Conduct Disorder underachiever tended to perceive herself as dependent and sensitive. Thus, diagnostic category affiliation produced different personality results on certain HSPQ factors depending upon whether the underachievers in question were male or female.

Within the NAS diagnostic category, Hartley found a significant achievement effect. Achieving and overachieving NAS students perceived themselves as having greater ego strength (Factor C) than the underachieving NAS students. Overachieving NAS students also perceived themselves as having greater superego strength (Factor Q3: Self-control), yet all groups still produced mean scores in the midrange.

Hartley also reported statistically significant sex-by-achievement effects on Factors C (Ego strength), E (Dominance), H (Boldness), I (Emotional sensitivity), O (Guilt-proneness), Q2 (Group dependent vs. self-sufficient), and Anxiety-adjustment. Female NAS students tended to perceive themselves as more sensitive, while male NAS students tended to perceive themselves as possessing greater ego strength and being more stubborn (i.e., less accommodating). Male NAS students tended to score lower on Guilt-prone-ness and Anxiety-adjustment than did female NAS students. Female NAS students tended to perceive themselves as more group dependent than did male NAS students. Even with these significant effects, all NAS subjects still scored within the midrange. These differences can be understood within the context of the NAS personality structure as well as within the context of general sex role differences in society.

McKay (1985) used a one-way analysis of variance to compare the O-LSAT scores for male and female suburban high school students. The mean O-LSAT score for 92 males was 110.42 (SD = 11.15), and for 108 females it was 106.27 (SD = 11.44). The resulting F value of 6.71 (df = 1,198) was significant at the .01 level. Nevertheless, there were no significant achieve-ment differences between males and females from Grade 1 through Grade 10. Here again, a significant mean O-LSAT score difference measured in Grade 10 did not correlate with performance differences between male and female students over a 10-year period. Therefore, factors other than intel-lective or sex differences appeared to have played a decisive role in the resulting equal achievement levels, even though intellective levels of male and female students had been statistically different.

These findings held for males and females within diagnostic categories. Male and female NAS students exhibited the identical achievement patterns in Grades 1 through 10. Similarly, no differences in the achievement patterns were found between male and female Overanxious Disorder students or between male and female Healthy Adolescents, yet there were striking dif-ferences in academic performance levels between the NAS students (male and female combined) and the other diagnostic categories (male and female combined). In other words, personality factors played a more powerful role in academic performance from Grades 1 through 10 than did sex differences.

Academic History and Differential Diagnosis

When McKay (1985) began to subdivide her high school sample into per-sonality categories, she found that Overanxious Disorder students and Healthy Adolescents showed no decline in GPA from Grade 1 through 10, whereas NAS students showed a steady decline in GPA beginning at Grade 6. In addition, she found that the mean GPA for the NAS group was consistently below the mean for the Overanxious and Healthy groups at all grade levels.

Theoretically, these results provide further support for the differential diagnostic model hypothesized in this book. For the Healthy Adolescent group, achievement patterns established in early elementary school should be maintained, and in fact they were. For the Overanxious Disorder student, even when anxiety increases, there would be an expected increase and continued effort to maintain an adequate academic performance level; i.e., the motivational level of the Overanxious Disorder student to perform well should remain high. It is hypothesized that only for the NAS students does the motivation to reduce perceived expectations of the future and resist increasing responsibility result in deteriorating academic performance through the high school years. This can even begin as early as Grades 4 through 6, during the latency years.

Statistically partialing out the effect of the O-LSAT score (i.e., intellectual capacity), McKay also found an increasingly significant relationship between diagnostic category and GPA from Grade 4 through Grade 6. According to the Developmental Theory Model, this is the age range which normally would be the signpost for the expression of expectations involved in a demand for significant academic responsibility in the form of homework. This would certainly be true for all individuals, but in particular for the NAS. Therefore, it appears logical that it is at this age that GPA should begin to correlate significantly with personality structure.

The McKay study pinpoints what we believe are crucial ties between personality development and academic achievement. If reliable predictions about etiology for certain groups can be made on the basis of differential personality diagnosis, the implications for rapid differential intervention and prevention are obvious.

Mandel (1986) studied the academic performance histories (Grades 6 through 10) of differentially diagnosed underachieving groups of equal intellectual capacity. Forty-one underachieving 10th graders were identified by means of a regression equation which included a measure of ability (O-LSAT) and academic performance (Grade 9 achievement). Each student had agreed to an individual tape-recorded interview, and permission was also sought from parents to obtain the GPAs for each student from Grade 6 through Grade 10. The diagnostic categories and O-LSAT intellectual capacity scores are presented in Table 8.5.

Mean GPAs for each group were calculated for each grade from 6 through 10. The results (Fig. 8.2) show equal levels of achievement (60–64%) for all groups at Grade 6, with the exception of the Healthy Adolescent females, included here as a control group. By the time the underachieving students complete Grade 10, however, there are marked performance differences across the diagnostic categories.

TABLE 8.5. Mean O-LSAT Scores of
Differentially Diagnosed Underachieving High
School Students

Diagnostic Category	N	O-LSAT
Healthy Adolescent females	12	110.3
NAS males	17	110.1
NAS females	24	104.7
Conduct Disorder males	8	108.2

Note: From Mandel (1986).

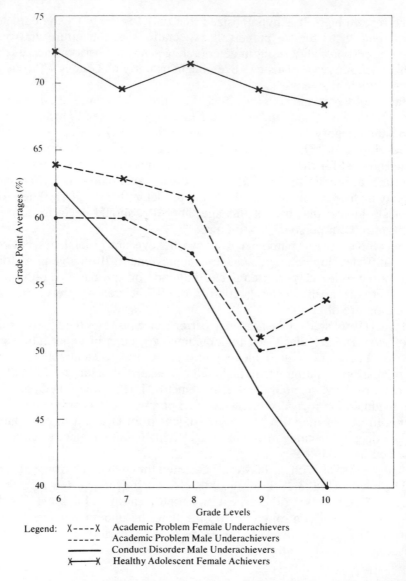

Figure 8.2. Academic histories of differentially diagnosed underachievers. From Mandel (1986).

The achievement patterns of NAS male and female students were similar. They began in Grade 4 with a mean GPA of 64.5%, and between Grades 5 and 7 generally held their performance in that range. In Grade 8 the mean GPA fell to 58.5%, and the most dramatic drop in achievement occurred in Grade 9 (mean GPA, 50.5%). In Grade 10, the mean GPA for NAS students had increased slightly (52.5%). When these NAS underachievers entered

Grade 9, they began rotating through high school classes and teachers, rather than staying with one homeroom teacher and one classroom. In other words, the Grade 9 teachers did not get to know each student as well as the teachers in the earlier grades had. It is possible, therefore, that these Grade 9 teachers would not have "rescued" or have been misled by the NAS students' potential as had previous teachers in earlier grades. The actual mean Grade 9 GPA for the NAS students may have been a more accurate measure of actual performance. Another possibility is that Grade 9 work was significantly harder for these NAS students. Further research is needed to uncover the sources of this dramatic Grade 9 performance decrease.

The most striking academic performance curve changes were produced by the Conduct Disorder underachievers. Their academic performance in Grade 6 is equivalent to the Academic Problem diagnostic group (mean GPA, 63%). By Grade 8, however, their mean GPA has dropped to 56%, and they fail Grade 9 (mean GPA, 47%). In Grade 10, this dramatic drop continues, producing a mean GPA of 40%. Clearly, by Grade 10 the Conduct Disorder student has dropped any real commitment to academic achievement.

As a group, the academic record of the Healthy Adolescent females is fairly even, averaging approximately 70%. The absence of pathology or motivational difficulties may have permitted them to spend more productive time studying, while leaving time and energy to pursue extracurricular interests. All of the previously reported underachieving groups had intellectual capacities equivalent to these healthy female achievers, and thus intellectual capacity could not have produced differential achievement patterns.

Although the sample sizes of some of the other diagnostic categories are too small to report statistical results, we have begun to see parallel trends in the other personality groups. It appears that each type of underachieving group has its own unique academic history pattern. We are currently gathering data to confirm these preliminary clinical impressions. Without replication with larger samples, the small number of subjects in some categories makes these results tentative, but the initial results are certainly in the direction predicted by the Developmental Theory Model.

Family Variables and Differential Diagnosis

Through the use of diagnostic interviews, Mandel (1984) placed students into DSM-III categories (Normal Adolescent, Conduct Disorder, NAS, Identity Disorder, and Overanxious Disorder). He found that the greatest proportion of negative attitudes regarding school came from the Conduct Disorder and NAS students, while most positive attitudes came from Overanxious Disorder and Normal Adolescent students. These findings can be predicted by the Developmental Model, other theories, mental health workers, and educational professionals. Thus, differing levels of positive or negative attitudes towards school which have an impact on academic performance were related to personality dynamics. Differential treatment should take into consideration these different attitudinal patterns.

McRoberts (1985) studied affective parent-child relationships in a sample of differentially diagnosed Grade 10 suburban high school students. Her sample consisted of 99 middle-class Caucasian families that were intact. She administered a measure of affective relationship, the Inventory of Family Feelings (Lowman, 1981), to both parents and the diagnosed student in each family. She also used two objective personality questionnaires: the Sixteen Personality Factors (16PF) for parents and the HSPQ for students. The 16PF was developed by Cattell, Eber, and Tatsuko (1970), and the HSPQ (adapted for adolescents from the 16PF) was developed by Cattell and Cattell (1975). Using individual tape-recorded interviews, two trained clinical judges independently diagnosed each interviewee.

McRoberts found that affective dyadic relationships between Overanxious Disorder students and their parents were closer and more perfectionistic than the more moderate and at times discrepant relationship reported for NAS students and their parents. This finding is consistent with the dynamics of these two personality styles. The Overanxious Disorder student wants to perceive his or her family relationships as "normal," whereas the NAS student has no such priority.

NAS Achievement and Differential Diagnosis

Cohen (1986) studied 96 NAS high school students of varying achievement levels to ascertain factors which might account for the differences in achievement. Of the 47 NAS males and 49 NAS females, the average age was 15 years 7 months, with a range of 14 years 6 months to 17 years.

Through the use of individual tape-recorded interviews, trained clinical judges' independent ratings identified the NAS students. The NAS students had also been given the O-LSAT as a measure of intellectual potential and the HSPQ as an objective measure of personality. The parents of each participating NAS student were asked to complete the Life History Questionnaire (LHQ), which provided developmental information about the student and the family. A regression formula incorporating both ability and performance measures was used to classify each NAS student as an underachiever, achiever, or overachiever.

No significant differences were found between underachieving, achieving, and overachieving NAS students on the O-LSAT scores, suggesting that intellectual capacity did not determine achievement level. Cohen had predicted that there would be a significant frequency distribution effect across the achievement levels for the NAS student, with overachievers having the smallest percentage. Because the dynamics of the NAS student are not likely to be consistent with the profile of an overachiever, it is least likely to find such students in this group. In fact, Cohen found a significantly greater number of NAS students among underachievers and achievers.

On the HSPQ, only one factor differentiated the various achievement levels. Underachieving NAS students scored in the low end of the middle range and overachieving NAS students scored at the upper end of the middle range on Factor G (Expedient vs. conscientious). Again, NAS students tend to score in the middle ranges of the HSPQ, although the differences between overachievers and the other two achievement groups has face validity. For NAS students to be classified as overachievers, they would need a greater degree of self-control, and this prediction was supported by the data.

None of the other variables which Cohen studied differentiated achievement levels for NAS high school students. The demographic variables she studied included family size, ordinal position, length of time at present dwelling, religious affiliation, and significant life events. None predicted NAS achievement level. Neither father's nor mother's educational history predicted, and the same held true for father's and mother's employment history. Further, developmental difficulties (e.g., pregnancy and delivery difficulties, toilet training, speech, walking, hearing, etc.) did not predict. All achievement levels had approximately equal and low levels of developmental difficulties. Finally, and perhaps most surprising, the presence or absence of marital disruption within the families of these students did not predict achievement level. These findings suggest that other factors determine achievement level in NAS students, and future research should focus on more complex and subtle family variables.

Occupational Fit and Differential Diagnosis

Bennett (1968) studied occupational fit in relation to academic achievement and diagnostic category. The subjects (all males) consisted of 35 underachievers and 36 achievers from IIT. The underachievers were enrolled in the underachievement program at the IIT Counseling Center; the achievers were volunteer undergraduates. Each was given a tape-recorded diagnostic interview and was asked to complete the Hershenson Occupational Plans Questionnaire (1967), a measure of perceived occupational fit. In the underachieving group, there were 11 Neurotic (i.e., Overanxious Disorder), 14 NAS (i.e., Academic Problem), and 10 Adolescent Reaction (i.e., Identity Disorder) students. In the achieving group, there were 12 Neurotic, 2 NAS, and 22 Normal Adolescent students.

Bennett found that for underachievers, there was no increase in occupational fit from freshman to senior year in high school, but that for achievers, there was an increase. He also found that the NAS underachievers did not perceive themselves as fitting into their stated occupational choices as much as did students from the other diagnostic categories. Bennett concluded that underachieving NAS students tend to make unrealistic occupational choices and then not question this lower occupational fit, a finding which is consistent with an understanding of NAS personality structure and dynamics.

Cross-Cultural Factors and Differential Diagnosis

Fraser (1987) examined the relationship between underachieving personality type and cultural factors. He studied two different high school samples, a Caucasian Canadian sample and one of West Indian origin currently living and attending school in Toronto. Clinical judges independently diagnosed each subject from the tape-recorded interviews.

Due to small numbers in the other diagnostic categories, Fraser was able to compare statistically only the Overanxious Disorder and NAS groups. He found identical patterns for the NAS and Overanxious Disorder personality types across the West Indian ($n = 21$ and 9 respectively) and Caucasian ($n = 96$ and 46 respectively) groups. There were no statistical differences in mean age, ratio of males to females, mean number of students from intact versus nonintact homes, and mean number of years living in Canada. The distributions Fraser found are similar to those in an earlier study (Pomp, 1971) in which the subjects were American high school students. Fraser's findings suggest that some underachieving personality types (especially the NAS) may be identical across many Western cultural and racial groups, even though frequencies may differ somewhat.

Future Research

Future research may address the following questions: How do each of these cultural groups perceive each of the underachieving personality types? For example, how do West Indian parents perceive their Overanxious Disorder underachieving sons or daughters, and are these perceptions different from the teachers' perceptions? How does each culture actually deal with each of the underachieving personality types? How do parents of NAS Asian or Italian or Jewish students actually deal with their underachieving sons or daughters? What are the perceptions of the larger majority culture about each of the underachieving personality types from each background, and are the factors producing differences in perceptions by the majority culture dependent upon the subculture which is the particular focus of attention?

As of this writing, a number of differential diagnostic studies are being conducted. Phillips (1987) is testing whether or not alternative methods to the diagnostic interview can be developed that can differentially diagnose various types of underachieving personality types. The instruments include classroom checklists completed by teachers, study habits checklists and personality inventories completed by students, and parent checklists in which parents rate their children's behavioral styles. Preliminary findings suggest that several instruments (e.g., the behavioral checklists) may have statistical power to accurately predict diagnostic group.

Other studies already in process or actively planned include: (a) underachieving personality styles in the adult work world and differential managerial/supervisory methods that affect productivity (Winthrope, 1988);

TABLE 8.6.   Summary of Research on Differential Diagnosis of
Personality Variables Using a Multifactorial Model

Variables Studied	Research Studies
Reliability/validity	Berenbaum (1969)
	Fraser (1987)
	Garfield (1967)
	Hartley (1985)
	Mandel (1969)
	Mandel & Marcus (1984b)
	Marcus (1969)
	Phillips (1987)
Psychometric personality assessment	Hartley (1985)
	Kaminska (1984)
	Kearney (1971)
	Nixon (1972)
	Pomp (1968, 1971)
	Tirman (1971)
Intellectual functioning	Cohen (1986)
	Freeman (1984)
	Hartley (1985)
	McKay (1985)
Sex differences	Hartley (1985)
	McKay (1985)
Academic history	Mandel (1986)
	McKay (1985)
Parents and family	Mandel (1984)
	McRoberts (1985)
Achievement levels	Cohen (1986)
Occupational plans	Bennett (1968)
Cross-cultural	Fraser (1987)
Noninterview differential identification	Phillips (1987)
	Tirman (1971)
Differential identification by teachers	Iddiols (1985)
	Phillips (1987)

(b) more detailed family research, especially based on a systems analysis of
family interaction for each of the underachieving personality types
(Schwartzbein, 1988); (c) differences in interrater clinician reliability between
male and female diagnostic judges (Fraser, 1988); and (d) the relationship between learning disabilities and personality types of underachievers
(Solursh, 1988).

Summary

In summary, a number of studies have focused on a wide range of variables
related to differential diagnosis of underachievement. These are summarized
in Table 8.6.

CHAPTER 9

Differential Treatment Research

We have presented in detail the range and depth of studies which we and our colleagues have conducted on differential diagnosis. In this chapter we will present studies by the same group of researchers on differential treatment of underachievers. Generally, there have been fewer psychotherapeutic than diagnostic studies, but those that have been completed support the concept that differential diagnosis can lead to effective differential treatment.

Creativity and Mental Health

Garfield (1967) completed one of the earliest therapy studies related to the original Developmental Theory model. He was interested in the relationship between creativity and mental health. More specifically, he wanted to test whether increases in creativity were positively correlated with personality growth. First, Garfield selected male underachievers at IIT. These students had been identified through the Academic Dean's office as having been high achievers when they had entered IIT, but who were doing poorly academically at the time of the study. They were invited by letter to participate in a remedial achievement service program at the IIT Counseling Center. Each student was asked to participate in a tape-recorded diagnostic interview and to complete several personality and creativity measures.

Garfield then had three clinicians independently listen to each tape-recorded interview and diagnose each subject according to personality type. He chose only those subjects on whom there had been interjudge agreement. Twenty-three were eventually selected, ranging in age from 18 through 24. Garfield then formed four different groups based on the diagnoses: one Neurotic (Overanxious Disorder) ($n = 6$), two Behavior Disorder (NAS) (combined $n = 12$), and one Adolescent Reaction (Identity Disorder) ($n = 5$).

Garfield did not provide any details regarding the types of psychotherapeutic approaches that were used for each of the therapy groups, probably because his main interest was to look closely at those individuals who had improved or had significantly changed as a result of group therapy, regardless of personality diagnosis or method of treatment.

Those subjects who had been rated by their therapists as improved, who were in the upper 33% of improvement scores on the Self-Ideal Q-Sort, and who were in the upper 33% of improvement scales on the Q-Adjustment Test, were labeled "improved." Those who did not meet these criteria were placed in the "nonimproved" group. Garfield employed the Original Uses Test, The Different Uses Test, and the Barron Welsh Test as creativity measures.

Garfield reported a significant positive correlation between level of psychological health (as rated by the clinicians) and creativity measures. He also reported a significant positive correlation between improvement in group psychotherapy and increase in creativity scores.

Garfield, Cohen, Roth, and Berenbaum (1971) then conducted essentially the identical study, but on a larger scale. His new subject total was 47, and he also included a no-treatment control group. He found the identical results as he had in his earlier work. The no-treatment control group and nonimproved treatment groups produced similar results. The improved treatment group showed a significant relationship between positive changes in group psychotherapy and increased creativity levels. Garfield concluded that there was both a relationship between creativity and mental health in general and that those individuals who improved as a result of successful psychotherapy tended to show creativity level increases. He discussed his findings in the context of Carl Rogers' concepts regarding the development of self and the releasing of creative forces within the individual.

Although Garfield used a differential diagnosis model in dealing with underachieving students, his results focus only on the relationship between mental health and creativity across diagnostic categories.

NAS, Group Therapy, and Achievement Change

Roth, Mauksch, and Peiser (1967) did an outcome study in which 104 male underachievers at IIT were provided group counseling as an alternative to being asked to withdraw academically from the university. The students (ranging in age from 18 through 24) were randomly divided into two sections: 52 in the experimental section received two hours of group therapy per week, while the other 52 were designated the noncounseled control section. The ratio of freshman and sophomores to juniors and seniors was about 3:1.

No diagnostic interviews were done because it was assumed from previous research and clinical work at the IIT Counseling Center that the majority of such underachieving students would fit the NAS pattern. This assumption was made in order to choose the most appropriate therapy approach for the greatest number of underachieving students. A confrontational intervention therapy approach was used (Roth & Meyersburg, 1963). Each therapy group consisted of approximately 6–8 underachieving students and met for two 1-hour sessions per week for 15 weeks.

The counseled students showed a significant increase in GPA, while the noncounseled control group did not. Further, the significant changes observed in the experimental section held for those who were carrying a heavier as well as for those who were carrying a lighter academic load (i.e., more vs. fewer courses). GPAs were obtained approximately four months after the end of counseling, and the results had held to that point. These findings strongly support the effectiveness of small group counseling in changing grade point average.

Further refinement of the question of the relationship between differential diagnosis and differential treatment was reported by Mandel, Roth, and Berenbaum (1968). They assumed that not all students who were underachieving due to personality and motivational factors were doing so for the same reasons, so that the relationship between personality and achievement should vary across diagnostic categories. More specifically, only the NAS underachiever was hypothesized as doing poorly in school to avoid the responsibilities of the future. Therefore, even if therapy were to produce significant personality changes in most other types of underachievers, only for the NAS student would there be a corresponding change in GPA because of the direct relationship between motivation and poor grades. For the other types of underachievers, poor academic performance was hypothesized as a by-product of priorities in other motivational and personality issues.

Sixty-seven male underachieving IIT students who were about to be dismissed from the university were given the opportunity of enrolling in the special group counseling program at the IIT Counseling Center. Each student agreed to a tape-recorded diagnostic interview, as well as to completion of the Self-Ideal Q-Sort before and after counseling. Two clinical judges were asked to reach a diagnostic decision about the personality type of each underachiever based on the information contained in the tape-recorded interviews. In a previous study (Garfield, 1967), these same clinical judges were able to independently agree on 36 of 37 diagnostic judgements. Thus, it was assumed that the interjudge reliability would remain high. Diagnostic categories were: Neurotic (Overanxious Disorder) ($n = 18$), Non-Achievement Syndrome ($n = 26$), and Adolescent Reaction (Identity Disorder) ($n = 23$).

The major hypothesis of this study was that for the NAS category would there be a significant statistical relationship between personality change and achievement change (measured by GPA), and that for the Overanxious Disorder and Identity Disorder diagnostic categories no such relationship would exist. For these two latter categories, individuals might change personality style and motivational focus, but there would be no statistical relationship between these personality changes and GPA. Table 9.1 illustrates the clear support for this hypothesis.

These findings strongly suggest differential relationships across certain factors (e.g., achievement), depending upon the type of personality structure. Only for the NAS student can one predict that changes in personality as a result of successful psychotherapy will parallel changes in academic performance as measured by GPA. This relationship does not hold for the other two personality categories studied: the Overanxious Disorder and Iden-

TABLE 9.1. Biserial Correlations Between Personality Change and Achievement Change as a
Function of Diagnostic Category

	Change in Personality Measures		
Diagnostic Category	Q-Sort	Therapist Rating	Diagnosis
Neurotic (Overanxious Disorder)	−0.24	−0.05	−0.05
Non-Achievement Syndrome	0.73*	0.85*	0.45
Adolescent Reaction (Identity Disorder)	0.03	−0.25	0.20

Note. From Mandel, Roth, and Berenbaum (1968, p. 504). Copyright 1968 by the American
Psychological Association. Reprinted by permission of the author.
*p = .01.

tity Disorder. Perhaps successful psychotherapy with Overanxious and Identity Disorder underachievers shows itself in other ways. In any case, the
differential model allows for assumptions specific to each diagnostic category.

    In an unusual therapy study, Fikso (1970) examined whether differentially
diagnosed underachievers observing group counseling of other differentially
diagnosed underachievers would show changes in achievement. He used
only two diagnostic categories: Neurotic (i.e., Overanxious Disorder) and
Non-Achievement Syndrome (i.e., Academic Disorder). All were college
students. Of the observing students, only the Neurotic students watching
the Neurotic groups showed significant improvement in GPA. Fikso concluded that vicarious learning could be effective, depending upon the particular diagnostic category. Presumably, the Neurotics would be more subject to modeling influences.

Personality Change and Types of Therapy

Two major studies (Goodstein, 1969; Noy, 1969) strongly supported the
relevance of basing differential treatment on differential diagnosis.

    Goodstein (1969) utilized differential diagnosis during assessment and then
hypothesized which types of therapeutic systems would produce the maximum positive change in clients. His sample consisted of 48 male underachievers on academic probation at IIT who were enrolled in the achievement
problem counseling program at the IIT Counseling Center. Each agreed to
a tape-recorded diagnostic interview, and each was asked to complete the
Self-Ideal Q-Sort, the Manifest Anxiety Scale (MAS), and the Thematic
Apperception Test (TAT). All were seen in small group therapy (N = 8/group)
for a total of four therapy groups (Table 9.2). Two no-treatment control
groups (N = 8/group) were also identified according to the diagnostic category. Two experienced therapists participated, each of whom had at least
5 years of clinical experience. The first was a practicing analytically oriented
therapist, the second a practicing client-centered therapist.

TABLE 9.2.   Research Design for Goodstein Study

Group[a]	Diagnostic category	Type of therapy	Appropriate vs. inappropriate[b]
Experimental	Neurotic (Overanxious Disorder)	Analytically oriented	Appropriate
Experimental	Adolescent Reaction (Identity Disorder)	Client-centered	Appropriate
Control I	Neurotic	Client-centered	Inappropriate
Control I	Adolescent Reaction	Analytically oriented	Inappropriate
Control II	Neurotic	No treatment	—
Control II	Adolescent Reaction	No treatment	—

Note. From Goodstein (1969).
[a]$N = 8$ for each group.
[b]Appropriate versus Inappropriate therapeutic system as hypothesized at outset of study.

Goodstein used two independent methods to determine whether the therapists were counseling within their stated therapeutic mode. First, clinicians who were not participating as therapists independently rated the tape recordings of 20 therapy sessions from each therapist to judge the type of therapy. These clinicians' ratings agreed statistically that the two therapists were conducting the type of therapy that they had been asked to use. Second, Goodstein asked each subject to complete a self-report on the type of group therapy experience and type of leadership. He reported predicted differences in clients' self-reports on the group atmosphere and structure measures between client-centered and analytically oriented group therapy. This confirmed that the type of therapy which was requested of the two therapists was in fact implemented and allowed Goodstein to place a greater degree of confidence in the outcome findings. The theory predicted that Neurotic clients would benefit most from analytically oriented treatment, and Adolescent Reaction clients would benefit most from client-centered.

Goodstein found that the Neurotic (Overanxious Disorder) subjects ($N = 8$) who received analytically oriented group therapy showed significantly more change on the Self-Ideal Q-Sort than Neurotic subjects ($N = 8$) who received client-centered group therapy. Likewise, Adolescent Reaction (Identity Disorder) subjects ($N = 8$) who received client-centered group therapy showed significantly more change on the Self-Ideal Q-Sort than Adolescent Reaction subjects ($N = 8$) receiving analytically oriented group therapy. Thus the results using the Q-Sort method lent support to the appropriateness of differential therapy based on differential diagnosis.

Interestingly, Goodstein found no relation between therapeutic system and change in GPA for either the Neurotic or the Adolescent Reaction subjects. This is consistent with previous findings (Mandel, Roth, & Berenbaum, 1968) that only for the NAS student is there a relationship between personality change and change in GPA.

On the Manifest Anxiety Scale (MAS), Goodstein found that Neurotic underachievers ($N = 8$) who had received analytically oriented group therapy showed a greater amount of change when compared with Neurotic underachievers ($N = 8$) who had received client-centered group therapy. This relationship was not found for the Adolescent Reaction subjects. This pattern was also found for the Neurotics on the Q-Adjustment scale but was not found for the Adolescent Reaction subjects.

Neurotic subjects who had received analytically oriented group therapy were rated by their therapist as having made significantly greater positive change ($p = .001$) than Neurotic subjects who had received client-centered group therapy. This relationship was not found for the client-centered therapist ratings, but a bias was found in this therapist's ratings which tended to invalidate this data.

Goodstein included no-treatment control groups in order to provide another method of comparison across appropriate treatment, inappropriate treatment, and no-treatment conditions. He found statistical significance for the Self-Ideal Q-Sort, the Q-Adjustment score, the MAS, and GPA. In other words (with the exception of their results on the TAT), subjects who received the appropriate group therapy approach showed significantly greater change than the no-treatment control groups.

Goodstein analyzed the findings from those subjects who had received inappropriate group therapy to ascertain the effects (if any). The only diagnostic group which showed significant increase in anxiety level was the Neurotic group that received client-centered group therapy (i.e., inappropriate). Even the no-treatment Neurotic group exhibited slight decreases in anxiety levels as measured on the MAS. The Neurotic group that received inappropriate treatment also reported a significant mean decrease in both the Q-Adjustment score and the Self-Ideal Q-Sort. Thus, for this group, an hypothesized inappropriate form of group therapy produced negative results.

Goodstein's findings strongly support the notion that differential treatment effects are related to differential diagnosis. Analytically oriented group therapy produced significantly more positive change in subjects diagnosed as Neurotic when compared to Neurotic subjects who received either client-centered group therapy or no treatment. Similar but less statistically significant support was found for the Adolescent Reaction subjects receiving client-centered group therapy. The appropriate form of group therapy produced significantly more positive change than either of the no-treatment control groups, thus supporting the notion that appropriate treatment is more effective than the mere passage of time.

The second major study in this area was reported by Noy (1969), who used an elegant research design to explore changes both during and at the end of therapy. A range of different treatment approaches were used with clients from one diagnostic category. Eight control subjects (underachieving students at IIT) were diagnosed as NAS students according to standard diagnostic procedures mentioned in the previous IIT studies. These NAS underachievers (who received no treatment) and the experimental subjects completed all of the psychological measures within the same time period. The experimental group consisted of 6 NAS underachieving IIT students who were offered individual counseling at the IIT Counseling Center. The assignment of students to the control and experimental groups was random.

Three male therapists were used, all of whom were senior clinical psychology graduate interns at the IIT Counseling Center. All had been trained in differential treatment methods for underachieving students and all had already completed clinical internships. During the course of this research, the three therapists were individually supervised by the same licensed clinical psychologist in order to ensure that the treatment approaches required were in fact being followed.

The design Noy used was a replicated 3×3 counterbalanced matrix "where each patient sees each of the therapists for a block of sessions, and each of the therapists sees each of the patients for the same time. In each new block of sessions, every patient is treated with another therapeutic approach. Thus, at the end of the experiment, each of the patients has been exposed to all the three methods of therapy in a counterbalanced fashion. Similarly, therapists use all the techniques equally" (p. 42). In other words, each therapist, using a particular therapy approach, saw two clients individually for a block of 8 sessions; using a second therapeutic approach, saw two more clients for a block of 8 sessions; and, using yet a third therapy modality, saw two final clients for 8 sessions. "The therapists alternated their therapeutic methods in a pre-determined systematized manner so that each therapist has used twice each of the techniques of therapy which were tested here" (p. 40).

The three therapeutic approaches used were psychoanalytically oriented, confrontation-intervention, and client-centered.

> In this study, the type of therapy is defined in terms of the constructs used and the concepts the therapist had of the patient. Thus, psychoanalytic approach consists of interpretation which emphasizes the past. It focuses on problems of aggression, of sexuality, transference, and defenses, etc. Intervention therapy emphasizes game playing in the present as meaningful in preventing future decision. Thus it is more teleological. The client centered therapist perceives the patient was being able to integrate his experiences alone in order to find his identity. He uses constructs of self and meanings while providing a non-directive warm atmosphere (pp. 40–41).

What was held constant in this research was the sex and personality diagnosis of the underachieving students, in that only male NAS underachievers were used. Noy was then able to study personality changes (if any) in this type of student when three different treatment approaches were used. From previous research it was hypothesized that the most appropriate therapy modality for the NAS was the confrontation-intervention approach, and that both analytically oriented and client-centered nondirective approaches were inappropriate.

In order to study changes during and at the end of therapy, Noy chose a number of measures: the Self-ideal Q-Sort discrepancy score, the Q-Adjustment score, Dana's Objective scoring of the TAT, pre- and posttherapy diagnostic interviews, therapists' ratings of clients, patients' self-ratings of overall improvement, patients' post hoc comparisons of improvement in each therapy approach, patients' descriptions of overall therapy experience, patients' post hoc comparisons of experience in each therapy approach, therapists' rankings of own discomfort in each therapy approach, therapists' rankings of own involvement amount in each therapy approach, and Boyd's content analysis of therapy transcripts.

The first hypothesis was that NAS students who received the appropriate (i.e., confrontation-intervention) therapy would show more growth than when they received either analytically oriented or client-centered therapy. This hypothesis was supported for all but two of the measures (Table 9.3).

Noy graphically represented the Boyd content analysis results for three of the six treatment clients (Figures 9.1–9.3). These graphs depict changes over time for each client and clearly show that much more growth occurs when a therapeutic relationship appropriate to the dynamics of an NAS client is provided.

Boyd's Content Analysis is based on Erik Erikson's (1963) concept of psychosocial development. Thus, in Figures 9.1 through 9.3, Stages 1–8 refer to Erikson's developmental stages:

Stage 1: Trust versus mistrust

Stage 2: Autonomy versus shame

TABLE 9.3. **Appropriate versus Inappropriate Therapy**

Measure	χ^2	Level of significance	Sum of ranks[a]		
			C.I.	P.A.	C.C.
Q-Adjustment	0.40	N.S.	13.5	11.0	11.5
Self-ideal Q-Sort	0.33	N.S.	12.0	11.0	13.0
TAT	9.00	0.01	18.0	9.5	8.5
Boyd's content analysis	9.33	0.01	18.0	9.0	9.0
Diagnostic interview	7.70	0.05	17.5	8.5	10.0
Therapist rating of improvement	7.70	0.05	17.5	8.5	10.0
Students' report of gains	9.08	0.01	18.0	9.5	8.5
Students' ranking of gains	10.17	0.01	18.0	10.0	9.0

Note. Adapted from Noy, 1969, p. 61.
[a]C.I. = confrontation-intervention therapy approach; P.A. = psychoanalytically oriented therapy approach; C.C. − client-centered therapy approach.

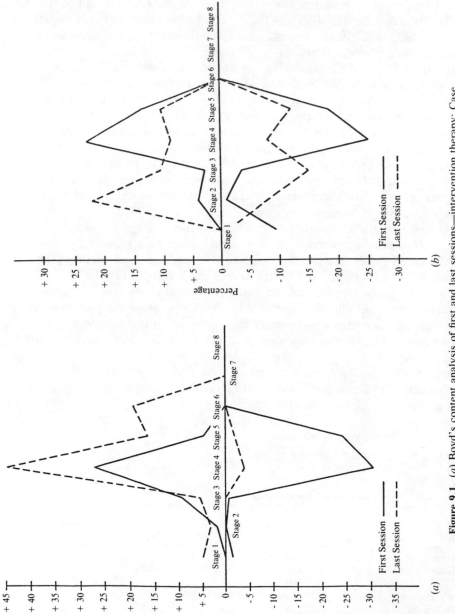

Figure 9.1. (*a*) Boyd's content analysis of first and last sessions—intervention therapy: Case 1. (*b*) Boyd's content analysis of first and last sessions—psychoanalytic therapy: Case 1. From Noy (1969). By permission of the author.

202

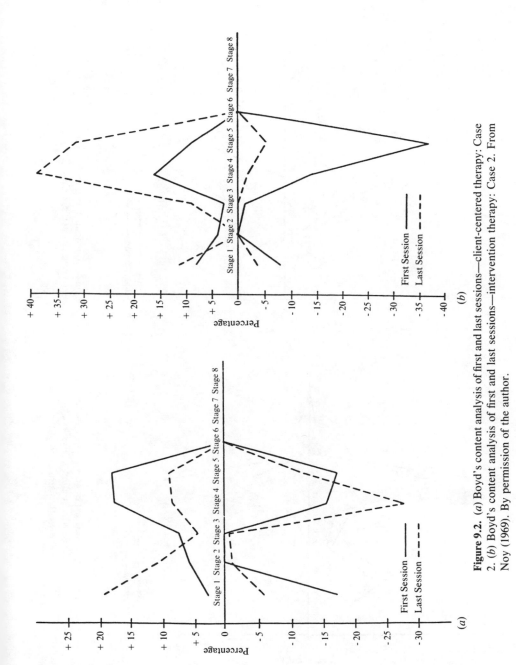

Figure 9.2. (*a*) Boyd's content analysis of first and last sessions—client-centered therapy: Case 2. (*b*) Boyd's content analysis of first and last sessions—intervention therapy: Case 2. From Noy (1969). By permission of the author.

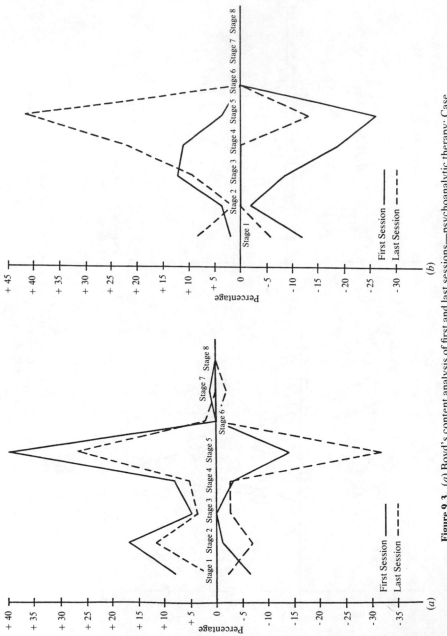

Figure 9.3. (a) Boyd's content analysis of first and last sessions—psychoanalytic therapy: Case 3. (b) Boyd's content analysis of first and last sessions—intervention therapy: Case 3. From Noy (1969). By permission of the author.

Stage 3:   Initiative versus guilt
Stage 4:   Industry versus inferiority
Stage 5:   Identity versus identity diffusion
Stage 6:   Integrity versus isolation
Stage 7:   Generativity versus stagnation
Stage 8:   Integrity versus despair

The content analysis involves scoring each client comment, and assumes that individuals who occupy a given stage produce a significantly greater number of comments which are associated with that stage. The vertical axis contains percentages of a client's positive and negative statements that relate to each stage. These statements are drawn from the initial and from final therapy sessions. The reader should note the type of therapy approach represented in each graph. For example, Figure 9.1a depicts the results of an NAS underachiever (Case 1) who received eight sessions of the appropriate confrontation-intervention therapeutic approach. In the initial therapy session, there were approximately equal percentages of positive and negative comments, focused almost entirely at Stages 4 and 5. Conceptually, this supports the notion of the NAS student's ambivalence regarding issues of industry and identity. From the final confrontation-intervention therapy session percentages, it is clear that this individual had dramatically increased his percentage of positive utterances centered in Stage 4 and exhibited far less ambivalence concerning the major issues in this stage. There was even evidence of beginning to resolve Stage 5 issues. These results contrast with the findings from the same NAS subject during the period of time when psychoanalytically oriented therapy was offered (Figure 9.1b). Here this subject began the new treatment block with a similar ambivalence about Stage 4 issues, but ended with an increased percentage of negative comments, focused at Stages 2–3. In other words, psychoanalytically oriented treatment produced a regression in stage placement for Case 1. Similar findings are depicted in the other graphs.

Noy also tested whether NAS subjects who received confrontation-intervention therapy would show a significantly greater amount of personal growth than the no-therapy control group of NAS underachievers. He found this to be supported by two of the three measures he used. For the appropriate treatment NAS group, Q-Adjustment scores and Dana's TAT analysis clearly showed significant positive changes when compared to the no-treatment NAS group. The Self-ideal Q-Sort analysis, although in the predicted direction, did not reach statistical significance.

Noy hypothesized no significant differences between the NAS no-treatment control group and the NAS inappropriate treatment group. There was support for this hypothesis, with Q-Adjustment, Self-ideal Q-Sort, TAT, and diagnostic interviews showing no differences between groups.

Noy found no differences across all three therapists with regard to client improvement, thus eliminating the therapist as a confounding variable. He also found that whether an NAS underachiever received confrontation-intervention therapy in the first, middle, or last 8 sessions made no difference in therapy outcome. Gains were noted at each of the three appropriate therapy blocks on all of the instruments used.

Noy reported that the therapists all felt more involved with their NAS clients when they were using a confrontation-intervention approach than when using either the analytically oriented or client-centered therapy.

Noy's design allowed for each subject to act as his own therapy control, and the findings were both striking and provocative. NAS underachievers receiving confrontation-intervention treatment showed significantly more personality change than the NAS underachievers in the no-therapy control group. This type of treatment was found to be significantly more effective for the NAS underachievers than the analytically oriented or client-centered approaches. Further, the use of analytically oriented or client-centered therapy with NAS underachievers produced results which paralleled the no-treatment NAS group.

NAS Qualitative Therapy Research

Two case studies (Mandel & Marcus, 1984a; Mandel & Uebner, 1971) have focused on changes in confrontation-intervention therapy with NAS underachievers. Based on a single clinical case, Mandel and Uebner published a collaborative report by therapist and NAS client. The therapist provided the conceptual framework for a theoretical understanding of the NAS underachiever and the type of approach which is appropriate for such a client. The NAS student, unbeknown to the therapist, had composed poetry during the course of counseling, and at the conclusion of counseling had presented the therapist with the poems as a gift. Upon reading the poems, the therapist invited the client to coauthor a professional article. Through his poems, the client had captured much of what he had experienced during the four months he had been in confrontive therapy. In the jointly authored professional article, the poems are in chronological order following a theoretical introduction. This article provides a qualitative view of the experiences, perceptions, and internal struggles for change of an NAS student in therapy, mostly from the client's perspective.

The second study (Mandel & Marcus, 1984a) was also based on a single case study of individual confrontation therapy with an NAS underachiever. This clinical training manual provides detailed transcripts of ten consecutive therapy sessions, along with commentary. The manual contains specific information about the initial, middle, and termination phases of NAS treatment, along with a focus on issues in effective confrontation technique. This study, like the Mandel and Uebner (1971) study, provides a qualitative perspective on the unfolding stages and issues of NAS therapy using the single case method.

Teacher Methods of Coping with Different Types of Underachievers

Although teachers are not usually trained in the techniques of differential diagnosis of underachievers, many competent and experienced teachers intuitively distinguish the different types of underachieving students by the students' differing needs in the classroom. These teachers do not use the DSM professional labels, but they do recognize the major types of underachievers in their daily teaching experiences.

A recent study by Iddiols (1985) was not a differential treatment study in the traditional context of psychotherapy, yet it did focus on whether or not teachers differentiate the most frequently seen types of underachievers. Iddiols focused on whether or not teachers used different approaches with each of these underachieving types and explored the relationship between these differential teaching strategies and the differential psychotherapy approaches developed by other members of the clinical research team over the previous 20 years.

Iddiols' subjects consisted of 23 experienced high school English teachers of predominantly middle-class students in the greater metropolitan Toronto area. Fifteen of these teachers were male, eight female. Overall, they averaged about 13 years of teaching experience.

Iddiols constructed four vignettes, each of which described one type of underachieving student; i.e., Overanxious Disorder, Conduct Disorder, NAS, and Identity Disorder underachievers. No professional labels or categorization were presented, only the vignettes. An example of one of these vignettes (which describes an Overanxious Disorder underachiever) is as follows:

> Kim is the kind of student who wants to do well. She works hard to get her work done on time and I feel that she'd sincerely like to improve her class standing. She seldom makes excuses for a poor performance and usually listens to any advice I might have to offer. But I think she may get depressed when things aren't going well: she probably worries about not succeeding.
>
> When Kim hands in an assignment she rarely seems happy with its presentation; she seeks constant reassurance from me that she's tackled the project correctly. As I evaluate her paper I can't help feeling that she often writes what she thinks I want her to write.
>
> I've also noticed that Kim appears anxious about how she'll appear in front of her peers. Although she pays attention and seems interested, she looks tense and unable to relax. When I call on Kim to answer a question she looks somewhat nervous. I really feel quite sorry for her.
>
> I've spoken with Kim's previous English teacher. Apparently her performance was quite positive during the first half of the semester, but then she seemed to get more "uptight." Her marks began to slide. I'd like to think that Kim's confidence will grow in time. Her "heart" is in the right place and I generally enjoy working with her (Iddiols, 1985, p. 72).

Because of the small number of female teachers, Iddiols decided to provide the male teachers with male student vignettes, and female teachers with female student vignettes, thus focusing his study exclusively on how a same-sex teacher would deal with each of the underachieving personality types.

He gave the four vignettes to each teacher and asked a number of questions. First, he asked how frequently the teacher had contact with the type of student described in each vignette. Second, the teacher was asked which of the four types was the most difficult to teach, which was the easiest, and why this was so? Finally, each teacher was asked to describe the methods usually used with each type.

Teachers reported that the vignette depicting the NAS student contained a description of the most frequent type of underachiever they encountered. This finding is consistent with other clinical and research findings on the prevalence of the NAS student in high school and university underachieving samples.

The vignettes of the Overanxious Disorder and Identity Disorder under-achievers were rated easiest types to teach. The teachers reported that the Overanxious Disorder underachiever was easier to work with because this student was receptive to teacher assistance and conformed readily to accepted standards of behavior. The teachers perceived this type of student as having a positive attitude toward school and as someone who responded to positive reinforcement techniques. Actually, teachers described many of the same reasons clinicians have mentioned for preferring to work with the Overanxious Disorder underachiever. For the Overanxious Disorder student, motivation to do well was perceived to be high, and a sense of partnership with this type of student was noted. Teachers typically reported being able to handle such a student within the resources of the classroom, and cited approaches such as liberal use of positive reinforcement and encouragement.

For the Identity Disorder underachiever, teachers valued certain personality characteristics: a willingness to risk and experiment, a curious mind, and a willingness to be a catalyst for meaningful classroom discussions. From clinical reports, these same characteristics have also proven intriguing to psychotherapists. This student disagrees with adults, but the nature and quality of such disagreements are open and exploratory and are viewed positively by most teachers and therapists. In-class teaching strategies included conferencing, advising, and student-focused discussions. Referral to guidance and counseling personnel was also mentioned, not because of a belief on the teachers' part that this student is seriously in need of mental health assistance, but to provide another source of sensitive adult support.

The vignette which described the Conduct Disorder underachiever was rated by teachers as the most difficult to teach. They felt they did not have enough time to adequately deal with such a student and pointed to the dismal "track record" as predicting future difficulties. Teachers felt that this type of underachiever exhibited an attitude which was at cross purposes with the school system and concluded that a partnership with such a student was rarely possible. The major teaching strategies for the Conduct Disorder included removal from the classroom and referral to the principal and vice-principal. In-class strategies included a tightening of classroom structure and closer monitoring.

As mentioned earlier, teachers rated the NAS vignette as the most frequently encountered type of underachiever. This type was rated as "easy to like" because of the normal personality, but this was the only type of student for whom teachers had little to suggest in terms of teaching strategies. They felt that such students lack commitment, even though they appear easy to get along with. Teachers suggested private conferencing and problem-solving sessions, but they obviously had tried such approaches with limited success when dealing with NAS underachievers. Some teachers recommended benign neglect in which the NAS underachiever is left to deal with natural consequences of inaction. Some recommended widening the curriculum choices for the NAS student, while several others recommended lectures on responsibility. Overall, teachers perceived themselves to be the least effective in helping this most frequently seen type of underachiever.

Iddiols' study contains two findings relevant to the question of differential diagnosis: First, the teachers intuitively differentiated across various personality and motivational types of students; second, the teachers perceived that each of these types needs to be dealt with in a unique manner. These findings strongly parallel clinicians' reports of therapy with these underachieving types and provide further consensual validation that there are indeed different types of underachievers each needing to be treated differently.

Summary

All of the above studies add evidence to the importance and effectiveness of differential treatment based on differential diagnosis. Specific therapeutic modalities have been shown to be maximally effective with specific personality types of academic underachievers. A summary of focus of these studies is presented in Table 9.4.

CRITIQUE OF MULTIFACTORIAL RESEARCH

In this section, we briefly critique 25 years of research from the first appearance of a description of the Non-Achievement Syndrome (Roth & Meyersburg, 1963). In general, the multifactorial model (Mandel & Marcus, 1984, 1985) used in most of the studies reviewed in Part Three is based on a developmental perspective of psychopathology and a differential psychotherapy conceptualization (Roth et al., 1967). This model has added meaningfully to clinical practice with underachieving adolescents and young adults. However, the value of any clinical speculation, theoretical formulation, or

TABLE 9.4.   Summary of Research on Differential Treatment of Underachiever Personality Types, Using a Multifactorial Model

Variable	Study
Creativity and mental health	Garfield (1967)
Differential individual psychotherapy	Mandel & Marcus (1984a)
	Mandel & Uebner (1971)
	Noy (1969)
Differential group psychotherapy	Goodstein (1969)
	Mandel, Roth, & Berenbaum (1968)
	Roth, Mauksch, & Peiser (1967)
Individual therapy outcome	Mandel & Marcus (1984a)
	Mandel & Uebner (1971)
	Noy (1969)
Group therapy outcome	Goodstein (1969)
	Mandel, Roth, & Berenbaum (1968)
	Roth, Mauksch, & Peiser (1967)
Vicarious therapy	Fikso (1970)

conceptualization lies also in its ability to suggest testable research questions and designs.

Studies on reliability and validity have supported many of the personality and motivational concepts. Further, a number of studies have dramatically highlighted the value of differential diagnosis and differential treatment. For the most part, these studies have contained adequate sample sizes, allowing for meaningful statistical analyses. The more recent studies have included a statistical method (i.e., regression equation) to differentiate underachievers from achievers and overachievers, making it possible to study the entire range of discrepant achievement, rather than to focus on gifted achievers only. Most of the studies have included a control group (usually achievers, sometimes differentially diagnosed as well), which has permitted meaningful comparisons.

The earlier studies (in the 1960s and early 1970s) focused exclusively on male underachievers, but the more recent work has begun to redress this imbalance. Other areas of research, however, have remained relatively neglected, such as family dynamics and the manner in which school systems and the wider culture perceive and deal with the underachieving types.

As the research focus has shifted away from identified underachievers in universities to random samples of students in suburban high schools and liberal arts colleges, we have begun to see a change in the relative percentages of various personality types. This provides a more representative sample of underachievers and may paint a clearer picture of underachievement than would emerge from studying a mental health population.

Recent studies have investigated similar personality types at different levels of achievement, e.g., factors that differentiate between underachieving and achieving or overachieving students from the same diagnostic category, with similar intellectual capacity, with similar academic histories, and from identical socioeconomic backgrounds. Undoubtedly there is a subtle inter-action among personality, family, school, and cultural variables.

There has also been an absence of more rigorous follow-up research to substantiate long-term personality changes as a result of therapy, to deter-mine whether such presumed changes are equally maintained across all diagnostic types of underachievers, and to define the role of the family and other support networks in maintaining or altering these changes. Longitu-dinal comparisons also need to be made within diagnostic category between those individual underachievers treated and those not treated.

Few studies have attempted to differentially diagnose on the basis of standardized personality tests or behavior inventories. The diagnostic in-terview remains the primary method of differentially grouping underachiev-ers on the basis of personality and motivational factors. This procedure is time consuming and requires not only a high degree of general clinical ex-perience, but also expert professional training in this type of differential diagnosis. Perhaps with further research to find psychological tests that can differentiate, a less time consuming and more widely used method can be constructed. Some research has provided hints of such a possibility, but much more is needed. Even when standardized personality assessment mea-sures have been used (such as the TAT, Rorschach, MMPI, 16PF, and HSPQ), they have not always been fully utilized, or they have been part of research designs which limited their focus. More systematic comparisons are needed.

Finally, it is obvious that more research has been devoted to differential diagnosis, less to differential treatment. The major reason for this appears to have been a practical one: It is much easier to mount and complete a diagnostic study than a treatment study, especially at a dissertation level.

These brief comments summarize some of the more obvious gaps in pre-vious research, and provide a base for the many studies waiting to be done. In any case, we hope that Part Three has given the reader a comprehensive look at the range of research in an area which, to our knowledge, has never been reviewed before.

Personality Types of Underachievers

In Part Four we take a detailed look at each of the major personality types, which together are likely to account for the majority of underachievers. Except for Chapter 14 (Oppositional Defiant Disorder Underachiever), these are presented in the order predicted by the Developmental Theory, as one moves up the developmental continuum from early childhood through young adulthood.

Each chapter will contain information about general characteristics, the phenomenological world of the student, criteria for differential diagnosis and treatment considerations, questions pertaining to the practical diagnosis, and a description of what each type of underachiever might be like as an adult should the personality characteristics and motivational levels remain relatively unchanged. We begin with a description of the Overanxious Disorder underachiever.

CHAPTER 10

The Overanxious Disorder Underachiever

General Characteristics

This category corresponds generally to the broad area of the neuroses as defined by classical psychoanalytic theory, and specifically to the DSM-III-R category labeled Overanxious Disorder (313.00). The major feature is a chronic anxiety or state of worrying that is excessive and neither linked directly to recent stressors in the psychosocial environment nor centered on a specific event or object (DSM-III-R, p. 63). An anxious student not in this category is one who may be temporarily worried and anxious but who is not a chronic worrier and in whom the only source of the anxiety is some clearly defined environmental or social situation (such as being involved in an auto accident or facing a major exam which determines his or her admission to college).

According to DSM-III-R (p. 64), four of the following seven symptoms must be present for at least 6 months in order to justify the diagnosis of Overanxious Disorder:

1. Unrealistic worry about future events
2. Preoccupation with the appropriateness of the individual's behavior in the past
3. Overconcern about competence in a variety of areas, e.g., academic, athletic, social
4. Excessive need for reassurance about a variety of worries
5. Somatic complaints, such as headaches or stomachaches, for which no physical basis can be established
6. Marked self-consciousness or susceptibility to embarrassment or humiliation
7. Marked feelings of tension or inability to relax.

After the age of 18, this type of individual may fit the description of the Generalized Anxiety Disorder, which has similar features but includes motoric anxiety symptoms (shakiness, muscle aches, etc.) and autonomic hyperactivity (sweating, dizziness, dry mouth, etc.).

Other characteristics of the Overanxious Disorder may include chronic and sometimes debilitating anxiety, obsessive rumination and compulsive behavior, and an everpresent need for approval from parental and authority figures. Certainly, as students, these individuals are obviously anxious, worried, and nervous. The actual degree of anxiety will vary over time, but it appears to be a chronic characteristic of this student's life and one that appears to adversely affect his or her academic performance. The anxiety may be focused on areas other than school performance (such as performance in sports and acceptance in social situations).

It is evident from the above DSM-III-R description that this category is directly related to historical notions of neurosis dating back to the early days of Freud and even earlier. The intense and debilitating anxiety, the constant need for approval, the likelihood of tics or other somatic symptoms, and other classic neurotic features all find their way into the DSM-III-R description of the Overanxious Disorder.

However, as students in a school setting, these individuals may or may not show the overt symptoms which would make it obvious that they belong in this category. More often than not, particularly in a brief interview and within a school setting where the student may be concerned about the reactions of peers, overt symptomology and psychosexual conflicts (which from a psychoanalytical point of view are crucial for the diagnosis of the neuroses and an understanding of its genesis) may be hidden or kept secret by the student. Therefore, the interpersonal characteristics, style of interaction, and perceptions of the Overanxious Disorder underachiever in the interview may be the only available means of detecting the presence of this type of personality.

Relationships with Overanxious Disorder underachievers are characterized by ambivalent conflicts around issues of hostility, acceptance and rejection, sexual attraction, dependency on authority figures, adequacy and competence, and superego demands in the form of "shoulds and shouldn'ts." The interviewer may observe minor compulsive behavior patterns and rituals, obsessive worry over particular events, constant and repetitive rumination over the details of whatever is being discussed, statements reflecting guilt and depression, generalized anxiety, dependency on the opinions of the interviewer, and psychosomatic complaints. This student tends to be more concerned with the opinions, feelings, and expectations of others than with personal needs and values.

All of these characteristics can be inferred from a careful analysis of the diagnostic interview: the choice of words, the particular responses to interviewer questions or comments, the quality and intensity of emotion in the voice, the attitude towards the interviewer, and so forth. It is particularly for this reason that taped (and indeed videotaped) interviews can be so valuable in the diagnostic process.

The Phenomenological World of the Overanxious Disorder Underachiever

Anxiety is one of those pervasive, everyday, ordinary affects (along with emotions such as depression, hostility, and love) which touch the lives of everyone in ways that are important and crucial as well as trifling and fleeting. Who among us does not feel at least a twinge of anxiety when trying to get to an appointment on time, thinking about unpaid bills, worrying "what the boss will think," wondering where our children have run off to, becoming ill, hearing unusual noises emanate from under the hood of the car, having a disagreement with a spouse or parent, noticing that the roof leaks. Anxiety is as ordinary and common an emotion as there is in life, and the experience of it is familiar to every human being. This has been observed for centuries by philosophers, theologians, writers, and physicians, and in the past 100 years by psychologists, psychiatrists, sociologists, and other social scientists.

In considering the world of the Overanxious Disorder underachiever, the reader's ordinary experience of anxiety can be both a hindrance and an aid. It can be a hindrance in that the level and quality of the anxiety we experience in everyday life is much less complex and intense than that experienced by the Overanxious Disorder Underachiever, and we may underestimate both its devastating impact and its resistance to treatment. It can be an aid, however, in that we can utilize our experience of everyday anxiety as a kind of experiential approximation of the inner tension-ridden world of the Overanxious Disorder student.

Nevertheless, to build a picture of the world as experienced by the Overanxious Disorder is a most complex and formidable undertaking, and perhaps we can best approach that world by considering, one by one, the various interpersonal issues involved and adding each, in turn, to the full pattern. We believe these issues to be: ambivalent feelings (i.e., love and hate) toward the parents, the need for approval from parents, dependency, expectations and superego demands, issues of adequacy and competence, the experience of affect (primarily anxiety, depression, and hostility), obsessive-compulsiveness, and the pattern of underachievement that may result from this picture.

The term ambivalence in modern common usage has come to mean something like indecision. We consider a person who is having trouble making a decision ambivalent, and we consider the ambivalence resolved when that decision is made. The technical psychological and psychiatric concept of ambivalence, however, has little to do with decision making; it has more to do with an emotional state. This state is one in which a person maintains two contradictory and conflicting emotions toward the same person or object. The classic example (and one that is in fact the central ambivalence in the Overanxious Disorder) is an individual who feels love and hate simultaneously for the same person.

Historically, in psychiatric usage, the term ambivalence is applied only to the most serious and severe psychopathologies: psychoses, borderline states, and the like. People with these problems exhibit such extreme and intensely conflicting emotions that the term ambivalence when used clinically is usually reserved only for these severe pathologies.

In daily practice, many therapists and counselors consider the ambivalence resolved when a decision is made. Therapists seem to believe that if only the client would make a decision—end that relationship with the other person, make the decision to leave home, and so forth—then their feelings would follow suit and the internal conflict would be resolved. Sometimes, of course, this is exactly what happens. However, especially when the relationship in question is intense and of great personal significance, a decision not only fails to resolve the ambivalence but may in fact result in more internal emotional turmoil.

The technical psychological and psychiatric concept of ambivalence, however, has little to do with decision making; it has more to do with an emotional state. Ambivalences may also exist around an endless array of emotions and issues: the question of whether or not to enter counseling, the pros and cons of choosing a particular career, feelings of revulsion and yet attraction for particular forms of behavior, and so on. The human being lives in a world of ambivalences: big and small, important and unimportant, emotionally draining and merely annoying, lifelong and momentary. The authors believe that ambivalences are so ordinary and everyday a phenomenon that it is much too limiting to consider the concept as only applicable to severe psychopathological states.

Some ambivalences indeed may be resolved by making a decision, but we believe that most instances of what we are calling ambivalence—the simultaneous presence of opposite or conflicting emotions toward the same person or object—are *not* resolved when one or the other end of the ambivalence is chosen. We believe that the ambivalence is resolved through the experience of a relationship in which *both* ends of the ambivalence are fully accepted. A classic example is the healthy marriage, where issues of acceptance and rejection, independence and togetherness, love and hate, and many other important dimensions of human emotionality become mutually accepted and interwoven into the fabric of the relationship. This is not a new idea; it is one goal (although not always expressed in this form) of many of the classic forms of dynamic psychotherapy and counseling, from psychoanalytic to client centered.

There is yet another wrinkle in this concept of ambivalence which is necessary if we are to fully understand the inner world of the Overanxious Disorder underachiever: a particular ambivalence may be divided in awareness. What this means is that the person may be aware of one end of the ambivalence, yet totally unaware that the other end is equally significant and may represent legitimate psychological needs. For example, a psychotherapy client may be well aware of wanting and needing counseling, but at the same time may be unaware of fears of becoming too dependent on or involved with the therapist. Therefore, he or she starts off therapy with great involvement and an apparent commitment, but then begins to "forget" to come to the appointments. In his early work on character analysis, Wilhelm Reich (1945) explored this issue brilliantly within the context of psychoanalytic psychotherapy. Another all too familiar example is the so-called "perfect marriage" which suddenly and for no apparent reason ends in divorce after many years of an apparently ideal relationship in which the couple never even had an argument. Undoubtedly, one factor is the failure to integrate hostility, even in the form of petty annoyances, into the daily give-and-take of the marital relationship.

We would stress here that this concept of a division in awareness is not necessarily the fully subconscious process assumed in psychoanalytic theory nor the fracture of the personality seen in, for example, borderline states. We would consider it more in the nature of a normal aspect of everyday psychic life, so normal and mundane that mental health professionals either fail to recognize it or misinterpret it as indecision.

Armed with this concept of strong ambivalences which may be divided in awareness, one can now sense the currents of emotional tension which drive the Overanxious Disorder. The individual with Overanxious Disorder, like the neurotic in classic psychoanalytic literature, both loves and fears significant others and transfers this emotional reaction onto authority figures in particular. Thus as an underachieving student, his or her reaction to an interviewer is likely to be respectful, attentive, and dependent, and yet highly anxious and uncomfortable.

The Overanxious Disorder underachiever may feel extremely ambivalent regarding the issue of achievement. To achieve for another person, say a parent or teacher, may be an important goal, and yet to achieve may also represent a "giving in" to the demands of this powerful and feared person. Therefore, the underachievement itself may be an expression of a passive-aggressive conflict, an unrecognized but real punishment of the person in authority by withholding the desired behavior—achievement. Because of the split in ambivalence, however, what the Overanxious Disorder student is aware of is not the anger and resentment, but only the need for approval. There is an awareness only of desperately needing and wanting to achieve and yet having something which blocks those activities leading to achievement. This student may agonize over homework, only to find that it is impossible to concentrate.

At the same time, there is an extreme dependency on other people, causing the student's own choices, needs, goals, objectives, and perceptions to take a back seat to the opinions and reactions of other persons. It is almost as if the Overanxious Disorder student needs the approval of others in order to exist. This type of individual may fret for days if a favorite teacher gives one disapproving look or comment. This student is always on edge, trying mightily to impress and win the approval of others, and yet highly anxious over losing this approval because of one mistake, one wrong word or action.

Therefore, the opinions and expectations of others are all important, and the Overanxious Disorder student lives in a world of endless shoulds and shouldn'ts, rules and guidelines, mores and norms, all of which become the standard of conduct. Even certain emotional reactions are suppressed if they do not conform to the "proper" feeling. This is very much the kind of personality factor referred to as *superego* in classical psychoanalytic literature. These students have developed a rigid view of what is right and wrong, good and bad, acceptable and unacceptable, a narrowly defined view which often corresponds to that of significant adults in their lives. These students are simply trying to be the good persons they think authority and parental figures expect to see.

There may be an inner expectation that the only achievement level acceptable to those in authority is so high that it is virtually unattainable: in short, the student may expect perfection. This perfection is not simply a goal to strive for but in fact becomes equated with adequacy itself. The student feels that anything less than perfection is totally unacceptable, and this contributes to feelings of intense pressure. This factor is often involved in suicides of students who are doing extremely well in school but feel that they can never be "good enough." In the Overanxious Disorder underachiever, however, the striving for perfection is so anxiety-ridden that studying cannot be performed well.

The Overanxious Disorder Underachiever feels an intense need to be accepted by the authority figure, to be approved of, in short to be loved. The student also feels as if this approval will be forthcoming only on condition that expectations are met, especially the expectation of perfection. At the same time, there is a great fear that to really attain this is impossible. These fears, expectations, needs, and insecurities, coupled with deep feelings of inadequacy, make this person's inner emotional life a nightmare of anxiety and uncertainty, much like Kafka's (1947) fictional character K in *The Trial*, who is always being vaguely accused of something but is never sure what or by whom. The Overanxious Disorder underachiever is driven by this obsessive complex of fears and concerns and has little free energy left over to concentrate adequately on studying.

Criteria for Differential Diagnosis

A. *Background Information*

For the past 20 years researchers have found that among underachievers, Overanxious Disorders are likely to be found more frequently than any other diagnostic group except Academic Problem Disorders. Among overachievers, there is some evidence that Overanxious Disorders will also be found in large percentages, second only to normal adolescents.

Teachers are likely to indicate that they encounter this type of underachiever frequently but that the Overanxious Disorder student is easier to teach and to help than students in any of the other diagnostic categories. This is undoubtedly because more than any other personality type, the Overanxious Disorder underachiever seeks approval, follows directions, wants to achieve, and is most likely to become an active partner in any remediation process. In fact, Overanxious Disorder underachievers are likely to maintain positive attitudes about school (Mandel, 1984).

B.   Diagnostic Testing

Overanxious Disorder underachievers typically score high on a variety of tests or scales that measure anxiety. For example, they may have elevated scores on the *Hs, Hy,* or *Pt* scales of the MMPI (Duckworth & Anderson, 1984) or on the Taylor Manifest Anxiety Scale. They may also show elevations on state-trait anxiety measures, particularly on trait scales. These types of responses are well known and well reported in the literature. Without the stresses of poor achievement, Overanxious Disorder achievers may or may not produce the same levels of anxiety scores.

In our experience, Overanxious Disorder underachievers will typically choose items on the *Mooney Problem Checklist* such as the following:

Feeling tired much of the time
Sleeping poorly
Lacking self-confidence
Not really being smart enough
Taking things too seriously
Being physically unattractive
Worried about a member of my family
Not doing anything well
Trying to forget an unpleasant experience
Constant worrying
Too nervous or high strung
Feelings too easily hurt
Feeling inferior
Feeling I am a failure
Working too hard
Having a troubled or guilty conscience

These items share common themes of feelings of inadequacy, sensitivity to the reactions of others, self-denigration, anxiety, and related issues.

On objective personality measures such as the HSPQ, we have found few specific sex differences within diagnostic category. Hartley (1985) found that only one HSPQ factor (Factor I, Suspiciousness) showed significantly different mean scores between male and female Overanxious Disorders. Males scored at the sensitive and dependent end of the scale, whereas the females scored at the tough-minded end. Hartley also reported that the female Overanxious Disorder underachievers were the only diagnostic group to score at the extremes on Factors C (Emotional stability), E (Dominance, aggressiveness, and assertiveness), O (Self-assured), Q_3 (Controlled, compulsive), Exvia (Extroversion).

Because of their needs for approval from others, Overanxious Disorder students are likely to answer diagnostic tests of personality with socially acceptable responses; i.e., they are likely to present stereotyped notions of what they think is expected of them (Kearney, 1971). Therefore, they may show higher than average scores on measures of social desirability.

Overanxious Disorders are also more likely than other diagnostic groups to have high scores on certain measures of dependency, as well as an external rather than an internal locus of control on such measures (Nixon, 1972).

Often on diagnostic tests, Overanxious Disorder underachievers will score much the same as Identity Disorder underachievers. Tirman's (1971) study concluded that Overanxious and Identity Disorder underachievers had similar MMPI profiles. It is possible that the intensity experienced by the Identity Disorder underachiever and the anxiety experienced by the Overanxious Disorder underachiever produce similar test responses.

On projective tests, such as the Rorschach Test, the TAT, and sentence completion tests, Overanxious Disorder underachievers are frequently diagnosed in a manner consistent with anxiety-related disorders.

Card 1 of the TAT shows "a young boy contemplating a violin which rests on a table in front of him" (Murray, 1971, p. 18). The stories which subjects create in response to this picture are usually interpreted as reflecting their attitudes, perceptions, and feelings about achievement and motivation. Incidentally, the drawing is actually a copy of a photograph of twelve-year-old Yehudi Menuhin, a world-famous prodigy.

A typical Overanxious Disorder underachiever's story about Card 1 is as follows:*

> This young boy has been having trouble in practicing his violin. He has been trying to get ready for a concert, and has been putting in extra time. But he still hasn't been able to get it right. He's worried that he won't be ready for the concert, and that he will disappoint his parents. . . . He continues to practice and everyone at the concert tells him that he did very well.

We see in this story the elements of disruptive anxiety, concern about others' opinions of him, concerns and doubts regarding personal adequacy, unquestioned dependency on parents, and at the end of the story a hint of lingering self-doubt even though others praise him.

---

* Anonymous quotations from students and interview dialogues throughout Chapter 10–13 are adapted from clinical case histories in the authors' files.

C. Interview Characteristics

In Chapter 4 (The Diagnostic Interview) we presented a format for a semi-structured interview consisting of five points of focus: (1) the nature of school performance and related issues, especially if they are problem areas; (2) the nature of family relationships; (3) the nature of social relationships (peers, the opposite sex, etc.); (4) the nature of the student's self-perceptions and affect; (5) the student's perceptions of and plans for the future. We will now consider how in an interview the Overanxious Disorder underachiever might typically respond in each of these areas.

1. *The nature of school performance and related issues, especially if they are a problem area*

Basically, the Overanxious Disorder underachiever is likely to be straightforward and candid about actual grades and other tangible evidence of performance but is also likely to present this data in an apologetic and somewhat embarrassed way, almost as if confessing some minor indescretion. Rarely will the student hedge or engage in distortions of the truth, however minor, in presenting information. One gets the impression that these individuals feel honor bound to confess, whether or not the information is asked for. This is likely to be related to the issues of guilt, anxiety, and dependency already discussed.

When asked the reasons for receiving particular grades, the student will typically stress how hard he or she has tried to achieve and how frustrating it has been not to perform up to the expected standards. Through all of this, there are indirect (and sometimes quite direct) statements of inadequacy, coupled with great anxiety and concern. For example, consider this excerpt from a diagnostic interview with a male Overanxious Disorder underachiever. (The interviewer has just asked why the student received a *D* in math.)

STUDENT: Well . . . well, it's basically understanding. Understanding and learning. I dunno, it's like a mental block on tests and things like that. I dunno; little things . . . have a really . . . are really strange in that class. I dunno . . . You know, sometimes you don't do the homework at nights, and . . . I'll always study for tests, and I always . . . I don't know. The teacher, she's really nice about it and everything like that, but I dunno. I can't concentrate, I just can't . . . I try to concentrate but I can't concentrate, and it just doesn't come easily when that happens [tension is noted in his voice].

INTERVIEWER: Have you always had marks like that in math?

STUDENT: No, not at all. I had a *C+* in math last year. Like, the geometry was what pulled the mark up last year. This year, geometry, the same thing, is pulling me down. I don't know—I don't understand that. I try to remember everything, but I just can't this year, it just. . . .

Even without actually hearing the voice of this student, one can sense the tension this student feels from the several pauses, repeated phrases, and the almost obsessive quality of the way he goes over things again and again. He is truly perplexed by and concerned over his predicament, and the small phrases reflecting feelings of inadequacy stand out ("I can't concentrate," "I try to remember everything, but I just can't this year," etc.). Even if his statements indicated apparent adequacy, the implication that he is expending so much effort in a doubtful cause sounds more like someone up against hopeless odds than like someone who is working hard to achieve goals. For example, he states, "I try to concentrate but I can't concentrate." Experts in the area of clinical hypnosis have long known that the use of the word "try" implies the expectation that so much effort is needed that a successful outcome is rather dubious.

The student in our example talks about mental blocks and an inability to concentrate, difficulties remembering, and other related inadequacies with a sense that something has happened to him beyond his capacity to understand. There is a sense here that he is not giving excuses for his underachievement but rather is confessing a terrible failure. He is truly perplexed.

An often overlooked aspect of the Overanxious Disorder underachiever's responses in an interview is the fact that there may be more material offered than implied in the question. For many underachievers with a different personality structure, the response to questions about poor grades might well be a shrug of the shoulders and a simple statement such as "I guess I didn't study hard enough." In the Overanxious Disorder, however, the simplest of questions might unleash the kind of lengthy, anxious, self-damning response given by the student in this example.

Conversely, the Overanxious Disorder underachiever is likely to dwell on successes, taking great pride in adequacy. For example, when this student was asked about a particularly good grade in a creative writing class, he responded:

STUDENT: Well, that's . . . I guess that's the kind of mind that I have, in a way. I always try to do things like that, think about things like that, or learn things about things you experience, you know, things like that.

INTERVIEWER: Sort of like Creative Writing is your cup of tea?

STUDENT: Yeah, like my cup of tea. Theater's like that, too, and I'm getting an *A* in it, too. You see, Theater's a challenge because I like seeing . . . I like . . . It's a challenge because it's the class I really take the most seriously. Some people don't take it seriously, and take it as a really easy credit. But not me.

2. *The nature of family relationships*

When discussing the family, the Overanxious Disorder underachiever typically focuses on parents, especially their expectations of his or her achievement level, as has already been indicated. It is almost as if the student is less concerned with an inner point of view than with seeing situations from the point of view of the parents and their expectations.

In the following example, when asked about his parents' reaction to how he was doing in school, an Overanxious Disorder student responded only around the issue of expectations. Notice how in all of the excerpts from interviews with this student, his own reactions toward others, especially his parents, are either totally absent or phrased only in terms of trying to live up to their expectations:

INTERVIEWEE: My parents? . . . Well, in public school, I mean elementary school, my parents were always good to me. I guess in high school that they find it hard to say anything . . . because of the *A*'s and *D*'s in some subjects. All they can do really is push. All they can say is, "You have to pick up your math and those other important subjects." So, really, you know, it's more pressure and put more concentration on. They . . . ah, they feel pretty good, I guess. I think that they're . . . satisfied, except that they wished I would do better in those two subjects. [Sighs].

As with most Overanxious Disorder students we have interviewed over the years, the attitude toward the parents appears to be one of an almost obsequious attention to them and their expectations. There is little to indicate any needs for any real psychological independence from the parents, and total attention is on parental goals rather than the student's own goals and needs.

Consider this interchange, for example:

INTERVIEWER: How far do you think your parents want you to go in school?

INTERVIEWEE: I think that they want me to go to university. I do want to go to university. I'm going to try for university. I think that they expect me to go to university.

INTERVIEWER: OK, staying with the focus on your family for a moment— what's your Mom like; what kind of a person is she?

INTERVIEWEE: She's . . . she's always been very intelligent, right; she's very smart. Like she's always on top of things . . . Like sometimes she acts like she doesn't know what's going on, and then later she'll prove that she does know. She's very smart; like she was always very smart in school, straight *A*'s. Is that what you mean?

INTERVIEWER: Mm hmm. How would you describe Dad?

INTERVIEWEE: Like he's also a straight *A* student when he was in school. He's . . . he's a very hard worker. He works very hard at business . . . He'll sacrifice a lot. It's surprising sometimes the incredible things sometimes he's planning to do.

INTERVIEWER: Like, incredible in what ways?

INTERVIEWEE: Just that he has some very good ideas, ways of improving his business.

This is a good example of the Overanxious Disorder underachiever's *other directedness*. He is so dependent on others (in this case his parents) for approval and guidance, that he leaves himself out of the discussion almost entirely. It is as if his own feelings, perceptions, and needs are nonexistent. He explains almost everything exclusively from his parents' point of view: *their* expectations, *their* wishes, *their* needs, *their* goals.

There is another aspect of self which the student presents that often escapes unnoticed. One of the reasons for asking in which ways an interviewee is like or unlike parents is that it gives some indication of the extent to which the student identifies or does not identify with the personality of the parents. When asked about similarities with his parents, this Overanxious Disorder underachiever said:

INTERVIEWEE: Well, I suppose I'm more like my dad in most ways. . . . But mostly, I'm like my dad. Like I pull off some surprising things every now and then [chuckles], you know, surprise some people. Like when people don't expect you to make an accomplishment. Then I totally concentrate, smarten up, really work hard to show somebody that I can do it. And they probably didn't expect me to make it.

INTERVIEWER: Are there ways in which you think you are like your mother?

INTERVIEWEE: Um . . . kind of like my mother. It's kind of like watching. My mother likes to watch situations and be on top of things. Sometimes I like to be like that sometimes, too—like watch situations and be on top of things, too. But mostly, I'm like my Dad.

INTERVIEWER: So in the way in which you surprise people sometimes, you're like your Dad.

INTERVIEWEE: Ya. He's a perfectionist, a real perfectionist. He always tries to be perfect, not missing anything.

INTERVIEWER: How do you feel about that style of his?

INTERVIEWEE: Well, sometimes . . . when he makes an error . . . well, he can't handle it, and it gets to him. Other than that I think it's good to be a perfectionist.

The aspect of parents' expectations has already been discussed, but what is interesting here is that this student identifies with his father in terms of similar personality characteristics. While it is not always true that the Overanxious Disorder student identifies with the parent of the same sex, it is a common interview response. In the Developmental Theory aspect of the model we have been presenting in this book, we have linked the Overanxious Disorder diagnostically to classic psychoanalytic definitions of neurosis. These state that the Oedipal child will identify with the parent of the same sex as a way of dealing with Oedipal conflicts and as a way of establishing a sense of identity to use in coping with the outside world (Freud, 1966). While Overanxious Disorder students will often identify also with the opposite sex parent, the primary identification is usually with the same-sex parent.

Notice how this student has taken great pleasure in identifying with his father, almost in the sense of borrowing a strength and then bragging about it. Thus while seeming to be describing himself and his own personality, he is actually doing so only because he has his father's personality to emulate. The interviewer would do well to be alert for this subtlety when interviewees describe themselves: Is this a description of a psychologically independent person, or is the person merely identifying with similar characteristics in others (particularly parents)? The latter type of response is often characteristic of the Overanxious Disorder student.

In the preceding interchange, even when the student does discuss himself, it is only in relation to his parents' expectations or in rather obvious attempts to see himself as being like them. Aside from some obvious fantasies of expecting perfection as the only sign of adequacy, it is as if this student is constantly trying to crawl into other people's heads and see the world through their eyes rather than his own. This characteristic can be readily observed in interviews with Overanxious Disorder students, especially if the interviewer pays particular attention to the student's point of view as reflected in choice of language.

The interviewer should be thinking, "Through whose eyes is this student trying to see the world?" If the answer is consistently that the interviewee is trying to see the world through the eyes of others in a dependent and obsequious manner—especially authority figures such as parents and teachers—this is a strong indication that one may be dealing with an Overanxious Disorder student.

In discussing relationships with siblings, the Overanxious Disorder student displays some of the same characteristics and appears ever mindful of the different roles expected in the family. There may be an attempt to look at things from the point of view of the sibling rather than from the point of view of the self. Probably because the sibling is in a less authoritative role than the parent, the Overanxious Disorder is also likely to be somewhat more judgmental and evaluative when talking about siblings, and this can be either positive or negative.

INTERVIEWEE: Well, my brother . . . He takes a lot of things seriously; he's ambitious about things, and that's really good, don't you think?

INTERVIEWER: Well, it can be if he's comfortable with that. Are you comfortable with his taking things seriously?

INTERVIEWEE: Yes.

INTERVIEWER: Does his taking things seriously affect you in any way?

INTERVIEWEE: No, why should it? I just have to keep pushing hard, that's all. But it's good for me; it keeps some of the pressure on.

Here we see an almost complete avoidance of the Overanxious Disorder underachiever's feelings towards a sibling who is doing better in school. The Overanxious Disorder is dealing with this issue by measuring himself and his sibling only in terms of expectations and standards of achievement.

INTERVIEWER: And how do you get along with him?

INTERVIEWEE: Oh . . . I get along well. We've been getting. . . . The odd morning where we argue some. . . . But it's nothing serious. We usually end up sitting down and talking to each other.

INTERVIEWER: About what sorts of things?

INTERVIEWEE: Oh, about the future, about our plans. He's always trying to get ahead, be successful—you know, the younger brother bit.

Differences are downplayed and glossed over. Notice how the Overanxious Disorder individual attempts to place the behavior of his sibling in the context of an expected family role, the "younger brother bit."

Many of these students attempt to portray their family life as a sort of fixed, smoothly running hierarchy in which each person has a well-defined role. Conflicts, differences of opinion, and dissatisfactions may be mentioned, but the Overanxious Disorder underachiever generally will attempt to minimize these by explaining them away or by giving the impression that his or her task in the situation is to somehow learn to live with it. The student gives the underlying impression that what is going on at home is unchangeable.

3. *The nature of social relationships (peers, the opposite sex, etc.)*

The student with Overanxious Disorder, especially in the high school and early college years, is less comfortable with an emerging adult psychosexual role in society than are his or her contemporaries. The student is either bewildered by the new demands for heterosexual adolescent social life, or deals with the opposite sex with stereotyped and simplistic expectations of an adult relationship.

INTERVIEWEE: Actually, I broke up with my girlfriend about six weeks ago.

INTERVIEWER: What happened to the relationship with your girl friend?

INTERVIEWEE: Oh . . . it's. . . . It started off with a friendship; at least it
started off as like a friendship kind of like . . . and it started to feel
closer and closer, you know. And then . . . I just don't know . . . I felt
that I had to . . . get more serious, like a real boyfriend and girl friend
should be to one another. You know, caring about each other. Not
physical stuff—just being closer.

INTERVIEWER: And what happened?

INTERVIEWEE: I don't know. I never really had a girl friend before. It was
new to me.

INTERVIEWER: I'm not sure exactly what you mean.

INTERVIEWEE: It wasn't. . . . It was . . . it was a friendship, you know
. . . a girl friend . . . like you're supposed to be doing this and that . . .
I never really had that kind of relationship before.

INTERVIEWER: You mean, it changed?

INTERVIEWEE: Right. Yeah . . . and then she ended it, just like that.

INTERVIEWER: Do you know why?

INTERVIEWEE: I suppose she wasn't ready for a serious relationship, like
. . . to talk about the future, and stuff like that. It wasn't about . . .
about sex, if that's what you're thinking, because I wouldn't, until we
decided to get married. So . . . it must have been . . . just about her
not wanting to get tied down.

This student is truly perplexed and obviously in a relationship "over his
head." One can sense the strong sexual issues which are practically denied
awareness and the discomfort with an intimate psychosexual relationship
(even on a young adolescent level). The comments about the "future," a
"serious relationship," and marriage clearly imply that the student is using
these adult expectations of what a romantic relationship *should* be as a clear
role he can rely on in the midst of an overwhelmingly provocative and
confusing relationship.

As students with Overanxious Disorder get older and have more social
experience with the opposite sex, there is likely to be less confusion and
panic but more reliance on rigid and "appropriate" patterns of heterosexual
interaction. Their discomfort with psychosexual or romantic relationships
can arise not only when members of the opposite sex are attracted to them,
but when they are attracted to members of the opposite sex, as appears to
have happened in the above example.

The Overanxious Disorder underachiever is more likely to be comfortable
with friendships that do not have a strong romantic or psychosexual component. Notice the expressions of greater comfort and ease expressed by
the student in the example when asked about ordinary friendships. The

Overanxious Disorder student is usually more comfortable with friendships than with romantic or sexual relationships.

INTERVIEWEE: Like the group I hang around with is at work. I like those people. They're real interesting. And my best friend I hang around with is sportswise, going to the movies together. And I spend time walking near the lake, jogging sometimes. I find that it calms me down a lot to do that. I can unwind doing that.

As has been mentioned previously, peer relationships tend to be anxiety arousing if they have a sexual and romantic component. On the other hand, because of the level of anxiety, degree of dependency, and kind of inter-personal insecurities typical of Overanxious Disorder students, they are not likely to be totally comfortable even with peers. Like anyone else, they may have one or two close friendships, but in any description of their social life with peers, there is likely to be some indication of discomfort, awkwardness, or avoidance. Since Overanxious Disorder students are likely to attempt to minimize conflicts or insecurities in these relationships, they are likely to paint a rosy picture of their friendships, and the interviewer should listen carefully for areas of conflict.

INTERVIEWEE: . . . I have, like I have a best friend . . . I hang around with a group of guys, and I also spend time alone, a lot of time alone.

This student's emphasis on that last phrase—"a lot of time alone"—is suggestive of a conflict area involving relationships with others, especially since the comment is offered in the context of discussing his peer relation-ships. This is the kind of comment that the interviewer could follow up on and clarify.

As pointed out earlier, notice how, in discussing his best friend, this student volunteers that one important aspect of the things he does with his best friend is the tension-reducing aspect:

INTERVIEWEE: . . . And my best friend I hang around with is sportswise, going to the movies together. And I spend time walking near the lake, jogging sometimes. I find that it calms me down a lot to do that. I can unwind doing that.

Certainly, many people with many different kinds of personalities and motivations will find activities that are relaxing. What is significant here is that this student's emphasis on tension reduction is somehow brought up in the context of his relationship with his best friend.

   4. *The nature of the student's self-perceptions and affect*

As would be predicted, the Overanxious Disorder underachiever is likely to describe the self in terms of the issues already discussed: need for approval, insecurities due to inadequacy feelings, the need to be the "right" kind of person and do the "right" kinds of things, dependency on others, the need to fulfill the expectations of others, and certainly a need (overt or covert) to gain the approval of the interviewer. There is not likely to be an introspective, well-considered, independent evaluation of the self; everything is presented in relation to the implied or stated expectations of significant others.

INTERVIEWER: How would you describe yourself? What kind of person do you see yourself as?

STUDENT: I'd say that . . . I watch . . . like I'm sort of just someone who's like a watcher. I like to watch things, and learn that way. My personality is . . . it's like I'm just there. And maybe, all of a sudden, I'll start talking and try to be nice to people, try to be polite to people.

Within the dynamics of the interview, we assume that people will respond to issues not only in the content of their verbalizations, but also in their choice of certain words and their particular arrangement of those words. Their verbalizations will have associative connections or implications for aspects of the here-and-now relationship with the interviewer. We might hypothesize, for example, that an Overanxious Disorder student's choice of words and phrases might reflect insecurity with the ambiguity of the interview format. In the preceding excerpt, the student might have utilized a discussion of politeness as an unconscious attempt to gain approval by trying to behave in a manner that the interviewer presumably wanted.

In any case, one senses in the above example that the student is presenting the self in terms of what others may expect from him, rather than how he would objectively and independently describe himself. In fact, he does not really describe himself, but rather who he is trying to become. ("I'll . . . try to be nice to people, try to be polite to people.")

As with other Overanxious Disorder students, there is the sense of impossibly high standards which the student feels obligated to attain in order to feel adequate and be acceptable to himself and others. In fact, Overanxious Disorder students generally present themselves as more perfectionistic than any of the other diagnostic categories (with the exception of Obsessive-Compulsive individuals).

There is nothing inherently pathological, abnormal, or unhealthy about striving for excellence or even perfection. Throughout history a vast number of outstanding individuals were never satisfied until their achievements reached (or at least approached) perfection. Without this attitude, the world would never have had any outstanding scientists, artists, musicians, leaders, teachers, athletes, and others in every conceiveable field of human endeavor. One cannot conclude that each and every one of these people suffered from

Overanxious Disorder simply because of the importance of this trait in their vocations.

What we are suggesting here is that Overanxious Disorder individuals measure themselves against a standard of perfection in every aspect of their lives, not just in their careers. Their entire sense of self-esteem appears predicated on the actual attainment of perfection, not merely the striving. Since the intrusion of perfectionistic standards into one's interpersonal relationships has the potential to damage any relationship, this may explain why these students dwell on shoulds and shouldn'ts, socially appropriate conduct, and evaluations of self and others according to externally appropriate criteria.

The diagnostician looks for signs of this characteristic particularly in the student's interpersonal attitudes, ideas, and reactions, where the very concept of perfection as a dominant need is unique to this type of personality.

One would hypothesize that these students harbor some resentment against parents and others for making these supposed perfectionistic demands, but often there does not appear to be obvious resentment. In fact, in contrast to other diagnostic groups, Overanxious Disorder students are likely to present themselves as having significantly close relationships with their parents. There is usually little hint of resentment unless it is directed against someone who is doing something "wrong" or counter to the expected standards. Usually in these situations, there is a tone of righteous indignation in the voice and manner of relating, sometimes out of proportion to the deed in question.

5. *The student's perceptions of and plans for the future*

In contrast to the other diagnostic categories, Overanxious Disorder students more consistently have specific plans for the future, particularly in terms of a career. These plans, even in the underachieving Overanxious Disorder students, are usually for successful, high status or high visibility careers. It is extremely unusual, for example, for such students to say something like, "Oh, I don't know . . . maybe an auto mechanic." More often, the response is like the following:

INTERVIEWER: What kind of person would you like to be when you're 26, in 10 years? What do you think you'll be doing?

INTERVIEWEE: Twenty-six? Wow, let me see. I'm at the university . . . of . . . I guess I'll be out of university by that time. And then my plan was to be . . . was not just to be an English teacher, but to be a head English teacher. And I'll stick with writing manuscripts, always stick with that, and teaching English. That's what I'd be doing.

For the Overanxious Disorder underachiever, the emphasis on a successful future career combined with the current lack of satisfactory grades may result in a deeply felt sense of failure and worthlessness, which may explain why such students freely discuss their academic inadequacies and frustrations almost as if they are confessing a sin.

Yet there is another element that the interviewer is bound to notice in the way that these students present themselves. The student in the example not only has detailed plans which involve what he views as a successful and prestigious career (although Head English Teachers might disagree), but he also goes out of his way to clear up a minor detail: that he will be out of (not in) the university at age 26. In our experience, this is another characteristic of Overanxious Disorder students in interviews. They feel compelled to continually clarify details and qualify statements made, as if they have to give the interviewer the entire story. Sometimes their need to provide a detailed background for the simplest of questions is obvious enough to make it clear that one is dealing with an Overanxious Disorder student, since the other diagnostic categories of students are not as likely to be so detail oriented.

However detailed these students may be in discussing their career plans, they are a little less certain about their interpersonal future. For reasons discussed earlier in this chapter, the Overanxious Disorder is uncomfortable discussing interpersonal relationships, particularly intimate relationships. Note how the student who was so involved and energetic in discussing his future career plans becomes uncertain and uncomfortable in discussing marriage in his future, even though he still focuses on details.

INTERVIEWER: Can you see yourself married [in the future]?

INTERVIEWEE: I'll be married. I've always planned to be married. Like it seemed like I'd be 20, 21, somewhere in there that I was supposed to be married. But then I thought that I don't really want to end this. Like I don't look at marriage in any bad way at all. Yeah, I do . . . I think . . . I'll be married, all right. I think so.

INTERVIEWER: And do you see yourself having any children by the time you're 26?

INTERVIEWEE: Mmmmm . . . Yes, but I'll have one or two—not too many kids.

INTERVIEWER: OK. And do you think that your wife would work, or would she stay at home?

INTERVIEWEE: I think, work . . . work . . . I think that work makes anyone a more interesting person . . . work . . . work . . . but she'd have to stay home some when the kids were born.

The details are there, but so is the discomfort with the topic, as is clear by the many pauses and halting responses. It is likely that the number of socially appropriate shoulds here (e.g., ". . . somewhere in there that I was supposed to be married") are his way of covering up his discomfort with this issue. In fact, for the Overanxious Disorder student, the greater the anxiety and discomfort around a given topic, the more likely the appearance of shoulds and shouldn'ts.

Practical Diagnosis

The personality characteristics and treatment approaches relevant to Overanxious Disorder underachievers are generally standardized and well defined. More than most other groups we will discuss, however, they present a wide variety of individual differences and treatment needs. Therefore, the practical diagnosis with this group will be more effective if idiosyncratic, situational, and other individual factors are taken into consideration.

Each Overanxious Disorder underachiever may have a preference for a particular approach. For example, some will prefer help with alleviating anxiety through noninsight oriented approaches. Such individuals are often amenable to behavioral techniques and will benefit from them. Others, although somewhat apprehensive, may be quite curious to discover the psychological origins of their difficulties. For such individuals, behavioral techniques alone will be unsatisfying. For many, the most beneficial treatment is often a combination of a direct tension reduction technique (such as a behaviorally oriented relaxation technique) coupled with some counseling to discover the underlying reasons for the anxiety. Depending on many factors such as age, ego strength, and ability to conceptualize, family involvement may or may not be indicated or desired.

There are students, of course, who fit the diagnostic criteria of the Overanxious Disorder but who are achievers. Such individuals often contain the anxiety by keeping occupied and productive so as not to have to face any underlying feelings of insecurity. Such students may simply have learned more successful anxiety management techniques than have the underachieving overanxious students. Overanxious Disorder achievers may never need professional help (at least for achievement problems), until and unless something occurs in their lives which jolts them into facing the underlying worries and self-doubts, such as the death of a parent, a divorce, or a serious illness. At those times, such individuals often report a heightened anxiety level, without insight into the underlying causes or precipitating events. As with the overanxious underachiever, the precipitating event often involves a situation in which a significant person in an authority position judges them harshly, or when bottled-up tension breaks through to the surface, causing troublesome symptoms. Because such individuals tend to have high standards by which they judge themselves, they often struggle alone with their growing tensions for a long time before reaching out for help.

For example, one Overanxious Disorder student referred for counseling because of underachievement had a history of adequate achievement up until the year before the referral. Prior to that time, he had always been a highly responsible and somewhat anxious teenager. By the time he was referred, he was already avoiding some classes and was completing fewer and fewer school assignments. In the diagnostic interview, he said that his girl friend had ended their relationship abruptly about the time his school difficulties began. Ever since, he had been obsessed with the loss and had spent considerable time and energy attempting to reestablish the relationship. Fortunately, he was introspective enough to wonder why his reaction was so extreme. Through exploration in counseling, he realized that he had forgotten the intense pain and sense of loss he had experienced when his grandmother had died five years earlier. Once he was able to recognize the similarity and meaning in his reactions to both significant losses, his obsessions and anxieties decreased and his commitment to achievement returned to its previous level.

Beyond helping the Overanxious Disorder underachiever to reduce tension, any other treatment goals are in the realm of standard psychotherapeutic theory and practice, and it is not our intention here to recap the myriad and often conflicting approaches which flood the professional literature. We merely state that helping the student to reduce the tension level is the key to helping overcome the underachievement, whether or not this results in personality change. The individual practitioner, in partnership with the student, must decide whether tension reduction and improved achievement level are sufficient therapeutic goals.

Differential Treatment Considerations

Performing well in school, or indeed in anything, requires some optimal level of tension. Without any internal tension, performance is usually not as high as it could be. Too much inner tension, on the other hand, diminishes the quality of performance. As anxiety increases, performance rises until an optimal level is reached; above that level of anxiety, performance begins to decrease.

For the Overanxious Disorder underachiever, the level of anxiety has far exceeded the optimal performance range. Therefore, a major focus in treating the underachievement problems of Overanxious Disorder students is to help lower the anxiety level until it reaches the range of optimal performance. Counselors, teachers, parents, and friends can help such students identify the sources of excessive anxiety and/or provide solutions that will diminish it. It should be noted that reducing the anxiety level in these students may or may not have an impact on basic personality structure. Some remain much the same sort of persons, except that they are now somewhat less anxious and are freer to achieve. Others, as a result of diminished anxiety, will experience changes in other interpersonal aspects of their lives, not simply in their academic performance.

This is a fairly well-defined problem area; numerous methods, techniques, and approaches to anxiety reduction have been developed since the problem of psychological anxiety was first emphasized by Freud and his colleagues.

Today, the overanxious student has many possible treatment approaches available if the goal is simply the reduction of tension. These include behavioral relaxation techniques, hypnosis and self-hypnosis, newer and more powerful study skills training, various techniques for cognitively restructuring the anxiety-arousing situation, dynamically oriented supportive counseling to help the student understand the sources of anxiety, medication, and many others. It is beyond the scope of this book to provide detailed information regarding tension-reduction approaches, but the reader is encouraged to seek out the many excellent and varied programs, therapies, and techniques available from a wide range of sources.

The Overanxious Disorder Underachiever as an Adult

If the Overanxious Disorder underachiever as an adult is diagnosed according to DSM-III-R, he or she is likely to be classified as having Generalized Anxiety Disorder (300.02) or one of the other anxiety disorders. Such a person is likely to maintain anxiety as a predominant trait. Among the symptoms which DSM-III-R (pp. 251–253) lists for this category are somatic symptoms (motor tension and autonomic hyperactivity such as sweating and heart pounding), as well as phenomena such as apprehensive expectation, hyperattentiveness, and depression. Usually there is only a mild impairment in social or occupational functioning. Our interest here, however, is not necessarily general psychological functioning, but the issues of adult achievement and underachievement analogous to these issues during the school years.

One can be an achiever or an underachiever and still have the same essential characteristics of anxiety, depression, and so forth. In a work situation, however, overanxious underachievers are likely to show many of the same characteristics they did as overanxious underachievers in school. These include anxiety which is at such a high level that it inhibits performance, major concerns about approval from administrative superiors and supervisors, attention to details not relevant to the job, and related characteristics. Supervisors accurately rate these employees as highly responsible individuals who could be valuable team members if they could harness their inner tension and excessive dependence on their superiors.

CHAPTER 11

The Conduct Disorder Underachiever

General Characteristics

DSM-III-R lists several related problems under this category. They differ in the degree of aggression and socialization but all have as a common characteristic a repetitive and "persistent pattern of conduct in which either the basic rights of others and major age-appropriate societal norms or rules are violated. The behavior pattern typically is present in the home, at school, with peers, and in the community" (DSM-III-R, p. 53). DSM-III-R lists other common characteristics as a repetitive and persistent pattern of aggressive behavior, lack of guilt or remorse, or paucity of meaningful relationships with others. As adults, these individuals are likely to be classified in the category of Antisocial Personality Disorder (301.70).

Long before the advent of the DSM series, the Conduct Disorder personality was initially labeled as moral insanity. More recently, such individuals were perceived as exhibiting a psychopathic or sociopathic personality, along the lines of Cleckley's classic description (1964). His description of this type of individual includes characteristics such as superficial charm and good intelligence, absence of irrational thinking, unreliability, inadequately motivated antisocial behavior, lack of remorse or shame, untruthfulness and insincerity, poor judgment and failure to learn by experience, and other similar and expected characteristics. Generally, such individuals have been perceived as lacking a sense of conscience. The overriding concern is for immediate gratification.

As an underachiever in school (or indeed as an underachieving adult on the job), Conduct Disorder individuals are likely to be quite open—almost to the point of a kind of nonchalant bragging—about past and current antisocial, immoral, or otherwise unacceptable behavior. They generally blame others for their own failures and often maintain that they have been treated unfairly by those in authority.

Conduct Disorder underachievers often have a pervasive impulsiveness in which their needs of the moment must be immediately satisfied. They have a low tolerance for frustration or for the kind of persistent mental attention to detail required for successful academic performance. They may exhibit obvious acting-out behavior, cutting classes when they feel like it, disobeying formal behavioral rules of the school, having frequent arguments or even fights with other students, stealing and cheating, and behaving in improper or even dangerous ways (often on a dare from friends). In the extreme, this impulsiveness can be seen in precocious and indiscriminate sexual acting out, involvement in drugs (as a user and often as a seller), alcohol abuse, abusive temper outbursts, or outright criminal activities. Such individuals seem not even to care if they are punished for any of these behaviors.

Issues of power and control over others are of paramount importance. The manipulation of others in order to satisfy specific, short-term needs is common, and the Conduct Disorder underachiever is usually quite effective in sensing who around them is vulnerable to manipulation. This manipulation includes a seductive charm, which is used when it suits the purpose. Even the defiance of authority has a gamelike quality to it, as if the major goal is to win a battle of wits rather than to persevere for the sake of some meaningful principle.

Obviously, in the welter created by this kind of behavior, underachievement may be seen as the least of the problems created by Conduct Disorder. Often the turmoil in the classroom far transcends the more mundane problem of underachievement. Indeed, to Conduct Disorder underachievers themselves issues of academic achievement are often irrelevant.

DSM-III-R lists a number of factors which may predispose an individual to this type of personality. These factors include parental rejection, inconsistent management with harsh discipline, early institutional living, frequent shifts of parent figures (e.g., from parents to stepparents to grandparents, etc.), large family size, involvement with delinquent groups, or the presence of an alcoholic father or mother. In our clinical experience, fathers of such students are often punitive and rejecting: no matter what the child does, his or her very presence is unacceptable to the father. The mother, on the other hand, gives in to every whim and is often the one to bail the child out of trouble. Sometimes these parental roles are reversed, but we have seen this pattern much too often over the years to consider it a coincidence.

Through the use of adoption studies, more recent research findings (Reid, Dorr, Walker, & Bonner, 1986) point to genetic antecedents of alcohol abuse and antisocial behavior. For example, similar antisocial behavior has been shown to be higher in monozygotic twins reared apart than in dizygotic twins reared apart. Yet many of these studies reported by Reid and his colleagues have also uncovered the importance of the gene-environment interaction.

The Conduct Disorder is far more commonly diagnosed in males than in females. It has been our experience both in clinical work and research that approximately ten to fifteen percent of high school and college or university students labeled as underachievers fit the Conduct Disorder description.

It should also be noted that there are many achieving individuals who, except for the more blatant forms of acting out and manipulation, function on an interpersonal basis like Conduct Disorders. These individuals are not always reliable, may be quite manipulative, can be deceptively charming when they want to be, and may be impulsive in the sense of pursuing the objects of their desires. Such individuals, in fact, may be quite successful in their achievements in life. Some mental health experts even argue that the people we label as psychopaths and sociopaths are only the unsuccessful ones; the successful ones are running the corporations, countries, and armies of the world (Greenwald, 1967). While we are not certain that we would carry the argument that far, it is certainly true that Conduct Disorder underachievers have many deviant and self-defeating characteristics which, if turned to their genuine advantage, could result in extremely successful vocational and interpersonal lives.

The Phenomenological World of the Conduct Disorder Underachiever

The brief but classic article by Harold Greenwald, "Treatment of the Psychopath" (1974), and the more recent edited work by Reid, et al. (1986) represent attempts to perceive the world through the eyes of the psychopathic personality. Many of Greenwald's observations and speculations can be applied equally (although often to a somewhat lesser degree of acting out) to the Conduct Disorder underachiever.

Greenwald points out that because of the psychopath's antisocial behavior, interpersonal manipulation, impulsiveness, apparent poverty in human relationships (considering other people only as objects to be manipulated), and lack of conscience or guilt, it has been difficult for mental health professionals to develop the same kind of empathy for the psychopath that they develop for individuals with other problems. Mental health professionals, after all, are human beings themselves, and are as likely as anyone else to become victims of the psychopath's manipulations. In fact, some of the sociopaths the authors have encountered in their own professional work over the years seem to have saved their most subtle and effective manipulations for use on mental health professionals. This lack of empathy often results in a tendency for the professional to morally evaluate the psychopath, even to the point of being convinced that such an individual is beyond treatment, as was the opinion of the field for many decades.

There is, of course, a delicate and subtle line to be drawn here. The criminal psychopath or the psychopath who commits heinous crimes and other illegal or immoral acts which injure other people or flout basic human standards of conduct cannot be forgiven for this behavior simply because of having a manipulative personality with a label in DSM-III-R or any other diagnostic system. Ultimately, each of us is responsible for our own behavior and must answer for it: morally, legally, socially, personally, and spiritually. Psychological and psychiatric theory and practice do not supplant this personal accountability, but it is a different dimension which coexists. If we are to arrive at an understanding of human beings in their full range of possibilities and even attempt to have a constructive impact on them, we as mental health professionals need to utilize our capacity to empathize with these individuals as much as possible without using this empathy as an excuse for behavior which society finds unacceptable.

An example of this kind of balance between developing empathy for individuals without losing the moral outrage at (in this case) their heinous crimes can be found in Dicks (1972). For a project sponsored by Britain's Centre for Research in Collective Psychopathology, Dicks and his colleagues used semistructured interviews of Nazi concentration camp guards and officers (that is, those who actually carried out the barbarous deeds in the camps) who had been tried and convicted after World War II and were still in prison for their crimes. The reader will find in Dicks' book a model for a professional yet empathetic interviewing approach coupled with a clear and unyielding moral judgment as to the barbarous and unforgivable crimes the interviewees had committed.

Ironically, considering the above example, Greenwald gives his readers some sense of the inner emotional world of the psychopath by asking the readers to imagine being a Jew dropped suddenly into the middle of Nazi Germany. Greenwald describes the likely feelings of mistrust of everyone, unwillingness in these circumstances to postpone gratification of impulses, and the dire need to lie and to manipulate others. He concludes that the psychopath feels surrounded by deadly enemies, and that his life experience has confirmed this belief. While this appears to be a description less of a psychopath than of a paranoid individual, Greenwald stresses that the psychopath deals with enemies by deciding that there is no hope beyond survival and immediate gratification.

Greenwald's analogy is compelling and fits much of the psychopath's behavior, especially considering the paranoid characteristics which often emerge during therapy with these individuals. However, the basis of the analogy—a Jew dropped into Nazi Germany—is fear. We believe, on the other hand, that one more element is necessary to get a clear picture of the inner world of the psychopathic personality; it is an element not likely to be a dominating force in a person motivated almost totally by excruciating, everpresent fear. That element is hostility.

A child who knows only angry rejection and indifference is likely to grow up with an intense and overpowering anger and related needs to get even with the world, especially if everyone in it is perceived as not really caring anyway. The psychopath's behavior, after all, is dripping with hostility. Manipulating the emotional sensibilities of other people, callously using other people, flagrantly disregarding accepted rules of civilized conduct, thinking only of self first and everyone else second, adopting an attitude of indifference and callousness even to those trying to help—these are the actions of a person who is driven by unforgiving rage. The world, therefore, does not represent an experience of constant fear, but rather an endless opportunity to vent one's anger, gratify impulses, and use people. Any human closeness will indeed cause discomfort and anxiety.

We hope that the reader who can empathize with the feelings of this inner maelstrom will understand in human terms that the psychopath is usually unmoved by ordinary attempts of others to reach out in a caring, human way. The readers who can empathize with the psychopath are those who can search within themselves, locate, and relish even the smallest self-characteristics of manipulating others, gratifying impulses, and, above all, getting even with the world. The reader who arrives at this empathy may not (and certainly should not) excuse the psychopath from the consequences of his or her behavior but may gain the understanding that will make possible constructive, therapeutic treatment.

Our more mundane example of the Conduct Disorder underachiever is on a less severe level of intensity than the criminal psychopath but shares many of the same interpersonal and inner emotional characteristics. These are people who feel angry at the world and believe that people are to be used. They will twist the truth, avoid close relationships with others, and attempt to satisfy their immediate needs without thinking of the consequences. They do not feel guilty, since they justify their actions on the basis of their immediate needs or on the basis of whatever rationalization happens to occur to them at the time. Studying and getting good grades are simply a nuisance; there's no immediate payoff.

The reader who imagines seeing the world in these ways will understand what it must be like to be a Conduct Disorder underachiever.

Criteria for Differential Diagnosis

A. Background Information

Background information, as we have indicated earlier, often involves family lives characterized by turmoil. There is often a history of family breakups, substance abuse, and the like. Fathers of Conduct Disorder students tend to be rejecting to the extreme. They blame the Conduct Disorder for everything and are abusive (verbally if not physically) and hostile to their children no matter what they do or say. From such a parent, the child learns that nobody likes anybody else, and one might as well get what gratification one can. The mother, on the other hand, tends to be a guilty neurotic type. She may be equally angry at the child but uses her relationship with the child as a weapon against the father, presumably to show how much she cares and how little the father does. The mother may also feel guilty for her anger or for having exposed her child to a problematic environment; in any case she is likely to get the child "off the hook" when the latter gets into trouble. Mother is always there to make excuses for the Conduct Disorder underachiever, bail him or her out of trouble, and overlook many indiscretions. From this parent, the child learns that anyone can be manipulated. Occasionally, we find that the parental roles are reversed, with the mother being the hostile rejecting one and the father being the pushover.

B. Diagnostic Testing

In keeping with their candidness about their antisocial behavior or motivation, Conduct Disorder underachievers will consistently agree with test items that tap these characteristics. For example, in our experience, they will typically select the following *Mooney Problem Checklist* items or others which collectively state or imply antisocial, impulsive characteristics:

Sometimes not being as honest as I should be

Wanting to quit school

Being tempted to cheat in class

Parents not trusting me

Concerned over proper sex behavior

Not taking some things seriously enough

Worrying how I impress people

Getting into trouble

Getting into arguments

Losing my temper

Giving in to temptations

Trying to stop a bad habit

Lacking self control

Family quarrels

Getting too excited

Too little chance to do what I want to do

On the HSPQ, there were significant sex differences on only one personality factor: Factor I (Suspiciousness). Conduct Disorder males scored at the tough-minded end of the scale, females at the sensitive and dependent end (Hartley, 1985). The reader may recall that in Chapter 10, this finding was reversed for the Overanxious Disorder males and females. In addition to the Suspiciousness scale, female Conduct Disorder underachievers score high on Factor A (Warm, outgoing).

Perhaps the most notable feature of Duckworth and Anderson's (1984), MMPI profile is the high "4" scale (Psychopathic Deviate). Sometimes this is in conjunction with other MMPI scales such as the classic "4-9" profile, but whatever other scales may be elevated, Scale 4 is a fairly reliable measure of the kind of personality tendencies of the Conduct Disorder underachiever.

Typical conclusions about Conduct Disorders based on measures such as the Rorschach Test may include poor judgment in how or what the individual divulges and the use of manipulation to impress or intimidate others. Another is superficial, distanced, or limited social relationships. Conduct Disorder individuals may show indications of carelessness and a simplistic view of the environment. They tend to avoid attempts to integrate the world around them in a coherent and meaningful manner and will not address all available environmental information. Other Rorschach conclusions may include perceptual inefficiency or cognitive laziness in which irrelevant features of the environment receive primary attention. Although they tend to be affectively guarded, rigid, and inflexible, when they do respond emotionally they do so intensively and with little impulse control.

A representative example of a Conduct Disorder underachiever's story regarding TAT Card 1 (boy with a violin) is as follows:

> This boy's name is John. His mom always wanted him to play in the orchestra, and he's sick of it. One day, he got very mad at his mother, and he chucked the violin at the wall and broke some of it, and now he is looking forlorn. . . . His mother makes him take up the tuba—a sturdy instrument.

His lack of impulse control here is blatant. Obviously, his solution to this problem is to have his mother, an external agent, choose an instrument that would be less vulnerable to his destructive tendencies, rather than for him to develop greater impulse control.

C.   Interview Characteristics

1. *The nature of school performance and related issues, especially if they are problem areas*

Issues of performance in school, unless having some immediate utility (i.e., payoff) for the Conduct Disorder, are considered as more of a nuisance than anything else. Conduct Disorder underachievers are often quite blunt about their situation and motives, almost as if they are flaunting their personality and situation, but they do so with a kind of nonchalant, indifferent manner. The interviewee in the following example is a 14-year-old female, and the interviewer is a female clinician.

INTERVIEWER: How are you doing [in school]?

INTERVIEWEE: I'm not doing good at school.

INTERVIEWER: How come?

INTERVIEWEE: Cause I don't like it.

INTERVIEWER: What is it about school that you don't like?

INTERVIEWEE: I don't know . . . I guess I'd rather be working.

INTERVIEWER: You'd rather be working. How come you're not?

INTERVIEWEE: Well, right now I'm in a foster home, and they won't let me drop out of school until I'm 16.

INTERVIEWER: Oh, so you've got to hang in in school until then. How old are you now?

INTERVIEWEE: I'm 14, but I'll be 15 in two weeks.

INTERVIEWER: Couldn't you get permission for an early school leave?
INTERVIEWEE: No way! And besides, I don't want to talk about it.

One can already sense from this student that the issue of needing the approval of the interviewer is nonexistent. In a few moments, she has indicated that she is not doing well at school, that she does not like school, that she would like to drop out of school, that the foster home she is in will not let her, and then after volunteering all of this "juicy" information, she states that she does not want to talk about it. Let us examine the nature of the communication process going on.

Certainly, her lack of concern for school and academic achievement is rather obvious. Also, her perception that she has no real control over her situation (that it is all up to the decisions of authority figures in her foster home, school, etc.) fits the Conduct Disorder description. In addition, there is the straightforward nonchalance and complete candor about her situation. In addition, within a few seconds and by virtue of an admirable economy of language, she has managed to get the interviewer involved in the problem of getting her foster parents to give her permission to quit school and get a job.

Then, when she has the interviewer good and "hooked" into this outside problem (outside of the interview, that is), she suddenly states that she does not want to talk about it. This last comment is, in our experience, so typical of Conduct Disorder underachievers that we find it occurring with monotonous regularity. It is, in our experience, unique to the Conduct Disorder. The interviewer, with a little introspection and a willingness to look at the details of the communication process, will find that this one characteristic often is sufficient to detect the Conduct Disorder personality.

Notice that by the end of this excerpt, the interviewer has been put in a real bind. On the one hand, the student's almost disdainful comment, "And besides, I don't want to talk about it," has now made it impossible for the interviewer to pursue this important topic without becoming intrusive, even downright pushy. On the other hand, the student has freely offered so much information relating to this situation, that the interviewer's interest is inevitable. Thus the bind that the interviewer is in is as follows:

If the interviewer continues to probe the situation of the foster home, then the Conduct Disorder student can rightly become upset at this "noseyness," and use the interviewer's intrusiveness as a sign that the interviewer doesn't really care about the student's feelings. If, on the other hand, the interviewer takes the hint and avoids the topic, it is clearly still on the interviewer's mind. Both the interviewer and the interviewee know this. The interviewer by holding back on her curiosity, creates a kind of hypocrisy in the interview. She is keeping her interest in the topic to herself and is therefore not being open, honest, or genuine. The Conduct Disorder underachiever, knowing this (since she set it up this way), can now justify not trusting the interviewer because she is not being open or honest. The student reasons, "If she isn't being open, why should I be?" Therefore, no matter how the interviewer reacts, the chance for an open and honest communication is blocked.

One might be tempted to criticize the above interpretation. Didn't the student ask to terminate the discussion? Isn't it obvious that she was not comfortable with the topic? The response to this is that if she genuinely was upset by the topic, why did she bring it up in the first place? Review again the details this young student brought up within a few minutes: not doing well at school, doesn't like it, rather be working, in a foster home, won't let her drop out. That is a great deal of information for someone who says she "doesn't want to talk about it." In addition, if she really did want to solve this problem, why did she not respond when the interviewer offered a solution? Instead, she rejected it out of hand.

The interviewer will find this bind occurring again and again in dealing with the Conduct Disorder. Often it will occur when the student confides information about behavior that is inappropriate, immoral, or otherwise against formal and informal values and codes of conduct. The interviewer is then in the bind of either agreeing with the student in order to maintain rapport and thereby entering into a hypocritical game in the interaction or disagreeing and thereby destroying rapport altogether.

Consider the following example from later in the same interview.

INTERVIEWER: So I take it that you didn't do much homework last year in math?

INTERVIEWEE: None. I never did any homework.

INTERVIEWER: O.K.; what's happening in Geography?

INTERVIEWEE: Hew! . . . about in the 30s. I just don't like Geography, or the teacher. She thinks she knows everything. I don't like that at all [student looks agitated].

INTERVIEWER: That aggravates you?

INTERVIEWEE: Yeah. I haven't been doing any work in that class for about two months now. I haven't been to class much either.

INTERVIEWER: What happens when you don't go to class?

INTERVIEWEE: I get caught [she smiles].

INTERVIEWER: And then what happens?

INTERVIEWEE: Well, I haven't said too much, but today I got caught for skipping out yesterday, and I got a detention.

INTERVIEWER: Oh, so sometimes you end up with a detention. Anything worse?

INTERVIEWEE: Yeah. Sometimes they threaten to throw me out of class, but I really don't give a shit. It doesn't matter much to me. It's basically her fault anyway; she doesn't let me get away with anything, but lets other kids get away with things.

INTERVIEWER: So you're being picked on unfairly.
INTERVIEWEE: Yes, all the time.

Predictably, she has now given a litany of trouble that she has gotten into: not showing up for class, not doing any homework unless forced to, getting caught for skipping, getting detentions, being threatened with getting thrown out of school, all of which she blames on others. She is, as we have suggested, putting the interviewer in yet another bind, since, in order to maintain rapport, the interviewer must either side with her regarding the indiscretions or act in an adversarial manner.

In addition, notice how the Conduct Disorder underachiever justifies her behavior by stating that the teacher "lets other kids get away with things." Somehow that makes her behavior acceptable. This is also a common sort of reasoning in the Conduct Disorder: the assumption that since everyone else is unfair, it supposedly provides permission to act out.

Overall, however, notice how questions about school, homework, academic performance, and intellectual attainments have little meaning for the Conduct Disorder underachiever. Instead, the focus is shifted immediately to the typical Conduct Disorder agenda: manipulation of the interviewer, impulsive acting out, and inappropriate behavior.

2. *The nature of family relationships*

Even when the child does not come from a broken home or a home in which there is obvious abuse, family relationships are likely to be equally conflictual and negative. Generally, the Conduct Disorder underachiever displays the same sort of detached hostility toward parents and siblings as toward other people. Note the callous and almost indifferent attitude with which this student talks about some of her disruptive family history.

INTERVIEWEE: Well, my mom and dad were always fighting. They would both drink a little too much and then start arguing about something or other, about almost nothing, really. It got so that the neighbors called the police a number of times. I guess we got known in the area as a pretty rough family. . . . After my aunt called the cops and told them that we hadn't been to school for three days and that she had taken me in to feed me, they stepped in and I was taken away. My dad was charged with hitting my mom, and she couldn't take care of us during that time. She had been beaten up pretty bad. . . . I get to see my mom about once every two weeks. We're talking about getting together again. My brother's gone to Chicago. . . . He [her brother] was bad news for everybody. He used to take things even from us. He would see a dollar laying around the table, or on my desk, and he would rip it off. No one trusted him. We were glad when he left home.

There is a cool, relatively detached, nonemotional attitude towards her family members. There is little hint of warmth or interpersonal need, except where she comments on trying to protect her parents from the police. She also has some protective feelings towards a younger sister.

3. *The nature of social relationships*

Generally, Conduct Disorder underachievers will have as friends other Conduct Disorder underachievers. In the way these students discuss these relationships, they sound more like the relationships of gang members rather than genuine friendships. There is always that element of mistrust, of distance.

INTERVIEWER: No? You don't have a best friend? How come?

INTERVIEWEE: My friends are all the same to me. . . . You should have more than one friend. Like it's stupid to have a best friend. I've been pretty close to some friends, but not never a best friend. It doesn't pay.

With typical Conduct Disorder bluntness, she states that she is uncomfortable with friendships that get too close, and that this is very clearly something she would like to avoid. She is bluntly manipulative even about her relationship with her boyfriend.

INTERVIEWER: Tell me about him. What kind of a guy is he?

INTERVIEWEE: Well, he's good looking; he's out working on his own; he's 19 . . . has a car [she smiles].

INTERVIEWER: Were you thinking about something just then?

INTERVIEWEE: Well, no, really. He likes me, likes to make love to me.

INTERVIEWER: So you have slept together.

INTERVIEWEE: Oh, yes, many times. It's really great.

INTERVIEWER: Have you taken any precautions to avoid pregnancy?

INTERVIEWEE: Sometimes. Other times, I guess I've just been lucky. Besides, I don't really want any kids right now; maybe never. I don't even think that I'll stay with him that long, either. I just want to see if he's for real about being able to get me in touch with some people in music, like a band or something.

4. *The nature of the student's self-perceptions and affect*

We have found that a fairly reliable interview characteristic of the Conduct Disorder underachiever is the tendency to explain his or her situation in a long, involved, and complex story. This explanation, depending on who said what when and to whom, becomes so confusing that the interviewer begins to get a blurred picture of the story and to get suspicious that the interviewee is playing fast and loose with the truth. There is a natural tendency for the interviewer to want to sort out this story and "nail down" exactly what happened to whom and when and why and how. In our experience, the interviewer who follows this course in the interview is being led down the garden path of irrelevancies, which, in any case, are impossible to validate and which deflect from more important aspects of the interview, such as the interviewee's relationship style and interaction. We have yet to untangle one of these Conduct Disorder stories so that we can separate truth from falsehood. We have learned, however, that the presence of such stories and our inclination to want to follow up on them are fairly reliable indications that the interviewee has a Conduct Disorder type of personality.

Conduct Disorder underachievers will consider changing their ways only if there is some immediate payoff, as in the following example, where the student will consider behaving more appropriately in school only if she is in danger of being thrown out of her foster home.

INTERVIEWEE: My foster mother is actually OK. She tells me not to get into any more trouble, and that might help the situation a little. She's also said that the day I get suspended from school is the day I have to leave—out!!

INTERVIEWER: OK, so the bottom line is that you can't get suspended. Now, can you get suspended for skipping class?

INTERVIEWEE: No, I really don't think so. They haven't warned me yet, and once you get a warning, that means you're close to getting suspended from that class. That's when I'll smarten up. I don't really want to have to leave the foster home.

It is clear to this student that when it suits her needs (that is, before she gets displaced from the foster home), she will change her behavior of not showing up for class. This blatant manipulative behavior clearly indicates the most obvious characteristic of the Conduct Disorder personality: the apparent lack of conscience or sense of morality. In her account of her situation, there is no place for any larger sense of values (such as fairness, honesty, or altruism) or any more sophisticated reasoning for her decisions beyond immediate need. Her decisions appear based solely on the immediacy and expediency of satisfying a current impulsive need.

Recall the many comments this student has made indicating almost total surrender to the needs of the moment, such as her statements about sleeping with her boyfriend or not cutting class only if she is directly threatened with being thrown out of her foster home. Note, too, that Conduct Disorders are only too ready to expose their indiscretions to the interviewer. We have found this a consistent and reliable criterion for differential diagnosis. In fact, problems in their acting-out behaviors are usually offered unsolicited and in an easy, endless stream of boastful confessions. Conduct Disorder underachievers may not talk about their behavior readily; but if they do, it is an almost certain diagnostic sign to the experienced interviewer.

Introspective self-concept is an area which Conduct Disorders consistently avoid. Within their inner emotional lives, they have such self-negative and self-rejecting opinions that they believe that they themselves are worthless—unworthy of the most elementary human kindnesses, incapable of any genuine accomplishments, undeserving of any earned successes. Every so often in the interview, these negative self-percepts will arise, usually in the form of a seemingly unimportant aside which is not elaborated on. The interviewer who is alert to these comments will find them consistently but infrequently in the interview.

INTERVIEWER: If I were to ask one of your female friends . . . to describe you, to tell me what kind of a person you were, what do you think they'd tell me?

INTERVIEWEE: Probably a bitch—No, I don't know [laughs].

INTERVIEWER: They wouldn't say that!

INTERVIEWEE: No, I guess they'd say I was a good kid.

INTERVIEWER: And would you say the same thing? Would you describe yourself in the same way as they had?

INTERVIEWEE: I guess I would say that I was a moody person.

INTERVIEWER: What kinds of things make you moody?

INTERVIEWEE: Just different kinds of people. Like some people will be, you know, real nice to you, and you turn around and those same people are talking about you.

Note here not only the self-disparaging remark (the "bitch"), but that the entire topic of how she perceives herself is avoided by shifting the focus, in typical Conduct Disorder fashion, to how she is being treated by other people. In fact, the implication of her statements is that she can't really trust anybody. Since presumably the interviewer is part of "anybody" (especially someone who is at the moment being nice to her), she is stating that she does not trust the interviewer.

The Conduct Disorder underachiever characteristics discussed in this entire chapter are omnipresent in the interview. No matter what the topic raised by the interviewer, the Conduct Disorder quickly changes the format to the collection of issues described here: immediate gratification of impulses, manipulation of others, disregard for values and rules of conduct, the blaming of others for current problems, a series of incidents of improper behavior, long and convoluted stories about a variety of situations, and so on. The interviewer alerted to this personality structure will find these issues a reliable guide to proper diagnosis.

5. *The student's perceptions of and plans for the future*

Sometimes Conduct Disorder underachievers will have few plans for the future. A question about career goals may elicit a shrug of the shoulders and an "I don't know," or even some small self-disparaging comment such as, "Maybe an auto mechanic. I'm not much good for anything, anyway." While there is nothing inherently inferior about being an auto mechanic, the perception of Conduct Disorder underachievers deep in their heart of hearts is that they are basically no good and therefore not likely to achieve anything worthwhile if it depends on their own genuine talent and abilities. Consider an example from the same female Conduct Disorder underachiever, who *does* appear to have career plans:

INTERVIEWEE: [when asked about future career]:   I think I'd like to be an actress or singer when I get out of here. My boyfriend, he mentioned that he would like to get me connected to a band or something, so I could begin my career.

INTERVIEWER: Let's talk about that dream you have, about acting or singing professionally. Have you had that dream for a long time?

INTERVIEWEE: Well, I've always liked singing and stuff. But no, I guess I've had this idea for years now. It's nothing real big yet; I mean, I haven't done anything about it yet, but I think my boyfriend, he has a few connections; that will get me going. . . .

INTERVIEWER: What kind of training do you think you'll need in order to accomplish your aim?

INTERVIEWEE: Well, I've never taken any kind of lessons. I don't think that I really need anything. Just a few good connections with the right people, and I'll be on my way. Actually, there is a school or two I could go to, just to learn a few things. . . .

INTERVIEWER: What kinds of things would you like to be doing when you're 25?

INTERVIEWEE: I'll have lots of money, stereos, good coats, a fast car, that sort of thing. . . . I'll become famous with my acting and singing.

Even though this student has a clear future goal, it is more a fantasy or wish rather than a goal requiring planned effort and consistent achievement over a long period of time. It is obvious that she feels that if she accomplishes anything it will be by virtue of various manipulations and connections performed by someone else. Conduct Disorder underachievers feel so inadequate that they rationalize the adequacy issue out of existence by their particular mode of thinking. Questions about her competence, training, education, and talent are almost totally avoided. There is also the clear implication that talent isn't worth much anyway, except at one point in the interview when she states that although she cannot read music, she feels she does have a "good ear" (not even a "good voice"). Yet even here, while she will admit to some talent, she is not likely to follow through on achieving the skills that require persistent and regular work: reading music. After all, reading music is not an inborn ability (except perhaps for Mozart); it is a learned skill. Conduct Disorder underachievers rarely acknowledge their own ability or patience for acquiring academic skills.

Practical Diagnosis

There is wide individual variation in the personality characteristics of Conduct Disorder underachievers. Some do not behave in overtly antisocial ways, but show the typical interpersonal manipulativeness. Some do not act out to the point where they conflict openly with authority figures. Some may be extremely aggressive and hostile, others less provocative and challenging. Some may be involved with a cohesive peer group, although such groups are often insulated from other peers and authority figures; others may not associate themselves with any peer group. Safer (1984) studied differences in severity within a group of seriously conduct-disordered adolescents. Those who exhibited antisocial behavior at earlier ages tended to have more serious educational and social problems by their junior high school years. Rutter (1980) notes that conduct-disordered adolescents who began their misconduct early in their development were more likely to have academic difficulties than those who began such behavior at a later age.

DSM-III-R (p. 56) has divided Conduct Disorders into three basic types, based on research findings. These types include the group type (312.20), the solitary aggressive type (312.00), and the undifferentiated type (312.90).

In addition, the diagnostician should be alert to the fact that Conduct Disorder underachievers may show characteristics that lead to incorrect diagnoses. Some, for example, will present the interviewer with so many excuses for their underachievement that they will be misdiagnosed as an Academic Problem underachiever (see Chapter 12), when these excuses are in fact a calculated attempt to manipulate the interviewer. Excuses in and of themselves are not diagnostically differentiating. The excuses of both the Academic Problem and the Conduct Disorder underachiever share the element of externalization: blaming external factors for the underachievement. Other Conduct Disorder underachievers will be so candid about their dislike of school or their need to act on their impulses that they can be misperceived as Identity Disorder underachievers (see Chapter 13) who are struggling with an emerging sense of identity. The externalization of blame and responsibility and the defiance of authority may also lead to a misdiagnosis of Oppositional Defiant Disorder underachiever (see Chapter 14). The key issue here is whether the basic rights of others have been violated, which would provide support for the Conduct Disorder underachiever diagnosis. The interviewer must be alert for the Conduct Disorder underachiever's manipulativeness in the interview, shallowness of relationships, lack of broadly held social values, and other more typical characteristics.

In our experience and that of others, such as Greenwald (1967), Conduct Disorder individuals who are achieving are rarely diagnosed, not only because they are unlikely to come to the attention of psychologists and other professionals, but also because professionals rarely consider the possibility that Conduct Disorder permits success. Achieving conduct-disordered individuals are more likely to come to the attention of professionals when the manipulative pattern begins to affect interpersonal relationships. For example, many people initially attracted to successful persons with Conduct Disorders often become disillusioned because of the impossibility of forming intimate and lasting relationships with these individuals. This resulting disruption may bring the conduct-disordered person into marital counseling or other types of treatment.

Differential Treatment Considerations

Historically there has been a great deal of controversy in the literature as to appropriate treatment modes, even questioning whether psychological treatment of this category can be effective.

The first and, in many ways, still classic detailed account of psychotherapy with a psychopathic personality is Robert M. Lindner's *Rebel Without A Cause* (1944). He utilized hypnotherapy as a primary approach, but it is only in recent years that hypnosis has gained more widespread credibility as a treatment modality. Even today, it is unlikely that hypnosis would be considered as standard a treatment for a widespread problem as are other therapeutic approaches such as behavioral, client centered, or cognitively oriented. Lindner's account stands as a fascinating and effective but idiosyncratic treatment approach.

Traditional individual and group psychotherapies, institutional placement and treatment, even psychopharmacological approaches—all have been considered relatively ineffective in treating the antisocial personality. In the case of psychotherapy almost any individual or group experience requires the kind of commitment to an interpersonal process that is specifically what the sociopath lacks (Freedman, Kaplan, & Sadock, 1976). Occasionally, single case studies report success. (McCord & McCord, 1964).

What makes Greenwald's (1967) therapeutic approach to the psychopathic personality so compelling is that it is not simply a modification of a standard therapeutic approach to a particularly difficult type of patient, but rather a specific procedure geared to the unique needs of a particular personality. The treatment approach he recommends involves identifying with the basic motives of the psychopath (for example, the need for money or status), teaching the psychopath more effective and less self-defeating ways of meeting those needs, strengthening the psychopath's confidence and skills in impulse-control techniques, and ultimately providing support for the underlying issues of dependency, insecurity, and anger.

We have found that the manipulated bind with which the Conduct Disorder underachiever immobilizes the interviewer is a crucial focus of treatment. Recall that the Conduct Disorder interviewee regularly shares with the interviewer a stream of instances of antisocial acting out, often subtly enlisting the interviewer's agreement in the apparent good sense of such behavior. In order to maintain rapport, the interviewer must then either go along with the interviewee's way of thinking, thereby interacting in a hypocritical and actually dishonest way by withholding obvious value judgments, or confront the wrongness of the behavior, thereby creating an antagonistic rather than supportive relationship. In either case, the Conduct Disorder does not have to face the uncomfortable prospect of a genuine, open, candid, supportive relationship with another human being.

In our experience, the interviewer bent on counseling or therapy (as opposed simply to diagnosis) can deal with this bind by verbalizing it whenever it occurs. The therapist needs to point out to Conduct Disorder underachievers that their admission of some antisocial type of behavior places the therapist in the bind of either lying (by agreeing with behavior which the interviewer feels is wrong) or confronting. The therapist then emphasizes that neither of these choices is acceptable, since what the therapist wants to do is to establish a helpful relationship with the student. The therapist also points out that this bind was created by the student and recounts the exact words the student used to "set up" the bind.

The counselor or therapist who follows this tack, either in individual or group psychotherapy, combined perhaps with the approach advocated by Greenwald, might well find a greater percentage of successful therapeutic outcomes with Conduct Disorder underachievers. The therapist might also find this group much less frustrating to deal with, since these techniques and approaches result in a more tolerant attitude towards students' impulsiveness and less likelihood of being successfully manipulated by them. Reid, et al. (1986) have edited an excellent collection of essays, some of which discuss the many troublesome countertransference issues in dealing with this type of underachiever.

The Conduct Disorder Underachiever as an Adult

The adult form of the Conduct Disorder will likely be described by DSM-III-R as the Antisocial Personality Disorder (301.70, pp. 342–346). This person shows the same kinds of behavioral patterns as the younger individual with Conduct Disorder: drug or alchohol abuse, lying, inappropriately aggressive behavior, and the like. DSM-III-R includes in this description failure to sustain adequate job performance over a period of years, and it is with this aspect of the Conduct Disorder as an adult that we will concern ourselves.

As adults, these individuals can be characterized as having the charm and often charisma to make an excellent first impression. Subsequent contact, however, reveals many of the Conduct Disorder's negative qualities. Work performance is thus characterized by promising and often impressive beginnings. These persons may interview well for the job, to the point where a great deal of achievement is expected of them. They have plenty of energy, often impressive-looking resumes and other letters of reference, obvious competence (at least from the knowledgeable way in which they talk), and an ingratiating manner. In short, these are people who can "sell themselves" exceptionally well.

The honeymoon is over rather quickly, however; too soon they begin to reveal their impulsive side. They may be caught telling lies or exaggerating the truth; some of their background documentation may prove to be false; they may irritate co-workers by an indifferent and hostile attitude; they may not complete projects on time and create elaborate stories explaining why someone else was responsible; they may even begin "putting the make" on co-workers of the opposite sex. Whatever the behavior is, it will become more and more destructive, no matter how many times these individuals are called into the boss's office for a chat. Finally, they will reach the point of being fired, after botching their job and alienating almost everyone.

Many adults, however, may have some or all of these characteristics and yet may not underachieve or be destructive in their interpersonal lives or careers. For example, the Conduct Disorder's charm and manipulative ability, if incorporated into a person who cares about others and has good relationship skills, can be excellent qualities to have in areas such as sales, public relations, personnel work, labor relations, or other similar careers. And who among us could not use some of the Conduct Disorder's narcissistic impulsiveness to accomplish our own goals and lead more satisfying lives? As in so many other areas of life, it becomes a matter of balance, values, and choice. Conduct-disordered children or adults do not have the balance, the values, or the choice. They are driven to behave in the ways predicted in this chapter, and the qualities of the Conduct Disorder guide every aspect of their lives.

It has been our clinical experience that when individuals who have been diagnosed as exhibiting the Antisocial Personality Disorder characteristics reach middle age, some seek psychotherapy on their own. The major issues which usually precipitate such requests revolve around concerns that the individual no longer has the energy required to maintain previous methods of operating, combined with a growing sense of social isolation and aloneness, which is a direct consequence of their past actions.

CHAPTER 12

The Academic Problem Underachiever

General Characteristics

In 1980, for the first time in the DSM series (DSM-III), there appeared a description of a condition labeled "Academic Problem" (V62.30). Its brevity allows it to be easily repeated here:

> This category can be used when a focus of attention or treatment is an academic problem that is apparently not due to a mental disorder. An example is a pattern of failing grades or of significant underachievement in an individual with adequate intellectual capacity, in the absence of a Specific Developmental Disorder or any other mental disorder to account for the problem (APA, 1980, p. 332).

No other data or guidelines for this condition are provided by DSM-III-R. We believe that this is a thumbnail description of what the Developmental Theory Model calls the Non-Achievement Syndrome, or NAS, as we have indicated earlier in Chapters 5, 6, 8 and 9. We and other researchers and clinicians who have examined this problem in detail have focused on a world of additional characteristics and symptoms (as well as recommended treatment approaches) that apply to the Academic Problem underachiever. We shall devote more attention to Academic Problem underachiever than the other types in this book, because there is generally much more information and understanding of the other diagnostic categories. This one, however, is little understood outside of the comparatively small circle of researchers who have worked with the particular problem and have published in this area.

The typical and consistent description of Academic Problem underachievers given by parents, teachers, counselors, and the underachievers themselves is that these students are lazy and unmotivated procrastinators, who could do better in school "if only they would try harder." When questioned about problems such as procrastination, Academic Problem underachievers usually promise sincerely to do better "next time," but these apparently good intentions are rarely followed by consistently successful actions.

In and out of the classroom, at almost any age after 10, such individuals seem to "coast, cruise, and float" through life. They appear to lack a sense of purpose or meaning in their lives, although they are quite content to spend hours in activities such as sports, music, computers, tinkering with machinery and automobiles, or simply in social activities. They generally are well liked, followers rather than leaders, and individuals who rarely act out in an antisocial manner. In fact, except for their mediocre achievement pattern, they appear to be easygoing, well-adjusted, friendly, and without severe anxieties, depressions, or mental disturbances.

Academic Problem underachievers rarely initiate requests for assistance, and most often state that all they need to do is to try harder and their grades will improve. In fact, their assessment appears to be correct, but they rarely work hard enough or consistently enough to improve. They tend to procrastinate, to give up easily at the first sign of difficulty, and to avoid following through on most projects or tasks. They express only a vague sense of personal identity, usually avoiding the introspective process. Nevertheless, they appear sincere in their intentions to improve and in their belief that if only certain roadblocks had not appeared in their path, they would have been able to achieve. Little seems to bother or concern them, and they simply appear content with their mediocre performance not only in school but in most areas of their lives.

Perhaps the most telling and obvious characteristic of these individuals is their seemingly endless series of rationalizations or excuses as to why they failed to achieve up to their potential. Among Academic Problem students, these rationalizations typically include problems such as forgetting books, studying the wrong material for tests, having a difficult or impossible teacher, not being "good in math" or some other subject, being lazy, getting bored with certain subjects, quite often losing interest, having trouble concentrating, being unable to take good notes, making stupid mistakes on tests, and a variety of similar statements. Granted, any young adolescent may utter the same kinds of statements, but the Academic Problem underachiever makes them constantly and links them to a consistent pattern of underachievement—day after day, month after month, year after year. We will have more to say about these excuses later in this chapter.

Our recent research (see Chapter 8) suggests that about 80% of all Academic Problem underachievers come from intact families in which one or both parents value academic achievement and education. We have identified this syndrome across the entire socioeconomic range and across different cultures (Fraser, 1987). We have found few family characteristics unique to this personality pattern: Academic Problem underachievers can be an oldest, middle, youngest, or only child; they can come from intact families or broken homes; they can appear in many religious, ethnic, or racial groups. Yet each Academic Problem underachiever seems to fit the predicted description with an astounding consistency.

As we have said, such individuals do not suffer from any serious identifiable mental disorder—clinical depression, retardation, severe and debilitating anxiety, manic-depressive mood swings—but tend to be fairly even-keeled in their temperament. They do not seem to be emotionally torn apart by internal turmoil. They hardly ever evidence suicidal ideation, phobias, hallucinations, delusions, or other classic psychiatric symptoms. They are not seriously antisocial or delinquent. All of their physical signs are within normal limits, and they do not show evidence of learning disabilities, attention deficit disorders, or related speech, hearing, or visual problems. We might add, however, that our clinical experience suggests that while Academic Problem underachievers infrequently show the presence of learning disabilities, some learning-disabled students show the motivational characteristics of Academic Problem underachievers.

When the Non-Achievement Syndrome, or NAS (the likely antecedent diagnostic term for the Academic Problem underachiever), was first described (Roth & Meyersburg, 1963), the NAS male to female ratio was thought to be on the order of 6:1. This estimate, however, was based on the sample of students referred for assessment or counseling. In more recent evaluations of demographic data (Hartley, 1985; Mandel, 1984; McRoberts, 1985; Phillips, 1987) it appears that the male to female ratio of Academic Problem underachievers (or NAS students) is closer to 1:1. Research demographics also indicate that in any random group of underachieving high school and college students *not* suffering from learning disabilities, neurological deficits, or other organic conditions, reliably 40 to 50% have the personality structure that we call *Academic Problem* and older research calls *Non-Achievement Syndrome*. The remainder is made up of a variety of personality constellations, primarily those outlined in this book (Overanxious Disorder, Conduct Disorder, Identity Disorder, Oppositional Defiant Disorder).

The Phenomenological World of the Academic Problem Underachiever

Typically, Academic Problem underachievers have not responded to varied attempts at remediation, counseling, parental intervention, or other approaches. We believe that this has occurred for several reasons, the most important of which is that these students have been approached as if they would respond positively to incentives or to the internal rewards of successful performance. Teachers, parents, counselors, and even peers have assumed that if Academic Problem underachievers tasted some success, if something were found to spark their interest, then this would awaken their dormant desire for success and that in turn would trigger the emergence of initiative. In short, it has been assumed that these students were unmotivated, and that what was needed was something to motivate them.

If these students were truly unmotivated but harbored the motivation toward achievement and success, then all of the measures used to motivate them should at least be moderately successful. But this is not the case. In spite of all of the pressure from teachers, parents, counselors, and others, Academic Problem underachievers do not change either in their academic performance or their apparent lack of motivation.

Yet the single most important factor in understanding the inner personal world of Academic Problem underachievers is realizing it is not that they lack motivation, but that they are *highly motivated,* and in fact achieve their particular goals with incredible perseverance, dedication, energy, cleverness, and sophistication. This strong motivation, however, is aimed at *continuing the poor or mediocre performance.* They may not want to fail, but they certainly want to avoid success as much as is possible. This is why these students rarely achieve outstanding academic success or complete failure, but steer a middle course and get mediocre grades. The very fact that their underachievement continues so tenaciously in the face of considerable family and school pressure is not a sign of a *lack* of achievement, but a sign of a powerful, overwhelming singleness of purpose. For the Academic Problem underachiever, the low grades do not *cause* a problem; they *solve* one.

But what kind of problem is it? What would cause someone to actually seek underachievement and to avoid doing well in school (or in anything else, for that matter)? We believe that Academic Problem underachievers are not only highly motivated, but that their motivation and actions involve an active—albeit unconscious—choice. In spite of these students' perceptions that their level of achievement is something that happens to them for reasons outside of their ability to control, these students are indeed making an active choice to underachieve. To understand why, we have to look at the reasons for academic achievement.

Any student prepares successfully to take a test by knowing all of the material assigned, memorizing all relevant data, understanding the concepts and theories, knowing how to perform all of the required mental operations (e.g., mathematical), anticipating the particular type of test to be given (multiple-choice, essay, math), and so forth. A student so prepared is highly likely to do well on the test and get a good grade.

What does getting a good grade on a test *not* depend on? It *does not matter* how the student prepared for the test, how many hours the student studied, what time of the day or night the student prepared, where the student prepared, whether the environment was quiet or noisy, whether the student studied lying down (or standing up or sitting at a desk), or whether the student studied every day from the beginning of the term or just the night before the test. It does not matter whether the student hates the subject, is indifferent and bored, or is intensely interested. It does not matter whether the test material is directly linked to a future career or not. It does not even matter how competent or incompetent the teacher is.

To get a good grade on a test, the only thing that matters is how well prepared the student is for the test!

After all, if school is to become a preparation for the "real world," we must make at least some effort to expect real achievement and not dwell solely on the process of education. If you are a child who puts together a bridge out of blocks, and that bridge then falls down, you can be excused because it was just play. What was important was the industry you showed, how you felt about it, and what you learned from it. As an adult, however, if you are an architect or a construction engineer, and the bridge you designed or built collapses, there is no excuse that is acceptable. It will not have mattered that you did not feel well the day you designed the plans or that you got bored with the details of erecting the bridge. All that will have mattered is how well or how poorly you prepared the blueprints or supervised the construction. As a parent, nobody gives you a day off because you happen to lose interest in being a parent for that day. As a teacher, nobody allows you to miss a day just because for that day you are bored with teaching. As a worker in the adult world, lack of interest is no excuse for less than adequate job performance.

Success in all of these endeavors may be made more pleasant and trouble-free by high interest, teacher support, and so forth, but all that really matter for success are *adequate preparation and execution*. One can succeed without interest, without a competent teacher, without a quiet room to study, and without a lot of extra time, but *no one can succeed without adequate preparation and execution*. And it is in the matter of adequate preparation and execution that the choice for achievement or underachievement is made.

Academic Problem underachievers seem to forget that the grades they get at the end of the semester are directly determined by how well they prepare, how much homework they accomplish, how much assigned material they learn and memorize, how much they anticipate test questions, how many assignments they turn in on time, how carefully they read, and how much they use these activities in taking tests. These are actions. To avoid these actions is a choice (albeit an unconscious one for Academic Problem underachievers), and to choose to avoid these actions is to choose failure or mediocre performance. Underachievement is the only possible outcome if one is not prepared and one does not execute on an exam or paper. Academic Problem underachievers do not prepare; they do not execute. This pattern pervades their daily school activities, their after school homework activities, and other aspects of their lives.

We have mentioned that the choice is unconscious, a term we use not necessarily in the Freudian sense of being so deeply repressed that only years of psychoanalysis will release the percept into consciousness. We do mean that the Academic Problem underachiever is unaware of this aspect of the motivation and decision-making processes and avoids this awareness. Although it is not gained easily, in psychoanalytic terms the awareness is more preconscious than unconscious.

The question, however, is why Academic Problem underachievers are unaware of their motivation to avoid those activities that would lead to success? Why do these students always have reasons for the underachievement, and why do these reasons make it seem as if the students had no choice or that events were beyond their control and understanding? Why should they be so bewildered by it all if there is indeed a highly motivated choice to underachieve?

We believe that the answer is as follows: While these students are making a careful, deliberate, and strongly motivated effort to underachieve, they are also making an equally motivated effort to convince themselves (that is, to pretend) that the underachievement is *not* a choice at all, but actually is the product of forces beyond their control. The mind plays a trick on itself. The students have chosen failure and have convinced themselves that the failure is not a choice but only something that happened beyond their capacity to respond to or change. An elaborate series of excuses, seemingly endless, appear to explain why the students failed and why they should not be held responsible for the failure.

Listen carefully to these excuses and rationalizations, however, and notice that the Academic Problem underachievers are *not really explaining what happened at all* but are merely *providing a description* of what happened. As a classic example, ask such a student the reason for doing poorly on a test, and the response may be (as we have heard hundreds of times over the years), ''I don't know. I thought I was prepared, but then I went in to take the test, and it had stuff from chapters I didn't think were going to be on the test.'' The answer appears to be that the student studied the wrong material. If, however, the reader will carefully study the wording of this response, it becomes obvious that this answer to a question of why the student did poorly is not a real explanation; it is an accounting of what happened. What happened was that the student did not study the right material; the question is, *why* did the student not study the right material? Why did the student think that particular material would not appear on the test?

As another typical example, a student will answer that a poor grade was received on a particular test because ''everybody did bad on that test.'' While on the surface, this seems to be an answer, it isn't. It is a description of the overall grade profile of the class on that test; it does not answer why this particular student did poorly on this particular test.

These excuses for failure permeate the thinking of Academic Problem underachievers, but the actual reasons they do poorly are: They do not prepare adequately for school, or else they do not execute properly what they prepare for. The sad aspect of their habitual pattern of excuses and rationalizations is that Academic Problem underachievers come to believe them, and the excuses are so plausible that others come to believe them also. This is why Academic Problem underachievers are so convincing when presenting their excuses—they believe them and therefore are not lying, in the sense of knowingly and maliciously presenting falsehoods.

This psychological sleight-of-hand keeps Academic Problem underachievers trapped. New excuses justify each new failure. The students believe these new excuses and add them to their arsenal of reasons for failure to achieve. The excuses permit these underachievers to distance themselves from understanding the actual situation, so that, more and more, they lose a sense of control over their achievements. Gradually, they lose touch with the underlying motivation and the choices that go along with this motivation. Ultimately, they are able to delay taking on more responsibility in school and anywhere else, convinced that "something always seems to happen" to make achievement impossible. Yet thanks to the excuses and the lack of personal responsibility these excuses imply, these underachievers can do all this while convincing themselves consciously that they really *want* to do better.

Why do Academic Problem underachievers need to pretend that their mediocre performance is not a choice they are making? Why do they deny their active role in the grades they actually get? Why can't they simply say, "I don't want to get good grades," and let it go at that? After all, good grades aren't everything. There are many other worthwhile goals in life to pursue, and getting high grades in school isn't the only path toward fulfillment and success.

The reason why Academic Problem underachievers need to pretend that they are not making the choice to underachieve is that they also need to avoid thinking about themselves. These are among the most nonintrospective individuals on earth; the last thing in the world they want to do is to talk seriously and in depth about themselves. They do not want to think deeply about who they are, where they plan to go, what they plan to do, who they want to travel with through life, what their values are, or what ideals they stand for. They do not want to take a serious look at their inner selves. After all, if they realize that they could have done something about the grades they got, then they might have to ask themselves why they did not try in the first place. And this is exactly the type of question these students avoid. Therefore, when asked to describe themselves, these students understand very well the nature of the question but find it uncomfortable and frightening, and so they respond with superficial answers such as, "I guess I'm just average; there's nothing much to tell, really."

Academic Problem underachievers are afraid of achievement. Their fears drive them to avoid academic success. This is why the usual attempts of rewards and punishments, attempts which have an impact on most people, are ineffective with these individuals. Therefore, when they do have some successes, Academic Problem underachievers do not become self-motivating. This is also why such students quickly lose interest once a commitment to achieve is made. Making commitments, keeping up the energy level, taking in the fruits of success produce serious crises for these students: the pressure of being expected to achieve. Achievement is not rewarding or self-motivating or pleasurable or satisfying; it is something to be postponed for as long as possible.

This is not to say that these students really enjoy poor performance or failure. They are not masochists or self-destructive in the sense that they enjoy pain and humiliation. They get "no thrill out of champagne," but they also get no thrill out of poor grades. It is simply that their fears of achievement are a stronger motivating force within them than any disappointment or failure. They are willing to endure failure as a means of avoiding success. But what is so terrifying about success? Isn't success what everyone wants? Aren't the rewards of success one of the strongest motivations in the human character?

Success is indeed wonderfully positive, but it also has its dark side. If you succeed, then there is the *expectation* that you have the ability to do it again, that you should do it again (and even better next time), and that you ought to keep on doing it again and again and again. In other words, success brings with it a lifetime burden of additional expectations. You are now stuck with these expectations to be responsible for repeating this success from now on into the distant future. The child who never seems to remember to take out the garbage and who continually needs to be reminded or pushed is trying to avoid the following perspective:

1. I am capable of remembering this chore.
2. I am responsible, in that I can remember this chore without needing reminders from others.
3. I have the physical strength to actually carry out this chore.
4. I have the commitment to follow through on both remembering and carrying out this chore from this day forward.
5. I am now responsible for the garbage for the rest of my life.

By forgetting, the child is sending a different message: he or she is not really responsible for having either the capability or the maturity to make a commitment to or carry out this chore. In other words, the child has developed a problem (the faulty memory) which precludes taking out the garbage, convinces everyone (including the child) that there was no choice involved in not taking out the garbage, keeps anyone from expecting the child to be responsible for taking out the garbage, and of course keeps the child from having to accept this responsibility.

Armed with this reasoning and these psychological methods of avoiding personal responsibility by avoiding success, Academic Problem underachievers not only avoid the burdens of taking out the garbage, but also avoid carrying the burdens of academic achievement, paying the bills, doing the laundry, keeping the house clean, deciding what to cook for dinner, making the mortgage payments, and choosing a career. Academic Problem underachievers need not worry about any of these things because their parents, teachers, and friends are usually worrying about it for them. Academic achievement is to be avoided because each achievement hastens the day when a range of responsibilities will fall on the student's own shoulders, when major decisions will have to be addressed, when independence will thrust the student—alone and having to "do it all"—out into the world. It is the future brought on by higher grades that the Academic Problem underachiever is afraid of.

Academic Problem underachievers are usually nonchalant and unconcerned about poor grades, except perhaps at report card time, when they anticipate pressure from parents. It is the parents who are usually worried and upset; it is the parents who push the underachievers to the tutors, counselors, reading and math specialists, learning disability experts, psychiatrists, psychologists, social workers, and other specialists. The Academic Problem underachievers consider these actions unnecessary but usually will go along so as to diminish the pressure from their parents to do something about the slumping grades. So, except for this predictable report card confrontation with their parents, these students seem unconcerned about their poor grades. This is puzzling only if we assume, as most people do, that these are unmotivated students. If, however, we recognize that they are highly motivated to avoid academic success then their lack of concern begins to make sense. Of course they are unconcerned! Their poor grades are exactly what they want, and the responsibility for achievement (a worry which should be theirs) has gradually fallen on their parents' shoulders.

This pattern filters down to personal habits and household chores as well as schoolwork. Academic Problem underachievers will flatly state that they need others to remind them to take their books to school, clean up their rooms, take out the garbage, walk the dog, finish homework assignments, study for tests, fill up the car with gas, and so on. It is not a perfect arrangement, because they do not like others "on their backs" (i.e., reminding them of their responsibilities and expecting them to produce), but it does allow these underachievers to minimize the expectations for achievement and personal responsibility.

In a way, Academic Problem underachievers are afraid of growing up, somewhat like Peter Pan. However, these underachievers and Peter Pan differ in some crucial aspects. Peter Pan avoided growing up because he believed that the life of a child was more fun than the life of an adult, whereas Academic Problem underachievers certainly get no fun from their continued underachievement and avoidance of responsibility. Peter Pan *chose* his lifestyle, whereas Academic Problem underachievers avoid perceiving themselves as having a choice. Peter Pan was not so much frightened by the future as bored by it, whereas Academic Problem underachievers are deeply fearful of the responsibility the future might bring. Lastly, for Peter Pan *childhood* meant freedom and independence, whereas for Academic Problem underachievers *adulthood* means freedom and independence, and they want no part of it.

Excuses and rationalizations protect Academic Problem underachievers from recognizing their own inner attempts to keep from achieving, from assuming more personal responsibility, from becoming more independent, from growing up. As long as you believe that if you lose interest in something, you therefore become unable to accomplish it; as long as you really believe that if you forget your books, there is nothing you can do about it; as long as you believe that you are inherently lazy—as long as you really believe these things—you can go on underachieving, avoid growing up, and at the same time convince yourself that you had no choice in the matter; it just happened. After all, if there is nothing you can do about a situation, why bother to try?

What better way to put off the future than to underachieve, thereby making it impossible to expect yourself to get into that future, and what better way to underachieve than to convince yourself that it was because of forces beyond your control. These are the two central characteristics of the inner personality defensive structure of the Academic Problem underachiever: One is behavioral (the underachievement itself), and the other is mental (the wall of excuses which makes the underachievement seem beyond the student's ability to control or change). These two characteristics form a core element in the personality of these individuals, and together they become the key to explaining and understanding almost every aspect of these underachievers' lives.

Yet if this is true, why is it that Academic Problem underachievers can put so much time, energy, and intelligence into sports, cars, music, or computers, and then turn around and seem to lose these same abilities and skills in school? To begin to understand how to answer this question, watch what happens when you begin to suggest to such an individual that perhaps a certain hobby could be a possible career. Typically, these underachievers will play down their own abilities, raise other factors that would minimize the possibility, or suddenly lose interest. Even if they agree that this might be a good career choice, a little more probing will show that they are not putting in the effort that will give them mastery in this area: They don't practice their musical instruments, for example.

Therefore, we can summarize the inner motivation of Academic Problem underachievers as follows:

1. The underachievement is not due to a lack of motivation, but is an unconscious, highly motivated choice—more powerful than rewards and incentives, punishments, or interest level.
2. Academic Problem underachievers have convinced themselves (and usually convince everyone else) that this "lack of motivation" is beyond their own inner control or understanding. According to them, their poor grades are somehow due to forces they can do nothing about, and therefore these students are victims of circumstance. Hundreds of specific excuses and rationalizations in specific instances of underachievement support this belief.
3. Since they have hidden their real motivation from their own awareness, these individuals may continue to go through life never having quite

the energy or the apparent willpower to follow through and achieve much. The students remain unaware of *what* they are doing and *why* they are doing it. This becomes a depressing puzzle both to them and to those around them.

Academic Problem underachievers are highly motivated to slow down their future, to maintain their status quo as long as possible, to avoid issues of genuine independence.

Criteria for Differential Diagnosis

A. Background Information

General diagnostic criteria, much of which are reports by these underachievers and others of behavior and characteristics outside of the interview and testing situation, are as follows:

1. A consistent pattern of underachievement in recent years, preceded by a relatively satisfactory achievement pattern
2. Consistent procrastination about personal responsibilities at home and at school (household chores, studying and completing homework)
3. Failure to complete commitments: academic projects, promises to complete household chores
4. Gradual or precipitous loss of interest in almost any long-term area of commitment (school subjects, music lessons, daily practice in some activity, etc.)
5. When working on any project, a tendency to give up easily at the first sign of any difficulty, setback, or loss of interest
6. Selective memory: i.e., forgetting responsibilities (household chores, homework, school books, assignments, test materials) but remembering in other areas (hobbies, sports statistics, activities with friends, etc.)
7. Verbal statements, made in apparent good faith, of intentions to improve academic performance or follow through with household chores in the future (Occasionally this will include remedial plans, but usually it is encapsulated in statements such as, "I've really got to try harder next time.")
8. Tendency to distraction, especially when doing homework or when about to do household chores
9. A multitude of excuses for poor performance (The nature of these is discussed elsewhere in this chapter.)
10. Laziness and lack of motivation, typically noted by parents, teachers, friends, and even Academic Problem underachievers themselves

11. Absence of diagnostic signs of significant mental disorders or distur-
    bances: little or no anxiety, depression, delusions, hallucinations,
    phobias, mood swings, thought disorders, etc.

12. Seeming lack of concern about poor performance, except at exam
    and report card time

13. Generally good relationships with parents, siblings, friends and other
    peers, and teachers

14. Almost complete lack of introspection about self and future

15. A sense of comfort or contentment about self; usually described as
    coasting or cruising through life

16. More responsibility shown for others than for self (e.g., will forget
    to do homework, but will remember to run errands for teachers or
    friends)

17. Episodes of real trouble, serious antisocial or delinquent acting out
    seldom seen

18. No evidence of measurable learning disabilities or attention deficit
    disorders

19. Tendency to overestimate school performance (Usually, if asked how
    things are going in school, they will state that they are OK.)

20. A need to be reminded of personal responsibilities, particularly
    schoolwork and household chores

21. No significant alteration of mediocre achievement patterns, even in
    the face of substantial rewards or punishments

22. In verbalizations, use of passive voice, vaguenesses and generalities,
    and other unique linguistic characteristics

B. Diagnostic Testing

As we have noted in Chapter 8, Academic Problem underachievers tend to
appear nonpathological on personality tests. They show little evidence of
severe anxiety, depression, thought disorders, or other classical signs of
mental or emotional problems. In fact, their personality profiles tend to
appear free of pathology, with only mild signs occasionally surfacing.

In our clinical experience, certain *Mooney Problem Checklist* items are
likely to be selected:

Not spending enough time in study

Made to take subjects I don't like

Being careless

Forgetting things

Being lazy

Not getting studies done on time

Not interested in some subjects

Can't keep my mind on my studies

Not being allowed to use the family car

Having bad luck

Parents expecting too much of me

Don't like to study

Getting low grades

Just can't get some subjects

Lacking ambition

Confused as to what I really want

On the HSPQ, Hartley (1985) found that male and female Academic Problem underachievers differed on Factor C (Ego strength). Females scored in the average range on this scale, while males scored at the emotionally stable pole of the scale.

One personality test which has shown some evidence of isolating the Academic Problem underachiever is the MMPI (Tirman, 1971). Clinical experience suggests either a completely normal profile or a slightly elevated Scale 4 (*Pd*). Previous research has also suggested that academic underachievers (without other significant problems) may have Scale 4 elevated (Haun, 1965). However, Kaminska (1984) gave the MMPI to a diagnosed sample of 15 Academic Problem underachievers and found that none of the clinical scale group means were elevated. She did find variability on each scale, suggesting a subtle range of personality characteristics even in a diagnostic group such as this one where all of the individuals seem alike.

As noted in Chapter 8, Tirman, using the MMPI in an attempt to discriminate between Neurotic (or Overanxious Disorder), Adolescent Reaction (or Identity Disorder), and Non-Achievement Syndrome (NAS, or Academic Problem) students, constructed an NAS scale consisting of 11 MMPI items: 1 True (242) and 10 False (10, 78, 132, 172, 179, 204, 217, 133, 361, and 507). Scales were also constructed for the other two diagnostic categories, and various statistical tests were used to test whether the MMPI could be used to discriminate among the three groups, but the results did not support the use of the MMPI for this purpose. Tirman did find that if the Adolescent Reaction group could be excluded, his analysis could more clearly differentiate between the Neurotic and NAS groups, but this analysis is not definitive enough for use on a daily basis with specific individuals.

On projective tests, such as the TAT, Academic Problem underachievers will show their characteristic attitudes and perceptions, often quite transparently. For example, on Card 1 (the boy with the violin), one such student wrote:

His mother signed him up for violin lessons. He has gone for the lessons, but doesn't like the violin, and doesn't like to practice. So, he's just sitting there, looking at the violin. His mother comes home (It's always the mother), and yells at him because he has not been practicing as he should. She stands over him and makes him practice and go to lessons. He doesn't like her for this, but has to keep going. There's a time warp—twenty years later. He's a star violinist, playing in the London Orchestra.

Many of the classic elements of the Academic Problem are in this brief story: the nonchalant dependence upon the parent, the lack of responsibility for decisions, the consistent underachievement (even in the face of considerable pressure), and the optimistic outcome which seems to just happen without any effort on his part. (Apparently, the underachievement disappeared in a time warp.) These and other elements can be found as recurrent themes in many Academic Problem TAT protocols: being "stalled," showing some degree of passive-aggressiveness, being a victim of circumstance, and reluctantly but quietly acquiescing to demands for at least minimally acceptable achievement.

A recent case report based on the Rorschach protocol of an Academic Problem underachiever states the following:

> While there are no serious signs of pathology, he is currently not using his resources efficiently to interact with others or achieve at a satisfactory level. Oppositional tendencies, coupled with a cautious response style, suggest that he is currently spending energy defending himself from perceived external pressures. Faced with an intellectual or emotional challenge, his primary tendency will be to withdraw and/or avoid. There appears to be little energy directed toward self-evaluation.

The diagnostician in this case was not aware that the student had been previously diagnosed as an Academic Problem underachiever and in fact was not trained to identify this diagnostic category. Therefore, this interpretation was an independent confirmation of the Academic Problem personality structure.

C. Interview Characteristics

Like no other underachievers in any other diagnostic category, Academic Problem underachievers relate in predictable, stereotyped ways. When interviewers learn to recognize the particulars of these relationship characteristics in just a handful of cases, they will find no trouble diagnosing this particular problem with a high degree of accuracy in almost any random group of underachievers. This kind of predictability does not occur to the same extent with other personality categories, in part because Academic Problem underachievers tend to use language in a unique and characteristic way specific to their needs.

Primarily, they use the language of hope rather than the language of decision. For example, if asked how they will do in the coming semester, the word "hope" appears again and again in their responses: I hope I can do better; I really hope to bring up my grades. In addition, there are always qualifiers beginning with the word "if": If I can put in more effort, I really hope to bring up my grades; if I can get myself to get down to business, I hope I can do better; if I try harder, maybe my grades will improve. This phraseology, so typical of Academic Problem underachievers, is carefully worded so that a commitment to achieve is never made; rarely will one of these students say in a strong and convincing manner, "I *will* bring up those grades."

Secondly, this wording is designed to avoid questions which require commitment, choice, goals, and responsibility in the answer. Note that the statement, "If I can put in more effort, I really hope to bring up my grades," is not really an answer to the question, "How will you do in the coming semester?" The "answer" is not a prediction based on a commitment to achieve, but rather a statement of fact based on certain conditions being met.

Another linguistic characteristic of these students is their vagueness in the use of language. What, for example, does "try harder" mean? In what ways and under what conditions does one need to "try harder"? What does "do better" mean? Does it mean going from a *D* to an *A* or a *C*? Does it mean anything about grades at all? Could it mean simply, "I'll try to study more," or some similar statement? Since many Academic Problem underachievers rely on idiomatic cliches in their excuses, the interviewer should be alert to these and not let them go by without questioning what they really mean. Carefully note such everyday phrases: try harder, do better, hope to do better, study enough (How much is "enough," and for what?), hard to concentrate, tough teacher, and so forth.

These verbalizations can be found throughout this section in the examples from interviews with these types of students. The reader might also notice that there is a definite humorous element to the thinking, verbalizations, and relationship style of Academic Problem underachievers. The excuses and rationalizations, the nonchalant style, the calmness in the face of academic catastrophe—all have a certain incongruous quality which, in actual interviews, are sometimes so patently silly that both the interviewer and the interviewee smile.

One of the reasons for this almost comic way of dealing with life may be that Academic Problem underachievers have some knowledge that their excuses are illogical, but we suspect that it may also have something to do with the nonintrospective nature of these individuals. If they truly need to avoid introspection, then they are not going to use their ordinarily good intelligence to examine their own statements and beliefs, especially where it concerns reasons for nonachievement. Therefore, their excuses will have cliches that are believed without any real critical thought. A statement such as, "I can't study if I'm not interested," flies in the face of human experience; most people do things every day and do them rather well, without having the slightest bit of interest. Or consider the Academic Problem underachiever who, when asked how he was doing in school, told us, "Yeah, I'm going to go down to the office to see how my grades are doing." The interviewer in this case was tempted to reply, "Yes, your grades have been asking about you." Whatever the reason for this obvious humorous quality to this category of underachiever, we have noted its consistent presence.

The interviewer's "knee-jerk" countertransference reaction may be anxiety when interviewing an Overanxious Disorder student, anger when interviewing a Conduct Disorder student, or depression when interviewing an Identity Disorder student, but all of these reactions reflect the interviewer's recognition that one is dealing with a person who has serious problems. On the other hand, the interviewer's reaction to an Academic Problem underachiever may be amusement at the incongruous and often ridiculous logic. The interviewer should be aware, however, that while in that amusement there is a recognition of differential diagnostic signs, there is also the potential for ridicule and rejection of a person who is, after all, trapped in a cycle of puzzling failure and fear. Academic Problem underachievers may be amusing and apparently contented with their nonachieving ways, but they are not happy individuals.

1. *The nature of the school performance and related issues, especially if they are problem areas*

Academic Problem underachievers are rather vague in their responses to questions or comments in this area. They usually want the interviewer to know that their grades aren't really terribly good, but that there is little more to say about the matter. Consider this interchange between an interviewer and a male Academic Problem underachieving high school student.

INTERVIEWER:　How are things going with you in school?

INTERVIEWEE:　Well, most subjects, it's OK. But there's a little trouble in a few. I'm doing good in a few.

INTERVIEWER:　Could you tell me which ones you're doing well at, and which ones are giving you some trouble?

INTERVIEWEE:　Calculus is OK. Analysis is also OK. But biology, chemistry, physics, and algebra . . . I'm not doing good in that.

INTERVIEWER:　What seems to be the problem in algebra?

INTERVIEWEE:　It's just not coming.

INTERVIEWER:　Tell me more about what you mean.

INTERVIEWEE:　Well, I'm sort of interested, but not really, so I don't try as hard in it. It's easier to work in something you're interested in.

Note the vagueness in the above. To begin with, what does "OK" mean here? Does it mean that the student is getting *A*'s or *B*'s? Most likely, as with so many Academic Problem underachievers, "OK" means a *C* or that they are just passing the course (a vast improvement, to them, over the previous term). However, the term "OK," which seems to be a perfectly adequate answer to the question of how one is doing in school, is actually a vague response which could mean any grade from barely passing all the way up to an *A*.

In the subjects that are not OK, he states that he's having "a little trouble." Once again, while this seems to be a clear response to the question, it does not begin to answer it. Indeed, what does "a little trouble" really mean? Does it mean he's flunking, or that he already has an *A* and is having trouble getting an *A + ?* What about the response, "It's just not coming," in response to a question about his difficulties in algebra? What exactly does this mean? In this instance, the interviewer wisely follows up and asks. The Academic Problem underachiever's answer is our old friend "lack of interest."

Four times within this brief interchange, this student has used vague language which seems to communicate his situation, but which hardly begins to make things clear. How much does he study? What does he actually do when he studies? What work has he missed? What work has he completed? How does he do on tests? On homework? From his responses thus far, we have no inkling of these answers, and generally this is exactly the way Academic Problem underachievers want to leave us: feeling that our questions have been answered when in fact they have not been.

Note also in the above excerpt that the student, even in the use of grammatical structure and vocabulary, avoids the language of choice. For example, rather than describing what *he* does or does not do in regard to algebra, he says "*It's* just not coming," as if all he has to do is sit back and wait for *it*. There is no perception of action, initiative, or responsibility on his part; he merely waits for *it* to arrive. It is almost as if he is describing the actions of someone else, without any real understanding of how or why it happened. His very choice of language ("It's easier to work at something you're interested in") removes him from any personal responsibility, any choice, and therefore any real control over his preparation and study."

These same characteristics—vagueness in language and avoidance of responsibility or choice—can be seen in an interview excerpt with another such student.

INTERVIEWER: How are things going at school?

INTERVIEWEE: Well, they're all right. I find that there's a heavier work load this year over last year. I've got a part-time job, and I ski quite a bit. Usually, the part-time job and skiing come before school, ahead of school.

INTERVIEWER: It does! So do you find that quite often you don't get homework done?

INTERVIEWEE: Well, I only do the necessary homework, only the stuff that counts, you know.

INTERVIEWER: Is that the reason that the job and skiing come first, because you enjoy those other things more?

INTERVIEWEE: Yeah, I'd rather do those things.

INTERVIEWER: So school is a bit of a drag.

INTERVIEWEE: Well, I've got to do it.

INTERVIEWER: Does that mean that you end up doing pretty much the minimum to get by?

INTERVIEWEE: Yes; that's about it.

INTERVIEWER: Well, how are your grades?

IINTERVIEWEE: [Sighs] Well, last term I got about 60 average. This term I should be getting about 68.

From the outset, this student is vague about how he is actually doing in school; he talks about "all right" and "heavier work load" and "necessary homework," terms which once again *seem* to tell the interviewer how he is doing, but actually are vague and almost meaningless in giving a clear picture of how he is actually doing in school. It is only when the interviewer becomes more and more specific that this student finally yields up (with a sigh) his actual grades, which are predictably dismal.

Note also that from the outset he wants the interviewer to know that there are other kinds of activities that get in the way of schoolwork. That, at least, is what he seems to be saying, but the actual wording of his initial response—"Usually, the part-time job and skiing come before school, ahead of school"—clearly means that it is his schoolwork that gets in the way of these other activities. Yet when the interviewer attempts to clarify whether the job and skiing represent a more important commitment to him ("because you sort of enjoy those things more?"), he ends up saying about school, "Well, I've got to do it." Like all Academic Problem underachievers, he is trying to give the interviewer the impression that he (the student) is doing adequate work: After all, he's "got to do it." But when pressed further, he first acknowledges that he is doing only just enough to "get by" and then states his actual grades, which are neither "all right" nor "just enough to get by." He admitted soon after this excerpt that he is, in fact, failing some of his courses. Therefore, while he is trying to give the impression that he is doing adequate work because he's "got to" (not because he is interested), the reality is that he is *not* doing adequate work.

Note the curious logic in the following excerpt in which the same student is asked about courses he does not like.

INTERVIEWEE: Well, Geography and Chemistry. There's really nothing I don't like. Like Chemistry, I figured I was going to drop it, but I figured, what the hell, may as well stay with it.

INTERVIEWER: What is it exactly about the Chemistry course that gives you difficulty?

INTERVIEWEE: It's kind of boring. We seem to be doing the same stuff all the time, and never getting anywhere—just reading. I find it boring, just boring.

INTERVIEWER: So you really seem to like the more practical shop courses. If you put time into schoolwork at all, would you be putting more time into these courses?

INTERVIEWEE: Well, in those courses we really don't have the emphasis on homework. In English, Man and Society, Geography: those are the subjects we get homework in. That's where it takes up more time. Now, I don't think that's what influences my liking or disliking a course, that's just the way it is.

Academic Problem underachievers will subtly try to convince the interviewer that their low grades are unavoidable and in every way beyond their capacity to change through any sort of voluntary choice or action. Note how this student starts by mentioning two subjects which he does not like but then adds that "there are no subjects I don't like." We believe that the reason for this contradiction is that the interviewer is clearly assuming in this excerpt that if this student is interested in a particular course, he will choose to work in that course as opposed to others. The student, on the other hand, is trying to convince the interviewer that he is making no choices whatsoever. If the subject is boring, he cannot be expected to put forth any effort because of some immutable laws of nature which govern his behavior. Therefore he tries first to use the argument that if he is not interested he somehow becomes unable to study, but when the interviewer interprets the interest issue as relating to motivation and choice, the Academic Problem underachiever has to backtrack and state that interest is not a factor ("that's just the way it is").

Another Academic Problem underachiever volunteers the following:

INTERVIEWEE: I guess I would say that I was sort of lazy in my attitudes towards school . . . just getting by. I don't think I am like that with a bunch of other things, like my job. I'm not that way with my job. I'm not apathetic; I don't like sitting around the house watching TV. I don't like being idle.

INTERVIEWER: How do you feel about that "laziness" as far as school goes? Do you feel badly about it?

INTERVIEWEE: Oh, yeah. Like, I see others who are just as lazy as I am, but who are getting marks in the 80s.

INTERVIEWER: Why would that be?

INTERVIEWEE: Well, they're more intelligent than I am—higher IQ, or something—which makes it simple for them, you know. They don't try any harder than I do and they're getting better marks.

Regarding excuses for underachieving, this student is "hauling out the big guns": laziness and stupidity. Rarely will any except Academic Problem underachievers be so willing to voluntarily discuss their supposedly inherent laziness and apparent lack of intelligence and to do so in such a nonchalant and nonanxious manner. Remember, too, that this is information which the interviewee has *volunteered,* meaning that it is information that he has wanted very much to impart to the interviewer. The reason is that of all of the different personality categories of underachievers, Academic Problem underachievers take particular comfort in admitting flaws that lower the expectation for any substantial achievement. After all, if one is lazy, then it is something almost built into one's genes and chromosomes and therefore cannot be changed; it is now unreasonable to expect achievement. If one lacks intelligence, then there is also nothing that can be done about it; it is now doubly unreasonable to expect achievement.

The kinds of linguistic mazes quoted in this section are quite sophisticated in their logical traps for the interviewer and are also typical of the use of language by Academic Problem underachievers. The sophisticated use of cliches and idiomatic truisms of academic life, the vagueness of language regarding actual academic achievement, the endless series of rationalizations and excuses, the avoidance of assuming personal responsibility or any real choice over grades, the attempt to present a picture that somehow everything is "all right," and above all the message to the interviewer that expectations for this interviewee to achieve must be lowered—all of these characteristics are present in almost any excerpt from interviews with Academic Problem underachievers where the topic is academic performance.

2. *The nature of family relationships*

In our theoretical discussions of this personality type, we have stressed that Academic Problem underachievers (at high school and college ages in particular) are trying to maintain their dependence upon their role as a child in the family, so that they can avoid the increased self-responsibility, independence, and decision making that comes with a more adult role. By the time they have become teenagers (and certainly after the age of 18), they have an actual choice of leaving home and beginning to establish their own independent adult lives. However, this is an option which Academic Problem underachievers avoid at all costs, and this in turn requires minimizing any arguments or disagreements at home. Arguments with their siblings may be perfectly acceptable, but if they openly disagree with their parents, these students always have the option of leaving home, with or without their parents' blessings.

Therefore, in the interests of avoiding this option, Academic Problem underachievers consistently and characteristically will attempt to maintain positive relationships with their parents; they will minimize the significance of any differences, disagreements, or confrontations. Usually, everything at home is "fine," and everyone "gets along real well." There is one exception to this pattern: these students will draw the line if their parents push them to achieve. Typically, the interviewer who asks an Academic Problem underachiever if there are any disagreements at home will have an interaction remarkably close to the following:

INTERVIEWER: Do you ever have any disagreements with your parents?

INTERVIEWEE: Sure; doesn't everybody?

INTERVIEWER: Well, when you have disagreements, what are they usually about? Give me an example.

INTERVIEWEE: It's usually about school. They're usually on my back to study more, or something.

INTERVIEWER: I see; and who usually wins these arguments?

INTERVIEWEE: Oh, they do [placidly].

INTERVIEWER: That's interesting. How come they win?

INTERVIEWEE: Well, they're usually right; I mean, I really should try harder in school, I know.

This may seem like the response of a healthy, well-adjusted youngster, but it usually comes out of the mouths of Academic Problem underachievers in their adolescent years, a time of life when one is *least* likely to acquiesce to parental demands and opinions. One may even suggest the following rule of thumb: "Show me an adolescent who—without anxiety, without guilt, without bitterness, without hostility, without depression—so calmly and pleasantly agrees with his or her parents, and I'll show you an Academic Problem underachiever."

Academic Problem underachievers cannot afford to win such arguments with their parents or to be angry about losing, because then they always have the option of walking out, and this is what they do not want to do. Therefore, they must maintain a fiction that everything is fine and that everyone gets along well. Consider the following excerpt, in which an 18-year-old Academic Problem underachiever sounds more like a typical 10-year-old:

INTERVIEWER: Tell me a bit about your family life. How are things there?

INTERVIEWEE: Things are really good.

INTERVIEWER: Could you tell me a bit about members of your family?

INTERVIEWEE: My dad is really good. We go golfing all summer. He takes me out every Saturday and Sunday. We do a lot of sports together.

INTERVIEWER: So you get along really well with him.

INTERVIEWEE: I really get along well with both my parents.

INTERVIEWER: What about your mom?

INTERVIEWEE: She's a secretary.

INTERVIEWER: Any brothers or sisters?

INTERVIEWEE: I have two little sisters: one is 16, the other is 13.

INTERVIEWER: How do you get along with them?

INTERVIEWEE: Well, I don't get along too well with the 16-year-old, but I do with the other one.

Like their answers to questions about school, their answers to questions about homelife are vague, glossed over, and nonspecific. Yet the diagnostic value here is not to make sure to get specific answers, but rather to evaluate the nature of these vague presentations.

3. *The nature of social relationships (peers, the opposite sex, etc.)*

There seems to be an unspoken commitment among Academic Problem underachievers to avoid discussing anything having to do with achievement, school, responsibility, or so forth. As indicated in the chapter on the Developmental Theory Model, one can make a case for linking this particular personality type to a preadolescent stage of development, and the way in which these underachievers describe their social lives indeed sounds like the social lives of 10-year-olds. Activities with peers are usually unplanned and involve little active or constructive participation: going out, "hanging around," sports, rock concerts, movies, and so forth.

INTERVIEWER: What do you do with your time after school?

INTERVIEWEE: Not much. I go out a lot.

INTERVIEWER: Do you play sports at all?

INTERVIEWEE: No, not this year. I used to play football all the time, but not anymore.

INTERVIEWER: Well, what sorts of things do you do when you go out?

INTERVIEWEE: Well, I've got a lot of buddies; a lot of us hang around together.

The above is a fairly typical response. Not only are there no real activities, but there is the same sort of vagueness and lack of meaningful activity which is so characteristic of these students. What, for example, does "hang around" really mean? He states that he goes out "a lot." He is so vague about his activities that it is understandable why the interviewer here was tempted to follow up and ask what sorts of things he does. The answer, of course, was "hang around," which again does not really answer the question.

What is somewhat unusual here is that a few moments later, when asked what he does with his buddies, the student replied:

INTERVIEWEE: Well, one of them is a promoter for a music group, and if there's a dance anywhere in the city, I go along with him. That takes care of Friday and Saturday.

While it seems as if this student is engaged in some productive activity here, notice that it is his friend who is the promoter, his friend who is involved and does the work, while our Academic Problem underachiever merely tags along wherever he happens to be led. Once again, there is no expression of responsibility, initiative, achievement, or even interest. Then he adds, "That takes care of Friday and Saturday," as if those two days are accounted for now; he does not have to worry about them. In fact, the above interchange and student responses make little sense except in the context of an avoidance of responsibility, choice, commitment, independence, and achievement, a context which even includes relationships with friends outside of school. The "taking care of Friday and Saturday" becomes not so much amusing as it is tragic, since we are listening to a person whose major goal in life is to let each day go by without any real life accomplishments: academic, career, or personal.

Relationships with the opposite sex tend to be described in equally vague and noninvolved terms. Note how this Academic Problem underachiever sidesteps a direct answer to a question about his attitudes toward love and sex as regards his relationship with his girl friend:

INTERVIEWEE: I think it depends how you feel about the person. If you feel that you like her, well, I guess it also depends on whether you respect her or not. It's hard to say.

4. The nature of the student's self-perceptions and affect

At first, Academic Problem underachievers appear to relate in a normal affective manner. They do not evidence significant anxiety or depression, delusions or other thought disorders, or neurotic disturbances in their relationships (as might be evidenced, for example, by "pulling" at the interviewer for approval or other transference phenomena). They seem normal, well adjusted, and reasonably in control of their emotions. In short, they appear to have good ego strength, and indeed they do.

Taking a closer look, however, it becomes clear that Academic Problem underachievers rarely display or even admit to strong emotions or reactions, no matter what the topic. Everything is too nonchalant; they rarely express great elation or deep unhappiness. That they are not generally anxious (although they may appear a bit uneasy at times) may seem at first an index of psychological health, but they seem at ease when discussing the major problem in their lives: their poor academic performance. They speak in a kind of monotonous monotone, which upon close scrutiny the interviewer will recognize as a persistent although not particularly intense depression.

When they do describe their emotions, they are again vague, cliche-ridden, and nonspecific. Because of their almost total avoidance of any meaningful introspection, Academic Problem underachievers give such little attention to self-concept that they tend to describe themselves in characteristically terse terms. Typical self-descriptions (usually said unemotionally and with a shrug of the shoulders) are:

"I don't know; I guess I never thought about it."

"I'm average."

"I get along with people."

"I'm a nice guy."

"I'm happy-go-lucky" (usually uttered in a joyless and slightly depressed manner).

"I don't know. I guess I'm kind of easygoing, but sort of lazy."

Only Academic Problem underachievers describe themselves in such lackadaisical, terse, and bland terms. Notice also how they are careful even in a few words to paint a picture of blissful status quo, as if they are saying, "Everything is going fine; don't expect too much from me; don't rock my boat." These kinds of self-description occur with such regularity that they are diagnostically significant. Consider the following excerpt.

INTERVIEWER: If I were to ask your friend to describe you, what do you think he would say about you?

INTERVIEWEE: Probably the same way I view him: meaning, a really good friend; really get along. If he's in trouble, I'll help him; if I'm in trouble, he'll help me.

INTERVIEWER: Now, if I ask you to describe yourself to me without his view, what sorts of things would you say about yourself?

INTERVIEWEE: Hmmm. Lazy, I suppose. I don't worry about things until they happen.

INTERVIEWER: When you say "lazy," what exactly do you mean?

INTERVIEWEE: Well, I'm not too energetic anymore.

We see the paucity of self-concept in this student. He describes himself only in terms of his lack of effort for achievement, and there seems no other way in which he introspects about who he is or what he is going to do with his life. Interviewers will find that despite their questioning, probing, reflecting, empathizing, or interpreting, Academic Problem underachievers will solidly resist anything more than these superficial but diagnostically significant statements. Rather than this difficulty in getting self-concept information being a problem in making the diagnosis, it is a unique index of this personality category.

5. *The student's perceptions of and plans for the future*

Since Academic Problem underachievers try to avoid committing themselves to their future as adults (in establishing both a career and adult social and interpersonal roles), one of the topics they will avoid introspecting about is the future. To keep even themselves from recognizing this as willful avoidance, they will maintain future "goals" but make sure that these are so unlikely (given the present level of achievement), have so many preconditions, or are so unrelated to their present situation that such goals do not require any immediate action or any commitment in the near future.

In addition, they use the same selective reasoning they employed with regard to getting better grades, in not linking current behavior to future outcome. For example, the Academic Problem underachiever who gets poor math grades because he claims that he's "not good at math" will in the next breath state with some conviction that he wants to become an electrical engineer. If the interviewer should suggest that poor grades in math and a genuine inability to do math would make a career in engineering unlikely, this type of student will reply, "Yeah, I know," or "Yeah, you're right; I didn't think of that."

Here is a fairly typical interview response to the question of the future:

INTERVIEWER: When you said that you don't worry about things until you have to, I guess you mean that you don't do a lot of planning.

INTERVIEWEE: Yeah, it's more on a day-by-day basis. Like, we [his family] don't know until 5 or 10 minutes before we're going that we're going somewhere.

INTERVIEWER: Do you prefer it that way, rather than having things planned out?

INTERVIEWEE: Yeah, because if you plan something out, you've got to do it, and you got to rely on it. This way you just do what you want to do at the time. . . .

INTERVIEWER: What sorts of things would you like to be doing 10 years from now?

INTERVIEWEE: I'd like to travel—like to enjoy myself.

INTERVIEWER: Would you perhaps be married or not be married by then?

INTERVIEWEE: [Immediate response] I won't be married by then; I'd rather wait a while.

INTERVIEWER: What about a job?

INTERVIEWEE: I guess I would take any job I could get, really.

INTERVIEWER: So it's not as if you're planning any one type of work.

INTERVIEWEE: No, right.

INTERVIEWER: When you do get married, what kind of girl would you like to marry?

INTERVIEWEE: It's hard to say . . . I suppose someone like me who doesn't want to be tied down too much.

This Academic Problem underachiever is displaying his avoidance of dealing with any kind of future commitment in every important area of his life. For him, even making day-to-day plans involves a frightening commitment. In fact, in his statement about the type of person he would want as a spouse, he makes *lack* of commitment a primary requirement.

Another kind of response which allows the student to avoid the issue is "I don't know," or "I'm not sure what I'm going to want to do in the future." True to the typical and predictable thought processes of Academic Problem underachievers, they reason that if they are not sure what their career interest will be, then there is no point in even thinking about it. In other words, the "I don't know" becomes just another excuse for avoiding important life questions. In reality, of course, uncertainty about a future career is the very reason one *should* think intensely about it.

The following excerpt is, again, rather typical, although somewhat more wordy than these students usually are.

INTERVIEWER: What about 10 years from now? What kinds of things would you like to be doing in 10 years?

INTERVIEWEE: Well, I hope to be single, still. Well, about that time thinking about marriage. That, and I guess I'd like to be successful. But then, you sort of get into a rut. I don't know. It's really hard to say. I guess I'll just have to see what comes along.

INTERVIEWER: When you say you'd want to be single, you mean that for a good long while you'd like to stay single?

INTERVIEWEE: Yeah. You see, my parents got married at 20, and had kids right away, and then that's it. As soon as they got married, life was over. And if you do decide to get married, you do pretty well have to be financially well off to have a child. Whereas, if you're single, you don't have to be making that much. You can still be doing what you want to do, and holding a job here and holding a job there, and be single, you're all right.

INTERVIEWER: What kind of a girl would you like to marry?

INTERVIEWEE: Well, not sort of a member of my hippie friends, sort of. But then again, not too straight a girl. Someone who is the same as I am—sort of average, in the middle.

Once again we see this student avoiding specific commitments or plans for the future, with the excuse that one cannot predict the future. The argument seems to be that if you cannot predict the future, you cannot be expected to make any plans, let alone stick to them.

In the preceding excerpt, we also get a glimpse of why Academic Problem underachievers perceive the future as so threatening that they need to avoid it: the burdensome commitments of marriage, the rut of a career, and so on.

Practical Diagnosis

As with other diagnostic categories, there are variations in personality style, affect, cognition, and behavior within the Academic Problem group. Academic Problem underachievers can be found across a wide range of cognitive abilities. Even though they usually tend to show little anxiety, depression, or energy, there is still variability within these characteristics. In fact, there is likely to be variability depending, for example, upon the particular time in the academic year. At the beginning of a school term, Academic Problem underachievers are likely to be more optimistic, energetic, and happy than they are towards the end of the term when academic deadlines loom. Age differences are also likely to result in some variation: older Academic Problem underachievers have more sophisticated and logical excuses and may be less content with their pattern of underachievement. Yet the characteristics of this category are so consistent that there is little likelihood of a misdiagnosis. Even individuals with this personality structure who are achieving present themselves with the same classic features as their underachieving counterparts.

Differential Treatment Considerations

The treatment approaches to the other personality categories we discuss in this book—such as psychoanalytic, cognitive, or client centered—are generally well known, much utilized and researched. On the other hand, the particular psychotherapeutic approach most successful with the Academic Problem underachiever is not generally known outside of the circle of professionals who have been trained in the Developmental Theory Model. Nor is there as yet widespread familiarity with the research in this area, which we reviewed in Chapter 9. Therefore, we are expanding the Differential Treatment section in this chapter.

The reader will see that the approach recommended is neither unique nor unfamiliar in its specifics, since it embraces elements of cognitive and behavioral principles, psychoanalytic and other dynamic approaches, and directive as well as nondirective techniques. It differs from these traditional approaches mostly in its organization and focus. It uses a particular combination of techniques and approaches geared specifically to the unique characteristics of Academic Problem underachievers. The major treatment component that is unique is the judicious use of different forms of constructive confrontation, which have been described in Mandel and Marcus (1984).

In successfully counseling Academic Problem underachievers, the therapist must be alert for two countertransference reactions that not only will impede therapeutic progress but will also perpetuate the underachiever's avoidance of personal responsibility. The first reaction is the tendency to want to "take over," tell the student how to solve particular study problems, assume that the student has agreed (by a nod of the head or a brief comment like, "Yeah, that's a good idea" or "I'll try"), and then expect that the student will follow these simple and self-evident solutions. This direct rec-ommending of solutions may seem the easiest and most sensible approach to start out with, but one must remember that Academic Problem under-achievers are highly motivated to avoid following through successfully on any such recommendations. The therapist who takes this directive approach is falling into the trap of filling a "responsibility vacuum." The student is not taking the responsibility even for generating solutions to academic prob-lems, and so it is natural for the therapist to want to "jump in" and start giving suggestions. However, the student will not follow the suggestions, and the therapist will have taken over an area of personal responsibility that rightfully belongs to the student. Indeed, Academic Problem underachievers are perfectly capable of developing their own effective problem-solving strat-egies, but they usually create a responsibility vacuum as a method of enticing others to suggest and even carry out part of the solutions. Simply stated, the therapist should avoid taking over for Academic Problem underachiev-ers; to do so will only enhance their dependency and inhibit the development of independent thought and action.

The second countertransference reaction which the therapist is likely to experience follows from the first: When these students fail to follow through even on the simplest and most self-evident recommendations for improved academic performance, the therapist is likely to feel disappointed, frustrated, and angry, usually because the students have not done what they promised to do. The therapist's frustration, of course, is caused by assuming that these students have made a commitment to follow through on therapist recom-mendations, improve their academic performance, and take responsibility for themselves. These are the very things that Academic Problem under-achievers are *least* likely to do.

Because of this therapist tendency to want to fill the responsibility vacuum and the resulting frustration at the inevitable failure of this approach, many therapists (like parents, teachers, and others) eventually gravitate to one of two approaches. They either give up and abandon a commitment to work with these students, or they simply fill the responsibility vacuum and take over. Even experienced therapists, especially if they do not fully understand the inner motivation of these underachievers, begin to sound like frustrated parents, either in abandoning ("I give up; I can't get anywhere with this kid") or in taking over ("Don't forget your homework").

Therapist frustration often results in a third approach: simply telling the Academic Problem underachievers what their inner motivation is. We have heard many a frustrated and angry therapist make statements such as the following to these underachievers:

"I think that you don't really *want* to do well; you want to do crummy."

"You're just trying to avoid some responsibility here."

"You are purposely failing, and you know it!"

"You forgot to do that assignment because you didn't really want to do it!"

"You say you like school, but you don't really, do you?"

Such direct confrontation may relieve a great deal of therapist frustration and may seem like an effective way to cut through superficialities and speak to the real issues, but Academic Problem underachievers have a cognitive framework that allows them to successfully (if not always comfortably) defend against any such incursions into their psyches. In fact, they are likely to have already heard such statements uttered with considerably more anger by their parents. As long as Academic Problem underachievers maintain their endless series of excuses and rationalizations which allow them to maintain the belief that *they are not responsible for their achievement,* no such direct confrontation or interpretation will be effective.

The approach we will discuss here is a combination of the one briefly discussed in the chapter on the Developmental Theory Model plus techniques, perceptions, and approaches which we have clinically tested and utilized over the years. The major goal is not to abandon the student, fill the responsibility gap, or directly confront the motivation, but rather to help the student gradually uncover and expose the gap between what he or she says will happen (i.e., *intentions*) and what actually does happen (i.e., *actions*). This requires the therapist take a nonjudgmental and supportive tack, yet confront and intervene on the student's cognitions (*not* the student's underlying motivation). The therapist must narrow what we have half-humorously called the "crap gap": the gap between a person's statements of intent and their ultimate actions.

The steps in this approach are: (1) Set an agreed-upon goal, (2) take detailed stock, (3) focus on specific problem areas and isolate each excuse within each area, (4) link each excuse to its natural consequence, (5) request solutions for each stumbling block or hindrance, (6) call for action, (7) follow up on actions called for, (8) keep repeating Steps 3–7 with one different excuse each time, and (9) shift to a nondirective approach. We will now discuss each of these steps in detail.

1. Set an Agreed-Upon Goal

The first step is to ask the Academic Problem underachiever if he or she wants to get better grades in school during the current term. The student may simply answer yes or make some noncommital statement such as, "Doesn't everyone?" Almost all Academic Problem underachievers will answer affirmatively to this question, because the alternative is to recognize their own responsibility for their low grades. If the student does not offer even the slightest response, then the question should be pressed until an answer is given. No matter how nonchalant or grudging the student's attitude, the therapist should follow this with a simple statement of the therapeutic objective: to help the student achieve *his or her own stated goal*.

The interaction typically runs like this:

INTERVIEWER: What kind of grades would you like to get? Would you like to get different grades?

INTERVIEWEE: Yeah, sure. Doesn't everybody?

INTERVIEWER: No, not everyone. If that's what you want; my job here is to help you get what you want.

This may seem like a small or even meaningless step, and the student's reaction to this may be indifference, but it is the single most necessary step in the counseling process. From the very outset it shifts the responsibility for setting goals away from the therapist and directly onto the student's shoulders. In addition, every therapeutic intervention from this point on will be linked back to this stated, agreed-upon goal, without which little progress is likely.

As the example above indicates, this initial step is often quite easy to complete, occurs in just a few moments, and appears almost superficial, but its importance should not be confused with a genuine commitment for therapy on the part of the student. Academic Problem underachievers do everything in their power to avoid following through on improving grades even when they are convinced that they want to do better. This initial step does begin the process of keeping the responsibility where it belongs: with the student. It also places the therapist in the role of helper rather than educational overseer.

What if the student answers differently?

"I don't want to do better; I'm happy with the grades I'm getting now. I don't want your help."

Students who make this statement are taking responsibility for what they want, how they feel, and what they are doing about it. They are, in fact, recognizing that their underachievement is an important choice. Such responses are not going to be made by Academic Problem underachievers. If a student makes a response such as the one above, the interviewer would be well advised to reconsider the diagnosis, because recognition of this kind of choice is the very thing that Academic Problem underachievers are motivated to avoid.

2. *Take Detailed Stock*

Getting the most detailed information possible, the therapist should now find out what courses the student is currently taking, what the requirements are in each, how many of those requirements the student has met, what problems have arisen already in the courses, how much the student studies, where and when the student studies, how much is accomplished at each study period, and all the other particulars about what the student is required to do and how the student actually studies.

The therapist should not settle for generalities which may seem to answer these questions but actually do not. For example, students may state that they study "about an hour and a half a night."

Such general statements should not be taken at face value. The therapist should ask for details and specific instances: "Well, then, tell me how much time you studied last night? And how much did you actually accomplish in that time? What about the night before that? And the night before that? Did you take any breaks?"

At this point, too, the therapist should make no evaluative or confrontive comments. The task here, unlike the task in a diagnostic interview, is to gather specific information about the student's handling of a particular problem area: academic performance. Since Academic Problem underachievers will not volunteer specific details, the therapist must probe for such information. This probing should be made clearly within the therapist role as someone "here to help you get what you said you want, which is better grades."

However probing and directive, the therapist must make no judgmental or evaluative statements to the student, nor give any interpretations, recommendations, or advice. At this point the therapist elicits as many details as possible, listens and documents the information, and tries to get as complete a picture as possible of *how the student actually prepares for and executes academic responsibilities.*

We have used a specific form for this purpose, which is presented in Figure 12.1.

Making and using a record of this information is important for later sessions, since much of this approach requires that the therapist become involved in the day-to-day details of how the student studies. Also, by asking for the details, the therapist will learn how many details the student is aware of. For example, the student may not know many course requirements.

This step requires great patience and determination to get all of the relevant details of the student's course work and work habits. It is a great temptation for the therapist to jump in and intervene early on "juicy" material. At this point it would be premature to do so.

3. Focus on Specific Problem Areas and Isolate Each Excuse Within Each Area

Once sufficient information about the actual study activities and academic situation is secured, the therapist asks the student which of these many areas or problems is standing in the way of getting good grades. The therapist may have to guide the student a bit, but usually the student is only too ready to

Student Name:		Grade:	Date:
Course Problems	Requirements	Current Status	Plans
1.			
2.			
3.			
4.			

Study Habits/Comments:

Figure 12.1. Therapist Record Form

mention one of the problems already elicited. It does not really matter which problem the student chooses to start with; the intervention process is the same.

The therapist then reviews the specific details of this problem: When does it happen? Where? How and in what ways? Are there any other individuals involved? Why does the student think this happens?

Sometimes this is simply a matter of reviewing what has already been discussed, but often there are even more details to elicit from the student. For example, if the student says that the reason for a poor grade in an English class is the teacher is inadequate or "too tough," do not let these judgments go by without asking the student in what ways the teacher is inadequate or too tough. Ask for specific instances. What the therapist is interested in here is not necessarily what actually happened, but rather *a full and detailed accounting from the student's own perspective.* Remember that the ultimate goal here is not to focus on and change the student's behavior, but to learn the student's perceptions of that behavior.

Does the student feel that the teacher speaks too rapidly or too slowly? Is the teacher demeaning or intimidating? Does the teacher explain the material well? If the student should claim that forgetting books was the reason for failing some tests, find out which books and which tests. Academic Problem underachievers often claim that they studied enough for a particular test but then flunked it. Ask them how much time was actually spent, on what days, and how much was actually accomplished each day. Ask the student if this kind of problem has ever happened before: When? Where? In which courses? Why? How did it happen?

If a time is mentioned (e.g., "I study an hour every day"), the therapist must probe carefully to see if this is actually true. Since Academic Problem underachievers will overestimate the actual time they spend studying, this level of detailed inquiry is absolutely necessary. Ask the student, "How much time did you study yesterday? How much did you get accomplished in that time? How many pages read? How many problems completed? How much material memorized? How many pages written? How much of this time was used for breaks? For watching television? For listening to music, or daydreaming, or thinking about other things? Were there any other interruptions or distractions? How much did they detract from that hour? Considering all this, how much time did you actually study yesterday? And now that you know about yesterday, what about the day before that? And the day before that?

Although many problem areas may arise, the therapist should try to limit the focus to one problem area (or excuse) and probe it in great detail and depth. The following is a fairly typical interaction:

THERAPIST: How come you got such lousy grades this term?

STUDENT: I don't know. I try to study, but maybe I don't study enough.

THERAPIST: You don't study enough?

STUDENT: Well, I study an hour every day; that should be enough.

THERAPIST: You study an hour every day. If I'm going to help you get the better grades you want, I'm going to have to have a better idea of what you mean. Can you give me an example? You say you study an hour every day. How much did you study yesterday?

STUDENT: Well, actually, yesterday I got home from school kind of late because of basketball practice, so by the time dinner was over I was kind of tired.

THERAPIST: Then how much did you actually study?

STUDENT: Well, I sat down to do some stuff, but I kind of got stuck on this one page, and I guess it just got harder to concentrate.

THERAPIST: Where was this?

STUDENT: At home. I can't study in the library: too quiet; I fall asleep.

THERAPIST: Where at home? What room?

STUDENT: The den. Actually, we were watching the playoff games on TV. I tried to study during the commercials.

THERAPIST: Then how much time did you actually study? I mean, how much actual time studying, not watching the playoffs?

STUDENT: Maybe, I guess, well, around 20 minutes, I'd say. But it was really hard to concentrate.

THERAPIST: OK, so yesterday you didn't put in an hour, just 20 minutes. What about the day before that?

STUDENT: I'm not really sure. I can't remember.

THERAPIST: Then how can you be sure you try and study for an hour each day?

STUDENT: Well, let's see. . . . The day before, I think I sat down to study right after supper, but my folks were bugging me to finish the dishes, and by the time I finished that, it was starting to get late.

THERAPIST: So how much time did you actually study?

STUDENT: I think maybe 15 minutes or so.

THERAPIST: I see. So yesterday you studied about 20 minutes, and the day before about 15. So it sounds like in the past 2 days you didn't put in the hour a day you thought you were doing.

STUDENT: Yeah, I guess not.

As is so often the case with Academic Problem underachievers, simply getting to the specifics (e.g., how much time the student studies each night) requires considerable persistence and singleness of purpose on the part of the therapist. In addition, the specifics turn out to be quite different from the generalities that sounded so logical, reasonable, and convincing. The therapist should keep in mind that these general statements and excuses sound logical and convincing because they tie in to idiomatic expressions we take for granted every day and because the student really believes them.

4.   Link Each Excuse to Its Natural Consequence

Once the excuse or rationale has been isolated, clarified, and made concrete by numerous recent examples, the excuse must then be linked to its future consequence. Academic Problem underachievers are masters at considering the studying they do today as one thing and the grades they get next month as another. The therapist must not take for granted that these students understand this link. It must be explained in the simplest, clearest, and most logical of terms, because these students do not make the elementary assumption that the grades they will get depend directly on the studying they do today. They may have an IQ of 180, but they will avoid this simple logical connection. The therapist must describe in a blunt but nonattacking manner what will happen if the student does not solve this particular problem in preparing schoolwork.

THERAPIST: You've been telling me that you did poorly in math because you haven't really been putting in the time at home that you thought you were, or that you should be putting in. Is that right?

STUDENT: Yeah, I guess so.

THERAPIST: But you also told me that you want to get better grades, and that you feel that studying an hour a day is enough.

STUDENT: Yeah.

THERAPIST: But as we've just seen, you haven't been putting in an hour a day; you haven't been doing enough work. What do you think will happen to your grade in math at the end of the school term if you don't do something to change this?

STUDENT: I guess I won't do good.

THERAPIST: Is that what you want to happen?

STUDENT: No, not really.

THERAPIST: Then what do you think the answer is?

STUDENT: I guess I need to put in more time.

The above may seem simpleminded, self-evident, and not worthy of discussing even with an 8-year-old, but it is crucial to help the student make the cognitive link between what is done today and the consequences tomorrow. In terms we have been discussing, the link must be established explicitly between adequate educational preparation and successful execution. Therapists who work with these students find themselves constantly saying, "And what do you think will happen if you *don't* solve this problem?"

5. Request Solutions for Each Stumbling Block or Hindrance

Only when the excuse is out in the open and there is a clear recognition of and agreement about the importance of doing something *specific* about it, can the therapist begin to broach the topic of solving the problem. At this point, however, many therapists lose track of the therapeutic role necessary to intervene on the Academic Problem underachiever. They attempt to fill the responsibility vacuum by showering the student with practical and reasonable solutions. Presenting these solutions at this point will be useless, because these students often do not pick up on these reasonable suggestions voluntarily.

In a tone of innocent helpfulness, the therapist simply *asks* the Academic Problem underachiever to generate possible solutions. This step is a problem-solving process, but it will not be mutual problem solving unless the therapist encourages the student to think of solutions. More often than not, Academic Problem underachievers will present effective solutions in response to this question. The therapist should now engage the student in a detailed discussion of these solutions, probing to clarify the practicalities, anticipating snags in the process, and refining the approach. For example, if the student states that the solution to a math difficulty would include speaking to the teacher *and* doing a little more homework in that subject, the therapist should explore both solutions to anticipate what could go wrong with each.

The therapist should provide a solution only if the student cannot think of at least one. In any case, the therapist should be willing to explore these alternatives in a way that can counter the student's statements of inability to deal with these situations. The object here is to place the student in a position where *the recognition of personal responsibility cannot be avoided*.

THERAPIST: Yes, forgetting your books is a real problem, and I can see where you can't think of anything to do about it. But I've got an idea: Suppose we write down "Remember math and English books" on fifty sheets of scratch paper, and then we stuff a sheet of paper in every pocket of every piece of clothing you own. We can put one in each shoe. We can tape one to your locker, your desk, your clothes, the TV set at home, and so on.

STUDENT: [Depressed] That's kind of silly.

THERAPIST: But you're saying that forgetting your books is really getting in the way of your getting good grades, right?

STUDENT: Yeah.

THERAPIST: Then if this works, then it's not silly at all; it's getting you something important that you want. And besides, some of the most famous and successful people have used this very technique to remember things. If it's good enough for them. . . .

STUDENT: Yeah, but other kids might laugh.

THERAPIST: They don't understand your problem. Besides, what's more important, getting good grades, or what other people think?

One must remember, as with the preceding example, that to treat the student's social life in such an apparently cavalier manner is not, in this case, as cruel as it seems. Academic Problem underachievers will use every possible aspect of their lives as a reason to continue their underachievement. It may start out as a good reason, but in the hands of these individuals it becomes just another excuse.

As part of the step, the therapist should ask what the student can do to counteract anything that may "go wrong" in the execution of the proposed solution. Due to their avoidance of introspection, Academic Problem underachievers simply have not spent time in this kind of problem solving. The therapist must make sure that each logical connection, each defined problem, each solution is verbally stated (by the student or the therapist) and is well defined.

Once the student "owns" the goal of better grades, has seen in specific terms the logic of a connection between the current problem and future consequences, and has a specific and workable solution, there is no way to "un-recognize" these connections again. The student has been placed in a position of having to accept personal responsibility for the grades, which can no longer be perceived as happening *to* the student (unless the student decides to let it happen, in which case there is the same level of personal responsibility).

Academic Problem underachievers often begin to show mild signs of depression and restlessness at this point, reflecting a more conscious or cognitive recognition of the conflicts inherent in their motivation to underachieve.

To summarize, the therapeutic approach to this point contains four key elements. In the first, the Academic Problem students are asked to state a goal regarding school, because they have declared that they want to do better academically. They are then asked to specify in detail how they plan to accomplish this goal. They are also asked to speculate about occurrences which might hinder or block them from reaching their goals. And finally, they are asked to figure out ways in which they can counteract the hindrances and problems which have arisen.

6. Call for Action

The therapist who has followed these steps with one excuse has now laid the groundwork for dealing directly with the Academic Problem underachiever's behavior. The therapist has asked for a statement of intention (the student's goal of wanting better grades), has illuminated the specifics about the present situation, has isolated a particular excuse which presumably keeps the student from achieving, has helped the student find a solution, and has worked out the details of that solution. The time has now come for action. Yet even here, the therapist must be careful not to demand or pressure the student to respond to the therapist's expectations. The important question to ask the student here is, "OK, now what do you propose to do?" This must also be followed up with questions about the specifics: when, how much, where, in what ways, and so forth.

Another trap awaits the therapist here. Going through this process and arriving at a mutual agreement as to what the student is going to do between sessions *is no guarantee that the student will follow through. Academic Problem underachievers are predictable in that no matter what plan they may have agreed to in the session, when they return for the next session they will have completed only a small part of it*. This is, after all, the nature of their pattern of behavior; it is not likely to change after a few sessions. The therapist who is under the illusion that the student has made a firm therapeutic contract to follow through on agreements is in for a profoundly disappointing experience during the following sessions. The therapist even runs the risk of taking the lack of follow-through by the student in a personal way. Parents often report a similar reaction of anger when they believe that their child has broken a personal promise about studying. The danger in such a reaction by a therapist is that it will color responses to the lack of follow-through and insert a negative element into the relationship.

The reader may well ask why the therapist should go through this elaborate and detailed process of dealing with an excuse if the student is almost guaranteed not to follow the recommendations. In other words, what is the value of this approach if it appears to have no impact on the student's behavior? This question can be answered by considering what in fact is happening within this therapeutic approach.

The reader who rereads in detail Steps 1 through 6 thus far will notice that a great deal of attention has been paid not to what the students actually do, but to how they *perceive* what they do. The direct confrontation in this approach is not aimed at the student's behavior or for that matter even at the student's motivation; what the therapist is confronting is the student's perceptions about his or her own responsibility for academic performance. Once those perceptions have been confronted in the manner suggested, the student can never again rely on those perceptions to fool himself or herself into believing that everything is all right and nothing can be done about grades. For example, students who really believe that they "try to study an hour every night" can no longer keep up this self-deception once this excuse has been subjected to the therapeutic process we have described thus far. The students are forced to recognize that in fact they *do not* study for an hour every night.

Let us explain this another way: The aim of this approach is not necessarily to get the student to do more, but to shrink the gap between what is promised and what is actually accomplished, the gap between intentions and actions, the "crap gap." It does not matter whether the stated intentions are decreased or the actions are increased; it is important that the students begin to develop a more realistic picture of their own role in their academic performance. Faced with this recognition, Academic Problem underachievers have one of three alternatives:

1. They can recognize the excuse for what it is, admit that they don't really want to achieve, that they have purposely failed, that they have priorities other than school, and begin to deal with those issues.
2. They can continue to underachieve but simply drop this one excuse and substitute another one.
3. They can begin to achieve just in this one area by studying an hour every day but make sure that not much else changes.

As to the first alternative, the student may continue to underachieve but is now willing to take the responsibility for it as a meaningful choice (rather than continuing to perceive academic performance as something that just happens), perhaps deciding that there are other genuine priorities. While one might question whether this student is making the right decision, there is no question that the student is indeed making a decision and facing the consequences of that decision. Although some Academic Problem underachievers will eventually opt for this decision, the majority do not. Taking responsibility to study less and then have to face one's parents with this choice has additional consequences which, say, a 16-year-old may not want to deal with. Basically, the choice that any students must face if they declare that they will not work any harder in school is whether or not to stay in school. That is a decision which most Academic Problem underachievers (especially those not yet in their 20s) do not wish to face, because it would throw them into the very situation they are making every effort to avoid: becoming independent and responsible for themselves.

It is much more likely that they will choose either the second or third alternative. These students will either continue to underachieve but substitute other excuses for the one that they can no longer justify, or they will begin to achieve just in this one area so as to avoid recognizing that the underachievement is a choice. If they choose Alternative 2, the therapist will find, for example, that they still are not studying an hour a day, but they have some different set of excuses for it. (For example, "There's no place to study: it's too noisy at home and too quiet at the library.") If they choose Alternative 3, they will indeed achieve, but only a small amount and only in the specific area of the specific excuse which the therapist so diligently confronted. In either case, it is unlikely that a successful intervention into one excuse will by itself foster dramatic changes in achievement or a radical change in the Academic Problem pattern. These students would rather work just a little harder in school and continue to "get by" without significant changes in their lives.

7.   Follow-Up on Actions Called For

There is no point in going through all of the steps so far if at the following session the therapist does not ask whether the student followed through, because the likelihood is that Academic Problem underachievers will not have done so. Specifics must again be sought to ascertain what may have gone wrong. As we have stated, these students will either maintain the same study problems but with a different excuse (e.g., "I now study closer to an hour every day, but I can't get much done because I keep forgetting my books") or achieve a little more but present a new problem area which sabotages overall achievement (e.g., "I studied an hour each day this past week, but I still flunked the test yesterday because I studied the wrong material"). In either case, Academic Problem underachievers *can no longer use last week's excuse because to do so would mean recognizing that the underachievement has been a choice,* and they are strongly motivated to avoid this insight.

Therefore, the results of following up are likely to be a deletion of the excuse from the student's arsenal of excuses and the calling up of other excuses to take its place. This should lead the therapist directly to the next step.

8.   *Keep Repeating Steps 3–7 with One Different Excuse Each Time*

From the welter of excuses the student presents, the therapist now chooses one and repeats Steps 3 through 7 (or the entire procedure if necessary) with this new excuse as a focus. When this new excuse is thus deleted from the student's repertoire, the therapist focuses on another, then another, then another, and so on. It does not really matter what particular excuses and in which order; the therapist focuses on the one excuse—no matter how small or seemingly insignificant—that he or she believes is most vulnerable to the intervention procedure at that moment. It is still important to focus on details rather than generalities and to avoid interpreting the student's motivation or affect. Counselors experienced in this approach can make a smooth and rapid transition from one excuse to the next.

THERAPIST: Let's take a look at the material from last week.

STUDENT: Yeah, I did it OK, but I forgot to bring it. I left it at home. I'll bring it next time.

THERAPIST: Fine, but how come you forgot it at home?

STUDENT: Well, I left it with a pile of things in the basement where I study, so that I wouldn't forget it.

THERAPIST: You mean school stuff?

STUDENT: Right. But it was in the pile of things that I didn't have to bring to school, so I left it at home.

THERAPIST: Hmmm. What do you think might happen if you keep forgetting to bring it?

STUDENT: I guess I might forget about it.

THERAPIST: Is that what you want to have happen?

STUDENT: No, not really.

THERAPIST: Then is there anything you can think of that you can do to ensure that you won't forget it next time?

STUDENT: Yeah. I guess I could put it in the right pile.

Each intervention is followed up at the next session. It may be that one or more excuses are focused on at a particular session, but if there are too many (say, four or five major excuses), the student's cognitive field becomes overloaded and the interventions lose their impact.

Eventually, as one excuse after another is rendered useless, the Academic Problem underachiever finds it *more and more difficult to avoid the perception that he or she is responsible for what happens.* The beginnings of insight can be seen in the following interchange.

THERAPIST: So, you're putting more time into math. Is it at the level you want it to be at?

STUDENT: Almost. I'm putting in the time I've said I would.

THERAPIST: So that means you'll end up getting the grades you want in math.

STUDENT: Well, not exactly.

THERAPIST: I'm not sure what you mean. You said last time that all you needed to do was to put in about one hour in math each night, and you'd be all right in math; you'd get that *B*.

STUDENT: Yeah, but I can't always finish it in an hour. Some of those problems are tough to crack.

THERAPIST: So, what do you think you can do about it?

STUDENT: [with a dejected attitude] I'll probably have to ask someone to help me with some of the problems.

THERAPIST: "Probably"? You don't sound as if you're convinced.

STUDENT: But I'll have to! Otherwise I won't be able to solve all of the problems.

THERAPIST: So, when do you plan to do something about it?

STUDENT: This week.

THERAPIST: What do you mean?

STUDENT: I guess I'll have to do it by Thursday.

THERAPIST: You mentioned a friend. Did you have someone specific in mind?

STUDENT: Yeah, Sam. He really knows his math.

THERAPIST: Sounds great. Can anything get in the way of your meeting with him on Thursday?

STUDENT: I guess the only thing that could interfere is his schedule. I don't know when he's free. . . . (to therapist) Yeah, Yeah, I know: I'll need to ask him right away.

While there is more than a hint that this Academic Problem underachiever has begun to take responsibility for thinking through the steps necessary to solve the "problem"—getting better grades—the therapist still needs to follow through on the specific steps each time a roadblock is mentioned. There is simply no shortcut that we have been able to discover that will lead the student to begin to take on and continue to accept personal responsibility for academic performance.

Up to this point, however, therapy has *not* consisted of deep emotional content or interchanges, focus on relationships with others, or any other problem area outside of the student's initial "goal" of getting better grades. The therapist must be content to patiently and methodically plod through excuse after excuse. It is only when the Academic Problem underachiever's fund of excuses is depleted that they can no longer successfully deny the more emotionally laden material lying beneath their relatively contented psychological surface.

When the point is reached that the student has had "enough" excuses taken away, there may be a variety of reactions that accompany the recognition of responsibility: panic, depression, anxiety, anger, regret, energy towards achievement, confusion, change in several areas (friendships, grades, relationships, etc.), and intense introspection. The therapist must now cease from cycling repeatedly through Steps 3 through 8, and must make the radical shift in approach outlined in Step 9.

9.   Shift to a Nondirective Approach.

The Academic Problem underachiever begins to see and understand how school-related behavioral patterns such as procrastination and avoidance of responsibility also occur in other areas of life. As the Academic Problem underachiever continues to take on more and more personal responsibility for achievement, the focus invariably shifts to the student's own choices and how those choices really will affect his or her future. Questions begin to emerge pertaining to personal identity, values and future goals, alternatives and choices, independence and meaning.

This shift by the student must be paralleled by a shift in therapeutic approach by the therapist. The original confrontations and interventions are no longer appropriate because the student has begun to take the personal responsibility previously avoided. Continuation of the confronting and problem-solving techniques at this stage will be counterproductive to a therapeutic relationship. This is why it is so important for the therapist to have maintained a supportive, confrontive stance from the very beginning. The therapist can now capitalize on this stance, in that a trusting relationship with the student has already been established, and the student can feel comfortable in exploring issues of significance without having to test the therapeutic relationship. This exploration can be done only in an atmosphere of mutual respect, with the student taking the lead and making productive use of the therapeutic relationship. The student begins to express and struggle with important life questions: Who am I? Where am I going? Why did I allow myself to get such crummy grades? What is it I really want? What do I want my future to be?

This can be a confusing and intense series of insights for these changing Academic Problem underachievers, partly because these kinds of questions are difficult to answer and partly because these students have been actively avoiding these questions for years and they "hit" consciousness seemingly all at once.

Therefore, the therapist at this point must shift away from confrontation, intervention, detailed problem solving, and "excuse-busting" and shift to becoming a supportive, nonjudgmental listener. Without advising the student or evaluating choices or attitudes the therapist acts as a kind of sounding board for the exploration of the pros and cons of choices, the risks and opportunities, the unknowns and anxieties, the hopes and dreams. This facilitates the student's delayed journey into maturity, which is marked by the emergence of a sense of identity and self and punctuated by a range of emotions. The original focus on problem-solving cognitions has given way to the emergence of genuine emotions, which in turn leads to a fuller use of both cognition and affect. In the process, the nature of the therapist's approach has shifted to a more supportive and reflective stance.

This, then, is the pattern of successful psychotherapeutic treatment of the Academic Problem underachiever. The approach may seem simple as compared to many traditional psychotherapies, and in fact it is fairly easily learned by counselors and other mental health professionals, teachers, and parents. Nevertheless, it requires an accurate diagnosis of Academic Problem, extreme patience and tolerance for frustration, a fund of intervention strategies that can counter at least half of the student's list of excuses, the sensitivity to maintain a supportive and respectful attitude toward the student even when confronting patently absurd excuses, and the flexibility to know when and how to "shift gears" and not impede the student's own genuine self-explorations. From the Developmental Theory perspective (see Chapter 6) on normal development, the student has moved from issues of preadolescent latency to issues of adolescence.

The Academic Problem Underachiever as An Adult

As we have indicated in the chapter on the Developmental Theory Model (Chapter 6), the vicissitudes of life often intervene on Academic Problem underachievers, forcing them to face issues of responsibility and independence. After all, whether students do well or poorly, rarely can they stay in school forever. At some point choices have to be made, and these individuals may at last be confronted with the responsibility for major decisions in their lives. However, if the pattern of coasting or cruising through life persists into adulthood, change is unlikely, except of course that the underachievement no longer has to do with school. More likely, it now involves similar patterns of underachievement in career and family life.

As adults, these individuals are usually described as well adjusted, content, easygoing, and friendly, just as they were described as youngsters. They are not anxious or depressed and are rarely outlandishly impulsive. They seldom take risks in relationships or otherwise. They are trustworthy except that they never seem to attain the level of success everyone was predicting. Nevertheless, they are pleasant individuals and appear to be happy and content with their lives.

Adult Academic Problem underachievers often settle for careers requiring little initiative, independence, variety, responsibility, or opportunity. They are content to remain doing what they have been doing—day after day, year after year—without aspiring to greater career success or advancement. While they may be quite competent in what they do, they rarely initiate projects on their own or place themselves in a leadership role. They often get along well with everyone on the job, and are well liked.

In their personal lives, adult Academic Problem underachievers who marry will often choose a spouse willing to take responsibility for planning and decision making. Usually these spouses are people with high drive and energy who take responsibility for others as well as themselves. This arrangement allows Academic Problem underachievers to continue having others take personal responsibility for them. They procrastinate (especially around issues that would lead to greater personal responsibility) and use their excuses when they need them. Although their natural interpersonal style is one of pleasantness and "getting along," these individuals can be caring and loving in their marriages and as parents. Incidentally, as parents they may avoid making strong demands on their children; their child-rearing motto might read, "Let it be."

One difference between adolescent and adult Academic Problem underachievers is that the adults are much more sophisticated and even worldly in their pattern of excuses and rationalizations. This should be expected, since any adult has a substantial advantage over an adolescent in years and breadth of experience. This sophistication can be seen especially in Academic Problem underachievers who have been in psychotherapy or counseling. They usually develop an additional arsenal of excuses and rationalizations to support their continued underachieving way of life.

Those adults who fit the Academic Problem pattern but who mature psychologically without the assistance of counseling, identify the turning points in their lives as moments when someone confronted them about the gaps between their statements of intention and actions. They also report that they have become more acutely aware of what Roth, et al. (1967) have termed "characterological remnants." These are characteristics which, although modified in intensity and frequency from earlier levels, persist into the present. For example, this might include the tendency to make lists of things to do, which in the past clearly resulted in little if any follow-through. These individuals may still make lists, but they know and are willing to admit the impossibility of accomplishing everything. On the other hand, they do follow through to a much larger extent, and in many instances, successfully complete what they have committed themselves to do. In other words, the gap between intentions and actions has narrowed.

CHAPTER 13

The Identity Disorder Underachiever

General Characteristics

Recall from Chapter 5 that DSM-III-R views the Identity Disorder as an individual not suffering from any other mental disorder, but who may show symptoms of depression and anxiety, "related to inner preoccupations rather than external events" (DSM-III-R, p. 89). The predominant focus is "severe subjective distress regarding inability to integrate aspects of the self into a relatively coherent and acceptable sense of self" (p. 89). DSM-III-R points out that the turmoil around these issues can result in impaired social or occupational decision making but that the problem has to do with normal maturation processes, particularly during adolescence and midlife crisis.

Note that this description correlates with the Developmental Theory Model (Chapter 6), particularly the stage of Late Adolescence, during which struggles over defining the self and achieving psychological independence are a dominant focus of the personality structure. Any underachievement for the Identity Disorder individual is usually due to a conscious choice to set achievement as a low priority. Total energy is directed towards the inner search for identity. The behavioral, social, and interpersonal events of life become stimuli for self-observation and introspection.

Indeed, "Who am I?" and "Where am I heading?" are typical questions, and the intensity of the attempt to answer these questions leaves few internal resources for conflict-free areas such as academic achievement. Thus Identity Disorder underachievers will let achievement slide in specific academic subjects, which they often consider meaningless anyway, while actively and creatively pondering and absorbing the more personally meaningful academic subjects.

Clinically, our experience is that these individuals have such a high level of ego strength, can tolerate so much introspection, and allow themselves to experience such intense inner affect, that they are often misdiagnosed as being far more disturbed than they actually are. The intensity and openness to emotions reflects a healthy sense of the developing self rather than a disturbed or primitive personality structure. What is often labeled "schizoid thinking" in these students is actually an intensive introspective search for self-definition. Usually the Identity Disorder underachiever is introspective and self-absorbed but may show some of the rebellious characteristics of the Oppositional Defiant Disorder underachiever (see Chapter 14). Often the younger the Identity Disorder underachiever, the more oppositional characteristics will be evident. This would be predicted by the Developmental Theory Model, since oppositional behavior is more often associated with younger adolescents and questions of identity more often found with older adolescents.

Intense anxiety and depression can be present and are caused by internal processes rather than external events. Identity Disorder underachievers have doubts about themselves and their futures. Such doubts may lead them to try different and uncharacteristic modes of behavior. "Such attempts may be manifested as transient experimental phases of widely divergent behavior as the individual 'tries on' various roles" (DSM-III-R, p. 89). On the other hand, many Identity Disorder underachievers may be immobilized by their confusion and be unable to take the steps that would test their internal perceptions of self.

DSM-III-R states that one diagnostic sign is severe subjective distress regarding uncertainty about three or more of the following issues:

1. Long term goals
2. Career choice
3. Friendship patterns
4. Sexual orientation and behavior
5. Religious identification
6. Moral value system
7. Group loyalties

Often the impact of ordinary life experiences will resolve these conflicts by the time the individual reaches the mid-20s. Our clinical experience to date predicts that 10 to 15% of underachieving high school, college, and university students have personality structures consistent with this diagnostic category.

The Phenomenological World of the Identity Disorder Underachiever

The adolescent's tumultous *sturm und drang* stage of life has been chronicled by social observers, historians, religious and literary authors, artists, poets, philosophers, medical experts and other scientists, political and other leaders, and, within the past century, by sociologists, anthropologists, psychologists, educators, psychiatrists, and other mental health professionals. Unlike the Conduct Disorder underachiever, who has received little empathetic understanding, the Identity Disorder underachiever's inner perceptual and emotional world has been an attractive subject for novelists, anthropologists, playwrights, human development experts, and others, perhaps because the issues of striving to define the self are not only important to the adolescent but also significant to the meaning of human life at almost any age. Therefore, one does not have to look far to find literary and case study examples of how the world looks through the eyes of someone with Identity Disorder. Those few examples we discuss here are a minute and fairly arbitrary selection from the many available.

Stephen Dedalus, James Joyce's fictional hero in *Portrait of the Artist as a Young Man* ([1916]1972), spends much time struggling with his growing sense of a meaningful self as he becomes psychologically independent from the Irish society in which he is growing up. Toward the end of the novel, Stephen and his friend Lynch engage in a long dialogue on the nature of art and life. At one point, Stephen says,

> The soul is born. . . . It has a slow and dark birth, more mysterious than the birth of the body. When the soul of a man is born in this country there are nets flung at it to hold it back from flight. You talk to me of nationality, language, religion. I shall try to fly by those nets (p. 203).

While the context of the lengthy passage from which this excerpt was drawn is the nature of art and the artist, there are many allusions to the development of the self-concept. For example, if for the word *soul* one substitutes the word *self,* this quotation could easily be interpreted as an expression of the inner emotional world of the Identity Disorder. The confusion and mystery of the self, the struggle to break free of the "nets" that hold it back, Stephen's defiance of those nets and his resolve to seek his own way—all of these could easily fit the Identity Disorder. Similar examples can be found in many other introspective literary works.

Dr. Allen Wheelis, the well-known psychiatrist and novelist, voices many of these issues through his own essays and through the mouths of the fictional characters he creates:

> If . . . I should take the view that what I shall decide is still open—not just unknown but really open, not fixed by antecedents, unpredictable at this point by any intelligence however superior, even by Laplace's omniscient demon— I would incline to continue the struggle, to anguish over it, try to think it out, find my way. Because the decision would be mine, something made, a creation (Wheelis, 1966, p. 157).

Here, too, is the lonely searcher within the self, confused by the definition of self but determined to solve the riddle. Although the Identity Disorder's attention is so completely self-absorbed, this does not mean that there is a loss of contact with the outside interpersonal and physical environment. Identity Disorder individuals are keenly sensitive to their surroundings, to the details of their interactions with others, to what they see, hear, feel, experience. They are, if anything, supersensitive to the world. They use this sensitivity, however, to process each event, each interpersonal interaction, each experience, as a kind of symbolic clue to help them figure out who they are. Everything said to them becomes a stimulus for self-exploration. They are looking constantly for the stimulus that will finally unlock the secret of who they really are.

One can think of the inner emotional world of the Identity disorder as a whirlpool, the center of which is the problem of defining the self as an independent being. All of the Identity Disorder's energies, goals, thoughts, emotions, and perceptions become swept up in that whirlpool and are drawn into its center. Nothing else is even remotely as important. Yet at the same time, the struggle is so confusing and impossible to comprehend that no sense can be made of it whatsoever. No wonder there is little energy left for as mundane and meaningless a task as getting good grades in all courses.

Criteria for Differential Diagnosis

A. Background Information

Many parents of Identity Disorder underachievers report great concern regarding their child's tendencies either to confront authority figures (parents, teachers, and others) or to be indifferent (that is, simply not pay attention) to authority directives, opinions, demands, rules, and so forth. Parents often acknowledge the depth and sensitivity of their child and may consider this independence a strength under different circumstances. Often these students become involved in long, rambling, emotional, philosophical discussions and arguments with parents, friends, and others. Identity Disorder underachievers may challenge their parents' values. For example, they may question whether their parents have "sold out" to some stereotyped negative aspects of society or they may confront their parents' child-rearing practices. The common thread here is the challenging of adult values and lifestyles, coupled with a confused striving for one's own.

Often there is a constant battle at home regarding the parents' expectations that the Identity Disorder underachiever take school more seriously, since the parents usually believe (rightly or wrongly) that although their child's striving for independence may be healthy and even admirable, the under-achievement is not. Often these parents want their child to get a diploma ("something to fall back on"), at the very least, and are worried that the rebellion or independence of mind they witness may work against this goal. In other words, even when the parents see the strengths of their under-achieving child, they are worried that such strengths may jeopardize the child's future.

B. Diagnostic Testing

The extent to which certain characteristics will show themselves in personality testing will vary depending upon several factors, including the degree of personal discomfort. Like Oppositional Defiant Disorder individuals, Identity Disorder underachievers often show conflict with authority, although the nature of this conflict may be dramatically different from conflicts with authority exhibited by Conduct Disorder underachievers. In the Conduct Disorder, such conflicts are characterized by manipulation and the satisfaction of current impulsive needs. For Identity Disorder underachievers, however, the conflict with authority often involves a need for having others recognize the personal independence these students feel they have achieved or are due. Even when not rebellious or in conflict with authority figures, Identity Disorder underachievers have no hesitation in voicing their independent opinions, agreeing or disagreeing directly and openly in almost any situation.

There is strong evidence of introspection: a developing sense of inner focus, strength, and definition. Because of this openness and degree of introspection, they may not hesitate to give test responses that reflect their confusion, mood swings, inner conflicts, and ambivalent range of emotions. Therefore, their results on personality tests can make these individuals appear more severely pathological than they really are, and the test interpreter should note that the often strong emotional test responses tend to be expressed in relation to a range of human experiences in which questions of value and meaning predominate. Also, the particulars of these responses tend to be transient rather than a more permanent feature, so that the details of this person's test responses may appear quite different if he or she were to be retested even a few days later. In addition, these individuals express themselves by taking personal responsibility for their choices, behavior, and individual characteristics. Solutions to problems involve the students' taking action, rather than others or "fate".

Many of the above characteristics become clear on tests which provide an opportunity both for self-description and self-expression. For example, our experience is that Identity Disorder underachievers are likely to choose *Mooney Problem Checklist* items such as the following:

Having clashes of opinion with my parents
Students not given enough responsibility
Family opposing some of my plans
Wanting to leave home
Unable to discuss certain problems at home
Friends not welcomed at home
Feeling that nobody understands me
Too little chance to do what I want to do
Teachers not practicing what they preach
Too many poor teachers
Teachers lacking personality
Teachers lacking interest in students
Not getting personal help from teachers

Not knowing the kind of person I want to be

Confused as to what I really want

Feeling I am too different

In terms of academically related test measures, such as study skills surveys, Identity Disorder underachievers tend to exhibit effective study skills in courses they deem meaningful but will not utilize these solid study skills in courses they deem meaningless. In other words, they often have adequate or even excellent study skills but use them selectively.

On our 60-item *Classroom Behavior Checklist,* teachers most often describe Identity Disorder underachievers as more likely to be leaders than followers, as not needing teacher approval or reassurance, and as rarely seeming indifferent but as having opinions about a wide range of topics. Teachers also report that these students can be moody and show signs of sadness or depression but become excited when involved in personally meaningful activities. Occasionally Identity Disorder underachievers are tense or anxious, which can be positive (as when they anticipate an activity in which they want to perform well) or negative (as when they find themselves in conflict with others or involved in activities which they deem meaningless). Teachers may also report that such students arrive at class upset or preoccupied.

There are specific comments on which teachers may disagree with regard to describing the Identity Disorder underachiever, depending upon whether or not the teacher teaches a course that the Identity Disorder underachiever has decided is worthwhile. In those courses which the student has decided to abandon, teachers report that he or she is either rebellious, perhaps disrupting the class to challenge the teacher on certain issues, or indifferent, daydreaming, not participating in class discussions, seemingly preoccupied. In either case, these teachers will report that the student does not complete work assignments. They would define the student as not taking responsibility for schoolwork. In fact such students have taken full responsibility for their decision *not* to work.

C. Interview Characteristics

1. *The nature of the school performance and related issues, especially if they are problem areas*

Generally, the grades these students get are not as important to them as the meaningfulness of the topic, or whether they are recognized as maturing, independent people. They will express pleasure, involvement, and a willingness to achieve in certain classes, while emphasizing boredom, anger, and even refusal to work in others. Often these opinions are presented strongly and directly, with little hesitation about sharing them with the interviewer.

The following interview excerpt is of a 16-year-old female whose grades range from barely passing to the 90th percentile. As noted earlier, the younger the Identity Disorder person, the more prominent the characteristics of an Oppositional Defiant Disorder person; this will be obvious from the examples in this section. Nevertheless, this student, as with other Identity Disorder interviewees, is verbal, thoughtful, at times pensive, and quite involved in the substance of the interview. General affect is appropriate to what is being discussed.

INTERVIEWEE: Well, my teacher and I didn't get along too good, so I really wasn't working much in his class. I let my work go . . . It wasn't the actual work in that class that was bothering me either. It was the teacher himself . . . that I was having difficulty coping with. . . . And the way it was resolved was, like, I was just told to do my work if I wanted to play on the tennis team. Basically, I was given an ultimatum, being as I play for the school team. I was told if I didn't get the work done, I wouldn't be allowed to play. I don't think that that's really fair—they're two separate issues—but I've decided to go along for now, until the tennis is over for the year.

Notice how open this student has been about her conflict with her teacher and how in this case it was this conflict which determined her level of work in that particular class. She forms her own independent judgment as to the meaning of this situation ("they're two separate issues") and evaluates it independently (in not thinking it is "fair"). Note also that her choice of language reflects her recognition that she is responsible for her own behavior and even her reactions in the situation. This is indicated in her remark that because she doesn't get along with her teacher, she was not working in his class. She also says that it was *she* who was having difficulty coping with this teacher. Notice also the comment, "*I've* decided to go along for now," which certainly indicates independent decision making and impulse control rather than rebellion as determining her decision. She is also not hesitant to share this with the interviewer. All of these characteristics are unique to the Identity Disorder underachiever and almost sufficient in and of themselves to reach an initial diagnostic speculation.

When the interviewer in this instance asks for more details about conflicts with the teacher, the student mentions that he is a "tyrant" whom other students "simply go along with":

INTERVIEWER: And you've found that difficult to do.
INTERVIEWEE: Yeah, mainly because I don't respect him.
INTERVIEWER: And what's that about?
INTERVIEWEE: Well, he tends to pick on other students who are not doing that well, even those who are trying. He tries to put them down. And I don't think that's right.

This Identity Disorder underachiever is clearly protesting an injustice by an authority figure as represented by the classroom teacher, and it is this conflict which initially determines how much the student will study in this class. Once again, the issue of academic achievement is a secondary consideration to this student. However, this rebellious pattern is also a characteristic of the Oppositional Defiant Disorder underachiever. The difference is that the Identity Disorder underachiever is less likely to feel the need to constantly confront the teacher openly and less likely to base a final decision on the need to rebel. If the above student were an Oppositional Disorder underachiever, for example, she never would have decided to study in order to protect her place on the tennis team. She would have openly opposed the teacher, even to the point of negative personal consequences.

Here is an example of an attitude towards a course in which the student is moderately interested.

INTERVIEWER: What else are you taking?

INTERVIEWEE: Theatre Arts. We learn about drama a bit, and about how the theater works. Right now we're learning the basics of acting, and what goes on on stage. Next year we're supposed to be doing more things in depth, and we'll be getting to the stuff I think is important for me—production of plays, building and designing sets, stuff like that.

INTERVIEWER: How are you doing in Theatre Arts?

INTERVIEWEE: Well, I'm not doing as well as I could, but I know why. The teacher thinks that there is only one way to express yourself on the stage, like only one method that really works. That's a bit out to lunch, you know. And she pushes all the students to fit into that one mold, which is kind of stupid.

INTERVIEWER: So how are you doing in it?

INTERVIEWEE: I'm getting about 60%. I've turned in a few assignments which I just knew she wouldn't look at because they weren't done exactly the way she wanted them done. So I lost marks because of it. I really don't care, though.

Obviously, she likes the course but not the teacher. She purposely does unacceptable work (although it is not clear whether the work is actually poor) because of her attitude towards the teacher, yet there is enough interest so that she is not failing the course. In courses that this Identity Disorder underachiever happens to like or in which the teacher is not objectionable, she is likely to achieve.

INTERVIEWEE: Man and Society is one course I really enjoy. We spend hours talking about different cultures, different societies, sort of different ways of living. I've spent a lot of time on that course. I'm getting about 90% in it . . . I just choose [in Physics] what to do from the assignment, and go after it. I really don't like things thrust on me if I can't do them in the way that I feel comfortable with them. I suppose that's less so for physics, but even there, I like to see how what we're learning connects to other things.

This student places such an overwhelming emphasis on the value and meaning of her relationship with her teachers as well as on the content of the courses, that she has a clear recognition that she is *choosing* her level of achievement—high or low—depending on the course and the teacher. She recognizes and takes full responsibility for her perceptions, her attitudes, her choices, and her behavior. At one point later in this interview, she states, "I know I could do better . . . but I don't want to do better." This is the type of statement which the Identity Disorder underachiever, more than any other category we discuss in this book, is likely to make.

For Identity Disorder underachievers, the underachievement is a by-product either of a lack of energy and focus (because the introspective process absorbs most of the student's inner resources) or of an act of rebellion (e.g., an action demonstrating that the tyrannical teacher has no control over the student and cannot force the student to do anything).

2. *The nature of family relationships*

More than in any other diagnostic category, a generation gap is most obvious here. While relationships with siblings can run the gamut from positive to negative and conflictual, relationships with parents are likely to be rocky, even when parents and children have a basically good relationship. Due to the intensified needs for psychological independence, Identity Disorder underachievers are likely to be overly sensitive to differences between themselves and their parents and see them as part of a past generation whose values may no longer be relevant.

INTERVIEWEE: Mom gets on my case more than Dad, but generally they think the same way anyway. They both think that I should do well and graduate. They don't seem to understand that it's not always easy dealing with teachers.

INTERVIEWER: What kind of people are your mom and dad?

INTERVIEWEE: Well, actually they're pretty good, generally; except that they are old-fashioned in their thinking. . . . They have all these rules and regulations about when I have to be in, who I can make friends with, that sort of stuff.

INTERVIEWER: How do you handle these limits?

INTERVIEWEE: Well, I keep at them about how unfair some of those rules are. And gradually they've changed some, but it's really been hard—taken a lot of my pushing.

Note here, too, how the Identity Disorder underachiever is dealing with parents almost as if she is an equal rather than simply as an underling looking up at authority figures. There is also for this particular individual a real sense of energy available to fully involve herself in goals and interactions with others. This may not be the case with those Identity Disorder underachievers who are less openly rebellious, more depressed, and more focused on introspective issues.

When discussing conflicts with parents, Identity Disorder underachievers are likely to focus on confrontations relating to independence issues. As in the preceding excerpt, the students' arguments with parents revolve around questions of following rules and regulations as opposed to having the freedom to make independent decisions. Identity Disorder underachievers do see these differences in terms of generation differences. They also feel that, in the interest of their own independent selves, they do not want to lead the same kind of lives as their parents have lived, which Identity Disorder students tend to perceive as superficial, meaningless, and somehow chained to boring rituals and patterns.

INTERVIEWEE: But you know, he [her father] is getting a little older, and he seems to be thinking about changing his line of work. I guess if I were him, I wouldn't want to do what he's been doing all of my life. He's gotten into a rut sort of. I think if he was 10 years younger and didn't have a family, he might risk something new. But it's like all the years seem to have caught up to him, if you know what I mean.

INTERVIEWER: So he just seems to be putting in his time.

INTERIVEWEE: Exactly. I'd never want to be caught in that situation. He has some good ideas, I think, but he doesn't seem ready to try them.

Except for conflict situations involving questions of independence and autonomy, Identity Disorder underachievers tend not to be involved with their parents or home life as much as with their lives outside the home. For example, when asked later in the interview how much time she spends with her parents, this student replies "Not a lot. We go out every so often to eat, or maybe to visit relatives. But mostly I like to spend my time with myself or with friends." In fact, the student's life outside the home is where most of the time and energy is focused, whether the person is an achieving or underachieving Identity Disorder.

3. *The nature of social relationships (peers, the opposite sex, etc.)*

Peer relationships tend to be intense, involved, and important to Identity Disorder underachievers. The endless discussions about the self, relationships with others, the future, and the meaning of life take place for the most part within close friendships, and the need for such friendships is strong.

Identity Disorder individuals receive understanding, support, and perspectives on identity from each other. Note how the student in our example even develops a similar relationship with her older sister.

INTERVIEWEE: She's [sister] older, by about three years. I guess because we're closer in our ideas about life, when compared with my parents' ideas, that we're close to each other.

INTERVIEWER: So if you had some serious problem that you wanted to talk to someone about. . . .

INTERVIEWEE: Right! I'd talk to my sister. Like she could give me advice, cause she's just gone through some of the things that I'm going through now. . . .

INTERVIEWER: Do you have any friends outside of your sister?

INTERVIEWEE: Sure, but not that many. I'm the type of person who likes to have a few really good friends, and we stick close to each other.

The peer relationships which Identity Disorders value most are those where there is respect for and curiosity about many experiences, a willingness to listen to and discuss issues of mutual importance, and a sense of understanding and acceptance. Interestingly, if Identity Disorder underachievers do have a good relationship with their parents, it tends to resemble more of a peer relationship than one between individuals of different generations. In such instances, it is not uncommon to hear students say that they can talk to their parents "like a friend," that their parents are understanding, and other such comments.

4. The nature of the student's self-perceptions and affect

For diagnostic purposes, it is not necessarily important what Identity Disorder underachievers say about how they perceive themselves. Some, in fact, may have little to say and actually be overwhelmed or confused by the question. What is important for the interviewer is to note the intense introspection around this question, the total inner involvement the student has in responding to it. This can even be seen in students who are practically silent on this issue. For example, the interviewer might say, "Describe yourself, as a person."

In response, some Identity Disorder underachievers may very well mumble "I don't know," or heave a heavy sigh, but the interviewer will notice that the student's body language, facial expression, eye focus, and momentary pause in responding indicate intense attention and concentration to inner processes, as if this interviewer's prompt has hit the student like a thunderbolt. This is as much a solid piece of evidence of openness, introspection, and involvement in self as the often extensive verbalizations of other Identity Disorder individuals. The students may not be defensive with the interviewer at all, but rather immediately use the interviewer's verbalizations as further opportunities for self-exploration.

In the following excerpt, the interviewer approaches the self-concept issue by inquiring how the student's friends perceive her.

INTERVIEWER: If I approached one of your friends and asked them to tell me what kind of a person you are, what do you think they would tell me?

INTERVIEWEE: Wow! That's a good question. I guess they would say that I'm . . . hmmm, yeah, I guess they would say that I'm the type of person who tells it like it is . . . [pauses] . . . I suppose they would also say that I care a lot about people—about things—that I'm a loyal friend; stuff like that.

INTERVIEWER: OK . . . How would you describe yourself? Would it be different from the ways they have described you?

INTERVIEWEE: [Pauses] Not really different, I guess . . . except that I would add that I can be very sensitive at times. I guess I'm *not* the type of person you would call dull . . . [pause] . . . And I also think that I'm not the type of girl who suppresses her intelligence just because of pressure from other girls. I'm the type of person who expresses herself a little more than others usually do.

Like many Identity Disorder underachievers, her responses to the questions of self-concept are introspective, elaborate, and have a thoughtful, considered quality, although these answers are not often systematic, well organized, or even clear. Yet these individuals are likely to spend a great deal of time and energy thinking about themselves in this confusing manner, always with the sense that they are trying to answer the question, "Who am I?"

Interviewers who question whether their interviewees spend a lot of time thinking about themselves will find that Identity Disorder underachievers generally respond affirmatively.

5. *The student's perceptions of and plans for the future*

Identity Disorder underachievers may or may not have future plans. If they do not, then their uncertainty usually becomes an expression of their confusion over their self-concept, almost as if they are saying, "If I can figure out who I am, then I can know what kind of career I will want and what my future will be. But I can't figure out who I am yet." Those who do have plans for the future express them in a variety of ways, and there is little of diagnostic significance in any particular response. However, Identity Disorder individuals will show the same kinds of independence and involvement in considering future plans as they do in other issues.

INTERVIEWER: What sorts of things do you think you'll be doing [10 years from now]?

INTERVIEWEE: Hmmm . . . I'm not absolutely positive, but I'd like to have a job as a draftsman.

INTERVIEWER: Anything else about the future?

INTERVIEWEE: Yes, I'd like to be involved with someone I love. We might not be married yet, but I'd like to find a guy who's special.

INTERVIEWER: What sort of guy would that be? What would he be like?

INTERVIEWEE: Thoughtful . . . willing to let me have my say, and not put me down for having my own ideas, even though some of my ideas may not agree with his . . . but, I'd want him to have some of his own ideas, too.

The general tone of the responses above is one of meeting the future directly and openly, even though future plans have not yet been worked out in detail.

Practical Diagnosis

Like Overanxious and Conduct Disorder underachievers, Identity Disorder underachievers present a wide variety of interpersonal, affective, cognitive, and behavioral characteristics. Even though Identity Disorder individuals share an intense introspection, independence of thought, responsibility for choices, and other characteristics we have already discussed, they can vary widely across most of the standard diagnostic dimensions: depression, hostility, anxiety, energy level, and so forth. For example, where one Identity Disorder underachiever may be talkative, argumentative, and energetic in the interview, another may be sad, quiet, and thoughtful. Some may appear overconcerned with their school performance or their relationships with parents, whereas others may not appear to be concerned about anything outside of an introspective struggle to define who they are.

The demands on the therapist will vary as widely as the various "shades and colors" of personality characteristics within this group. As we have already indicated, successful therapy with this group requires a nonjudgmental, accepting stance on the part of the therapist. However, some Identity Disorder underachievers will be helped more by a therapist who is active, energetic, and evocative; others by one who is quiet and simply an empathic listener.

Differential Treatment Considerations

As mentioned earlier, most attempts by adults to demand a specific response from the Identity Disorder underachiever are perceived as an expectation incongruent with the student's developing value system and are therefore rejected. This student does not seek out solutions that others have adopted but wishes to weigh and consider a full range of solutions prior to making a commitment. Pushing even what may appear to be an ideal solution may result in these individuals reacting negatively, at least initially.

A more productive approach might be to help the student develop a sense of self-concept, a process which depends on empathy with the student's internal struggle for self-definition. Phrasing ideas for *consideration* rather than automatic *acceptance* produces more effective outcomes. Points where the students have become stuck and immobilized in working out their sense of self can be explored in a nonjudgmental way. These students have the inner strength to generate alternatives, and will respond openly and constructively within a nonjudgmental interchange in which they can freely explore issues without feeling prejudged or evaluated. The client-centered approach pioneered by Carl Rogers (1951) appears tailor-made for this type of individual. This nondirective therapy is effective with Identity Disorder underachievers because it gives them an emotionally accepting sounding board which can allow them to focus on their internal self-perceptions and concerns.

Further, we have found that forming discussion groups comprised of students, all of whom fit the Identity Disorder personality style, can produce dramatic and rapid results. These students often thrive on in-depth discussions with like-minded individuals, especially if the group leader is expert enough to allow exploration of any and all relevant issues without projecting even the mildest of expectations and judgments.

The Identity Disorder Underachiever as an Adult

As we have indicated, the Identity Disorder problem usually becomes resolved by the time the person reaches the mid-20s. The personality structure here is so open to experience, so involved in intense personal relationships, so introspective and self-exploring, so invested in achieving a well-defined independent self, that resolution of this problem usually is inevitable within a few years. There is almost no controversy that this problem represents a stage in maturational development, and that its peak is the age range from midadolescence to the mid-20s. Identity Disorder underachievers spend so much energy and thought in productive resolution of this problem that, like an exploding star, their available energy eventually is dissipated. Time itself and familiarity with the problem soon cool the fires of intense introspection, and these people proceed with their lives.

Perhaps the above reasons explain why in clinical practice one is likely to encounter few adult Identity Disorder individuals, especially underachievers. Every so often, however, we will meet one, and the usual pattern is of a person who continues to experience difficulties in career commitments and personal relationships. The experience of these problems is much as one would expect: intense introspection, confusing questions about the definition of self, and almost painfully self-critical openness to exploring the nature of the inner self. Often there is quite an overlap between the Identity Disorder as an adult and the midlife crisis. DSM-III-R sees the midlife crisis as falling into the Identity Disorder category (p. 90), and there is indeed a significant similarity. However, there are also some important although subtle differences.

Adults in midlife crisis are painfully introspective and on a confusing inner search, but the issue of who they are (that is, how they would define themselves as individuals, what their "self-boundaries" are like) is less significant. For these older individuals, the major identity issues revolve around disappointments and the degree to which they have become disillusioned during the primary working years (ages 25–45). They are confronting themselves about the time and energy that they have already used and are struggling with how to resolve future energy commitments. Previously valued choices may no longer carry the same meaning they had 20 years earlier. The individual struggling with a midlife crisis is looking back, questioning the meaning of a life more than half over.

Identity Disorder underachievers are looking forward, questioning meaning, without yet having committed energy and time to the actual journey. They are much more specifically concerned with how they would define themselves.

To put this distinction another way, the person in midlife crisis is concerned about meaningful choices in the real world; the person with Identity Disorder is concerned about perceiving and defining the self. This is a subtle difference of focus, and in the diagnostic situation it may not always be clear or easy to discern, especially since both types of adults are talking about the same category of life events: marriage, family, career, and so forth.

Like their younger counterparts, adult Identity Disorder underachievers tend to be open to relationships and willing to involve themselves totally in a therapeutic dialogue. The prognosis is usually considered good.

CHAPTER 14

The Oppositional Defiant Disorder Underachiever

There are other personality types who may be classified as underachievers, but they occur infrequently and have problems that are considered far more important than underachievement. We will briefly discuss one in this chapter: the Oppositional Defiant Disorder underachiever (DSM-III-R 313.81).

This student shares certain characteristics with the Conduct Disorder underachiever and a few characteristics with the Identity Disorder underachiever, but there also features unique to this category. The major characteristic is a pattern of outright rebellion against anyone perceived as representing authority or "the system." This rebellion is often open in its provocativeness and its resistance to perceived rules and demands of authority figures. Unlike Conduct Disorders, however, Oppositional Defiant Disorders do *not* generally violate codes of conduct or the basic rights of others. In fact, there is a feeling of deep comaraderie with peers; the oppositional attitude is aimed squarely at teachers, parents, and other authority figures. This is the category which Chapter 6 on the Developmental Theory Model equates to an early adolescent stage of development, when the person externalizes the independence-dependence conflict and defines independence as doing the opposite of what is expected. These individuals are, in effect, in an ongoing, never-ending adolescent rebellion against the world.

On the other hand, it is important for the diagnostician to recognize that oppositionality in and of itself can be found in any diagnostic category, least likely perhaps in the Overanxious Disorder group. While oppositionality is the hallmark of the Oppositional Defiant Disorder underachiever, it alone is not sufficient to differentially diagnose this group. The nature of the oppositionality may vary across diagnostic categories: Identity Disorder underachievers may be more direct and open, whereas Academic Problem underachievers express their resistance in a more passive-aggressive manner. Conduct Disorder underachievers, of course, may be openly oppositional, not to assert independence but to manipulate others.

Examples of Oppositional Defiant Disorder behavior include the following:

1. When a suggestion is made by an authority figure, Oppositional Defiant Disorder underachievers are automatically against it. Conversely, when a like-minded friend makes a suggestion, they are automatically for it.

2. When any authority figure even politely invites these students to do something, they usually refuse or become embroiled in an argument as to why they should be free to refuse.
3. If asked to cease what they are doing, they will feel compelled to continue rather than stop the activity.

In other words, Oppositional Defiant Disorder underachievers base their actions on how they are treated by others rather than on their own internal goals. Obviously, with this kind of priority, academic achievement is often sacrificed in the battle. As youngsters, the students will often have had a history of temper tantrums and stubborn dawdling, sometimes having begun during the terrible-twos stage of development. But they themselves continue to see all of their problems as being caused by others. Nevertheless, they rarely exhibit persistent lying or violation of major rules of conduct (e.g., truancy), nor do they become involved in theft, vandalism, or other illegal or otherwise antisocial behavior.

DSM-III-R lists a number of diagnostic criteria for identifying the Oppositional Defiant Disorder, of which at least five must be present over a 6-month period. These include:

1. Loss of temper
2. Argumentativeness with adult authority figures
3. Active defiance of adult requests or limits
4. A pattern of deliberate annoyance of other people
5. Blame placed on others for own actions and problems
6. Easily annoyed by others
7. Frequently angry and bitter
8. Involved in spiteful or vindictive actions
9. Uses vulgar or coarse language

Oppositional Defiant Disorder underachievers do not have the same impulse-ridden, "me first" quality of Conduct Disorders, and are in fact quite altruistic when it comes to those they perceive as "victims of the system." However, Conduct Disorder underachievers do exhibit all of the characteristics of the Oppositional Defiant Disorder, and when violation of the basic rights of others are included, a diagnosis of Conduct Disorder underachiever is appropriate (i.e., will supercede a diagnosis of Oppositional Defiant Disorder underachiever).

Oppositional Defiant Disorder underachievers may also be misdiagnosed as Identity Disorder underachievers, in that they are vitally concerned about their independence and about making their own decisions. Unlike persons with Identity Disorder, however, they are rarely involved in cooperative activities with authority figures. Whereas Identity Disorder students may choose to involve themselves in a meaningful and cooperative way with a teacher they respect, Oppositional Defiant Disorder underachievers base everything on the fact that the teacher is an authority figure and they will generally refuse to cooperate. They are quick to specify what they will *not* do and what they are *against* but are not as proficient at delineating what they actually want to do or what they stand for. It is in opposition to others that they anchor behavior and attitude.

Their persistence in this response style has been noted by Rachman (1980), who discusses the compulsive component of oppositional behavior. This compulsive element maintains the problematic behavior even in the face of conflict and negative consequences. Meyer and Osborne (1987) view oppositional behavior as ". . . goal-directed (aimed toward emotional autonomy and independent thinking), but not goal attaining (usually resulting in descriptors such as immature or irresponsible)'' (p. 254).

Also, we suspect that the major affective component of Oppositional Defiant Disorder underachievers—anger—is not always masked or hidden, although it may not be directly expressed. For the Oppositional Defiant Disorder underachiever, satisfaction comes from making life difficult for others.

In any case, Oppositional Defiant Disorder underachievers are likely to give teachers, parents, and others so much trouble that they are readily identified. However, they may also be misdiagnosed due to characteristics that overlap with other personality categories. For example, their negativism and disobedience usually does not include a violation of the rights of others as is the case for Conduct Disorders. The Identity Disorder underachiever may also show negativism and disobedience, but this is usually based on questions of deeply felt values and principles.

It is difficult to gauge the prevalence of this personality type in the underachieving population because few of these students cooperate in research or clinical services run by those in authority. When they do appear, the adult diagnostic DSM-III-R label most often used would be Passive-Aggressive Personality Disorder (301.84), in which, among other things, intentional inefficiency is a differentiating personality characteristic.

PART FIVE

Conclusions

We have presented the research literature on underachievement and delineated theoretical, research, and clinical material related to our differential diagnosis and differential treatment model for underachievement. In this last section we will briefly summarize our work.

CHAPTER 15

A Final Word on Differential Diagnosis and Differential Treatment

Now that the reader has an understanding of each of the most frequently seen personality types of underachievers, we will briefly summarize the distinguishing features of each type. Table 15.1 provides an opportunity to rapidly assess the spectrum of crucial characteristics across diagnostic categories.

Our major aim throughout this book has been to emphasize the different personality types within the underachieving group. Table 15.1 focuses on these major qualitative differences. An understanding of these differences, when compared in this concise and direct manner, leads to strikingly different treatment goals for each personality type. Sensitivity to differential diagnosis and treatment can lead to greatly increased understanding of underachievement and improved clinical effectiveness.

The authors trust that this book has given the reader a more comprehensive (or at least more thought-provoking) look at the relationship between underachievement and personality. We also hope that the reader has a clearer picture of the personality types commonly found in underachieving students, a well-considered knowledge of differential diagnosis and its use, an appreciation of the direct link between differential diagnosis and differential treatment, an overview of professional literature relevant to this area, and an interest in research possibilities. Beyond all this, we hope that there will be an increased ability to balance diagnostic skills on the one hand with an appreciation of the uniqueness of each individual on the other. We believe that whether one agrees or disagrees with our model, it is possible to fill the gaps among theory, research, and practice and arrive at a coherent systematic approach that lends itself both to rigorous scientific research and to clinical practice.

Before concluding our discussion, however, we need to consider two additional aspects of this model: aspects of the diagnostic process itself, and the likelihood of multiple diagnoses.

Ideally, the diagnostic process should include the diagnostic interview, testing, and the procurement of relevant background information from the client and others. No matter how certain a clinician may be of a diagnostic judgment based on interview data, he or she should seek independent con-

TABLE 15.1.   Summary of Core Characteristics and Treatment Focus Specific to Each
Underachieving Type

Diagnostic category	Core characteristics	Treatment focus
Overanxious Disorder	Excessive anxiety Dependence upon approval and reassurance from authority	Reduction of anxiety
Conduct Disorder	Impulsivity Lack of conscience Manipulativeness	Delay of gratification Self-control
Academic Problem	Apparent lack of motivation Excuses for underachievement Procrastination	Closure of gap between intentions and performance

Identity Disorder	Introspective focus on self-
	  concept
	Emphasis on values and
	  choices
	Establishment of independence
		Enhancment of developing
		  self
		Support for independent
		  decision making

Oppositional Defiant
  Disorder
	Negativism
	Oppositionality
	Stubbornness
		Fostering of self-enhancing vs.
		  self-defeating choices
		Avoidance of power struggles

firmation from test data and from other sources (such as parents, teachers, or counselors). Only when the diagnosis made on the basis of the interview is clearly consistent with these other types of data can the clinician suggest, with some certainty, a diagnosis.

Yet even here, the diagnostic judgment may change, perhaps because of new information or a previously unnoticed type of interaction in the interview. The clinician must be willing at any point in the diagnostic process to question how well the diagnosis fits the data, and not vice versa. The data, after all, constitute actual events and reactions related to the client, whereas diagnostic theories do not. A practical rule of thumb is to consider a diagnosis accurate only if it can be meaningfully rationalized as explaining each and every item of client behavior, from every specific utterance in an interview to every response on assessment measures to every reported event in the client's background.

We believe that it is a mistake to disregard differential diagnostic questions after a diagnostic has been made. It is the clinician's continuing responsibility to scrutinize again and again every diagnostic judgment from the first minute of the first diagnostic session to the terminating session after two years of psychotherapy.

The second aspect of our model concerns multiple diagnoses as part of the Practical Diagnosis. Often in the real world, problems are not so easily or neatly categorized in the ways we have presented in this book. A given Academic Problem underachiever's school problems may be compounded by the presence of a learning disability, a family situation in which the parents are seeking a divorce, or perhaps both. An Overanxious Disorder underachiever may have transferred from a school in which he or she received inadequate preparation for the current school placement. A Conduct Disorder underachiever may currently be in legal trouble for shoplifting, and in addition may have a history of hyperactivity.

Any of these and other compounded problems require the most careful and thorough Practical Diagnosis to decide which aspect of the underachievement is due to what cause and then to decide which treatment modality has the highest priority. For example, as a result of a thorough differential diagnosis, it may be decided that the Conduct Disorder underachiever just described requires referral to a physician to assess the hyperactivity and immediate counseling to intervene on self-defeating behavior. On the other hand, it may be decided that this type of personality will not voluntarily follow any treatment recommendations, and that the first step is to seek legal guidance from the court to compel the student to accept treatment.

This book began with an historical analogy: the use of the early microscope to discover complexities in substances previously considered ordinary and uncomplicated. We hope that this book has now given the reader the metaphoric equivalent of a modern electron microscope—through which clearer and more comprehensive details can be seen. If as a result the reader has gained a clearer perception of our topic, we are of course pleased, but we are also gratified by the reader who may not agree with our presentation but who has been stimulated to approach underachievement in new and creative ways.

Bibliography

This list includes not only all references made in the text, but also a bibliographic listing of references on underachievement from 1927 to mid-1987.

Abicht, M. (1976). Black children and their environment. *College Student Journal, 10*(2), 142–152.

Abrams, D. (1949). When we know. . . . *Childhood Education, 25*, 350–353.

Adams, R. L., & Phillips, B. N. (1972). Motivation and achievement differences among children of various ordinal birth positions. *Child Development, 43*, 155–164.

Adas, A-R. (1964). Patterns of achievement in the Jordanian schools. *Dissertation Abstracts, 24*(12), 5524.

Adelman, H. S. (1966). The effects of social reinforcement upon achievement expectancy in underachieving and achieving boys. *Dissertation Abstracts, 27*(6-B), 2128.

Adelman, H. S. (1969). Reinforcing effects of adult non-reaction on expectancy of underachieving boys. *Child Development, 40*(1), 111–122.

Adelman, H. S. & Chaney, L. A. (1982). Impact of motivation on task performance of children with and without psychoeducational problems. *Journal of Learning Disabilities, 15*, 242–244.

Adler, A. (1951). *The Practice and Theory of Individual Psychology*, (P. Radin, Trans.) New York: Humanities Press.

Adlerblum, E. D. (1947). Mental hygiene begins in school. *Mental Hygiene, N.Y., 31*, 541–555.

Agarwal, S. K. (1977a). A psycho-social study of academic underachievement. *Indian Educational Review, 12*(2), 105–110.

Agarwal, S. K. (1977b). Personality traits of under- and over-achieving boys of Class XI. *Asian Journal of Psychology & Education, 2*(1), 42–44.

Aguilera, A. (1954). School failure—psychiatric complications. *Journal of Child Psychiatry, 3*, 88–92.

Ahmann, J. S., Smith, W. J., & Glock, M. D. (1958). Predicting academic success in college by means of a study habits and attitude inventory. *Educational & Psychological Measurement, 18*, 853–857.

Ahn, H. (1978). Electroencephalographic evoked potential comparisons of normal children and children with different modes of underachievement. *Dissertation Abstracts International, 38*(7-B), 3453.

Allbright, L. E., Glennon, J. R., & Siegert, P. A. (1963). Measuring achievement motivation at the time of employment. *Journal of Industrial Psychology, 1*(2), 59–65.

Allen, D. A. (1971). Underachievement is many-sided. *Personnel & Guidance Journal, 49*(7), 529–532.

Allen, R. F. (1975). The development of the Student Behavior Inventory: An instrument to aid in the identification and categorization of academic underachievers by observing their behavior. *Dissertation Abstracts International, 36*(1-A), 122–123.

Allen, V. L., & Atkinson, M. L. (1978). Encoding of nonverbal behavior by high-achieving and low-achieving children. *Journal of Educational Psychology, 70*(3), 298–305.

Allen, V. L., & Feldman, R. S. (1973). Learning through tutoring: Low-achieving children as tutors. *Journal of Experimental Education, 42*(1), 1–5.

Almeida, C. H. (1968). Children's perceptions of parental authority and love, school achievement and personality. *Dissertation Abstracts International, 29*, 3863-A.

Altmann, H. A., Conklin, R. C., & Hughes, D. C. (1972). Group counselling of underachievers. *Canadian Counsellor, 6*(2), 112–115.

Altus, W. (1948). A college achiever and non-achiever scale for the MMPI. *Journal of Applied Psychology, 32*, 385–397.

Altus, W. (1962). Sibling order and scholastic aptitude. *American Psychologist, 17*, 304–307.

Altus, W. (1965). Birth order and scholastic aptitude. *Journal of Consulting and Clinical Psychology, 29*, 202–205.

Alwin, D., & Thornton, A. (1984). Family origins and the schooling process: Early versus late influence of parental characteristics. *American Sociological Review, 49*, 784–802.

American Heritage Dictionary of the English Language. (1973). New York: Houghton Mifflin.

American Psychiatric Association. (1980). *Diagnostic and Statistical Manual* (3rd ed.). Washington, DC: Author.

American Psychiatric Association. (1987). *Diagnostic and Statistical Manual of Mental Disorders* (3rd ed.–Rev.). Washington, DC: Author.

Anastasi, A. (1956). Intelligence and family size. *Psychological Bulletin, 53*, 187–209.

Anastasi, A. (1965). *Individual differences,* New York: Wiley.

Anastasi, A. (1976). *Psychological Testing* (4th ed.). New York: MacMillan.

Anderson, C. A., & Jennings, D. L. (1980). When experiences of failure promote expectations of success: The impact of attributing failure to ineffective strategies. *Journal of Personality, 48*, 393–407.

Anderson, E. (1985). Forces influencing student persistence and achievement. In L. Noel, R. Levitz & D. Saluri, *Increasing student retention.* San Francisco: Jossey-Bass.

Anderson, J. P. (1970). Reading and writing can be fun for the underachiever. *English Journal, 59*, 1119–1121, 1127.

Anderson, J. R. (1954). Do college students lack motivation? *Personnel and Guidance Journal, 33*, 209–210.

Andrew, D. C. (1956). Relationship between academic load and scholastic success of deficient students. *Personnel and Guidance Journal, 34*, 268–270.

Andrews, W. R. (1971). Behavioral and client-centered counseling of high school underachievers. *Journal of Counseling Psychology, 18*(2), 93–96.

Anikeef, A. M. (1954). The relationship between class absences and college grades. *Journal of Educational Psychology, 45*, 244–249.

Annell, A-L. (1949). School problems in children of average or superior intelligence: a preliminary report. *Journal of Mental Science, 95*, 901–909.

Annesley, F., Odhmer, F., Madoff, E., & Chansky, N. (1970). Identifying the first grade underachiever. *Journal of Educational Research, 63*, 459–462.

Anthony, E. J., & Benedek, R. (Eds.). (1970). *Parenthood.* Boston: Little, Brown.

Arieti, S. (1974). An overview of schizophrenia from a predominantly psychological approach. *American Journal of Psychiatry, 131*, 241–249.

Arkava, M. L. (1969). Alterations in achievement motivation through counseling intervention. *Journal of Secondary Education, 44*, 74–80.

Armstrong, M. E. (1955). *A comparison of the interests and social adjustments of under-*

achievers at the secondary school level. Unpublished doctoral dissertation, University of Connecticut.

Aronson, E., & Carlsmith, J. (1962). Performance expectancy as a determinant of actual performance. *Journal of Abnormal and Social Psychology, 65,* 178–182.

Arulsigamoni, A. (1973). The relationship between self-concept and school achievement in low-achieving, junior high school children and the effect of counseling intervention on self-concept. *Dissertation Abstracts International, 34*(1-A), 187–188.

Asbury, C. A. (1973). A review of literature concerned with selected factors influencing over- and underachievement in young, school-age children. *Catalog of Selected Documents in Psychology, 3,* 62.

Asbury, C. A. (1974). Selected factors influencing over- and underachievement in young school-age children. *Review of Educational Research, 44*(4), 409–428.

Asbury, C. A. (1975). Maturity factors related to discrepant achievement of White and Black first graders. *Journal of Negro Education, 44*(4), 493–501.

Astin, A. W. (1964). Personal and environmental factors associated with college dropouts among high aptitude students. *Journal of Educational Psychology, 55*(4), 219–227.

Atkinson, J. W. (1950). Studies in projective measurement of achievement motivation. *Microfilm Abstracts, 10*(4), 290–291.

Atkinson, J. W., & Birch, D. (1978). *Introduction to motivation* (2nd ed.). New York: Van Nostrand.

Atkinson, J. W., & Feather, N. T. (1966). *A theory of achievement motivation.* New York: Wiley.

Attwell, A. A. (1968). Some factors that contribute to underachievement in school: A suggested remedy. *Elementary School Guidance & Counseling, 3*(2), 98–103.

Ausubel, D. P., Schiff, H. M., & Goldman, M. (1953). Qualitative characteristics in the learning process associated with anxiety. *Journal of Abnormal Social Psychology, 48,* 537–547.

Bach, P. W. (1976). A theory-based screening device for the identification and classification of underachieving children in the early elementary grades. *Dissertation Abstracts International, 36* (9-A), 5985.

Bachor, D. G. (1979). Suggestions for modifications in testing low-achieving adolescents. *Journal of Special Education, 13*(4), 443–452.

Bachtold, L. M. (1969). Personality differences among high ability underachievers. *Journal of Educational Research, 63*(1), 16–18.

Bagley, C. (1979). A comparative perspective on the education of Black children in Britain. *Comparative Education, 15,* 63–81.

Bahe, V. R. (1969). Reading-study instruction and college achievement. *Reading Improvement, 6*(3), 57–61.

Bailey, R. C. (1971). Self-concept differences in low and high achieving students. *Journal of Clinical Psychology, 27*(2), 188–191.

Baither, R. C., & Godsey, R. (1979). Rational emotive education and relaxation training in large group treatment of test anxiety. *Psychological Reports, 45*(1), 326.

Baker, G. S. (1949). I can learn to take care of myself—the case of Robert. *Childhood Education, 25,* 227–230.

Baker, H. S. (1975). The treatment of academic underachievement. *Journal of the American College Health Association, 24*(1), 4–7.

Baker, H. S. (1979). The conquering hero quits: Narcissistic factors in underachievement and failure. *American Journal of Psychotherapy, 33*(3), 418–427.

Baker, R. W., & Madell, T. O. (1965). Susceptibility to distraction in academically underachieving and achieving male college students. *Journal of Consulting Psychology, 29*(2), 173–177.

Bales, K. B. (1979). *Academic achievement and the broken home.* Paper presented at the Annual Meeting of the Southern Sociological Society, Atlanta, GA.

Bank, R. K. (1972). Formulation, application, and analysis of a method to study female underachievement. *Dissertation Abstracts International, 33*(1-A), 185–186.

Banretti-Fuchs, K. (1972). Attitudinal and situational correlates of academic achievement in young adolescents. *Canadian Journal of Behavioural Sciences, 4,* 156–164.

Bantam Medical Dictionary (1982). New York: Bantam Books.

Barcai, A., & Dreman, S. B. (1976). A comparison of three group approaches to underachieving children: Eleven school related tests. *Acta Paedopsychiatrica, 42*(2), 60–67.

Barcai, A., Umbarger, C., Thomas, W., & Chamberlain, P. (1973). A comparison of three group approaches to under-achieving children. *American Journal of Orthopsychiatry, 43*(1), 133–141.

Barclay, A., & Cervantes, L. F. (1969). The Thematic Apperception Test as an index of personality attributes characterizing the adolescent academic drop-out. *Adolescence, 4*(16), 525–540.

Bard, J. A., & Fisher, H. R. (1983). A rational-emotive approach to academic underachievement. In A. Ellis & M. E. Bernard (Eds.), *Rational-emotive approaches to the problems of childhood.* New York: Plenum.

Bar-Eli, N., & Raviv, A. (1982). Underachievers as tutors. *Journal of Educational Research, 75*(3), 139–143.

Barger, B., & Hall, E. (1964). Personality patterns and achievement in college. *Educational & Psychological Measurement, 24*(2), 339–346.

Barker, L. W. (1968). An analysis of achievement, motivational, and perceptual variables between students classified on the basis of success and persistence in college. *Dissertation Abstracts, 29*(4-A), 1100.

Barrett, H. O. (1950). Differences in intelligence between two- and four-year course pupils in a commercial high school. *Journal of Educational Research, 44,* 143–147.

Barrett, H. O. (1957). An intensive study of 32 gifted children. *Personnel and Guidance Journal, 36,* 192–194.

Bar-Tal, D. (1978). Attributional analysis of achievement related behavior. *Review of Educational Research, 48,* 259–271.

Bar-Tal, D. (1979). Interaction of teacher and pupils. In I. H. Frieze, D. Bar-Tal, & J. S. Carol, (Eds.). *New approaches to social problems: Applications of attribution theory* (pp. 337–358). San Francisco: Jossey-Bass.

Bar-Tal, D., & Frieze, I. H. (1977). Achievement motivation for males and females as a determinant of attribution for success and failure. *Sex Roles, 3,* 301–313.

Bartl, C. P., & Peltier, G. L. (1971). The academic underachiever in an industrialized world. *School and Society, 99,* 24–27.

Bartlett, E. W., & Smith, C. P. (1966). Childrearing practices, birth order, and the development of achievement-related motives. *Psychological Reports, 19,* 1207–1216.

Bartley, T. O. (1976). Tutorial program to aid secondary schools low-achieving students. *Dissertation Abstracts International, 37*(4-A), 2118.

Bateson, G., Jackson, D. D., Haley, J., & Weakland, J. (1956). Toward a theory of schizophrenia. *Behavioral Science, 1,* 251–264.

Battle, E. S. (1964). Achievement values, standards, and expectations: Their effect on children's task persistence and academic competence. *Dissertation Abstracts, 24*(11), 4790.

Baumgarten, F. (1945). Einseitig praktisch begabter Schulversager. II, III [One-sided practical aptitude in a school failure. I]. *Z. Kinderpsychiat., 11*, 166–180.

Baumgarten, F. (1945). Einseitig praktisch begabter Schulversager. II, III [One-sided practical aptitude in a school failure. II, III]. *Z. Kinderpsychiat., 12*, 7–22, 78–94.

Bayer, A. E. (1966). Birth order and college attendance. *Journal of Marriage and the Family, 28*, 480–484.

Baymur, F. B., & Patterson, C. H. (1960). A comparison of three methods of assisting underachieving high school students. *Journal of Counseling Psychology, 7*, 83–89.

Bayton, J. A., & Whyte, E. (1950). Personality dynamics during success-failure sequences. *Journal of Abnormal and Social Psychology, 45*, 583–591.

Bazemore, S. G., & Noblit, G. W. (1978). Class origins and academic achievement: An empirical critique of the cultural deprivation perspective. *Urban Education, 13*, 345–360.

Bean, A. G. (1971). Personality measures as multiple moderators in the prediction of college student attrition. *Dissertation Abstracts International, 32*(1-A), 229.

Beck, A. T., Emery, G., & Greenberg, R. L. (1985) *Anxiety disorders and phobias: A cognitive perspective*. New York: Basic Books.

Beckham, A. S. (1950). A Rorschach study of high school failures. *American Psychologist, 5*, 346.

Bednar, R. L., & Weinberg, S. L. (1970). Ingredients of successful treatment programs for underachievers. *Journal of Counseling Psychology, 17*(1), 1–7.

Behrens, L. T., & Vernon, P. E. (1978). Personality correlates of overachievement and underachievement. *British Journal of Educational Psychology, 48*(3), 290–297.

Belcastro, F. P. (1985). Use of behavior modification with academically gifted students: A review of the research. *Roeper Review, 7*, 184–189.

Bell, D. B. (1970). The motivational and personality factors in reading retardation among two racial groups of adolescent males. *Dissertation Abstracts International, 31*(2-B). 909–910.

Bell, J. E. (1945). Emotional factors in the treatment of reading difficulties. *Journal of Consulting Psychology, 9*, 125–131.

Bem, S. (1974). The measurement of psychological androgyny. *Journal of Consulting and Clinical Psychology, 42*, 155–162.

Bemelmans, F. (1971). Les troubles de l'apprentissage scolaire [Academic learning problems]. *Bulletin de Psychologie Scolaire et d'Orientation, 20*(4), 165–186.

Bender, P. S., & Ruiz, R. A. (1974). Race and class as differential determinants of underachievement and underaspiration among Mexican-Americans and Anglos. *Journal of Educational Research, 68*(2), 51–55.

Bender, W. N., Wyne, M. D., Stuck, G. B., & Bailey, D. B. (1984). Relative peer status of learning disabled, educable mentally handicapped, low achieving, and normally achieving children. *Child Study Journal, 13*(4), 209–216.

Bendig, A. W. (1958). Predictive and postdictive validity of need achievement measures. *Journal of Educational Research, 52*, 119–120.

Bendig, A. W., & Hughes, J. B., III. (1954). Student attitude and achievement in a course in introductory statistics. *Journal of Educational Psychology, 45*, 268–276.

Benedet, M. J. (1973). [Qualitative aspects of intellectual processes of normal or superior children who fail in school]. *Revista de Psicologia General y Aplicada, 28*(120–121), 41–69.

Bennett, B. E. (1968). *Perceived occupational fit, diagnostic categorization, and academic achievement*. Unpublished master's thesis, Illinois Institute of Technology, Chicago, IL.

Bennett, C. S. (1970). Relationship between selected personality variables and improvement in academic achievement for underachieving eighth grade boys in a residential school. *Dissertation Abstracts International, 30*(8-A), 3272–3273.

Bent, R. K. (1946). Scholastic records of non-high school graduates entering the University of Arkansas. *Journal of Educational Research, 40,* 108–115.

Benz, H., Pfeiffer, I., & Newman, I. (1981). Sex role expectations of classroom teachers, Grades 1–12. *American Educational Research Journal, 18,* 289–302.

Berenbaum, H. L. (1969). Validation of the Non-achievement Syndrome: A behavior disorder. *Dissertation Abstracts International, 29*(4-B), 1502.

Berg, I. A., Larsen, R. P., & Gilbert, W. M. (1944). Scholastic achievement of students entering college from the lowest quarter of their high school graduating class. *Journal of the American Association of College Registrars, 20,* 53–59.

Berg, R. C. (1968). The effect of group counseling on students placed on academic probation at Rock Valley College, Rockford, Illinois, 1966–1967. *Dissertation Abstracts, 29*(1-A), 115–116.

Berger, E. M. (1961). Willingness to accept limitations and college achievement. *Journal of Counseling Psychology, 8,* 140.

Berne, E. (1964). *Games people play.* New York: Grove Press.

Berne, E. (1966). *Principles of group treatment.* New York: Oxford University Press.

Bernstein, N. (1946). Why Richard dreaded school. *Understanding the Child, 15,* 114–117.

Bever, D. E. (1972). An analysis of selected intellectual and nonintellectual characteristics of dropouts and survivors in a private college. *Dissertation Abstracts International, 32*(7-A), 3773–3774.

Bey, T. M. (1986). Helping teachers achieve success with underachievers. *NASSP Bulletin, 70,* 91–93.

Bhatnagar, A. (1970). Teaching the underachiever. *Teaching, 43,* 20–23.

Bhatnagar, A. (1976). Effect of individual counselling on the achievement of bright under-achievers. *Indian Educational Review, 11*(4), 10–18.

Bhatty, R. (1978). Motivation in low-achiever and normal children. *Dissertation Abstracts International, 38*(7-A), 4034.

Bidwell, C. E., & Kasarda, J. D. (1975). School district organization and student achievement. *American Sociological Review, 40,* 55–70.

Biggs, B. E., & Felton, G. S. (1973). Use of an achievement motivation course to reduce test anxiety of academic low achievers. *College Student Journal, 7*(1), 12–16.

Billingslea, F. Y., & Bloom, H. (1950). The comparative effect of frustration and success on goal-directed behavior in the classroom. *Journal of Abnormal and Social Psychology, 45,* 510–515.

Birr, D. J. (1969). The effects of treatments by parents and teachers on the self-concept of ability held by underachieving early adolescent pupils. *Dissertation Abstracts International, 30*(4-A), 1429.

Blackman, S., & Goldstein, K. M. (1982). Cognitive styles and learning disabilities. *Journal of Learning Disabilities, 15*(2), 106–115.

Bladergroen, W. J. (1954). Children with learning difficulties. *Acta Psychother. and Psychosom. Orthopaedagog., 2,* 42–51.

Blai, B. (1976). Poor academic performance: Why? *Scientia Paedogogica Experimentalis, 13*(2), 186–202.

Blair, G. E. (1968). The relationship of selected ego functions and the academic achievement of Negro students. *Dissertation Abstracts, 28*(8-A), 3013.

Blair, J. R. (1971). The effectiveness of three classes of reinforcement on the performance of normal and low achieving middle-class boys. *Dissertation Abstracts International, 31*(12-A), 6394.

Blair, J. R. (1972). The effects of differential reinforcement on the discrimination learning of normal and low-achieving middle-class boys. *Child Development, 43*(1), 251–255.

Blake, R. R., & Mouton, J. S. (1959). Personality: Achievement, anxiety, and authoritarianism. *The Annual Review of Psychology, 10,* 203–232.

Blechman, E. A. (1981). Families and schools together: Early behavioral intervention with high risk children. *Behavior Therapy, 12*(3), 308–319.

Block, J. (1978). Effects of a rational-emotive mental health program on poorly achieving, disruptive high school students. *Journal of Counseling Psychology, 25,* 61–65.

Blos, P. (1946). Psychological counseling of college students. *American Journal of Orthopsychiatry, 16,* 571–580.

Blosser, C. R. (1972). A pilot study to explore the relationships between cognitive style, need achievement, and academic achievement motivation. *Dissertation Abstracts International, 32*(11-A), 6088.

Bluvol, H. (1973). Differences in patterns of autonomy in achieving and underachieving adolescent boys. *Dissertation Abstracts International, 33*(8-B), 3929.

Bocknek, G. L. (1959). The relationship between motivation and performance in achieving and underachieving college students. *Dissertation Abstracts, 20,* 1435.

Bohman, M., & Sigvardsson, S. (1981). A prospective, longitudinal study of children registered for adoption: A 15-year follow-up. *Annual Progress in Child Psychiatry and Child Development,* 217–237.

Bolyard, C. S., & Martin, C. J. (1973). High-risk freshmen. *Measurement & Evaluation in Guidance, 6*(1), 57–58.

Bond, J. A. (1952). Analysis of factors adversely affecting scholarship of high school pupils. *Journal of Educational Research, 46,* 1–15.

Bonnardel, R. (1964). [Behavior and scholarly success among students]. *Travail humain, 27*(3–4), 349–355.

Booth, J. P. (1978). The informal classroom: A working model designed for the underachieving pupil. *Dissertation Abstracts International, 39*(3-A), 1317–1318.

Borgen, W. A., Lacroix, H., & Goetz, E. (1978). Career exploration through group counselling. *School Guidance Worker, 34,* 46–49.

Borko, H., Cone, R., Russo, N., & Shavelson, R. (1979). Teachers' decision making. In P. Peterson & H. Walberg (Eds.). *Research on Teaching,* Berkeley, CA.: McCutcheon.

Borow, H. (1946a). Current problems in the prediction of college performance. *Journal of the American Association of College Registrars, 22,* 14–26.

Borow, H. (1946b). Non-intellectual correlates of college achievement. *American Psychologist, 1,* 249.

Borsilow, B. (1962). Self-evaluation and academic achievement. *Journal of Counseling Psychology, 9,* 246–254.

Boshier, R., & Hamid, P. N. (1968). Academic success and self-concept. *Psychological Reports, 22*(3, Pt. 2), 1191–1192.

Bost, J. M. (1984). Retaining students on academic probation: Effects of time management peer counseling on students' grades. *Journal of Learning Skills, 3*(2), 38–43.

Bouchillon, B. G. (1971). A comparison of four techniques in the modification of repressed self-concept for low achieving college students. *Dissertation Abstracts International, 31*(9-A), 4538.

Bowlby, J. (1969). *Attachment and loss* (Vol. 1). New York: Basic Books.

Bowlby, J. (1973). *Attachment and loss* (Vol. 2). New York: Basic Books.

Boyd, R. D. (1964). Analysis of the ego stage development of school age children. *Journal of Experimental Education, 32,* 249.

Bozak, I. M. (1969). A summer project for underachieving freshmen. *Improving College and University Teaching, 17,* 208–211.

Brandt, L. J., & Haden, M. E. (1974). Male and female teacher attitudes as a function of students' ascribed motivation and performance levels. *Journal of Educational Psychology, 66*(3), 309–314.

Brantley, D. (1969). Family stress and academic failure. *Social Casework, 50,* 287–290.

Bratton, D. (1945). Classroom guidance of pupils exhibiting behavior problems. *Elementary School, 45,* 286–292.

Braun, C. (1976). Teacher expectation: Sociopsychological dynamics. *Review of Educational Research, 46,* 185–213.

Breland, H. M. (1974). Birth order, family configuration, and verbal achievement. *Child Development, 45,* 1011–1019.

Bresee, C. W. (1957). Affective factors associated with academic underachievement in high-school students. *Dissertation Abstracts, 17,* 90–91.

Bridges, W. W. (1972). The use of peers as facilitators in small group procedures with under-achieving college freshmen. *Dissertation Abstracts International, 32*(9-A), 4936.

Bright, G. M. (1970). The adolescent with scholastic failure. *Bulletin of the Orton Society, 20,* 59–65.

Briscoe, J. (1977). Independent study for the "tuned out." *Adolescence, 12*(48), 529–532.

Bristow, W. H., & Hungerford, R. H. (1945). Slower-learning pupils—problems and issues. *High Points, 27,* 10–16.

Broderick, P. C., & Sewell, T. E. (1985). Attribution for success and failure in children of different social class. *Journal of Social Psychology, 5,* 591–599.

Broedel, J. W. (1959). A study of the effects of group counseling on the academic performance and mental health of underachieving gifted adolescents. *Dissertation Abstracts, 19,* 3019.

Broedel, J. W., Ohlsen, M., Proff, F., & Southard, C. (1960). The effects of group counseling on gifted underachieving adolescents. *Journal of Counseling Psychology, 7,* 163–170.

Broman, S., Bien, E., & Shaughnessy, P. (1985). *Low achieving children: The first several years.* Hillsdale, NJ: Lawrence Erlbaum.

Brooks, R. B., & Snow, D. L. (1972). Two case illustrations of the use of behavior-modification techniques in the school setting. *Behavior Therapy, 3,* 100–103.

Brophy, J. (1983). Research on the self-fulfilling prophecy and teacher expectations. *Journal of Educational Psychology, 75,* 631–661.

Brophy, J., & Everston, C. (1978). Context variables in teaching. *Educational Psychologist, 12,* 310–316.

Brophy, J., & Good, T. (1974). Teacher-Student Relationships. New York: Holt, Rinehart, & Winston.

Brower, D. (1967). Academic underachievement: A suggested theory. *Journal of Psychology, 66*(2), 299–302.

Brown, P. O. (1973). A comparison of self-esteem, anxiety, and behavior of Black and non-Black underachieving elementary school students in open and stratified classrooms. *Dissertation Abstracts International, 34*(6-A), 3011–3012.

Brown, R. D. (1969). Effects of structured and unstructured group counseling with high- and low-anxious college underachievers. *Journal of Counseling Psychology, 16,* 209–214.

Brown, R. I. (1969). Problems of learning with exceptional children. *Western Psychologist, 1*(1), 29–38.

Brown, W. F., Abeles, N., & Iscoe, I. (1954). Motivational differences between high and low scholarship students. *Journal of Educational Psychology, 45,* 215–223.

Bruck, M., & Bodwin, R. F. (1962). The relationship between self-concept and the presence and absence of scholastic underachievement. *Journal of Clinical Psychology, 18*(2), 181–182.

Brunner, E. DeS. (1948). Educational attainment and economic status. *Teach. Coll. Rec., 49,* 242–249.

Brusnahan, J. (1969). A study of the effects of small-group counseling on ninth-grade underachievers. *Dissertation Abstracts International, 30,* 3273–3274-A.

Buck, M. R., & Austrin, H. R. (1971). Factors related to school achievement in an economically disadvantaged group. *Child Development, 42,* 1813–1826.

Buck, T. D. (1969). Selected behavioral correlates of discrepant academic achievement. *Dissertation Abstracts, 29*(8-A), 2513–2514.

Bulcock, J. W. (1977). Evaluating social facts related to school achievement in Sweden and England. *Scandinavian Journal of Educational Research, 21,* 63–96.

Burchinal, L. G. (1959). Social status, measured intelligence, achievement, and personality adjustment of rural Iowa girls. *Sociometry, 22,* 75–80.

Burns, G. W. (1972). A factor analytic study of the revised edition of the Illinois Test of Psycholinguistic Abilities with underachieving children. *Dissertation Abstracts International, 33*(4-A), 1548.

Burns, G. W., & Watson, B. L. (1973). Factor analysis of the revised ITPA with underachieving children. *Journal of Learning Disabilities, 6*(6), 371–376.

Burrall, L. (1954). Variability in achievement of pupils at the fifth grade level. *California Journal of Educational Research, 5,* 68–73.

Bush, W. J. (1972). A comparative study of the WISC test patterns of the bright and gifted underachievers with test patterns of underachievers with normal intelligence. *Dissertation Abstracts International, 32*(9-A), 5066.

Bush, W. J., & Mattson, B. D. (1973). WISC test patterns and underachievers. *Journal of Learning Disabilities, 6*(4), 251–256.

Bushlow, P. A., & Sudwarth, C. A. (1970). Underachievers profit from pilot project in John Eaton School. *Delta Kappa Gamma Bulletin, 36,* 45–48.

Califf, S. N. (1968). Perception of college environment by achieving and nonachieving freshmen. *Dissertation Abstracts, 29*(2-B), 751–752.

Calvert, K. C. (1972). An investigation of relationships between the syntactic maturity of oral language and reading comprehension scores. *Dissertation Abstracts International, 32*(9-A), 4828–4829.

Campbell, J. R. (1969). Cognitive and affective process development and its relation to a teacher's interaction ratio: An investigation to determine the relationship between the affective and cognitive development of junior high low achievers and the interaction ratio employed by their instructors. *Dissertation Abstracts International, 30*(3-A), 1069–1070.

Campbell, W. J. (1952). The influence of home environment on the educational progress of selective secondary school children. *British Journal of Educational Psychology, 22,* 89–100.

Cantwell, D. P., & Satterfield, J. H. (1978). The prevalence of academic underachievement in hyperactive children. *Journal of Pediatric Psychology, 3*(4), 168–171.

Caplan, M. D. (1969). Resistance to learning. *Peabody Journal of Education, 47,* 36–39.

Capponi, A. (1974). The relation between academic underachievement and depression: An exploratory study. *Dissertation Abstracts International, 34*(7-B), 3488–3489.

Cardon, B. W. (1968). Sex differences in school achievement. *Elementary School Journal, 68*(8), 427–434.

Carmical, L. (1964). Characteristics of achievers and under-achievers of a large senior high school. *Personnel and Guidance Journal, 43*(4), 390–395.

Carney, R., Monn, P., & McCormick, R. (1966). Validation of an objective measure of achievement motivation. *Psychological Reports, 19,* 243–248.

Carroll, J. A., Fuller, G. B., & Carroll, J. L. (1979). Comparison of culturally deprived school achievers and underachievers on memory function and perception. *Perceptual and Motor Skills, 48*(1), 59–62.

Carter, H. D. (1948). Methods of learning as factors in prediction of school learning. *Journal of Psychology, 26,* 249–258.

Carter, H. D. (1958a). *California study methods survey: Untimed, 30–50 min., grades 7–13, 1 form.* Los Angeles, CA: California Test Bureau.

Carter, H. D. (1958b). The mechanics of study procedure. *California Journal of Educational Research, 9,* 8–13.

Carter, H. D. (1959). Improving the prediction of school achievement by the use of the California Study Methods Survey. *Educational Administration and Supervision, 45,* 255–260.

Carter, H. D. (1961). Overachievers and underachievers in the junior high school. *California Journal of Educational Research, 12,* 81–86.

Carter, H. D. (1964). Over- and underachievement in reading. *California Journal of Educational Research, 15*(4), 175–183.

Carwise, J. L. (1968). Aspirations and attitudes toward education of over- and under-achieving Negro junior high school students. *Dissertation Abstracts, 28*(10-A), 3878.

Castelyns, N. (1968). A study of the effectiveness of two procedures of group counseling with small groups of talented, underachieving seventh and eighth grade students. *Dissertation Abstracts, 28*(9-A), 3498.

Castenell, L. (1984). A cross-cultural look at achievement motivation research. *The Journal of Negro Education, 53,* 435–443.

Cattell, R. B., Cattell, M. D. (1975). *Handbook for the Jr.–Sr. High School Personality Questionnaire (HSPQ).* Champaign, Ill.: Institute for Personality and Ability Testing.

Cattell, R. B., Eber, H. W., & Tatsuoka, M. M. (1970). *Handbook for the Sixteen Personality Factor Questionnaire (16PF).* Champaign, Ill.: Institute for Personality and Ability Testing.

Caudill, W., & De Vos, G. (1956). Achievement, culture and personality: The case of the Japanese Americans. *American Anthropologist, 58,* 1102–1126.

Chabassol, D. J. (1959). Correlates of academic underachievement in male adolescents. *Alberta Journal of Educational Research, 5,* 130–146.

Chadwick, B. A., & Day, R. C. (1971). Systematic reinforcement: Academic performance of underachieving students. *Journal of Applied Behavior Analysis, 4*(4), 311–319.

Chahbazi, P. (1957). An analysis of the Cornell Orientation Inventory items on study habits and their relative value in prediction of college achievement. *Journal of Educational Research, 51,* 117–127.

Champaign Community Unit Schools, Department of Special Services (1961). *Exceptional Children, 28,* 167–175.

Chansky, N. M. (1964). Progress of promoted and repeating grade I failures. *Journal of Experimental Education, 32*(3), 225–237.

Chaplin, J. P. (1975). *Dictionary of psychology.* New York: Dell.

Chapman, R. S. (1959). Achievement and under-achievement in English language ten in an Alberta composite high school. *Alberta Journal of Educational Research, 5,* 41–49.

Cheatham, R. B. (1968). A study of the effects of group counseling on the self-concept and on the reading efficiency of low-achieving readers in a public-intermediate school. *Dissertation Abstracts, 29*(6-B), 2200.

Chestnut, W. J. (1965). The effects of structured and unstructured group counseling on male college students' underachievement. *Journal of Counseling Psychology, 12*(4), 388–394.

Chestnut, W., & Gilbreath, S. (1969). Differential group counseling with male college underachievers: A three-year follow-up. *Journal of Counseling Psychology, 16*(4), 365–367.

Cheuvront, H. L. (1975). Use of behavior modification concepts with adolescent underachievers to improve school achievement through attitude change. *Dissertation Abstracts International, 36*(4-B), 1940–1941.

Chopra, S. L. (1967). A comparative study of achieving and underachieving students of high intellectual ability. *Exceptional Children, 33*(9), 631–634.

Christensen, H. (1979). Test anxiety and academic achievement in high school students. *Perceptual & Motor Skills, 49*(2), 648.

Chronbach, L. J., & Webb, N. (1975). Between-class and within-class effects in a reported aptitude × treatment interaction: Reanalysis of a study by G. L. Anderson. *Journal of Educational Psychology, 67*(6), 717–724.

Cicirelli, V. G. (1967). Sibling constellation, creativity, I.Q., and academic achievement. *Child Development, 38,* 481–490.

Cicirelli, V. G. (1978). The relationship of sibling structure to intellectual abilities and achievement. *Review of Educational Research, 48,* 365–379.

Cipperly, J. W. (1969). An effort to refine the concept of academic underachievement through an investigative case study approach. *29*(9-A), 2957.

Claes, M. (1976). [Developing motivation in teenage academic nonachievers]. *Revue de Psychologie Appliquee, 26*(3), 551–566.

Claes, M., & Salame, R. (1975). [Motivation toward accomplishment and the self-evaluation of performances in relation to school achievement]. *Canadian Journal of Behavioural Science, 7*(4), 397–410.

Clark, K. B. (1972). *A possible reality: A design for the attainment of high academic achievement for inner-city students.* New York: Emerson Hall.

Cleckley, H. (1964). *The mask of sanity* (4th ed.). St. Louis, MO: C. V. Mosby.

Clifford, M. M., & Cleary, T. A. (1972). The relationship between children's academic performance and achievement accountability. *Child Development, 43*(2), 647–655.

Cocalis, J. D. (1973). An evaluation of peer group rewards as modifiers of academic underachievement. *Dissertation Abstracts International, 33*(7-A), 3371.

Coffin, B. S., Dietz, S. C., & Thompson, C. L. (1971). Academic achievement in a poverty area high school: Implications for counseling. *Journal of Negro Education, 40*(4), 365–368.

Cohen, R. (1978). The effects of self-monitoring on the academic and social behaviors of underachieving children. *Dissertation Abstracts International, 38*(9-A), 5390–5391.

Cohen, S. (1986). *Similarities and differences in underachieving, achieving, and overachieving Non-achievement Syndrome high school students.* Unpublished master's thesis, York University, Toronto, ON.

Cohen, T. B. (1963). Prediction of underachievement in kindergarten children. *Archives of General Psychiatry, 9*(5), 444–450.

Cohn, B., & Sniffen, A. M. (1962). A school report on group counseling. *Personnel Guidance Journal, 41*(2), 133–138.

Coie, J. D., & Krehbiel, G. (1984). Effects of academic tutoring on the social status of low-achieving socially rejected children. *Child Development, 55*(4), 1465–1478.

Colangelo, N. & Dettmann, D. F. (1983). A review of research on parents and families of gifted children. *Exceptional Children, 50,* 20–27.

Coleman, A. E., et al. (1972). Comparison of health knowledge of young adult under-achievers and their parents. *Journal of School Health, 42,* 354–355.

Coleman, H. A. (1940). The relationship of SES to the performance of junior high school students. *Journal of Experimental Education, 9,* 61–63.

Coleman, J. C. (1962). Learning method as a relevant subject variable in learning disorders. *Perceptual & Motor Skills, 14,* 263–269.

Coleman, J. C., & Hewitt, F. (1962). Treatment of underachieving adolescent boys who resist needed psychotherapy. *Journal of Clinical Psychology, 18,* 28–33.

Coleman, J. C., & Rasof, B. (1963). Intellectual factors in learning disorders. *Perceptual & Motor Skills, 16,* 139–152.

Coleman, J. S. (1960). The adolescent subculture and academic achievement. *American Journal of Sociology, 65,* 337–347.

Collier, K. L. (1969). The effect of selected response contingencies on paired-associate learning in educationally retarded school children. *Dissertation Abstracts International, 30*(4-A), 1429.

Collins, J. H., & Douglas, H. R. (1937). The SES of the home as a factor in success in the junior high school. *Elementary School Journal, 38,* 107–113.

Compton, M. F. (1982). The gifted underachiever in the middle school. *Roeper Review, 4*(4), 23–25.

Comrey, A. L. (1949). A factorial study of achievement in West Point courses. *Educ. Psychol. Measurement, 9,* 193–209.

Congdon, R. G. (1964). Personality factors and the capacity to meet curriculum demands. *Personnel & Guidance, 42*(8), 767–775.

Conklin, A. M. (1940). Failures of highly intelligent pupils. *Teacher's College Contribution to Education,* No. 792.

Connor, M. W. (1968). Learning characteristics of able nonachievers in audiolingual foreign language classes. *Dissertation Abstracts, 29*(5-A), 1446–1447.

Cook, E. S., Jr. (1956). An analysis of factors related to withdrawal from high school prior to graduation. *Journal of Educational Research, 50,* 191–196.

Cooper, H. (1979). Pygmalian grows up: A model for teacher expectation, communication, and performance influence. *Review of Educational Research, 49,* 389–410.

Corlis, R. B. (1963). Personality factors related to under achievement in college freshmen of high intellectual ability. *Dissertation Abstracts, 24*(2), 823–833.

Cortines, R. C. (1968). Reaching the underachiever through the media. *Audiovisual Instruction, 13*(9), 952–956.

Covington, M. V. (1983). Strategic thinking and the fear of failure. In S. F. Chipman, J. Segal, & R. Glaser (Eds.), *Thinking and learning skills: Current research and open questions* (Vol. 2). Hillsdale, NJ: Erlbaum.

Cowan, J. C. (1957). Dynamics of the underachievement of gifted students. *Exceptional Children, 24,* 98–101.

Crandall, V. C., Katkovsky, W., & Crandall, V. J. (1965). Children's beliefs in their own control of reinforcements in intellectual-academic situations. *Child Development, 36,* 91–106.

Crawford, A. B., & Burnham, P. S. (1946). *Forecasting college achievement; a survey of aptitude tests for higher education. Part I: General considerations in the measurement of academic promise.* New Haven: Yale University Press.

Creange, N. C. (1971). Group counseling for underachieving ninth graders. *School Counselor, 18,* 279–285.

Crescimbeni, J. (1964). Broken homes affect academic achievement. *Education, 84*(7), 437–441.

Crespi, L. P. (1944). Amount of reinforcement and level of performance. *Psychology Review, 51,* 341–357.

Cress, J. N. (1975). The relationship between self-concept and the discrepancy between actual and expected achievement: A comparative study of clinic-referred and non-referred underachievers, and normal achievers. *Dissertation Abstracts International, 35*(12-B, Pt. 1), 6090.

Crittenden, M. R., Kaplan, M. H., & Heim, J. K. (1984). Developing effective study skills and self-confidence in academically able young adolescents. *Gifted Child Quarterly, 28*(1), 25–30.

Cronbach, L. J., & Snow, R. E. (1977). *Aptitude and instructional methods: A handbook for research on interactions.* New York: Irvington.

Crootof, C. (1963). Bright underachievers' acceptance of self and their need for achievement. A study of three groups of high school boys—Bright Achievers, Normal Achievers, and Bright Underachievers—to determine the relationship of results elicited from them by Bill's Index of Adjustment and Values, Edward's Personal Preference Schedule and McClelland's Picture Story Test for measuring academic motivation. *Dissertation Abstracts, 24*(4), 1695–1696.

Crowe, J. G. (1947). "We look at the schools. . . ." *Surv. Midmon., 83,* 335–337.

Cubbedge, G. H., & Hall, M. M. (1964). A proposal for a workable approach in dealing with underachievers. *Psychology, 1*(4), 1–7.

Cummings, J. D. (1944). The incidence of emotional symptoms in school children. *British Journal of Educational Psychology, 14,* 151–161.

Cunningham, C. E., & Barkley, R. A. (1978). The role of academic failure in hyperactive behavior. *Journal of Learning Disabilities, 11*(5), 274–280.

Custenborder, C. R. (1969). An investigation of the structure and mode of classification strategies of retarded and achieving readers. *Dissertation Abstracts, 29*(9-A), 2998.

Dalton, S., Anastasiow, M., & Brigman, S. L. (1977). The relationship of underachievement and college attrition. *Journal of College Student Personnel, 18*(6), 501–505.

Dana, R. H., & Baker, D. H. (1961). High school achievement and the Bell Adjustment Inventory. *Psychological Reports, 8,* 353–356.

Dandapani, S. (1979). Guidance programmes for underachievers. *Indian Educational Review, 14*(1), 111–114.

Danesino, A., & Layman, W. A. (1969). Contrasting personality patterns of high and low achievers among college students of Italian and Irish descent. *Journal of Psychology, 72*(1), 71–83.

Darby, E. (1969a, August 14). They seek cures of the non-achiever. *Chicago Sun-Times* p. 104.

Darby, E. (1969b, August 15). Help for the do-nothing individual. *Chicago Sun-Times* p. 50.

Darrell, E., & Wheeler, M. (1984). Using art therapy techniques to help underachieving seventh grade junior high school students. *Art in Psychotherapy, 11*(4), 289–29.

Dasen, P. R., Berry, J. W., & Witkin, H. A. (1979). The use of developmental theories cross-culturally. In L. Eckensberger, W. Lonner, & Y. H. Poortinga (Eds.). *Cross-cultural contributions to psychology* (pp. 69–82). The Netherlands: Swets Publishing Service.

Davey, B. (1972). A psycholinguistic investigation of cognitive styles and oral reading strategies in achieving and underachieving fourth grade boys. *Dissertation Abstracts International, 32*(8-A), 4414.

Davids, A. (1966). Psychological characteristics of high school male and female potential scientists in comparison with academic underachievers. *Psychology in the Schools, 3*(1), 79–87.

Davids, A. (1968). Cognitive styles in potential scientists and in underachieving high school students. *Journal of Special Education, 2*(2), 197–201.

Davids, A., & Hainsworth, P. K. (1967). Maternal attitudes about family life and child rearing as avowed by mothers and perceived by their underachieving and high-achieving sons. *Journal of Consulting Psychology, 31*(1), 29–37.

Davids, A., & Sidman, J. (1962). A pilot study: Impulsivity, time orientation, and delayed gratification in future scientists and in under-achieving high school students. *Exceptional Children, 29*(4), 170–174.

Davids, A., Sidman, J., & Silverman, M. (1968). Tolerance of cognitive interference in underachieving and high achieving secondary school boys. *Psychology in the Schools, 5*(3), 222–229.

Davies, L. (1979). The social construction of underachievement. *B.C. Journal of Special Education, 3,* 203–217.

Davies, V. (1963). Investigation of under- and overachievement among Washington State freshmen. *Research Studies,* Washington State University, *31,* 18–42.

Davis, F. (1984). Understanding underachievers. *American Education, 20,* 12–14.

Davis, F. G. (1945). Capacity and achievement. *Occupations, 23,* 394–401.

Davis, H. B., & Connell, J. P. (1985). The effect of aptitude and achievement status on the self-system. *Gifted Child Quarterly, 29,* 131–136.

Dearborn, W. F. (1949). The student's background in relation to school success. In W. T. Donahue, C. H. Coombs, & R. M. W. Travers (Eds.), *The measurement of student adjustment and achievement* (pp. 191–200). Ann Arbor, MI: University of Michigan Press.

Deb, M., & Ghosh, M. (1971). Relation between scholastic achievement and intelligence. *Behaviorometric, 1*(2), 136–137.

Decker, T. W. (1978). Two approaches in the treatment of test anxious college underachievers. *Dissertation Abstracts International, 38*(8-A), 4675.

De Leon, C. S. (1970). The relationship between personal-social problems and under-achievement in high school. *Saint Louis University Research Journal, 1*(4), 601–620.

Delisle, J. (1982). Learning to underachieve. *Roeper Review, 4*(4), 16–18.

Demars, R. J. (1972). A comparative study of seventh grade low achievers' attitudes and achievement in mathematics under two approaches, UICSM and traditional. *Dissertation Abstracts International, 32*(9-A), 4832–4833.

Demichiell, R. L. (1973). The application of cluster-analytic techniques in the prediction of academic achievement and leadership from self-report personality data. *Dissertation Abstracts International, 33*(12-A), 6684–6685.

Denhoff, E., Hainsworth, P. K., & Siqueland, M. L. (1970). The measurement of psychoneurological factors contributing to learning efficiency. *Journal of Learning Disabilities, 1*(11), 636–644.

Dennis, S. (1985). *The relationship between parents as educational role models and students' academic achievement and academic performance.* Unpublished undergraduate thesis, York University, Toronto, ON.

Deo, P., & Gupta, A. K. (1972). A comparison of the criteria for identifying over and underachievers. *Indian Educational Review, 7*(1), 153–167.

Derevensky, J. L., Hart, S., & Farrell, M. (1983). An examination of achievement-related behavior of high- and low-achieving inner-city pupils. *Psychology in the Schools, 20*(3), 328–336.

De Sena, P. A. (1964). Comparison of consistent over-, under-, and normal-achieving college students on a Minnesota Multiphasic Personality Inventory special scale. *Psychology, 1*(1,2), 8–12.

De Sena, P. A. (1966). Problems of consistent over-, under-, and normal-achieving college students as identified by the Mooney Problem Check List. *Journal of Educational Research, 59*(8), 351–355.

Desiderato, O., & Koskinen, P. (1969). Anxiety, study habits, and academic achievement. *Journal of Counseling Psychology, 16*(2, Pt. 1), 162–165.

Despert, J. L., & Pierce, H. O. (1946). The relation of emotional adjustment to intellectual function. *Genetic Psychol. Monogr., 34,* 3–56.

Devane, J. R. (1973). An exploratory study of the relationship between factors of self-concept and over-under achievement in arithmetic. *Dissertation Abstracts International, 33*(9-A), 4932–4933.

De Venter, J. (1946). [What pupils can finish their studies with success?] *Vlaam. Opvoedk. Tijdschr., 26,* 274–287.

Dhaliwal, A. S., & Saini, B. S. (1975). A study of the prevalence of academic underachievement among high school students. *Indian Educational Review, 10*(1), 90–109.

Dhaliwal, A. S., & Sharma, J. P. (1975). Identification and measurement of academic over- and underachievement. *Psychologia: An International Journal of Psychology in the Orient, 18*(2), 95–103.

Dhaliwal, A. S., & Singh, G. (1974). The psychological concepts of over- and underachievement defined operationally in terms of residual achievement. *Psychological Studies, 19*(1), 43–45.

Dickenson, W. A., & Truax, C. B. (1966). Group counseling with college underachievers. *Personnel & Guidance Journal, 45*(3), 243–247.

Dicks, H. V. (1972). *Licensed mass murder.* New York: Basic Books.

Diener, C. L. (1957). A comparison of over-achieving and under-achieving students at the University of Arkansas. *Dissertation Abstracts, 17,* 1692.

Diener, C. L. (1960). Similarities and differences between over-achieving and under-achieving students. *Personnel and Guidance Journal, 38,* 396–400.

Diener, R. G., & Maroney, R. J. (1974). Relationship between Quick Test and WAIS for black male adolescent underachievers. *Psychological Reports, 34*(3, Pt. 2), 1232–1234.

Diethelm, O., & Jones, M. R. (1947). Influence of anxiety on attention, learning, retention and thinking. *Archives of Neurology and Psychiatry, 58,* 325–336.

Digna, S. (1953). Motivation in guiding the child. *Education, 74,* 138–142.

Dinger, M. A. (1974). Effectiveness of individual counseling using reinforcement techniques in raising the grade point averages of underachieving eleventh-grade students in the five high schools of Augusta County, Virginia. *Dissertation Abstracts International, 34*(9-A, Pt. 1), 5623.

DiVesta, F. J., Woodruff, A. D., & Hertel, J. P. (1949). Motivation as a predictor of college success. *Educational & Psychological Measurement, 9,* 339–348.

Dixon, J. L. (1977). Other-directedness and academic underachievement in bright adolescent girls. *Dissertation Abstracts International, 37*(8-A), 4979–4980.

Dodge, P. (1984). Sociological realism and educational achievement. *International Social Science Review, 59,* 134–138.

Dodson, D. W. (1947). The community and child development. *Journal of Educational Sociology, 20,* 264–271.

Dolan, L. (1978). The affective consequences of home support, instructional quality, and achievement. *Urban Education, 13,* 323–344.

Doll, E. A. (1953) Varieties of slow learners. *Exceptional Children, 20,* 61–64.

Dolph, E. J. (1966). A comparative study of the ordinal position of the child and his school achievement. *Dissertations Abstracts International, 26,* 6509A.

Domino, G. (1970). Interactive effects of achievement orientation and teaching style on academic achievement. *ACT Research Reports, 39,* 1–9.

Donahue, W. T., Coombs, C. H., & Travers, R. M. W. (Eds.). (1949). *The measurement of student adjustment and achievement.* Ann Arbor, MI: University of Michigan Press.

D'Orazio, D. E. (1968). Under-achieving: Slow learners in primary schools. *Scientia Paedagogica Experimentalis, 5*(2), 187–191.

Douvan, E. (1956). Social status and success strivings. *Journal of Abnormal and Social Psychology, 52,* 219–223.

Dowd, E. T., & Moerings, B. J. (1975). The underachiever and teacher consultation: A case study. *School Counselor, 22,* 263–265.

Dowdall, C. B., & Colangelo, N. (1982). Underachieving gifted students: Review and implications. *Gifted Child Quarterly, 26*(4), 179–184.

Doyle, R. E. (1978). Group-counseling and counselor-teacher consultation with poorly achieving ninth grade students. *Dissertation Abstracts International, 38*(11-A), 6531–6532.

Doyle, R. E., Gottlieb, B., & Schneider, D. (1979). Underachievers achieve—A case for intensive counseling. *School Counselor, 26*, 134–143.

Drake, L. E. (1962). MMPI patterns predictive of underachievement. *Journal of Counseling Psychology, 9*(2), 164–167.

Drakeford, G. C. (1971). Intensity of cross-modal meaning discrimination in academic achievers and under-achievers. *Dissertation Abstracts International, 31*(7-B), 4308.

Dragsow, J. (1957). Underachievers. *Journal of Counseling Psychology, 4*, 210–211.

Drevlow, R. R., & Krueger, A. H. (1972). Behavior modification of underachieving mathematics students. *Pupil Personnel Services Journal, 1*(3), 31–35.

Drews, E. M., & Teahan, J. E. (1957). Parental attitudes and academic achievement. *Journal of Clinical Psychology, 13*, 328–332.

Driscoll, J. A. (1952). *Factors in intelligence and achievement.* Washington, DC: The Catholic University of America Press.

Duckworth, J., & Anderson, W. (1984). *MMPI: Interpretation manual for counselors and clinicians (3rd ed.).* Muncie, IN: Accelerated Development, Inc.

Duclos, C. M. (1976). The effects of a model of systematic human relations training on a volunteer group of freshmen underachievers. *Dissertation Abstracts International, 37*(4-A), 2011–2012.

Dudek, S. Z., & Lester, E. P. (1968). The good child facade in chronic underachievers. *American Journal of Orthopsychiatry, 38*(1), 153–160.

Duff, O. L., & Siegel, L. (1960). Biographical factors associated with academic over- and under-achievement. *Journal of Educational Psychology, 51*, 43–46.

Duke, M. P., & Nowicki, S. (1974). Locus of control and achievement: The confirmation of a theoretical expectation. *Journal of Psychology, 87*, 263–267.

Dullaert, K. (1971). A holistically oriented twelve year longitudinal examination of negative-discrepant achievement. *Dissertation Abstracts International, 31*, 6189A.

Dunn, J. (1983). Relationship between birth category, achievement, and interpersonal orientation. *Journal of Personality and Social Psychology, 41*, 121–131.

Durrell, D. D. (1954). Learning difficulties among children of normal intelligence. *Elementary School Journal, 55*, 201–208.

Dusek, J. (1975). Do teachers bias children's learning? *Review of Educational Research, 45*, 661–684.

Dusek, J., & Joseph, S. (1983). The bases of teacher expectancies: A meta analysis. *Journal of Educational Psychology, 75*, 327–346.

Dweck, C. S., & Elliot, E. S. (1983). Achievement motivation. In E. M. Hetherington (Ed.), *Socialization, personality, and social development.* New York: Wiley.

Dziuban, C. D., Harrow, T. L., & Thompson, R. A. (1972). An experimental assessment of a language arts development program. *Southern Journal of Educational Research, 6*(4), 203–208.

Easton, J. (1959). Some personality traits of underachieving and achieving high school students of superior ability. *Bulletin of the Maritime Psychological Association, 8*, 34–39.

Easton, R. H. (1968). A model for counseling and its trial with a group of low-achieving high school students. *Dissertation Abstracts, 29*(6-A), 1752.

Eckhardt, E. P. (1975). Self-concept and achievement after counseling and remediation with upper elementary underachievers. *Dissertation Abstracts International, 35*(12, Pt. 1), 6091.

Edgerly, R. F. (1971). Parent counseling in Norwell Junior High School. *Journal of Education, 154*, 54–59.

Edgington, E. S. (1964). A normative approach to measurement of underachievement. *Journal of Experimental Education, 33*(2), 197–200.

Edmiston, R. W., & Jackson, L. A. (1949). The relationship of persistence to achievement. *Journal of Educational Psychology, 40*, 47–51.

Edwards, A. B. (1968). An analysis of the creative ability levels of the potential dropout in the average mental ability range. *Dissertation Abstracts, 29*, 3828-A.

Ehrbright, R. M. (1969). A descriptive study of underachievers as represented by students participating in the Upward Bound Program at the University of Montana. *Dissertation Abstracts International, 30*(6-A), 2246–2247.

Eichman, N. F. (1971). Academic achievement and student perception of importance of non-cognitive correlates. *Dissertation Abstracts International, 32*(1-A), 89–90.

Eisenman, R., & Platt, J. J. (1968). Underachievement and creativity in high school students. *Psychology, 5*(4), 52–55.

Eklof, K-R. (1973). Validation of a component theory of motivation to achieve in school among adolescents. *Dissertation Abstracts International, 33*(7-A), 3375–3376.

Elder, J. B. (1974). The ameliorative effects of reading and study methods courses on underachievers. *Dissertation Abstracts International, 35*(4-A), 2046–2047.

Eller, R. D. (1971). A comparison of the extent to which personal counseling and environmental manipulation affect the achievement and the adjustment of selected underachieving students attending a large suburban high school. *Dissertation Abstracts International, 32*(4-A), 1849.

Elliott, K. K. (1967). A cross-cultural study of non-intellectual correlates of achieving and low achieving boys. *Dissertation Abstracts International, 27*, 6872–6873-B.

Elliott, J. L., & Elliott, D. H. (1970). Effects of birth order and age gap on aspiration level. *Proceedings of the Annual Convention of the American Psychological Association, 5*, 369–370.

Ellis, A., & Grieger, R. (Eds.). (1977). *Handbook of rational-emotive therapy.* New York: Springer.

Entin, E. (1968). The relationship between the theory of achievement motivation and performance on a simple and complex task. *Dissertation Abstracts, 29*(3-B), 1160–1161.

Entwistle, N. J. (1968). Academic motivation and school attainment. *British Journal of Educational Psychology, 38*(2), 181–188.

Entwistle, N. J., & Welsh, J. (1969). Correlates of school attainment at different levels. *British Journal of Educational Psychology, 39*(1), 57–63.

Enzer, N. B. (1975). Parents as partners in behavior modification. *Journal of Research & Development in Education, 8*(2), 24–33.

Epps, E. G. (1969a). Correlates of academic achievement among Northern and Southern urban Negro students. *Journal of Social Issues, 25*(3), 55–70.

Epps, E. G. (1969b). Negro academic motivation and performance: An overview. *Journal of Social Issues, 25*(3), 5.

Epstein, M. H. (1976). Modification of impulsivity and arithmetic performance in underachieving children. *Dissertation Abstracts International, 36*(7-A), 4398–4399.

Erdewyk, Z. M. (1968). Academic and non-academic variables related to persistence, transfer, and attrition of engineering students. *Dissertation Abstracts, 28*(11-A), 4453–4454.

Erickson, M. H. (1980). *The collected papers of Milton H. Erickson* (E. L. Rossi, Ed.). New York: Irvington.

Erickson, M. H., Rossi, E. L., & Rossi, S. I. (1976). *Hypnotic Realities.* New York: Irvington.

Erickson, M. R., & Cromack, T. (1972). Evaluating a tutoring program. *Journal of Experimental Education, 41*(2), 27–31.

Erikson, E. (1963). *Childhood and society*. New York: Norton.

Esposito, R. A. (1968). Comparison of teacher and standardized test classification of students as under- and over-achievers. *Dissertation Abstracts, 29*(6-A), 1752–1753.

Estabrooks, G. H., & May, J. R. (1965). Hypnosis in integrative motivation. *American Journal of Clinical Hypnosis, 7*(4), 346–352.

Esterson, H., Feldman, C., Krigsman, N., & Warshaw, S. (1975). Time-limited group counseling with parents of pre-adolescent underachievers: A pilot program. *Psychology in the Schools, 12*(1), 79–84.

Etaugh, C. (1974). Effects of maternal employment on children. *Merrill-Palmer Quarterly, 20*, 71–80.

Evans, F. B., & Anderson, J. G. (1973). The psychocultural origins of achievement and achievement motivation: The Mexican-American family. *Sociology of Education, 46*, 396–416.

Exner, J. E., Jr. (1974). *The Rorschach* (Vol. 3). New York: Wiley.

Fagot, B., & Littman, I. (1976). Relation of preschool sex-typing to intellectual performance in elementary school. *Psychological Reports, 36*, 699–704.

Falbo, T. (1981). Relationships between birth category, achievement, and interpersonal orientation. *Journal of Personality and Social Psychology, 41*, 121–131.

Fanning, J. F. (1969). Effects of selected reporting practices on reading achievement, reading attitude, and anxiety of below average readers in grades three through six. *Dissertation Abstracts International, 30*(5-A), 1746.

Farls, R. J. (1967). High and low achievement of intellectually average intermediate grade students related to the self-concept and social approval. *Dissertation Abstracts International, 28*(4), 1205-A.

Farquhar, W. W., & Payne, D. A. (1964). A classification and comparison of techniques used in selecting under- and over-achievers. *Personnel & Guidance Journal, 42*(9), 874–884.

Farson, M. R. (1945). A program for low ability children in the regular grade; With special reference to the reading problem. *American Journal of Mental Deficiency, 50*, 107–114.

Fazel, M. K. (1969). Child's perception of parental attitude and its relationship to academic achievement and problem awareness. *Dissertation Abstracts, 29*(8-B), 3084–3085.

Fearn, L. (1982). Underachievement and rate of acceleration. *Gifted Child Quarterly, 26*(3), 121–125.

Feidi-Maskell, T. (1980). The problem of the underachievement of the English working class at school: Special reference to the "community school." *The Greek Review of Social Research, 38*, 53–63.

Feinberg, H. (1947). Achievement of a group of socially maladjusted boys as revealed by the Stanford Achievement Test. *Journal of Social Psychology, 26*, 203–212.

Felton, G. S. (1972). Changes in measured intelligence of academic low achievers in a process-oriented learning program. *Psychological Reports, 30*(1), 89–90.

Felton, G. S. (1973a). A brief scale for assessing affective correlates of academic low achievement. *College Student Journal, 7*(1), 58–63.

Felton, G. S. (1973b). Changes in I.Q. scores of Black low achievers in a process-oriented learning program. *College Student Journal, 7*(1), 83–86.

Felton, G. S. (1973c). Use of the MMPI Underachievement scale as an aid in counseling academic low achievers in college. *Psychological Reports, 32*(1), 151–157.

Fenner, E. D., Jr. (1966). An investigation of the concept of underachievement. *Dissertation Abstracts, 27*(3-A), 600.

Ferinden, W. E., & Seaber, J. A. (1971). Adlerian psychology as a basis for group counseling of socially maladjusted students. *National Catholic Guidance Conference Journal, 15*(2), 106–112.

Feshbach, N. (1969). Student teacher preferences for elementary school pupils varying in personality characteristics. *Journal of Educational Psychology, 60,* 126–132.

Feuerstein, R., Rand, Y., Jensen, M., Kaniel, S., Tzuriel, D., Benshacher, N., & Mintzker, Y. (1985–86). Learning potential assessment. *Special Services in the Schools, 2,* 85–106.

Fifer, G. (1952). Grade placement of secondary school pupils in relation to age and ability. *California Journal of Educational Research, 3,* 31–36.

Fikso, A. (1970). Vicarious vs. participant group psychotherapy of underachievers. *Dissertation Abstracts International, 31*(2-B), 912.

Finch, F. H. (1946). Enrollment increases and changes in the mental level of the high school population. *Appl. Psychol. Monogr., 10,* 75.

Fine, M. J. (1977). Facilitating parent-child relationships for creativity. *Gifted Child Quarterly, 21*(4), 487–500.

Fine, M. J., & Pitts, R. (1980). Intervention with underachieving gifted children: Rationale and strategies. *Gifted Child Quarterly, 24,* 51–55.

Fink, M. (1962). Self-concept as it relates to academic underachievement. *California Journal of Educational Research, 13,* 57–62.

Fink, M. (1963). Cross validation of an underachievement scale. *California Journal of Educational Research, 14*(4), 147–152.

Finkelstein, N. W., & Ramey, C. T. (1980). Information from birth certificates as a risk index for educational handicap. *American Journal of Mental Deficiency, 84,* 546–552.

Finlayson, D. S. (1970). How high and low achievers see teachers' and pupils' role behaviour. *Research in Education, 3,* 38–52.

Finn, J. D. (1972). Expectations and the educational environment. *Review of Educational Research, 42*(3), 387–410.

Finn, J. D., Gaier, E. L., Peng, S. S., & Banks, R. E. (1975). Teacher expectations and pupil achievement. A naturalistic study. *Urban Education, 10*(2), 175–197.

Finney, B. C., & Van Dalsem, E. (1969). Group counseling for gifted underachieving high school students. *Journal of Counseling Psychology, 16*(1), 87–94.

Fitzpatrick, J. L. (1978). Academic underachievement, other-direction, and attitudes toward women's roles in bright adolescent females. *Journal of Educational Psychology, 70*(4), 645–650.

Fitzpatrick, N. (1984). Secondary III core program is for underachieving average ability students. *NASSP Bulletin, 68,* 94–97.

Flaman, F., & McLaughlin, T. F. (1986). Token reinforcement: Effects for accuracy of math performance and generalization to social behavior with an adolescent student. *Technique, 2,* 39–47.

Flanders, N. A., Anderson, J. P., & Amidon, E. J. (1961). Measuring dependence proneness in the classroom. *Educational and Psychological Measurement, 21*(3), 575–587.

Flaugher, R. L., & Rock, D. A. (1969). A multiple moderator approach to the identification of over- and underachievers. *Journal of Educational Measurement, 6*(4), 223–228.

Fleming, R. S. (1951). Parents, too, can meet children's needs. *Understanding the Child, 20,* 74–75.

Fliegler, L. A. (1957). Understanding the underachieving gifted child. *Psychological Reports, 3,* 533–536.

Flory, M. D., & Symmes, C. B. (1964). Academic and emotional problems of college women: Low-effort and high-effort syndromes. *Psychiatry, 27*(3), 290–294.

Foreman, F. S. (1969). Study of self-reinforcement and study skills programs with bright college underachievers. *Dissertation Abstracts International, 30*(4-A), 1430.

Forlano, G., & Wrightstone, J. W. (1955). Measuring the quality of social acceptability within a class. *Educational & Psychological Measurement, 15,* 127–136.

Forrest, D. V. (1966). A comparative study of male secondary school underachievers matriculating at the University of South Dakota. *Dissertation Abstracts, 27*(3-A), 671–672.

Forsyth, D. R., & Strong, S. R. (1986). The scientific study of counseling and psychotherapy: A unificationist view. *American Psychologist, 41*(2), 113–119.

Fotheringham, J. B., & Creal, D. (1980). Family socio-economic and educational-emotional characteristics as predictors of school achievement. *Journal of Educational Research, 73,* 311–317.

Fowler, J. W., & Peterson, P. L. (1981). Increasing reading persistence and altering attributional style of learned helpless children. *Journal of Educational Psychology, 73,* 251–260.

Fowler, P. C., & Richards, H. C. (1978). Father absence, educational preparedness, and academic achievement. *Journal of Educational Psychology, 70*(4), 595–601.

Fox, R. G. (1975). The effects of peer tutoring on the oral reading behavior of underachieving fourth grade pupils. *Dissertation Abstracts International, 36*(2-A), 817.

Frankel, E. (1960). A comparative study of achieving and underachieving high school boys of high intellectual ability. *Journal of Educational Research, 53,* 172–180.

Frankel, E. (1964). Characteristics of working and non-working mothers among intellectually gifted high and low achievers. *Personnel & Guidance Journal, 42*(8), 776–780.

Frankl, A., & Snyder, M. L. (1978). Poor performance following unsolvable problems: Learned helplessness or egotism? *Journal of Personality and Social Psychology, 36,* 1415–1423.

Fransen, F. (1948). Les facteurs caracteriels dans le rendement pratique de l'intélligence [Character factors in practical intellectual achievement]. *Miscellanea psychologica Albert Michotte* (pp. 412–428).

Fraser, P. (1987). *The Non-achievement Syndrome in a Canadian West Indian high school sample.* Unpublished master's thesis, York University, Toronto, ON.

Fraser, P. (1988). *A comparison of interrater reliability between male and female clinicians in differentially diagnosed high school underachievers.* Unpublished doctoral proposal, Department of Psychology, York University, Toronto, ON.

Frederick, R. M. (1977). Self-selected versus randomly assigned programs for underachieving college students. *Dissertation Abstracts International, 37*(9-A), 5697.

Free, J., Marcus, S., Mandel, H., & Morrill, W. (1981). Student attrition and retention. *Proceedings of the 30th Conference of University and College Counseling Center Directors* (pp. 41–46). WI: AUCCCD.

Freedman, A. M., Kaplan, H. I., & Sadock, B. J. (1976). *Modern synopsis of comprehensive textbook of psychiatry/II.* Baltimore, MD: Williams & Wilkins.

Freeman, R-A. (1984). *Screening for learning disabilities in a Non-achievement Syndrome high school sample.* Unpublished undergraduate thesis, York University, Toronto, ON.

Freeman, W. J. (1970). Turning on bright underachievers. *Today's Education, 59,* 52–53.

Frelow, R. D., Charry, J., & Freilich, B. (1974). Academic progress and behavioral changes in low achieving pupils. *Journal of Educational Research, 67*(6), 263–266.

French, J. L. (Ed.). (1959). *Educating the gifted: A book of readings.* New York: Henry Holt.

Freud, S. (1966). *Standard edition of the complete psychological works of Sigmund Freud.* London: Hogarth Press.

Friedland, J. G. (1972). Intellective and personality variables in the differential diagnosis of underachievement. *Dissertation Abstracts International, 32,* 5512-B.

Friedland, J. G., & Marcus, S. I. (1986a). *The Developmental Inventory (DPI).* Unpublished psychological test, Chicago: Friedland & Marcus.

Friedland, J. G., & Marcus, S. I. (1986b). *The Motivational Analysis Inventory (MAI).* Unpublished psychological test, Chicago: Friedland & Marcus.

Friedman, S. B. (1971). Medical considerations in adolescent underachievement. *Journal of School Psychology, 9*(3), 235–240.

Froehlich, G. J. (1944). Mental development during the preadolescent and adolescent periods. *Review of Educational Research, 14,* 401–412.

Froehlich, H. P., & Mayo, G. D. (1963). A note on under- and overachievement measurement. *Personnel & Guidance, 41*(7), 621–623.

Fuchs, E. (1972). How teachers learn to help children fail. In J. M. Hunt (Ed.), *Human intelligence* (pp. 108–122). New Brunswick, NJ: Transaction Books.

Funke, T. M. (1970). The effectiveness of individual and multiple counseling approaches on the academic self-concept of older elementary school children with social, emotional, and learning problems. *Dissertation Abstracts International, 31*(5-A), 2103.

Gadzella, B. M., & Fournet, G. P. (1976). Differences between high and low achievers on self-perceptions. *Journal of Experimental Education, 44*(3), 44–48.

Galante, M. B., Flye, M. E., & Stephens, L. S. (1972). Cumulative minor deficits: A longitudinal study of the relation of physical factors to school achievement. *Journal of Learning Disabilities, 5*(2), 75–80.

Gale, A. (1974). Underachievement among Black and White male junior college students. *Dissertation Abstracts International, 35*(12-B, Pt. 1), 6070–6071.

Galton, F. (1874). *English men of science: Their nature and nurture.* London: MacMillan.

Gardner, J. B. (1968). A study of dropouts at Northwest Mississippi Junior College. *Dissertation Abstracts, 29*(4-A), 1104.

Garfield, S. J. (1967). *Creativity, mental health, and psychotherapy.* Unpublished doctoral dissertation, Illinois Institute of Technology, Chicago, IL.

Garfield, S. J., Cohen, H. A., & Roth, R. M. (1971). Creativity and mental health. *Journal of Educational Research, 63*(4), 147–149.

Garfield, S. J., Cohen, H. A., Roth, R. M., & Berenbaum, H. A. (1971). Effects of group counseling on creativity. *Journal of Educational Research, 64*(5), 235–237.

Garms, J. D. (1968). Predicting scholastic achievement with nonintellectual variables. *Dissertation Abstracts, 28,* 3460.

Gaudry, E., & Spielberger, C. D. (1971). *Anxiety and educational achievement.* Sydney, Australia: Wiley.

Geer, F. C. (1970). The experience of underachievement at the college level. *Dissertation Abstracts International, 31*(1-A), 219.

Gehman, W. S. (1955). Problems of college sophomores with serious scholastic difficulties. *Journal of Counseling Psychology, 2,* 137–141.

Gerler, E. R., Kenney, J., & Anderson, R. F. (1985). The effects of counseling on classroom performance. *Journal of Humanistic Education and Development, 23,* 155–165.

Gerolamo, N. C. (1976). A study of the relationship between academic underachievement and affective inhibition. *Dissertation Abstracts International, 36*(11-B), 5760.

Ghosh, S. N. (1972). Non-cognitive characteristics of over- and under-achievers: A review of studies. *Indian Educational Review, 7*(2), 78–91.

Gilbreath, S. H. (1967). Group counseling, dependence, and college male underachievement. *Journal of Counseling Psychology, 14*(5), 449–453.

Gilbreath, S. H. (1968). Appropriate and inappropriate group counseling with academic underachievers. *Journal of Counseling Psychology, 15*(6), 506–511.

Gilbreath, S. H. (1971). Comparison of responsive and nonresponsive underachievers to counseling service aid. *Journal of Counseling Psychology, 18*(1), 81–84.

Gilhousen, M. R. (1978). Psychological characteristics of the underachiever: A vocational approach. *Dissertation Abstracts International, 38*(8-A), 4770.

Gjesme, T. (1971). Motive to achieve success and motive to avoid failure in relation to school performance for pupils of different ability levels. *Scandanavian Journal of Educational Research, 15,* 81–89.

Glasser, W. (1971). Reaching the unmotivated. *Science Teacher, 38,* 18–22.

Glavach, M., & Stoner, D. (1970). Breaking down the failure pattern. *Journal of Learning Disabilities, 3*(2), 103–105.

Glavin, J. P., & Annesley, F. R. (1971). Reading and arithmetic correlates of conduct-problem and withdrawn children. *Journal of Special Education, 5*(3), 213–219.

Glenn, H. (1979). Investigation of factors related to academic underachievement among sixth grade pupils. *Dissertation Abstracts International, 39*(11-A), 6651.

Gnagney, T. (1970). The myth of underachievement. *Education Digest, 35,* 49–52.

Goebel, M. E. (1967). A comparison of the relative effectiveness of three types of counseling with high school underachievers. *Dissertation Abstracts, 27*(9-A), 2827.

Goldburgh, S. J., & Penney, J. F. (1962). A note on counseling underachieving college students. *Journal of Counseling Psychology, 9*(2), 133–138.

Golicz, H. J. (1982). Use of attitude scales with gifted underachievers. *Roeper, 4*(4), 22–23.

Good, T. (1980). Classroom expectations: Teacher-pupil interactions. In J. McMillan (Ed.), *The Social Psychology of School Learning,* New York: Academic Press.

Good, T., & Brophy, J. (1977). *Educational Psychology: A Realistic Approach.* New York: Holt, Rhinehart, & Winston.

Good, T., Cooper, H., & Blakey, S. (1980). Classroom interaction as a function of teacher expectations, student sex, and time of year. *Journal of Educational Psychology, 72,* 378–385.

Goodenough, F. L. (1946). The measurement of mental growth in childhood. In L. Carmichael (Ed.), *Manual of child psychology* (pp. 450–475). New York: Wiley.

Goodstein, L., & Crites, J. (1961). Brief counseling with poor college risks. *Journal of Counseling Psychology, 8,* 318–321.

Goodstein, M. A. (1969). The relationship of personality change to therapeutic system and diagnosis. *Dissertation Abstracts International, 30,* 2419-B.

Goodstein, M. A. (1980). The diagnosis and treatment of underachievement. *Journal of the International Association of Pupil Personnel Workers, 24,* 102–109.

Gopal, R. (1970). A study of some factors related to scholastic achievement. *Indian Journal of Psychology, 45,* 99–120.

Gordon, E., & Thomas, A. (1967). Children's behavioral style and teachers' appraisal of their intelligence. *Journal of School Psychology, 5,* 292–300.

Gordon, M. T. (1976). A different view of the IQ-achievement gap. *Sociology of Education, 49*(1), 4–11.

Gottsegen, M. G., & Gottsegen, G. B. (Eds.). (1969). *Professional school psychology* (Vols. 2 & 3). New York: Grune & Stratton.

Gough, H. G. (1946). The relationship of SES to personality inventory and achievement test scores. *Journal of Educational Psychology, 37,* 527–540.

Gough, H. G. (1953). What determines the academic achievement of high school students? *Journal of Educational Research, 46,* 321–331.

Gourley, M. H. (1971). The effects of individual counseling, group guidance, and verbal reinforcement on the academic progress of underachievers. *Dissertation Abstracts International, 31*(8-A), 3873.

Gowan, J. C. (1957). Intelligence, interests, and reading ability in relation to scholastic achievement. *Psychology Newsletter, 8,* 85–87.

Graaf, A. de (1951). [Some major causes of the decrease in achievement level of secondary school students.] *Psychol. Achtergr., 15/16,* 22–36.

Granlund, E., & Knowles, L. (1969). Child-parent identification and academic underachievement. *Journal of Consulting & Clinical Psychology, 33*(4), 495–496.

Granzow, K. R. (1954). A comparative study of under-, normal-, and overachievers in reading. *Dissertation Abstracts, 14,* 631–632.

Grau, P. N. (1985). Two causes of underachievement: The scapegoat phenomenon and the Peter Pan Syndrome. Part I. *Gifted Child Today, 8*(41), 47–50.

Grau, P. N. (1986). Two causes of underachievement: The scapegoat phenomenon and the Peter Pan Syndrome. Part II. *Gifted Child Today, 9*(1), 9–11.

Green, C. W. (1953). The relationship between intelligence and ability. *Journal of Educational Research, 47,* 191–200.

Greenberg, J. W., & Davidson, H. H. (1972). Home background and school achievement of Black urban ghetto children. *American Journal of Orthopsychiatry, 42*(5), 803–810.

Greenberg, M. (1970). Musical achievement and the self-concept. *Journal of Research in Music Education, 18*(1), 57–64.

Greenblatt, E. L. (1950). Relationship of mental health and social status. *Journal of Educational Research, 44,* 193–204.

Greenspan, S. B. (1975). Effectiveness of therapy for children's reversal confusions. *Academic Therapy, 20*(3), 169–178.

Greenwald, H. (1974). Treatment of the psychopath. In H. Greenwald (Ed.), *Active Psychotherapy,* (pp. 363–377). New York: Jason Aronson.

Griffin, P. A. (1979). Coping styles and life events: Etiological factors in adolescent adjustment. *Dissertation Abstracts International, 40*(3-A), 1278.

Griffiths, G. R. (1945). The relationship between scholastic achievement and personality adjustment of men college students. *Journal of Applied Psychology, 29,* 360–367.

Grimes, J. W., & Wesley, A. (1961). Compulsivity, anxiety, and school achievement. *Merrill-Palmer Quarterly, 7,* 247–273.

Grosenbach, M. J. (1977). An assessment of personality types of students who chose challenge curricula and students who are underachievers. *Dissertation Abstracts International, 37*(10-A), 6274.

Grossman, B. J. (1971). Counseling parents of senior high school students. *Journal of Education, 154,* 60–64.

Grossman, F. M. (1981). Cautions in interpreting WRAT standard scores as criterion measures of achievement in young children. *Psychology in the Schools, 18*(2), 144–146.

Grover, P. L., & Tessier, K. E. (1978). Diagnosis and treatment of academic frustration syndrome. *Journal of Medical Education, 53*(9), 734–740.

Growing up socially and emotionally in the elementary school. (1947). *Understanding the Child, 16,* 116–118.

Gruen, E. W. (1945). Level of aspiration in relation to personality factors in adolescents. *Child Development, 16,* 181–188.

Guay, J. (1974). Poverty and intellectual underachievement: A critical review and a suggested intervention. *Dissertation Abstracts International, 34*(10-B), 5167.

Gurman, A. S. (1969). Group counseling with underachievers: A review and evaluation of methodology. *International Journal of Group Psychotherapy, 19*(4), 463–474.

Gurman, A. S. (1970). The role of the family in underachievement. *Journal of School Psychology, 8*(1), 48–53.

Guth, P. S. (1977). A study of the characteristics of the fourth, fifth, and sixth grade subjects of two school districts who are underachievers in reading. *Dissertation Abstracts International, 37*(9-A), 5560–5561.

Guttman, J., & Bar-Tal, D. (1982). Stereotypic perceptions of teachers. *American Educational Research Journal, 19,* 519–528.

Haggerty, M. (1971). The effects of being a tutor and being a counselee in a group of self concept and achievement level of underachieving adolescent males. *Dissertation Abstracts International, 31*(9-A), 4460.

Haider, S. J. (1971). Parental attitudes and child-rearing practices as related to academic underachievement. *Dissertation Abstracts International, 31*(12-A), 6402.

Hale, R. L. (1979). The utility of WISC-R subtest scores in discriminating among adequate and underachieving children. *Multivariate Behavioral Research, 14*(2), 245–253.

Haley, J. (1969). *The power tactics of Jesus Christ.* New York: Grossman.

Hall, E. (1983). Recognizing gifted underachievers. *Roeper Review, 5,* 23–25.

Halpern, H. M. (1969). Psychodynamic correlates of underachievement. In M. G. Gottsegen & G. B. Gottsegen (Eds.), *Professional school psychology* (Vol. 3) (pp. 318–337). New York: Grune & Stratton.

Halsted, D. W. (1967). An initial survey of the attitudinal differences between the mothers of over-achieving and under-achieving eleventh-grade Puerto Rican students. *Dissertation Abstracts, 27*(12-A), 4127–4128.

Hammer, E. F. (Ed.). (1970). *Achievement perspectives on school dropouts.* Los Angeles, CA: Western Psychological Services.

Hanley, D. E. (1971). The effects of short-term counseling upon high school underachievers' measured self-concepts, academic achievement, and vocational maturity. *Dissertation Abstracts International, 31*(10-A), 5125–5126.

Harlow, H. F., & Harlow, M. K. (1962). The effect of rearing conditions on behavior. *Bulletin of the Menninger Clinic, 26,* 213–224.

Harari, H. and McDavid, J. (1973). Name stereotypes and teacher expectations. *Journal of Educational Psychology, 65,* 222–225.

Harris, B. R., Muir, R., Lester, E. P., Dudek, S. Z., & Goldberg, J. (1968). Intelligence, personality and achievement. *Canadian Psychiatric Association Journal, 13*(4), 335–339.

Harris, D. (1940). Factors affecting college grades: A review of the literature, 1930–1937. *Psychological Bulletin, 37,* 125–161.

Harris, M. (1969). Motivating underachievers. *Instruction, 78,* 138.

Harris, P., & Trotta, F. (1962). An experiment with underachievers. *Education, 82,* 347–349.

Harris, R. B. (1971). The effects of praise and/or reproof on serial learning in underachievers. *Dissertation Abstracts International, 32*(3-A), 1336.

Harrison, F. (1968). Aspirations as related to school performance and socioeconomic status. *Sociometry, 32*(1), 70–79.

Harrison, P. J. (1976). Intelligence and classroom behavior as predictors of achievement in the underachieving child. *Dissertation Abstracts International, 36*(7-B), 3607.

Hartley, L. (1985). *Academic underachievement in female high school students: A comparative analysis in differential diagnosed samples.* Unpublished doctoral dissertation, York University, Toronto, ON.

Hartman, R. D. (1969). An assessment of a program for underachievers. *Exceptional Children, 36*(1), 44–45.

Hartmann, H. (1958). *Ego psychology and the problem of adaptation.* New York: International Universities Press.

Hartmann, R. S. (1970). The effects of experimentally induced cognitive dissonance on the grade point average of selected underachievers. *Dissertation Abstracts International, 31*(4-A), 1621.

Harvey, W. A. (1966). In L. A. Pervin, L. E. Reik, & W. Dalrymple (Eds.), *Identity and depression in students who fail* (pp. 223–236). Princeton, NJ: Princeton University Press.

Hastings, J. M. (1982). A program for gifted underachievers. *Roeper Review, 4,* 42.

Haun, K. W. (1965). A note on the prediction of academic performance from personality test scores. *Psychological Reports, 16,* 294.

Havinghurst, R. J., & Breese, F. H. (1947). Relation between ability and social status in a midwestern community: III. Primary mental abilities. *Journal of Educational Psychology, 38,* 241–247.

Hawkins, D. B., & Horowitz, H. (1971). Variations in body image as a function of achievement level in school performance. *Perceptual & Motor Skills, 33*(3, Pt. 2), 1229–1302.

Hawkins, J. L. (1974). A comparison of the effects of two types of reinforcement techniques on academic and nonacademic classroom behaviors of underachieving elementary students. *Dissertation Abstracts International, 35*(5-B), 2404.

Haywood, H. C. (1968). Motivational orientation of overachieving and underachieving elementary school children. *American Journal of Mental Deficiency, 72*(5), 667.

Heck, R. A. (1972). Need for approval and its relationship to under, expected and over achievement. *Dissertation Abstracts International, 32*(7-A), 3688.

Hedley, W. H. (1968). Freshman survival and attrition at a small, private, liberal-arts college: A discriminant analysis of intellectual and nonintellectual variables. *Dissertation Abstracts, 29*(2-A), 461.

Heilbrun, A. B., Jr., Waters, D. B. (1968). Underachievement as related to perceived maternal child rearing and academic conditions of reinforcement. *Child Development, 39*(3), 913–921.

Helfenbein, L. N. (1970). Differences among differentially defined types of underachievers. *Dissertation Abstracts International, 30*(9-A), 3785–3786.

Henderson, E. H., & Long, B. H. (1971). Personal-social correlates of academic success among disadvantaged school beginners. *Journal of School Psychology, 9*(2), 101–113.

Hendin, H. (1972). The psychodynamics of flunking out. *Journal of Nervous and Mental Disease, 155*(2), 131–143.

Hepner, E. M. (1970). Self-concepts, values, and needs of Mexican-American underachievers. *Dissertation Abstracts International, 31*(6-A), 2736.

Hershenson, D. (1967). The Hershenson Occupational Plans Questionnaire. Unpublished test, Illinois Institute of Technology, Department of Psychology, Chicago.

Hess, T. (1970). A comparison of group counseling with individual counseling in the modification of self-adjustment and social adjustment of fifteen year old males identified as potential dropouts. *Dissertation Abstracts International, 31*(3-A), 998–999.

Heyneman, S. P., & Loxley, W. A. (1983). The effect of primary-school quality on academic achievement across twenty-nine high- and low-income countries. *American Journal of Sociology, 88,* 1162–1194.

Hieronymus, A. N. (1951). A study of social class motivation: relationships between anxiety for education and certain socio-economic and intellectual variables. *Journal of Educational Psychology, 42,* 193–205.

High, B. H. (1971). Group counseling with underachieving tenth graders. *Dissertation Abstracts International, 31*(10-A), 5127.

Hilgard, E. R. (1946). Aspirations after learning. *Childhood Education, 23,* 115–118.

Hill, A. H., & Grieneeks, L. (1966). An evaluation of academic counseling of under- and over-achievers. *Journal of Counseling Psychology, 13*(3), 325–328.

Hilliard, L. T. (1949). Educational types of mentally defective children. *Journal of Mental Science, 95,* 860–866.

Hilliard, T., & Roth, R. M. (1969). Maternal attitudes and the nonachievement syndrome. *Personnel & Guidance Journal, 47*(5), 424–428.

Himmel-Rossi, B., & Merrifield, P. (1977). Students' personality factors related to teacher reports of their interactions with students. *Journal of Educational Psychology, 69,* 375–380.

Himmelweit, H. T. (1950). Student selection—an experimental investigation: I. *British Journal of Sociology, 1,* 328–346.

Himmelweit, H. T., & Summerfield, A. (1951a). Student selection—an experimental investigation: II. *British Journal of Sociology, 2,* 59–75.

Himmelweit, H. T., & Summerfield, A. (1951b). Student selection—an experimental investigation: III. *British Journal of Sociology, 2,* 340–351.

Hinkelman, E. A. (1955). Relationship of intelligence to elementary school achievement. *Educational Administrative Supervisor, 41,* 176–179.

Hirsch, J. G., & Costello, J. (1970). School achievers and underachievers in an urban ghetto. *Elementary School Journal, 71*(2), 78–85.

Hobart, C. W. (1963). Underachievement among minority group students: An analysis and a proposal. *Phylon, 24,* 184–196.

Hocker, M. E. (1971). Visual-motor characteristics of retarded readers and the relationship to their classroom behavior. *Dissertation Abstracts International, 31*(9-A), 4383.

Hoeffel, E. C. (1978). The antiachieving adolescent. *Dissertation Abstracts International, 39*(5-A), 2867–2868.

Hoffman, J. L., Wasson, F. R., & Christianson, B. P. (1985). Personal development for the gifted underachiever. *Gifted Child Today, 38,* 12–14.

Hoffman, L. W. (1972). Early childhood experiences and women's achievement motives. *Journal of Social Issues, 28,* 129–155.

Hoffman, M. S. (1971). Early indications of learning problems. *Academic Therapy, 7*(1), 23–35.

Hogan, R., & Schroeder, D. (1980). The ambiguities of educational achievement. *Sociological Spectrum, 1,* 35–45.

Hoge, R. D. (1977). The use of observational data in elementary counseling. *Canadian Counsellor, 11*(2), 93–96.

Hollon, T. H. (1970). Poor school performance as a symptom of masked depression in children and adolescents. *American Journal of Psychotherapy, 25*(2), 258–263.

Holmstrom, E. I. (1973). Low achievers: Do they differ from "typical" undergraduates? *ACE Research Reports, 8*(6) 1–44.

Holt, M. F. (1978). Guilford's structure of intellect model applied to underachievement in gifted children. *Dissertation Abstracts International, 39*(2-A), 812.

Honor, S. H. (1971). TAT and direct methods of obtaining educational attitudes of high and low achieving high school boys. *Dissertation Abstracts International, 32*(2-B), 1213.

Hoopes, M. H. (1969). The effects of structuring goals in the process of group counseling for academic improvement. *Dissertation Abstracts International, 30,* 1012-A.

Hoover, B. (1967). College students who did not seek counseling during a period of academic difficulty. *Dissertation Abstracts, 28*(4-A), 1298-A.

Horace Mann-Lincoln Institute of School Experimentation. (1948). Child development and the curriculum. *Teach. Coll. Rec., 49,* 314–324.

Hornbostel, L. K., & McCall, J. N. (1980). Sibling differences in need-achievement associated with birth order, child-spacing, sex, and sibling's sex. *Journal of Individual Psychology, 36,* 36–43.

Horowitz, L. J. (1967). Parents' intervention in behavior modification of underachievers. *Dissertation Abstracts, 27*(12-A), 4129.

Horrall, B. M. (1957). Academic performance and personality adjustment of highly intelligent college students. *Genetic Psychological Monograph, 55,* 3–83.

House, G. (1972). Orientations to Achievement. *Unpublished Doctoral Dissertation,* University of Michigan.

Howell, W. L. (1972). The correlates of change in school integration with the academic achievement of eighth grade students. *Dissertation Abstracts International, 32*(12-B), 7292.

Hoyser, E. E. (1971). Therapeutic non-directive play with low achievers in reading. *Dissertation Abstracts International, 31*(8-A), 3875.

Hoyt, D. P., & Norman, W. T. (1954). Adjustment and academic predictability. *Journal of Counseling Psychology, 1,* 96–99.

Hughes, H. H. (1961). Expectancy, reward, and Differential Aptitude Tests performance of low and high achievers with high ability. *Dissertation Abstracts, 21,* 2358.

Hunter, M. C. (1973). Helping underachievers. *Educational Horizons, 52,* 23–25.

Hussain, M. D. (1971). A comparison of treatment methods for underachieving elementary students. *Dissertation Abstracts International, 32*(3-B), 1846.

Hvozdik, J. [Basic psychological problems of pupils failing in school]. (1972). *Jednotna Skola, 24*(6), 543–553.

Hymes, J. L., Jr. (1954). But he CAN learn facts. . . . *Education, 74,* 572–574.

Iddiols, J. (1985). *The relationship between different teacher helping strategies and different personality types of underachieving students.* Unpublished undergraduate thesis, York University, Toronto, ON.

Ignas, E. (1969). A comparison of the relative effectiveness of four different counseling approaches in short-term counseling with junior and senior high school underachieving students. *Dissertation Abstracts, 29*(10-A), 3419–3420.

Irvine, D. W. (1966). Relationship between the STEP tests and overachievement/underachievement. *Journal of Educational Research, 59*(7), 294–296.

Iscoe, I. (1964). "I told you so": The logical dilemma of the bright underachieving child. *Psychology in the Schools, 1,* 282–284.

Ivey, A. E. (1962). The academic performance of students counseled at a university counseling service. *Journal of Counseling Psychology, 9*(4), 347–352.

Izzo, T. E. (1976). Home parental assistance for underachieving readers in third grade using read-at-home program kits. *Dissertation Abstracts International, 37*(6-A), 3473.

Jack, R. M. (1975). The effect of reinforcement value in mixed and unmixed lists on the learning style of overachieving and underachieving female college students. *Dissertation Abstracts International, 35*(11-B), 5619.

Jackson, B. (1985). Lowered expectations: How schools reward incompetence. *Phi Delta Kappan, 67,* 304–305.

Jackson, K. R., & Clark, S. G. (1958). Thefts among college students. *Personnel & Guidance Journal, 36,* 557–562.

Jackson, R. M. (1968). In support of the concept of underachievement. *Personnel & Guidance Journal, 47*(1), 56–62.

Jackson, R. M., Cleveland, J. C., & Merenda, P. R. (1968–1969). The effects of early identification and counseling of underachievers. *Journal of School Psychology, 7*(2), 42–49.

Jackson, R. M., Cleveland, J. C., & Merenda, P. F. (1975), The longitudinal effects of early identification and counseling of underachievers. *Journal of School Psychology, 13*(2), 119–128.

Jain, S. K., & Robson, C. J. (1969). Study habits of high, middle, and low attainers. *Proceedings of the 77th Annual Convention of the American Psychological Association, 4*(2), 633–634.

Janes, G. D. (1971). Student perceptions, parent perceptions, and teacher perceptions of student abilities, aspirations, expectations, and motivations: Their relationship to under- and over-achievement. *Dissertation Abstracts International, 31*(9-A), 4548–4549.

Janos, P. M. (1986). "Underachievement" among markedly accelerated college students. *Journal of Youth and Adolescence, 15,* 303–313.

Janssen, J. W. (1970). The relative effectiveness of students at several college levels to lead small groups of low-achieving freshmen in academic adjustment counseling. *Dissertation Abstracts International, 31*(3-A), 1012.

Jeter, J. T. (1975). Can teacher expectations function as self-fulfilling prophecies? *Contemporary Education, 46,* 161–165.

Jhaj, D. S., & Grewal, J. S. (1983). Occupational aspirations of the achievers and underachievers in mathematics. *Asian Journal of Psychology and Education, 11*(1), 36–39.

Johnson, A. A. (1968). A study of the relationship between nonpromotion and the male student's self-concept of academic ability and his perceived parental, friends', and teachers' evaluations of his academic ability. *Dissertation Abstracts, 29*(2-A), 409.

Johnson, C. (1981). Smart kids have problems, too. *Today's Education, 70,* 26–27.

Johnson, E. G., Jr. (1967). A comparison of academically successful and unsuccessful college of education freshmen on two measures of "self." *Dissertation Abstracts, 28*(4-A), 1298–1299.

Johnson, E. K. (1968). The effects of client-centered group counseling utilizing play media on the intelligence, achievement, and psycho-linguistic abilities of under-achieving primary school children. *Dissertation Abstracts, 29*(5-A), 1425–1426.

Johnson, R. W. (1969). The development of an instrument to distinguish among four high school achievement groups in terms of their behavior. *Dissertation Abstracts, 29*(10-A), 3420.

Johnston, P. H., & Winograd, P. N. (1985). Passive failure in reading. *Journal of Reading Behavior, 17*(4), 279–301.

Jones, H. E. (1946). Environmental influences on mental development. In L. Carmichael (Ed.), *Manual of child psychology* (pp. 582–632). New York: Wiley.

Jordan, C. (1985). Translating culture: From ethnographic information to educational program. *Anthropology and Education Quarterly, 16,* 104–123.

Joyce, J. (1972). *Portrait of the artist as a young man.* New York: Viking Press. (Original work published 1916).

Joyce, J. F. (1970). An investigation of some personality characteristics of achieving high school students from lower socioeconomic environments. *Dissertation Abstracts International, 31*(4-A), 1623.

Kaess, W., & Long, L. (1954). An investigation of the effectiveness of vocational guidance. *Educational and Psychological Measurement, 14,* 423–433.

Kafka, F. (1947). *The trial.* London: Secker and Warburg.

Kahler, T. (1973). Predicting academic underachievement in ninth and twelfth grade males with the Kahler Transactional Analysis Script Checklist. *Dissertation Abstracts International, 33*(9-A), 4838–4839.

Kambly, A. H. (1967). Psychiatric treatment of adolescent underachievers. *Psychotherapy & Psychosomatics, 15*(1), 32.

Kaminska, A. (1984). *MMPI profiles in the Non-achievement Syndrome high school student.* Unpublished undergraduate thesis, York University, Toronto, ON.

Kanner, L. (1971). The integrative aspect of ability. *Acta Paedopsychiatrica, 38*(5–6), 134–144.

Kanoy, R. C., Johnson, B. W., & Kanoy, K. W. (1980). Locus of control and self-concept in achieving and underachieving bright elementary students. *Psychology in the Schools, 17*(3), 395–399.

Kanter, V. F. (1970). A study of the relationship between birth order and achievement by overachieving early school starters and underachieving late school starters at the sixth grade level. *Dissertation Abstracts International, 31*(1-A), 70–71.

Karlsen, B. (1955). A comparison of some educational and psychological characteristics of successful and unsuccessful readers at the elementary school level. *Dissertation Abstracts, 15,* 456–457.

Karnes, M. B., McCoy, G., Zehrbach, R. R., Wollersheim, J. P., & Clarizio, H. F. (1963). The efficacy of two organizational plans for underachieving intellectually gifted children. *Exceptional Children, 29*(9), 438–446.

Karolchuck, P. A., & Worell, L. (1956). Achievement motivation and learning. *Journal of Abnormal & Social Psychology, 53,* 255–257.

Katz, I. (1967). The socialization of academic motivation in minority group children. *Nebraska Symposium on Motivation, 15,* 133–191.

Kauffman, J. M., & Weaver, S. J. (1971). Age and intelligence as correlates of perceived family relationships of underachievers. *Psychological Reports, 28*(2), 522.

Kaul, L. (1971). Differences in some Edwards Personal Preference Schedule needs related with academic achievement among rural and urban adolescents. *Education and Psychology Review, 11,* 11–14.

Kearney, R. (1971). Erikson's concept of epigenesis: A statistical exploration. *Dissertation Abstracts International, 31*(12-B), 7600.

Kehle, T. J. (1972). Effect of student's physical attractiveness, sex, race, intelligence, and SES on teacher's expectations for student personality and academic performance. *Unpublished Doctoral Dissertation,* University of Kentucky.

Keimowitz, R. I., & Ansbacher, H. L. (1960). Personality and achievement in mathematics. *Journal of Individual Psychology, 16,* 84–87.

Keisler, E. R. (1955). Peer group rating of high school pupils with high and low school marks. *Journal of Experimental Education, 23,* 369–373.

Kemp, L. C. D. (1955). Environmental and other characteristics determining attainment in primary schools. *British Journal of Educational Psychology, 25,* 67–77.

Kender, J. P., et al. (1985). WAIS-R performance patterns of 565 incarcerated adults characterized as underachieving readers and adequate readers. *Journal of Learning Disabilities, 181,* 379–383.

Kennet, K. F., & Cropley, A. J. (1970). Intelligence, family size, and socioeconomic status. *Journal of Biosocial Science, 2,* 227–236.

Keogh, J., & Benson, D. (1964). Motor characteristics of underachieving boys. *Journal of Educational Research, 57*(7), 339–344.

Keppers, G. L., & Caplan, S. W. (1962). Group counseling with academically able underachieving students. *New Mexico Social Studies Education and Educational Research Bulletin, 1,* 12–17.

Kester, S. W., & Lethworth, G. A. (1972). Communication of teacher expectations and their effects on achievement and attitudes of secondary school students. *Journal of Educational Research, 66,* 51–55.

Ketchum, E. G. (1947). School disabilities. *Philadelphia Medicine, 42,* 1250–1256.

Khan, S. B. (1969). Affective correlates of academic achievement. *Journal of Educational Psychology, 60*(3), 216–221.

Kifer, E. (1975). Relationships between academic achievement and personality characteristics: A quasi-longitudinal study. *American Educational Research Journal, 12,* 191–210.

Kilmann, P. R., Henry, S. E., Scarbro, H., & Laughlin, J. E. (1979). The impact of affective education on elementary school underachievers. *Psychology in the Schools, 16*(2), 217–223.

Kim, Y. C. (1971). Factorial analysis of intellectual interest and measurement of its validity in the prediction of college success. *Dissertation Abstracts International, 32*(6-A), 3094.

Kimball, B. (1952). The sentence completion technique in a study of scholastic achievement. *Journal of Consulting Psychology, 16,* 353–358.

Kimball, B. (1953). Case studies in educational failure during adolescence. *American Journal of Orthopsychiatry, 23,* 406–415.

Kincaid, D. (1969). A study of highly gifted elementary pupils. *Gifted Child Quarterly, 13*(4), 264–267.

Kintzi, R. (1976). Successful management of specific ninth grade social and academic behavior. *SALT: School Applications of Learning Theory, 8*(2), 28–37.

Kipnis, D., & Resnick, J. H. (1969). *Experimental prevention of underachievement among intelligent impulsive college students.* Philadelphia, PA: Temple University Press.

Kipnis, D., & Resnick, J. H. (1971). Experimental prevention of underachievement among intelligent impulsive college students. *Journal of Consulting & Clinical Psychology, 36*(1), 53–60.

Kirk, B. (1952). Test versus academic performance in malfunctioning students. *Journal of Consulting Psychology, 16,* 213–216.

Kirkendall, D. R., & Gruber, J. J. (1970). Canonical relationships between motor and intellectual achievement domains in culturally deprived high school pupils. *Research Quarterly, 41*(4), 496–502.

Kisch, J. M. (1968). A comparative study of patterns of underachievement among male college students. *Dissertation Abstracts, 28*(8-B), 3461–3462.

Klausmeier, H. J. (1958). Physical, behavioral, and other characteristics of high- and low-achieving children in favored environments. *Journal of Educational Research, 51,* 573–581.

Klein, J. P., Quarter, J. J., & Laxer, R. M. (1969). Behavioral counseling of underachievers. *American Educational Research Journal, 6*(3), 415–424.

Klein, C. L. (1972). The adolescents with learning problems. How long must they wait? *Journal of Learning Disabilities, 5*(5), 262–284.

Klinge, V., Rennick, P. M., Lennox, K., & Hart, Z. (1977). A matched-subject comparison of underachievers with normals on intellectual, behavioral, and emotional variables. *Journal of Abnormal Child Psychology, 5,* 61–68.

Klinglehofer, E. L. (1954). The relationship of academic advisement to the scholastic performance of failing college students. *Journal of Counseling Psychology, 1,* 125–131.

Klohr, M. C. (1948). Personal problems of college students. *Journal of Home Economics, 40,* 447–448.

Klonsky, K. (1987). The psychology of school failure. *Forum: The Magazine for Secondary School Educators, 13*(1), 22–26.

Knauer, F. E. (1969). A study of the relationship of selected variables to persistence of academically capable former students of the University of South Dakota, *Dissertation Abstracts, 29*(8-A), 2527–2528.

Koch, H. L. (1954). The relation of ''primary mental abilities' in five- and six-year-olds to sex of child and characteristics of his siblings. *Child Development, 25,* 209–233.

Koelsche, C. L. (1956). A study of the student drop-out problem at Indiana University. *Journal of Educational Research, 49,* 357–364.

Kohl, H. (1979). Changing the ''Wanting-to-Fail'' syndrome. *Teacher, 97,* 14, 20, 22.

Kolb, D. (1965). Achievement motivation training for underachieving high school boys. *Journal of Personality and Social Psychology, 2,* 783–792.

Kornrich, M. (Ed.). (1965). *Underachievement.* Springfield, IL: Charles C. Thomas.

Kort, J. (1975). Underachievers and group counseling. *Journal of the International Association of Pupil Personnel Workers, 11,* 152–155.

Kosky, R. (1983). Childhood suicidal behavior. *Journal of Child Psychology & Psychiatry & Allied Disciplines, 24*(3), 457–468.

Kowitz, G. T. (1965). An analysis of underachievement. In M. Kornrich (Ed.), *Underachievement* (pp. 464–473). Springfield, IL: Charles C. Thomas.

Kozuch, J. A., & Garrison, H. H. (1980). A sociology of social problems approach to the literature on the decline in academic performance. *Sociological Spectrum, 1,* 115–136.

Kraft, A. (1969). A class for academic underachievers in high school. *Adolescence, 4*(15), 295–318.

Kraft, I. A. (1972). A child and adolescent in group therapy. In H. I. Kaplan & B. J. Sadock (Eds.), *Group treatment of mental illness* (pp. 47–77). New York: E. P. Dutton.

Krause, E. A. (1968). Trust, training, and the school dropout's world view. *Community Mental Health Journal, 4*(5), 369–375.

Kreutzer, V. O. (1973). A study of the use of underachieving students as tutors for emotionally disturbed children. *Dissertation Abstracts International, 34*(6-A), 3145.

Krige, P. (1976). Patterns of interaction in family triads with high-achieving and low-achieving children. *Psychological Reports, 39*(Pt. 2), 1291–1299.

Kroft, S. B., Ratzlaff, H. C., & Perks, B. A. (1986). Intelligence and early academic underachievement. *British Journal of Clinical Psychology, 25*(2), 147–148.

Krouse, J. H., & Krouse, H. J. (1981). Toward a multimodal theory of academic underachievement. *Educational Psychologist, 16*(3), 151–164.

Krout, M. H. (1946). Psychological standards in measuring achievement. *Sch. Sci. Math., 46,* 803–806.

Krug, R. E. (1959). Over- and under-achievement and the Edwards Personal Preference Schedule. *Journal of Applied Psychology, 43,* 133–136.

Krutop, J. O. (1971). An educational model to break the failure cycle. *Dissertation Abstracts International, 32*(4-A), 1918.

Kubany, E. S., & Sloggett, B. (1971). The role of motivation in test performance and remediation. *Journal of Learning Disabilities, 4,* 426–428.

Kukla, A. (1972). Attributional determinants of achievement-related behavior. *Journal of Personality and Social Psychology, 21*(2), 166–174.

Kunz, P. R., & Peterson, E. T. (1977). Family size, birth order, and academic achievement. *Social Biology, 24,* 144–148.

Lacher, M. (1971). The life styles of underachieving, overachieving and normal achieving college students. *Dissertation Abstracts International, 31*(8-B), 4999.

Lacher, M. (1973). The life styles of underachieving college students. *Journal of Counseling Psychology, 20*(3), 220–226.

Ladouceur, R., & Armstrong, J. (1983). Evaluation of a behavioral program for the improvement of grades among high school students. *Journal of Counseling Psychology, 30,* 100–103.

Laing, R. D. (1965). *The divided self.* Baltimore, MD: Penguin.

Laird, A. W. (1980). A comprehensive and innovative attack of action programs for delinquency prevention and classroom success. *Education, 101,* 118–122.

Laitman, R. J. (1975). Family relations as an intervening variable in the relationship of birth order and self-esteem. *Dissertation Abstracts International, 36,* 3051B.

Landsman, T., & Sheldon, W. D. (1949). Nondirective group psychotherapy with failing college students. *American Psychologist, 4,* 287.

Lane, M. E. (1971). Achievement motivation, level of academic achievement and therapy outcome. *Dissertation Abstracts International, 31*(11-B), 6906–6907.

Lantz, B. (1945). Some dynamic aspects of success and failure. *Psychological Monographs, 59*(1), vi–40.

Lardizabal, E. T. (1986). The ethnic home environment—Its impact on school attitudes and academic achievement. *Dissertation Abstracts International, 46*, 3553-A.

Larkin, M. A. (1975). A comparison of the differences on conventional audiological measures and selected auditory instruments between reading achievers and underachievers. *Dissertation Abstracts International, 35*(9-A), 5970–5971.

Larkin, R. W. (1980). *Sympathy for the devil: Student motivation and the socio-characterological revolution.* Paper presented at the annual meeting of the Society for the Study of Social Problems, New York.

Larsen, S. C., & Ehly, S. (1978). Teacher-student interactions: A factor in handicapping conditions. *Academic Therapy, 13*(3), 267–273.

Lauer, G. R. (1969). A comarison of attitudes of male underachievers and normal male high school students toward their teachers. *Dissertation Abstracts International, 30*(4-A), 1469.

Lavin, D. E. (1965). *The prediction of academic performance: A theoretical analysis and review of research.* New York: Russell Sage Foundation.

Lawrence, A. (1985). *The relationship between family stability and academic achievement in high school students.* Unpublished undergraduate thesis, York University, Toronto, ON.

Laxer, R. M., Kennedy, D. R., Quarter, J., & Isnor, C. (1966). Counselling small groups of underachievers in secondary schools: An experimental study. *Ontario Journal of Educational Research, 9*(1), 49–57.

Layton, J. R., & Chappell, L. (1976). An analysis of teacher opinion regarding student academic achievement and teacher ability to cope with underachievement. *Colorado Journal of Educational Research, 15*, 17–27.

Leland, B. (1948). Distinguishing the remedial child from the child in need of special education. *Journal of Exceptional Children, 14*, 225–230.

LeMay, M. L., & Damm, V. J. (1968). The Personal Orientation Inventory as a measure of the self-actualization of underachievers. *Measurement & Evaluation in Guidance, 1*(2), 110–114.

Lenn, T. I., Lane, P. A., Merritt, E. T., & Silverstone, L. (1967). Parent group therapy for adolescent rehabilitation. *V.O.C. Journal of Education, 7*(3), 17–26.

Lens, W. (1983). Achievement motivation, test anxiety, and academic achievement. *University of Leuven Psychological Reports,* (No. 2).

Leonard, G. E. (1968). Counselor—Being? *National Catholic Guidance Conference Journal, 13*(1), 33–38.

Lesnick, M. (1972). Reading and study behavior problems of college freshmen. *Reading World, 11*(4), 296–319.

Leverett, G. (1985). *Am I my brother's/sister's keeper? Sibling achievement patterns of overachieving, average achieving, and underachieving grade 9 high school students.* Unpublished undergraduate thesis, York University, Toronto, ON.

Levin, M. L., Van Loon, M., & Spitler, H. D. (1978). *Marital disruption and cognitive development and achievement in children and youth.* Paper presented at the Annual Meeting of the Society for the Study of Social Problems, New York.

Levin, W. J. (1972). The effectiveness and generalization of ability-oriented reinforcement for improving the academic performance of underachievers. *Dissertation Abstracts International, 32*(11-B), 6652.

Levine, E. M. (1980). The declining educational achievement of middle-class students, the deterioration of educational and social standards, and parents' negligence. *Sociological Spectrum, 1*, 17–34.

Levine, E. M. (1983). Why middle class students aren't learning. *Journal of Social, Political and Economic Studies, 8*, 411–425.

Levinson, D. J. (1978). *The seasons of a man's life.* New York: Knopf.

Levinson, E. A. (1965). Why do they drop out? *Teaching & Learning,* 25–32.

Levy, M. F. (1972). An analysis of a program designed to modify self concept and school of sentiment of low achieving students. *Dissertation Abstracts International, 33*(3-A), 930–931.

Lewis, B. (1969). Underachievers measure up. *American Education, 5,* 27–28.

Lewis, W. D. (1945). Influence of parental attitudes on children's personal inventory scores. *Journal of Genetic Psychology, 67,* 195–201.

Lichter, S. J. (1966). A comparison of group counseling with individual counseling for college underachievers: Effect on self concept and academic achievement. *Dissertation Abstracts, 27*(6-B), 2138–2139.

Liddicoat, J. P. (1972). Differences between under- and overachievers at a small liberal arts women's college. *Dissertation Abstracts International, 32*(11-A), 6133–6134.

Liebman, O. B. (1953). Relationship of personal and social adjustment to academic achievement in the elementary school. *Unpublished Doctoral Dissertation,* Columbia University.

Light, L. L., & Alexakos, C. E. (1970). Effect of individual and group counseling on study habits. *Journal of Educational Research, 63,* 450–454.

Lightfoot, G. F. (1951). Personality characteristics of bright and dull children. *Teach. Coll. Contr. Educ., 9,* 69–136.

Limbrick, E., McNaughton, S., & Glynn, T. (1985). Reading gains for underachieving tutors and tutees in a cross-age tutoring programme. *Journal of Child Psychology and Psychiatry and Allied Disciplines, 26,* 939–953.

Lindenbaum, L. (1978). The relationship of background factors to cognitive change in anti-achieving adolescents following one year's experience at the Center for Alternative Education. *Dissertation Abstracts International, 38*(12-A), 7234.

Lindgren, H. C., & Mello, M. J. (1965). Emotional problems of over- and underachieving children in a Brazilian elementary school. *Journal of Genetic Psychology, 106*(1), 59–65.

Lindner, R. M. (1944). *Rebel without a cause.* New York: Grune & Stratton.

Lindquist, E. F. (1949). Norms of achievement by schools. *Proc. 1948 Conf. Test. Probl., Educ. Test. Serv.,* 95–97.

Long, T. E. (1967). An experimental investigation of the effects of single contact problem counseling which included the first formal appraisal of ability and achievement data for underachieving high school boys. *Dissertation Abstracts, 27*(11-A), 3626.

Lowe, T. O. (1973). The utilization of verbal reinforcement by cadet teachers in the treatment of underachieving fourth-grade boys. *Dissertation Abstracts International, 33*(11-A), 6093–6094.

Lowe, T. O., & McLaughlin, E. C. (1974). The use of verbal reinforcement by paraprofessionals in the treatment of underachieving elementary school students. *Journal of the Student Personnel Association for Teacher Education, 12*(3), 95–101.

Lowell, E. L. (1952). The effect of need for achievement on learning and speed of performance. *Journal of Psychology, 33,* 31–40.

Lowenstein, L. F. (1976a). Helping children to achieve. *Journal of the Parents' National Educational Union, 11*(1), 20–21.

Lowenstein, L. F. (1976b). Helping children to achieve: II. *Journal of the Parents' National Educational Union, 11*(2), 59–61.

Lowenstein, L. F. (1979). Recent research in the identification, prevention and treatment of underachieving academic children. *Community Home & School Gazette, 73*(6), 243–246.

Lowenstein, L. F. (1982). An empirical study of the incidence, diagnosis, treatment and follow-up of academically under-achieving children. *School Psychology International, 3*(4), 219–230.

Lowenstein, L. F. (1983a). Could do better if he tried, or could he? *School Psychology International, 4*(2), 65–68.

Lowenstein, L. F. (1983b). Case study: The diagnosis, treatment and follow-up of an under-achieving child. *School Psychology International, 4*(2), 113–118.

Lowenstein, L. F., Meza, M., & Thorne, P. E. (1983). A study in the relationship between emotional stability, intellectual ability, academic attainment, personal contentment and vocational aspirations. *Acta Psychiatrica Scandinavica, 67*(1), 13–20.

Lowman, J. (1981). Love, hate, and the family: Measures of emotion. In E. Filsinger & R. Lewis (Eds.), *Assessing marriage: New behavioral approaches*. Beverly Hills, CA: Sage Publications.

Lowman, R. P., & Spuck, D. W. (1975). Predictors of college success for the disadvantaged Mexican-American. *Journal of College Student Personnel, 16*(1), 40–48.

Ludwig, S. (1981). [Are the concepts of over- and underachievement outdated?] *Psychologie in Erziehung und Unterricht, 28*(5), 282–292.

Lunneborg, P. W. (1968). Birth order, aptitude, and achievement. *Journal of Consulting and Clinical Psychology, 32*, 101.

Lynn, R. (1959). The relation between educational achievement and school size. *British Journal of Sociology, 10*, 129–136.

Maginnis, G. H. (1972). Measuring underachievement in reading. *Reading Teacher, 25*(8), 750–753.

Mahler, M. S. (1974). Symbiosis and individuation. *Psychoanalytic study of the child, 29*, 89–106.

Malloy, J. (1954). An investigation of scholastic over and underachievement among female college freshmen. *Journal of Counseling Psychology, 1*, 260–263.

Malpass, L. F. (1953). Some relationships between students' perception of school and their achievement. *Journal of Educational Psychology, 44*, 475–482.

Mandel, H. P. (1969). Validation of a developmental theory of psychopathology: Diagnostic categorization versus symptomatology. *Dissertation Abstracts International, 30*, 2911–2912-B.

Mandel, H. P. (1981). *Short-term psychotherapy and brief treatment techniques: An annotated bibliography: 1920–1980*. New York: Plenum.

Mandel, H. P. (1984). *The Durham County Achievement Research Project: Phase I: A sample description*. Toronto: Institute on Achievement and Motivation, York University.

Mandel, H. P. (1986). [Academic performance histories of differentially diagnosed high school underachievers of equal intellectual capacity]. Unpublished data. Toronto: Institute on Achievement and Motivation, York University.

Mandel, H. P., & Marcus, S. I. (1983). [Inter-judge rater reliability from diagnostic interviews of 28 underachieving high school students]. Unpublished data. Toronto: Institute on Achievement and Motivation, York University.

Mandel, H. P., & Marcus, S. I. (1984a). *Helping the Non-achievement Syndrome student: A clinical training manual*. Toronto: Institute on Achievement and Motivation, York University.

Mandel, H. P., & Marcus, S. I. (1984b). [Inter-judge rater reliability from diagnostic interviews of underachieving high school students]. Unpublished study. Toronto: Institute on Achievement and Motivation, York University.

Mandel, H. P., & Marcus, S. I. (1984c). [Parent checklist—Child focussed]. Unpublished paper. Toronto: Institute on Achievement and Motivation, York University.

Mandel, H. P., & Marcus, S. I. (1984d). [Student self-rating checklist]. Unpublished paper. Toronto: Institute on Achievement and Motivation, York University.

Mandel, H. P., & Marcus, S. I. (1985). *Identifying personality and motivational types of underachieving students: A clinical training manual*. Toronto: Institute on Achievement and Motivation, York University.

Mandel, H. P., Marcus, S. I., Hartley, L., McRoberts, P., & Phillips, B. (1984). [Classroom behavior checklist—Teacher form]. Unpublished paper. Toronto: Institute on Achievement and Motivation, York University.

Mandel, H. P., Marcus, S. I., Roth, R. M., & Berenbaum, H. L. (1971). Early infantile autism: A pre-ego psychopathology. *Psychotherapy: Theory, Research and Practice, 8*(2), 114–119.

Mandel, H. P., Roth, R. M., & Berenbaum, H. L. (1968). Relationship between personality change and achievement change as a function of psychodiagnosis. *Journal of Counseling Psychology, 15*, 500–505.

Mandel, H. P., & Uebner, J. (1971). "If you never chance for fear of losing . . ." *Personnel and Guidance Journal, 50*, 192–197.

Mandel, H. P., Weizmann, F., Millan, B., Greenhow, J., & Speirs, D. (1975). Reaching emotionally disturbed children: "Judo" principles in remedial education. *American Journal of Orthopsychiatry, 45*, 867–874.

Manhas, L. (1974). Guidance programme for underachievers. *Journal of Vocational & Educational Guidance, 16*(1–2), 33–38.

Manley, R. O. (1977). Parental warmth and hostility as related to sex differences in children's achievement orientation. *Psychology of Women Quarterly, 1*, 229–246.

Marcus, I. W. (1966). Family interaction in adolescents with learning difficulties. *Adolescence, 1*(3), 261–271.

Marcus, S. I. (1969). Diagnostic classification of alcoholics according to a developmental theory model. *Dissertation Abstracts International, 30*, 2424-B.

Marcus, S. I. (1971). Why some kids fail. *Newsletter: Council for Children with Behavior Disorders, 8*, 11–19.

Marcus, S. I. (1985). [Combined frequency distributions of 57 selected studies on underachievement from 1963–1985]. Unpublished data. Toronto: Institute on Achievement and Motivation, York University.

Marcus, S. I. (1986). [Frequency distribution by year of published articles and books on nonintellective factors and academic achievement]. Unpublished data. Toronto: Institute on Achievement and Motivation, York University.

Marcus, S. I., & Friedland, J. G. (1987). [Relationship between the Motivational Analysis Inventory and GPA in high school and college students]. Unpublished study.

Marcus, S. I., & Steele, C. (1985). Counseling services for students in engineering and the technological sciences. *Proceedings of the Association of University and College Counseling Center Directors* (pp. 102–103). Binghamton, NY: AUCCCD.

Margolis, H., Muhlfelder, C., & Brannigan, G. G. (1977). Reality therapy and underachievement: A case study. *Education, 98*(2), 153–155.

Marjoribanks, K. (1981). Family environments and children's academic achievement: Sex and social group differences. *The Journal of Psychology, 109*, 155–164.

Marshall, S. E. (1945). Solving individual problems of adjustment. *Journal of Educational Sociology, 19*, 36–39.

Martin, G. C. (1952). Interviewing the failing student. *Journal of Educational Research, 46*, 53–60.

Martin, J., Marx, R. W., & Martin, E. W. (1980). Instructional counseling for chronic underachievers. *School Counselor, 28*, 109–118.

Martin, J. G., & Davidson, J. (1964). Recall of completed and interrupted tasks by achievers and underachievers. *Journal of Educational Psychology, 55*(6), 314–316.

Martinez, D. H. (1974). A comparison of the behavior, during reading instruction, of teachers of high and low achieving first grade classes. *Dissertation Abstracts International, 34*(12-A, Pt. 1), 7520–7521.

Martz, E. W. (1945). Phenomenal spurt of mental development in a young child. *Psychiatric Quarterly, 19,* 52–59.

Masih, L. K. (1974). Manifest needs of high ability achieving and underachieving elementary school children in a culturally disadvantaged setting. *New York State Personnel and Guidance Journal, 9,* 55–61.

Maslow, A. (1954). *Motivation and Personality,* New York, Harper & Row.

Mason, R. L., Richmond, B. O., & Wheeler, E. E. (1972). Expressed needs of academically excluded students. *Journal of the Student Personnel Association for Teacher Education, 10*(3), 74–80.

Masterson, M. L. (1971). Family structure variables and need approval. *Journal of Consulting and Clinical Psychology, 36,* 12–13.

Matsunaga, A. S. (1972). A comparative study of ninth grade male underachievers and achievers on selected factors related to achievement. *Dissertation Abstracts International, 32*(10-A), 5614.

Maxwell, J. (1951). Intelligence and family size of college students. *Eugen. Review, 42,* 209–210.

Mayo, G. D., & Manning, W. (1961). Motivation measurement. *Education and Psychological Measurement, 21,* 73–83.

McArthur, C. (1965). The validity of the Yale Strong scores at Harvard. *Journal of Counseling Psychology, 12*(1), 35–38.

McCall, J. N., & Johnson, O. G. (1972). The independence of intelligence from size and birth order. *Journal of Genetic Psychology, 121,* 207–213.

McCandless, B. R., & Castenada, A. (1956). Anxiety in children, school achievement, and intelligence. *Child Development, 27,* 379–382.

McClelland, D. C., Atkinson, J. W., Clark, R. A., & Lowell, E. L. (1953). *The achievement motive.* New York: Appleton-Century Crofts.

McClelland, D. C. (1985a). How motives, skills, and values determine what people do. *American Psychologist, 40*(7), 812–825.

McClelland, D. C. (1985b). *Human motivation.* Glenview, IL: Scott Foresman.

McClelland, D. C., & Alschuler, A. S. (1971). *Final Report of Achievement Motivation Development Project,* Washington, DC: U.S. Office of Education, Bureau of Research.

McCloud, T. E. (1968). Persistency as a motivational factor of vocational interest in the prediction of academic success of twelfth-grade superior students. *Psychology, 5*(4), 34–46.

McClure, R. F. (1969). Birth order and school related attitudes. *Psychological Reports, 25,* 657–658.

McCord, W., & McCord, J. (1964). *The psychopath.* Princeton, NJ: D. Van Nostrand Reinhold.

McCrone, W. P. (1979). Learned helplessness and level of underachievement among deaf adolescents. *Psychology in the Schools, 16,* 430–434.

McCurdy, B., Ciucevich, M. T., & Walker, B. A. (1977). Human-relations training with seventh-grade boys identified as behavior problems. *School Counselor, 24*(4), 248–252.

McDermott, P. A. (1980). A computerized system for the classification of developmental, learning, and adjustment disorders in school children. *Educational & Psychological Measurement, 40*(3), 761–768.

McDonald, A. P. (1971). Birth order and personality. *Journal of Consulting and Clinical Psychology, 108,* 133–136.

McGhearty, L., & Womble, M. (1970). Case analysis: Consultation and counseling. *Elementary School Guidance and Counseling, 5,* 141–147.

McGillivray, R. H. (1964). Differences in home background between high-achieving and low-achieving gifted children. *Ontario Journal of Educational Research, 6*(2), 99–106.

McGowan, R. J. (1968). Group counseling with underachievers and their parents. *School Counselor, 16,* 30–45.

McGraw, J. J. (1966). A comparison of mean subtest raw scores on the Wechsler Intelligence Scale for Children of regular and over-achieving readers with under-achieving readers. *Dissertation Abstracts, 27*(6-K), 1552.

McGuigan, D. E. (1976). Academic underachievement of Mexican-American secondary students. *Dissertation Abstracts International, 37*(1-A), 75–76.

McGuire, D. E., & Lyons, J. S. (1985). A transcontexual model for intervention with problems of school underachievement. *American Journal of Family Therapy, 13,* 37–45.

McGuire, J. M. (1972). A study of the relationship between academic motivation and a counseling letter treatment on help-seeking behavior of low achieving college students, *Dissertation Abstracts International, 32*(7-B), 4190–4191.

McGuire, J. M., & Noble, F. C. (1973). Motivational level and response to academic encouragement among low-achieving college males. *Journal of Counseling Psychology, 20*(5), 425–430.

McKay, H., Sinisterra, L., McKay, A., Gomez, H., & Lloreda, P. (1978). Improving cognitive ability in chronically deprived children. *Science, 200,* 270–278.

McKay, J. (1985). *The relationships among sex, age, ability, and achievement patterns in differentially diagnosed high school students.* Unpublished master's thesis, York University, Toronto, ON.

McKeachie, W. J. (1951). Anxiety in the college classroom. *Journal of Educational Research, 45,* 153–160.

McKenzie, J. D., Jr. (1961). An attempt to develop Minnesota Multiphasic Personality Inventory scales predictive of academic over- and underachievement. *Dissertation Abstracts, 22,* 632.

McKenzie, J. D., Jr. (1964). The dynamics of deviant achievement. *Personnel & Guidance Journal, 42*(7), 683–686.

McKinney, F. (1947). Case history norms of unselected students and students with emotional problems. *Journal of Consulting Psychology, 11,* 258–269.

McLaughlin, R. E. (1977). Behaviorally oriented techniques for the remediation of academic underachievement in high potential intermediate school students. *Dissertation Abstracts International, 37*(11-A), 7046.

McLoed, J. (1979). Educational underachievement: Toward a defensible psychometric definition. *Journal of Learning Disabilities, 12*(5), 322–330.

McPherson, M. W. (1948). A survey of experimental studies of learning in individuals who achieve subnormal ratings on standardized psychometric measures. *American Journal of Mental Deficiency, 52,* 232–254.

McQuaid, M. L. (1971). The development and evaluation of a program designed to strengthen the secondary school underachiever in twenty work-study skills. *Dissertation Abstracts International, 32*(4-A), 1946.

McQuarry, J. P. (1953). Some relationships between non-intellectual characteristics and academic achievement. *Journal of Educational Psychology, 44,* 215–228.

McQuarry, J. P., & Truax, W. E., Jr. (1955). An under-achievement scale. *Journal of Educational Research, 48,* 393–399.

McReynolds, W. T., & Church, A. (1973). Self-control, study skills development and counseling approaches to the improvement of study behavior. *Behaviour Research & Therapy, 11*(2), 233–235.

McRoberts, P. (1985). *Affective parent-child relationships and personalities of parents of high school students of varying achievement levels*. Unpublished doctoral dissertation, York University, Toronto, ON.

McWilliams, S. A., & Finkel, N. J. (1973). High school students as mental health aides in the elementary school setting. *Journal of Consulting and Clinical Psychology, 40*(1), 39–42.

Meacham, R., & Lindemann, J. E. (1975). A summer program for underachieving adolescents. *American Journal of Occupational Therapy, 29,* 280–283.

Meeth, L. R., (1972). Expending faculty support for underachievers. *Junior College Journal, 42,* 25–28.

Mehdi, B. (1965a). What research has to say about under-achievement among the gifted. *Guidance Review, 2,* 6–23.

Mehdi, B. (1965b). Prediction of academic success: A review of research. *Guidance Review, 3,* 9–19.

Mehta, P. H. (1968). The self-concept of bright underachieving male high school students. *Indian Educational Review, 3*(2), 81–100.

Mehta, P., & Dandia, P. C. (1970). Motivation training for educational development: a follow-up study of bright underachievers. *Indian Educational Review, 5*(2), 64–73.

Meiselman, J. R. (1970). Variables related to the identification of underachievers. *Dissertation Abstracts International, 31*(1-A), 230.

Meltzer, M. L., & Levy, B. I. (1970). Self-esteem in a public school. *Psychology in the Schools, 7*(1), 14–20.

Meyer, E. D. (1972). The relationship between self-concept and underachievement. *Illinois Journal of Education, 63,* 63–68.

Meyer, R. G., Osborne, Y. (1987). *Case studies in abnormal behavior* (2nd ed.). Newton, MA: Allyn & Bacon.

Mezzano, J. (1968). Group counseling with low-motivated high school students–comparative effects of two uses of counselor time. *Journal of Educational Research, 61,* 222–224.

Michelson, L., and Ascher L. M. (Eds.), (1987). *Anxiety and stress disorders: Cognitive-behavioral assessment and treatment.* New York: Guilford Press.

Michielutte, W. L. (1977). The use of group tutorial and group counseling methods in the investigation of causal relationships between self concept and reading achievement among underachieving sixth-grade boys. *Dissertation Abstracts International, 37*(8-B), 4156.

Middleton, G. (1958). Personality syndromes and academic achievement. *Dissertation Abstracts, 19,* 1439.

Miller, G. W. (1970). Factors in school achievement and social class. *Journal of Educational Psychology, 61,* 260–269.

Miller, L. M. (Ed.). (1961). *Guidance for the underachiever with superior ability,* Washington, DC: U.S. Department of Health, Education, and Welfare.

Milligan, E. E., Lins, L. J., & Little, K. (1948). The success of non-high school graduates in degree programs at the University of Wisconsin. *School and Society, 67,* 27–29.

Mince-Ennis, J. A. (1980). The effect of parent training on academic achievement of low achieving adolescents. *Dissertation Abstracts International, 41,* (4-A), 1409.

Mirsky, A. F., & Ricks, N. L. (1974). Sustained attention and the effects of distraction in underachieving second grade children. *Journal of Education, 156,* 4–17.

Mishne, J. (1971). Group therapy in an elementary school. *Social Casework, 52*(1), 18–25.

Missildine, W. H. (1946). The emotional background of thirty children with reading disabilities with emphasis on its coercive aspects. *Nerv. Child., 5,* 263–272.

Mitchell, C. E. (1975). Use of self-actualization scales as a predictor of academic success with underachievers. *Dissertation Abstracts International, 35*(11-A), 7084.

Mitchell, K. R., Hall, R. F., & Piatkowska, O. E. (1975a). A group program for the treatment of failing college students. *Behavior Therapy, 6*(3), 324–336.

Mitchell, K. R., Hall, R. F., & Piatkowska, O. E. (1975b). A group program for bright failing underachievers. *Journal of College Student Personnel, 16,* 306–312.

Mitchell, K. R., & Piatowska, O. E. (1974a). Effective non-study methods for college students. *College Student Journal, 9*(3), 19–41.

Mitchell, K. R., & Piatowska, O. E. (1974b). Effects of group treatment for college under-achievers and bright failing underachievers. *Journal of Counseling Psychology, 21*(6), 494–501.

Mohan, V. (1974). Guidance for the underachiever. *Journal of Vocational and Educational Guidance, 16*(1–2), 39–43.

Moldowski, T. F. (1962). The effect of reinforcement upon level of expectancy of achievers and underachievers. *Dissertation Abstracts, 23*(3), 1075–1076.

Mondani, M. S., & Tutko, T. A. (1969). Relationship of academic underachievement to inci-dental learning. *Journal of Consulting & Clinical Psychology, 33*(5), 558–560.

Monderer, J. H., & Fenchel, G. H. (1950). The effect of college grades on motivation and status. *Journal of the Intercollegiate Psychological Association, 2,* 16–24.

Moon, R. A. (1951). The problem of success and failure in the school age child. *Journal of the Kansas Medical Society, 52,* 45–48.

Moore, J. E. (1950). Educational adjustment of the unstable boy. *Journal of Correctional Education, 2,* 17–21.

Mora, G., Talmadge, M., Bryant, F., & Brown, E. M. (1967). Psychiatric syndromes and neurological findings as related to academic underachievement: Implications for educational and treatment. *American Journal of Orthopsychiatry, 37*(2), 346–347.

Morgan, E. R. (1971). Behavior theory counseling with culturally disadvantaged, underachiev-ing youth. *Dissertation Abstracts International, 31*(7-A), 3274–3275.

Morgan, H. H. (1952). A psychometric comparison of achieving and nonachieving college students of high ability. *Journal of Consulting Psychology, 16,* 292–298.

Morgan, J. W. (1974). The differences between underachieving institutionalized male delin-quents and nondelinquents as measured by psychological tests, scales and inventories. *Dissertation Abstracts International, 34*(7-B), 3471.

Morgan, R. R. (1975). Prediction of college achievement using the need achievement scale from the Edwards Personal Preference Schedule. *Educational & Psychological Measurement, 35*(2), 387–392.

Morrison, E. (1967). Academic underachievement among preadolescent boys considered as a manifestation of passive aggression. *Dissertation Abstracts, 28*(4-A), 1304–1305.

Morrison, E. (1969). Underachievement among preadolescent boys considered in relationship to passive aggression. *Journal of Educational Psychology, 60*(3), 168–173.

Morrow, W. R. (1970). Academic underachievement. In C. C. Costello (Ed.), *Symptoms of psychopathology.* New York: Wiley.

Morrow, W. R., & Wilson, R. (1961a). Family relations of bright high-achieving and under-achieving high school boys. *Child Development, 32,* 501–510.

Morrow, W. R., & Wilson, R. (1961b). The self-reported personal and social adjustment of bright high-achieving and under-achieving high school boys. *Journal of Child Psychology and Psychiatry, 2,* 203–209.

Motto, J. L. (1959). A reply to Drasgow on underachievers. *Journal of Counseling Psychology, 6,* 245–247.

Moulin, E. K. (1971). The effects of client centered group counseling using play media on the intelligence, achievement, and psycholinguistic abilities of underachieving primary school children. *Elementary School Guidance and Counseling, 5,* 85–95.

Mukherjee, S. C. (1972). A comparative study of the parents of low and high achieving students. *Dissertation Abstracts International, 32*(11-B), 6624-B.

Mullen, F. A. (1950). Truancy and classroom disorder as symptoms of personality problems. *Journal of Educational Psychology, 41,* 97–109.

Mumpower, D. L., & Riggs, S. (1970). Overachievement in word accuracy as a result of parental pressure. *Reading Teacher, 23*(8), 741–747.

Munger, P. F., & Goeckerman, R. W. (1955). Collegiate persistence of upper- and lower-third high school graduates. *Journal of Counseling Psychology, 2,* 142–145.

Murakawa, N. (1968). Intellectual ability of underachievers. *Psychologia: An International Journal of Psychology in the Orient, 11*(1–2), 67–80.

Murakawa, N., & Pierce-Jones, J. (1969). Thinking and memory of underachievers. *Psychologia: An International Journal of Psychology in the Orient, 12*(2), 93–106.

Murphy, J. (1974). Teacher expectations and working-class under-achievement. *British Journal of Sociology, 25*(3), 326–344.

Murphy, L. B., & Ladd, H. (1944). *Emotional factors in learning.* New York: Columbia University Press.

Murray, C. B., & Jackson, J. S. (1982). The conditioned failure model of Black educational underachievement. *Humboldt Journal of Social Relations, 10*(1), 276–300.

Murray, H. A. (1971). *Thematic Apperception Test Manual.* Boston: Henry Alexander Murray.

Murray, M. A. (1983). Instructional strategies as part of the content domain of a criterion-referenced test. *Florida Journal of Educational Research, 25,* 15–31.

Muthayya, B. C. (1966–67). Some personal data and vocational choices of high and low achievers in the scholastic field. *Psychology Annual, 1*(1), 21–25.

Mutimer, D., Loughlin, L., & Powell, M. (1966). Some differences in the family relationships of achieving and underachieving readers. *Journal of Genetic Psychology, 109*(1), 67–74.

Myers, D. C. (1978). An analysis of specified attributes and characteristics of selected high and low achieving students affecting students' perception of teacher effectiveness. *Dissertation Abstracts International, 39*(4-A), 2037–2038.

Myers, E. J. (1971). Counseling the parents of sixth grade underachievers. *Journal of Education, 154,* 50–53.

Myers, J. E. (1944). Problems of dull and bright children. *Smith College Studies of Social Work, 15,* 123.

Mykelbust, H. R. (1973). Identification and diagnosis of children with learning disabilities: An interdisciplinary study of criteria. *Seminars in Psychiatry, 5*(1), 55–77.

Myrick, R. D., & Haight, D. A. (1972). Growth groups: An encounter with underachievers. *School Counselor, 20*(2), 115–121.

Nagaraja, J. (1972). The failing student. *Child Psychiatry Quarterly, 5*(3), 12–16.

Nam, C. B. (1965). Family patterns of educational attainment. *Sociology of Education. 38,* 393–403.

Narayana, R. S. (1964). A study of the sense of responsibility and its relation to academic achievement. *Psychological Studies, 9*(2), 109–118.

Neber, H. (1974). [Structure and intensity of spontaneous learning of under- and overachievers]. *Psychologie in Erziehung und Unterricht, 21*(6), 335–344.

Nelson, D. D. (1968). A study of school achievement and personality adjustment among adolescent children with working and non-working mothers. *Dissertation Abstracts, 29*(1-A), 153.

Nelson, D. E. (1971). The college environment: Its meaning to academically successful and unsuccessful undergraduates. *Journal of Educational Research, 64*(8), 355–358.

Nelson, M. O. (1967). Individual psychology as a basis for the counseling of low achieving students. *Personnel & Guidance Journal, 46*(3), 283–287.

Nemecek, F. D. (1972). A study of the effect of the human potential seminar on the self-actualization and academic achievement of college underachievers. *Dissertation Abstracts International, 33,* 6766-A.

Neubauer, W. (1981). [How teachers and psychologists do explain academic achievement: A critical discussion]. *Psychologie in Erziehung und Unterricht, 28*(2), 97–106.

Newman, A. P. (197?). Later achievement study of pupils underachieving in reading in first grade. *Reading Research Quarterly, 7*(3), 477–508.

Newman, C. (1969). A study of underachievement in an average college population. In M. G. Gottsegen, & G. B. Gottsegen (Eds.), *Professional school psychology* (Vol. 2, pp. 338–358). New York: Grune & Stratton.

Newman, C. J., Dember, C. F., & Krug, O. (1973). "He can but he won't": A psychodynamic study of so-called "gifted underachievers." *Psychoanalytic Study of the Child, 28,* 83–129.

Newman, R. C., & Pollack, D. (1973). Proxemics in deviant adolescents. *Journal of Consulting and Clinical Psychology, 40*(1), 6–8.

Nicholls, J. G. (1979). Development of perception of own attainment and causal attributions for success and failure in reading. *Journal of Educational Psychology, 71,* 94–99.

Nicholson, C. L. (1977). Correlations between the Quick Test and the Wechsler Intelligence Scale for Children: Revised. *Psychological Reports, 40*(2), 523–526.

Nixon, D. (1972). *A comparison of measures of psychological dependency and internal-external control of reinforcement among three categories of underachieving high school students.* Unpublished master's thesis, York University, Toronto, ON.

Noel, L. (1970). Selected factors related to underachievement of superior students in Illinois colleges. *Dissertation Abstracts International, 30*(7-A), 2808.

Noel, L., Levitz, R., & Saluri, D. (Eds.). (1985). *Increasing student retention.* San Francisco: Jossey-Bass.

Noland, S. A., Arnold, J., & Clement, W. (1980). Self-reinforcement by under-achieving, under-controlled girls. *Psychological Reports, 4,* 671–678.

Norfleet, M. A. (1968). Personality characteristics of achieving and underachieving high ability senior women. *Personnel & Guidance Journal, 46*(10), 976–980.

Norman, R. D., Clark, B. P., & Bessemer, D. W. (1962). Age, sex, IQ, and achievement patterns in achieving and nonachieving gifted children. *Exceptional Children, 29*(3), 116–123.

Nowakowski, J. A. (1980). The human factor. *Momentum, 11,* 20–22.

Nowicki, S., & Strickland, B. R. (1973). A locus of control scale for children, as related to achievement. *Journal of Consulting and Clinical Psychology, 40,* 148–154.

Noy, S. (1969). Comparison of three psychotherapies in promoting growth in behavior disorders. *Dissertation Abstracts International, 29,* 3919-B.

Nuttall, E. V., Nuttall, R. L., Polit, D., & Hunter, J. B. (1976). Effects of family size, birth order, sibling separation and crowding on the achievement of boys and girls. *American Educational Research Journal, 13*(3), 217–223.

Oak-Bruce, L. (1948). What do we know . . . for sure? *Childhood Education, 24,* 312–316.

Oakland, J. A. (1969). Measurement of personality correlates of academic achievement in high school students. *Journal of Counseling Psychology, 16*(5, Pt. 1), 452–457.

Obler, M., Francis, K., & Wishengrad, R. (1977). Combining of traditional counseling, instruction, and mentoring functions with academically deficient college freshmen. *Journal of Educational Research, 70*(3), 142–147.

O'Donnell, P. I. (1968). Predictors of freshman academic success and their relationship to attrition. *Dissertation Abstracts, 29*(3-A), 798.

Ogden, K. W. (1971). An evaluation of nonpromotion as a method of improving academic performance. *Dissertation Abstracts International, 32*(2-A), 795–796.

Ohlsen, M. M., & Gazda, G. M. (1965). Counseling underachieving bright pupils. *Education, 86,* 78–81.

Olsen, C. R. (1969). The effects of enrichment tutoring upon self-concept, educational achievement, and measured intelligence of male underachievers in an inner-city elementary school. *Dissertation Abstracts International, 30*(6-A), 2404.

O'Neil, M. B. (1974). The effect of Glasser peer group counseling upon academic performance, self satisfaction, personal worth, social interaction and self esteem of low achieving female college freshmen. *Dissertation Abstracts International, 34*(10-A), 6389.

Ono, K. (1958). Shōgakkō ni okeru gakugyō fushinji no kenkyū: (I) [An investigation on the underachievers in the elementary school]. *Japanese Journal of Educational Psychology, 5,* 234–243.

Onoda, L. (1976). Personality characteristics and attitudes toward achievement among mainland high achieving and underachieving Japanese-American Sanseis. *Journal of Educational Psychology, 68*(2), 151–156.

Onoda, L. (1977). Neurotic-stable tendencies among Japanese-American Sanseis and Caucasian students. *Journal of Non-White Concerns in Personnel and Guidance, 5,* 180–185.

Ontario Ministry of Community and Social Services. (1986). *Ontario child health study: Summary of initial findings.* Toronto: Queen's Printer for Ontario.

Orlando, C., & Lynch, J. (1974). Learning disabilities of educational casualties: Where do we go from here? *Elementary School Journal, 74*(8), 461–467.

Orlofsky, J. L. (1978). Identity formation, Achievement, and fear of success in college men and women. *Journal of Youth and Adolescence, 7,* 49–62.

Osborne, R. T., & Sanders, W. B. (1949). Multiple choice Rorschach responses of college achievers and non-achievers. *Educational & Psychological Measurement, 9,* 685–691.

O'Shea, A. J. (1968). Differences on certain non-intellective factors between academically bright junior high school male high and low achievers. *Dissertation Abstracts, 28*(9-A), 3515.

Osuala, E. C. (1981). Parental influences on academic achievement of students. *Asian Journal of Psychology & Education, 7*(1), 1–7.

Otop, J. (1977). Sources of school failure in gifted pupils as revealed by teachers' ratings. *Polish Psychological Bulletin, 8*(2), 107–113.

Ott, J. S., et al. (1982). Childhood cancer and vulnerability for significant academic underachievement. *Journal of Learning Disabilities, 15*(6), 363–364.

Owens, W. A., & Johnson, W. C. (1949). Some measured personality traits of collegiate underachievers. *Journal of Educational Psychology, 40,* 41–46.

Palermo, D. S., Castenada, A., & McCandless, B. R. (1956). The relationship of anxiety in children to performance in a complex learning task. *Child Development, 27,* 333–337.

Palkovitz, G. M. (1971). Differences between self-perceived academic achievers and academic non-achievers and the effects of a treatment program on increasing the level of achievement of self-perceived academic non-achievers. *Dissertation Abstracts International, 32*(6-A), 3037.

Palubinskas, A. L., & Eyde, L. D. (1961). SVIB patterns in medical school applicants. *Journal of Counseling Psychology, 8,* 159–163.

Parks, J. B. (1969). A working model for increasing self-awareness and achievement of junior high school students. *Dissertation Abstracts, 29* (10-A), 3468.

Paschel, B. J. (1968). The role of self concept in achievement. *Journal of Negro Education, 37,* 392–396.

Passi, B. K., & Lalithamma, M. S. (1973). Self-concept and creativity of over, normal and underachievers amongst grade ten students of Baroda. *Indian Journal of Psychometry & Education, 4*(1), 1–11.

Pathak, R. D. (1972). Comparative study of the scholastic achievement of various sociometric groups of children. *Indian Journal of Social Work, 33,* 199–203.

Pattie, F. A. (1946). Howells on the hereditary differential in learning—a criticism. *Psychological Review, 53,* 53–54.

Payne, D. A., & Farquhar, W. W. (1962). The dimensions of an objective measure of academic self-concept. *Journal of Educational Psychology, 53*(4), 187–192.

Payne, J. (1973). Counselling and academic achievement. *British Journal of Guidance and Counselling, 1*(2), 19–25.

Peaker, G. (1979). Assessing children's performance. *Special Education: Forward Trends, 6,* 31–34.

Pelton, L. H. (1978). Child abuse and neglect: The myth of classlessness. *American Journal of Orthopsychiatry, 48*(4), 608–617.

Pentecoste, J. C. (1975). An experiment relating locus of control to reading success for Black bright underachievers. *Reading Improvement, 12,* 81–86.

Pentecoste, J. C., & Nelson, N. J. (1975). Effects of small group counseling on cognitive growth of bright underachievers in an atypical educational situation. *Education, 96*(1), 89–94.

Pepinsky, P. H. (1960). A study of productive nonconformity. *Gifted Child Quarterly, 4,* 81–85.

Peppin, B. H. (1963). Parental understanding, parental acceptance, and the self concept of children as a function of academic over- and under-achievement. *Dissertation Abstracts, 23*(11), 4422–4423.

Perkins, D. N. (1981). *The Mind's Best Work,* Cambridge, MA: Harvard University Press.

Perkins, H. R. (1976). Gifted underachievers. *North Carolina Association for the Gifted and Talented Quarterly Journal, 2,* 39–44.

Perkins, J. A. (1970). Group counseling with bright underachievers and their mothers. *Dissertation Abstracts International, 30*(7-A), 2809.

Perkins, J. A., & Wicas, E. A. (1971). Group counseling bright underachievers and their mothers. *Journal of Counseling Psychology, 18*(3), 273–278.

Pervin, L. A., Reik, L. E., & Dalrymple, W. (1966). *The college dropout and the utilization of talent.* Princeton, NJ: Princeton University Press.

Peters, D. M. (1968). The self concept as a factor in over- and under-achievement. *Dissertation Abstracts, 29*(6-A), 1792–1793.

Peterson, D. J. (1972). The relationship between self-concept and self-disclosure of under-achieving college students in group counseling. *Dissertation Abstracts International, 33*(5-B), 2354.

Peterson, J. F. (1966). A study of the effects of giving teachers personal information about high-ability, low-performing, secondary school students. *Dissertation Abstracts, 27*(4-A), 963–964.

Phelps, M. O. (1957). An analysis of certain factors associated with under-achievement among high school students. *Dissertation Abstracts, 17,* 306–307.

Phillips, B. (1987). *The correlates of achievement: Relationships among achievement level, intellective, demographic, and personality factors in differentially categorized high school students.* Unpublished doctoral dissertation, York University, Toronto, ON.

Piacere, J., & Piacere, A. (1967). Une expérience d'observation psychologie et de rééducation préventive contre l'échec scolaire au cours préparatoire [Psychological observation experiment and preventive reeducation in contrast to academic underachievement at the preparatory level]. *Bulletin de Psychologie, 20,* 670–680.

Pigott, H. E., Fantuzzo, J. W., & Clement, P. W. (1986). The effects of reciprocal peer tutoring and group contingencies on the academic performance of elementary school children. *Journal of Applied Behavior Analysis, 19*(1), 93–98.

Pigott, H. E., Fantuzzo, J. W., Heggie, D. L., & Clement, P. W. (1984). A student-administered group-oriented contingency intervention: Its efficacy in a regular classroom. *Child & Family Behavior Therapy, 6*(4), 41–55.

Pigott, K. M. (1971). Parent counseling—Three case studies. *Journal of Education, 154,* 86–92.

Pines, S. F. (1981). A procedure for predicting underachievement in mathematics among female college students. *Educational and Psychological Measurement, 41,* 1137–1146.

Pippert, R., & Archer, N. S. (1963). A comparison of two methods for classifying underachievers with respect to selected criteria. *Personnel & Guidance, 41*(9), 788.

Pirozzo, R. (1982). Gifted underachievers. *Roeper Review, 4*(4), 18–21.

Pomp, A. M. (1969). *Self-concept, achievement level, and diagnostic category.* Unpublished master's thesis, Illinois Institute of Technology, Chicago, IL.

Pomp, A. M. (1971). Psychodiagnosis and psychosexual development in an adolescent population. *Dissertation Abstracts International, 31,* 6266-B.

Potter, S. R. (1968). A study of factors related to academic success in a selected population of 7th grade students. *Dissertation Abstracts, 29,*(6-A), 1829.

Powell, C. A. (1972). Simulated corporation shakes apathy in underachievers in agriculture. *American Vocational Journal, 47,* 75–76.

Powell, W. J., & Jourard, S. M. (1963). Some objective evidence of immaturity in underachieving college students. *Journal of Counseling Psychology, 10*(3), 276–282.

Powers, S., & Rossman, M. H. (1984). Attributions for school achievement of low-achieving Indian and Caucasian community college students. *Psychological Reports, 55*(2), 423–428.

Powers, W. J. (1971). An analysis and interpretation of the effects of vistherapy on the academic performance and attitude of a selected number of academically low-achieving adolescents in a public junior high school. *Dissertation Abstracts International, 32*(3-B), 1857–1858.

Prawat, R. S., Byers, J. L., & Anderson, A. H. (1983). An attributional analysis of teachers' affective reactions to students success and failure. *American Educational Research Journal, 20,* 137–152.

Prieto, A., & Zucker, S. (1980). The effects of race on teachers' perceptions of educational placement of behaviorally disorder children. *Resources in Education, 15,* ED 188427.

Propper, M. M., & Clark, E. T. (1970). Alienation: Another dimension of underachievement. *Journal of Psychology, 75*(1), 13–18.

Pugh, M. D. (1976). Statistical assumptions and social reality: A critical analysis of achievement models. *Sociology of Education, 49,* 34–40.

Purkey, W. W. (1969). Project Self Discovery: Its effect on bright but underachieving high school students. *Gifted Child Quarterly, 13*(4), 242–246.

Quigley, J. H. (1970). The effect of order of success reinforcement on problem-solving persistence of achievers and underachievers. *Dissertation Abstracts International, 30*(8-A), 3332–3333.

Quilter, J. M. (1979). The psychological processing of symbolic information by arithmetic underachievers. *Dissertation Abstracts International, 39*(8-B), 4049–4050.

Rachman, S. (1980). *Obsessions and compulsions.* Englewood Cliffs, NJ: Prentice-Hall.

Radin, S. S., & Masling, J. (1963). Tom: A gifted underachieving child. *Journal of Child Psychology & Psychiatry, 4*(3–4), 183–197.

Rand, M. E. (1970a). Rational-emotive approaches to academic underachievement. *Rational Living, 4*(2), 16–18.

Rand, M. E. (1970b). The use of didactic group therapy with academic achievers in a college setting. *Dissertation Abstracts International, 30*(9-B), 4379.

Ratchick, I. (1953). Achievement and capacity: a comparative study of pupils with low achievement and high intelligence quotients with pupils of high achievement and high intelligence quotients in a selected New York high school. *Dissertation Abstracts, 13,* 1049–1050.

Rausch, O. P. (1948). The effects of individual variability on achievement. *Journal of Educational Psychology, 39,* 469–478.

Rawson, H. E. (1973). Academic remediation and behavior modification in a summer-school camp. *Elementary School Journal, 74*(1), 34–43.

Raynor, J. O. (1970). Relationships between achievement-related motives, future orientation, and academic performance. *Journal of Personality and Social Psychology, 15,* 28–33.

Reck, M. (1968). The prediction of achievement in a college science curriculum. *Educational & Psychological Measurement, 28*(3), 943–944.

Redmond, N. J. (1971). Rorschach correlates of underachievement and cognitive deficits of underachievers. *Dissertation Abstracts International, 32*(5-B), 3015.

Redl, F., & Wineman, D. (1951). *Children who hate.* New York: Free Press.

Reed, C. E. (1955). A study of three groups of college preparatory students who differ in relative achievement. *Dissertation Abstracts, 15,* 2106.

Rehberg, R. A., Sinclair, J., & Schafer, W. E. (1970). Adolescent achievement behavior, family authority structure, and parental socialization practices. *American Journal of Sociology, 75,* 1012–1034.

Reich, W. (1945). *Character analysis.* New York: Orgone Institute Press.

Reid, W. H., Dorr, D., Walker, J. I., & Bonner, J. W., III. (Eds.). (1986). *Unmasking the psychopath: Antisocial personality and related syndromes.* New York: Norton.

Reisel, A. (1971). A comparison of group and individual factors in scholastic underachievement. *Dissertation Abstracts International, 31*(7-A), 3350.

Reiss, S. (1973). Transfer effects of success and failure training from one reinforcing agent to another. *Journal of Abnormal Psychology, 82*(3), 435–445.

Reiter, H. H. (1973). Some personality differences between under- and over-achievers. *International Review of Applied Psychology, 22*(2), 181–184.

Rennick, P. M., Klinge, V., Hart, Z., & Lennox, K. (1978). Evaluation of intellectual, linguistic, and achievement variables in normal, emotionally disturbed, and learning disabled children. *Adolescence, 13,* 755–766.

Resnick, J. (1951). A study of some relationships between high school grades and certain aspects of adjustment. *Journal of Educational Research, 44,* 321–340.

Reyes, R., & Clarke, R. B. (1968). Consistency as a factor in predicting grades. *Personnel & Guidance Journal, 47*(1), 50–55.

Richards, H. C., Gaver, D., & Golicz, H. (1984). Academically unpredictable school children: Their attitudes towards school subjects. *Journal of Educational Research, 77,* 273–276.

Richardson, C. M. (1981). Learning disability procedures: A human rights perspective. *Journal of Learning Disabilities, 14*(1), 7–8, 47.

Rickard, G. (1954). *The relationship between parental behavior and children's achievement behavior.* Unpublished doctoral dissertation, Harvard University, Cambridge, Ma.

Ricks, N. L. (1974). Sustained attention and the effects of distraction in underachieving second grade children. *Dissertation Abstracts International, 35*(3-A), 1535–1536.

Ricks, N. L., & Mirsky, A. F. (1974). Sustained attention and the effects of distraction in underachieving second grade children. *Journal of Education, Boston, 156*(4), 4–17.

Ridding, L. W. (1967). An investigation of personality measures associated with over and underachievement in English and arithmetic. *Journal of Educational Psychology, 37*(3), 397–398.

Rie, H. E., Rie, E. D., Stewart, S., & Ambuel, J. P. (1976). Effects of methylphenidate on underachieving children. *Journal of Consulting & Clinical Psychology, 44*(2), 250–260.

Rie, H. E., Rie, E. D., Stewart, S., & Ambuel, J. P. (1976). The effects of ritalin on underachieving children: A replication. *American Journal of Orthopsychiatry, 46,* 313–322.

Riedel, R. G., Grossman, J. H., & Burger, G. (1971). Special Incomplete Sentences Test for underachievers: Further research. *Psychological Reports, 29*(1), 251–257.

Riggs, R. O. (1970). A study of non-intellective characteristics associated with differential levels of academic over- and under-achievement. *Dissertation Abstracts International, 31*(6-A), 2745–2746.

Rimm, S. (1985a). Identifying underachievement: The characteristics approach. *Gifted Child Today, 41,* 2–5.

Rimm, S. (1985b). How to reach the underachiever. *Instructor, 95,* 73–74.

Ringness, T. A. (1965). Affective differences between successful and non-successful bright ninth grade boys. *Personnel & Guidance Journal, 43*(6), 600–606.

Ringness, T. A. (1967). Identification patterns, motivation and school achievement of bright junior school boys. *Journal of Educational Psychology, 58,* 93–102.

Ringness, T. A. (1970). Identifying figures, their achievement values and children's values as related to actual and predicted achievement. *Journal of Educational Psychology, 61*(3), 174–185.

Rittenhouse, J., Stephan, W. G., & Levine, E. (1984). Peer attributions and action plans for underachievement: Implications for peer counseling. *Personnel and Guidance Journal, 62,* 391–397.

Robbins, J. E. (1948). The home and family background of Ottawa public school children in relation to their IQ's. *Canadian Journal of Psychology, 2,* 35–41.

Robey, D., & Cody, J. (1966). A differential diagnosis of low and average academic 9th grade male students. *Journal of Experimental Education, 34,* 38–43.

Robin, A. L., Martello, J., Foxx, R. M., & Archable, C. (1977). Teaching note-taking skills to underachieving college students. *Journal of Educational Research, 71*(2), 81–85.

Robinowitz, R. (1956). Attributes of pupils achieving beyond their level of expectancy. *Journal of Personality, 24,* 308–317.

Robins, L. (1978). Sturdy childhood predictors of adult antisocial behaviour: replications from longitudinal studies. *Psychological Medicine, 8,* 611–622.

Robyak, J. E., & Downey, R. G. (1979). A discriminant analysis of the study skills and personality types of underachieving and nonunderachieving study skills students. *Journal of College Student Personnel, 20*(4), 306–309.

Rocks, S. (1985). Effects of counselor-directed relationship enhancement training on underachieving, poorly communicating students and their teachers. *School Counselor, 32*(3), 231–238.

Rodgers, B. (1983). The identification and prevalence of specific reading retardation. *British Journal of Educational Psychology, 53*(3), 369–373.

Rodgers, J. L. (1984). Confluence effects: Not here, not now! *Developmental Psychology, 20,* 321–331.

Rodick, J. D., & Henggeler, S. W. (1980). The short-term and long-term amelioration of academic and motivational deficiencies among low-achieving inner-city adolescents. *Child Development, 51*(4), 1126–1132.

Roesslein, C. G. (1953). *Differential patterns of intelligence traits between high achieving and low achieving high school boys.* Washington, DC: Catholic University of America Press.

Rogers, C. M. (1951). *Client-centered therapy.* Boston: Houghton Mifflin.

Rogers, C. M., Smith, M. D., & Coleman, J. M. (1978). Social comparison in the classroom: The relationship between academic achievement and self-concept. *Journal of Educational Psychology, 70*(1), 50–57.

Rogers, K. D., & Reese, G. (1965a). Health studies—presumably normal high school students: II. Absence from school. *American Journal of Diseases of Children, 109*(1), 9–27.

Rogers, K. D., & Reese, G. (1965b). Health studies—presumably normal high school students: III. Health room visits. *American Journal of Diseases of Children, 109*(1), 28–42.

Rolick, J. W. (1965). Scholastic achievement of teenagers and parental attitudes toward and interest in school-work. *Family Life Coordinator, 14*, 158–160.

Rollins, B. C., & Calder, C. (1975). Academic achievement, situational stress, and problem-solving flexibility. *Journal of Genetic Psychology, 126*(1), 93–105.

Romine, P. G., & Crowell, O. C. (1981). Personality correlates of under- and over-achievement at the university level. *Psychological Reports, 48*(3), 787–792.

Rosebrook, W. (1945). Identifying the slow learning child. *American Journal of Mental Deficiency, 50*, 307–312.

Rosen, B. C. (1959). Race, ethnicity, and the achievement syndrome. *American Sociological Review, 24*, 47–60.

Rosen, B. C. (1961). Family structure and achievement motivation. *American Sociological Review, 26*, 574–585.

Rosenbaum, J. E. (1980). Declining achievement: Lower standards or changing priorities? *Sociological Spectrum, 1*, 103–113.

Rosenberg, B. G., and Sutton-Smith, B. (1966). Sibling association, family size, and cognitive abilities. *Journal of Genetic Psychology, 109*, 271–279.

Rosenberg, B. G. & Sutton-Smith, B. (1969). Sibling age spacing effects upon cognition. *Developmental Psychology, 1*, 661–668.

Rosenfeld, H. M. (1966). Relationship of ordinal position to affiliation and achievement motives: Direction and generality. *Journal of Personality, 34*, 467–480.

Rosenshine, B. (1970). Enthusiastic teaching: A research review. *School Review, 78*, 499–514.

Rosenthal, R. & Jacobson, L. (1968). *Pygmalion in the classroom: Teacher expectations and pupil intellectual development*. New York: Holt, Rinehart, & Winston.

Rosentover, I. F. (1974). Group counseling of the underachieving high school student as related to self-image and academic success. *Dissertation Abstracts International, 35*(6-A), 3433–3434.

Rosmarin, M. S. (1966). Reaction to stress and anxiety in chronically underachieving high ability students. *Dissertation Abstracts, 27*(5-B), 1630.

Rosner, S. L. (1969). An investigation of certain aspects of self-related concept and personality of achieving readers and mildly underachieving readers and their mothers. *Dissertation Abstracts International, 30*(6-B), 2898–2899.

Rossi, A. O. (1968). The slow learner. *New York State Journal of Medicine, 68*(24), 3123–3128.

Rotella, R. J. (1985). Motivational concerns of high level gymnasts. In B. Bloom (Ed.), *Developing talent in young people* (pp. 67–85). New York: Ballantine Books.

Roth, R. M. (1959). The role of self-concept in achievement. *Journal of Experimental Education, 27*, 265–281.

Roth, R. M. (1970). *Underachieving students and guidance*. Boston: Houghton Mifflin.

Roth, R. M., Berenbaum, H. L., & Hershenson, D. (1967). *A developmental theory of psychotherapy: A systematic eclecticism*. Unpublished paper, Department of Psychology, Illinois Institute of Technology, Chicago, IL.

Roth, R. M., Mauksch, H. O., & Peiser, K. (1967). The non-achievement syndrome, group therapy, and achievement change. *Personnel & Guidance Journal, 46*(4), 393–398.

Roth, R. M., & Meyersburg, H. A. (1963). The Non-achievement syndrome. *Personnel & Guidance Journal, 41*, 535–540.

Roth, R. M., & Puri, P. (1967). Direction of aggression and the Non-achievement Syndrome. *Journal of Counseling Psychology, 14*, 277–281.

Rothburt, M., Dalfen, S. & Barrett, R. (1971). Effects of teacher expectancy on student-teacher interaction. *Journal of Educational Psychology, 62*, 49–54.

Rotheram, M. J. (1982). Social skills training with underachievers, disruptive, and exceptional children. *Psychology in the Schools, 19*(4), 532–539.

Rotter, J. (1966). Generalized expectancies for internal versus external control of reinforcement. *Psychological Monographs, 80*(1).

Rowan, B., & Miracle, A. W. (1983). Systems of ability grouping and the stratification of achievement in elementary schools. *Sociology of Education, 56,* 133–144.

Rowland, J. K. (1959). A psychometric study of student attitudes as a measure of academic motivation. *California Journal of Educational Research, 10,* 195–199.

Rowland, M. K., & Smith, J. L. (1966). Toward more accurate prediction of achievement. *Elementary School Journal, 67*(2), 104–107.

Rowzee, J. M. (1977). The effects of communication skill training on low socio-economic level underachieving secondary students' facilitative communication and self concept skills. *Dissertation Abstracts International, 37*(11-A), 7048–7049.

Rubin, D. S. (1968a). A comparison of the mother and father schemata of achievers and underachievers: A study of primary grades and achievement in arithmetic. *Dissertation Abstracts, 29*(6-A), 1794.

Rubin, D. S. (1968b). Mother and father schemata of achievers and underachievers in primary school arithmetic. *Psychological Reports, 23*(3, Pt. 2), 1215–1221.

Rubin, D. S. (1969). A comparison of the mother and father schemata of achievers and underachievers: A study of primary grades and achievement in arithmetic. *Journal of Social Psychology, 78*(2), 295–296.

Rubin, H. S., & Cohen, H. A. (1974). Group counseling and remediation: A two-faceted intervention approach to the problem of attrition in nursing education. *Journal of Educational Research, 67,* 195–198.

Ruckhaber, C. J. (1967). Differences and patterns of low achieving and high achieving intellectually able fourth grade boys on seventeen non-intellectual variables. *Dissertation Abstracts, 28*(1-A), 132.

Rugel, R. P. (1974). WISC subtest scores of disabled readers: A review with respect to Bannatyne's recategorization. *Journal of Learning Disabilities, 7*(1), 57–64.

Ruhland, D., & Feld, S. (1977). The development of achievement motivation in Black and White children. *Child Development, 48,* 1362–1368.

Rutter, M. (1980). *Changing youth in a changing society.* Cambridge, MA: Harvard University Press.

Rutter, M. (Ed.). (1980). *Scientific foundations of developmental psychiatry.* London: Hinemann Medical.

Rvals, K. (1975). Achievement motivation training for low-achieving eighth and tenth grade boys. *Journal of Experimental Education, 44*(2), 47–51.

Ryan, E. B., Ledger, G. W., Short, E. J., & Weed, K. A. (1982). Promoting the use of active comprehension strategies by poor readers. *Topics in Learning & Learning Disabilities, 2*(1), 53–60.

Ryan, E. D. (1963). Relative academic achievement and stabilometer performance. *Res. Quart. Amer. Ass. Hlth. Phys. Educ. Rec., 34*(2), 185–190.

Ryan, F. (1951). Personality differences between under and overachievers in college. *Dissertation Abstracts, 11,* 967–968.

Rychlak, J. F., & Tobin, T. J. (1971). Order effects in the affective learning styles of overachievers and underachievers. *Journal of Educational Psychology, 62*(2), 141–147.

Ryker, M. J. E., Rogers, C., & Beaujard, P. (1971). Six selected factors influencing educational achievement of children from broken homes. *Education, 91*(3), 200–211.

Safer, D. J. (1984). Subgrouping conduct disordered adolescents by early risk factors. *American Journal of Orthopsychiatry, 54*(4), 603–611.

Salend, S. J., & Henry, K. (1981). Response cost in mainstreamed settings. *Journal of School Psychology, 19*(3), 242–249.

Salvia, J., Algozinne, R., & Sheare, J. B. (1977). Attractiveness and school achievement. *Journal of School Psychology, 15*(1), 60–67.

Samph, T. (1974). Teacher behavior and the reading performance of below-average achievers. *Journal of Educational Research, 67*(6), 268–270.

Sampson, E. E., & Hancock, F. T. (1967). An examination of the relationship between ordinal position, personality, and conformity: An extension, replication, and partial verification. *Journal of Personality and Social Psychology, 5,* 398–407.

Sams, L. B. (1968). The relationship between anxiety, stress and the performance of nursing students. *Dissertation Abstracts, 29*(5-A), 1456.

Samson, J. E. (1976). Differential effects of task difficulty and reward contingencies on cheating and performance scores of academic underachievers and normal achievers. *Dissertation Abstracts International, 36*(9-B), 4707.

Sanders, W. B., Osborne, R. T., & Greene, J. E. (1955). Intelligence and academic performance of college students of urban, rural, and mixed backgrounds. *Journal of Educational Research, 49,* 185–193.

Sandin, A. A. (1944). Social and emotional adjustments of regularly promoted and non-promoted pupils. *Child Development Monograph, 32,* ix–142.

Sandler, I. N., Reich, J. W., & Doctolero, J. (1979). Utilization of college students to improve inner-city school children's academic behavior. *Journal of School Psychology, 171,* 283–291.

Sanford, E. G. (1952). The bright child who fails. *Understanding the Child, 21,* 85–88.

Sarnoff, I., & Raphael, T. (1955). Five failing college students. *American Journal of Orthopsychiatry, 25,* 343–372.

Sartain, A. Q. (1945). Relation of marks in college courses to the interestingness, value, and difficulty of the courses. *Journal of Educational Psychology, 36,* 561–566.

Saurenmann, D. A. & Michael, W. B. (1980). Differential placement of high-achieving and low-achieving gifted pupils in grades four, five, and six on measures of field dependence-field independence, creativity, and self-concept. *Gifted Child Quarterly, 24,* 81–86.

Savage, R. D. (1974). Personality and achievement in higher education professional training. *Educational Review, 27,* 3–15.

Sawyer, A. R. (1974). The effectiveness of token reinforcement, modeling, and traditional teaching techniques on achievement and self-concept of underachievers. *Dissertation Abstracts International, 34*(7-A), 3888.

Saxena, P. C. (1978). Adjustment of over and under achievers. *Indian Journal of Psychometry & Education, 9*(1-2), 25–33.

Schachter, M. (1949). La motivation psychodynamique dans un cas de "paresse" scolaire [The psychodynamic motivation in a case of scholastic "laziness"]. *Z. Kinderpsychiat., 16,* 83–85.

Schacter, F. F. (1982). Sibling deidenfication and split-parent identification: A family tetrad. In M. E. Lamb & B. Sutton-Smith (Eds.), *Sibling relationships: Their nature and significance across the lifespan.* Hillsdale, NJ, Erlbaum.

Schacter, S. (1963). Birth order, eminence, and high education. *American Sociological Review, 28,* 757–768.

Schaefer, C. E. (1977). Motivation: A major cause of school underachievement. *Devereux Forum, 12*(1), 16–29.

Schaefer, H. D. (1968). Group counseling of students exhibiting a significant discrepancy between ability and grade-point averages. *Dissertation Abstracts, 29*(4-A), 1138.

Schaeffer, B., Harris, A., & Greenbaum, M. (1968–1969). The treatment of socially oriented underachievers: A case study. *Journal of School Psychology, 7*(4), 70–73.

Scharf, M. C. (1969). Study of differences in selected personality and academic characteristics of low achieving college males. *Dissertation Abstracts International, 30*(4-A), 1405–1406.

Schilling, F. C. (1969). A description of the development and implementation of a curriculum-materials package for teaching mathematics to low achievers. *Dissertation Abstracts International, 30*(5-A), 1925–1926.

Schillo, R. J. (1964). Concept learning of achievers and underachievers as a function of task expectancy. *Dissertation Abstracts, 24*(9), 3841.

Schindler, A. W. (1948). Readiness for learning. *Childhood Education, 24*, 301–304.

Schlesser, G. E. (1946). Development of special abilities at the junior high school age. *Journal of Educational Research, 40*, 39–51.

Schmidt, B. G. (1945). The rehabilitation of feeble-minded adolescents. *School and Society, 62*, 409–412.

Schmidt, V. S. (1972). A comparison of children's aspirations and of parental expectations as a function of underachievement in the child. *Dissertation Abstracts International, 33*(5-A), 2181.

Schmieding, O. A. (1966). Efficacy of counseling and guidance procedures with failing junior high school students. *School Counselor, 14*, 74–80.

Schneider, J. M., Glasheen, J. D., & Hadley, D. W. (1979). Secondary school participation, institutional socialization, and student achievement. *Urban Education, 14*, 285–302.

Schoenhard, G. H. (1958). Home visitation put to a test. *Personnel & Guidance Journal, 36*, 480–485.

Schooler, C. (1972). Birth order effects: Not here, not now! *Psychological Bulletin, 78*, 161–175.

Schoonover, S. M. (1959). The relationship of intelligence and achievement to birth order, sex of sibling, and age interval. *Journal of Educational Psychology, 50*, 143–146.

Schreiber, P. R. (1945). Measurements of growth and adjustment after four years in high school. *Journal of Educational Research, 39*, 210–219.

Schroder, R. (1963). Academic achievement of the male college student. *Marriage and Family Living, 25*, 420–423.

Schultz, D. V. (1969). An evaluation of the effect of a United States Office of Education Talent Search Project on the academic performance of M-Scale-identified low-motivated ninth grade Michigan students. *Dissertation Abstracts, 29*(10-A), 3398–3399.

Schwab, F. J. (1969). A comparison of personality profiles of over- and under-achieving students at South Dakota State University. *Dissertation Abstracts International, 30*(6-A), 2343–2344.

Schwab, M. R., & Lundgren, D. C. (1978). Birth order, perceived appraisals by significant others, and self-esteem. *Psychological Reports, 43*, 443–454.

Schwartz, R. L. (1968). Effects of aggression and of evaluative instructions upon test performance of achievers and underachievers. *Dissertation Abstracts, 29*(1-B), 380–381.

Schwartzbein, D. (1988). *An analysis of family systems in differentially categorized underachievers.* Unpublished doctoral proposal, Department of Psychology, York University, Toronto, ON.

Scruggs, T. E., & Cohn, S. J. (1983). A university-based summer program for a highly able but poorly achieving Indian child. *Gifted Child Quarterly, 27*(2), 90–93.

Seabrooks, G. C. (1974). Factors related to admissions, low achievement, and early attrition of the disadvantaged student at the University of Notre Dame. *Dissertation Abstracts International, 35*(4-A), 1993.

Seagull, E. A., & Weinshank, A. B. (1984). Childhood depression in a selected group of low-achieving seventh-graders. *Journal of Clinical Child Psychology, 13*(2), 134–140.

Sears, W. J. (1968). The relation between the size high school and academic success of selected students at the University of Alabama. *Dissertation Abstracts, 29*(5-A), 1407.

Seaver, W. B. (1973). Effects of naturally induced teacher expectancies. *Journal of Personality and Social Psychology, 28*, 333–342.

Seeley, K. (1985). Gifted adolescents: Potential and problems. *NASSP Bulletin, 69*, 75–78.

Segel, D. (1951). Frustration in adolescent youth; its development and implications for the school program. *Office of Education Bulletin* (#1). Washington, DC: U.S. Office of Education.

Seiden, D. S. (1969). Some variables predictive of low achievement by high ability students. *Dissertation Abstracts, 29*(9-A), 3009.

Seipt, I. S. (1945). Sociological foundations of the psychiatric disorders of childhood. *Proc. Inst. Child Res. Clin. Woods Schs., 12*, 125.

Seltzer, C. C. (1948). Academic success in college of public and private school students: Freshman year at Harvard. *Journal of Psychology, 25*, 419–431.

Semke, C. W. (1968). A comparison of the outcomes of case study structured group counseling with high ability, underachieving freshmen. *Dissertation Abstracts, 29*(1-A), 128.

Sepie, A. C., & Keeling, B. (1978). The relationship between types of anxiety and under-achievement in mathematics. *Journal of Educational Research, 72*(1), 15–19.

Sewell, W. H., Haller, A. O., & Strauss, M. A. (1957). Social status and educational aspiration. *American Sociological Review, 22*, 67–73.

Shah, G. B. (1966). Causes of underachievement in mathematics. *Education & Psychology Review, 6*(2), 79–87.

Shanner, W. M. (1944). *Primary mental abilities and academic achievement*. Unpublished doctoral dissertation, University of Chicago.

Shapiro, B. K., Palmer, F. B., Wachtel, R. C., & Capute, A. J. (1984). Issues in the early identification of specific learning disability. *Journal of Development & Behavioral Pediatrics, 5*(1), 15–20.

Sharma, K. L. (1975). Rational group counseling with anxious underachievers. *Canadian Counsellor, 9*(2), 132–137.

Sharma, L. (1972). Academic underachievement: A reformulation and rectification. *Canadian Counselor, 6*, 205–213.

Sharma, V. P. (1970). Efficacy of evaluation procedures in relation to pupils' scholastic attainment. *Indian Psychological Review, 6*(2), 107–109.

Shavelson, R. J., & Stern, P. (1981). Research on teachers' pedagogical thoughts, judgements, decisions, and behavior. *Review of Educational Research*, 455–498.

Shaver, J. P., & Nuhn, D. (1971). The effectiveness of tutoring underachievers in reading and writing. *Journal of Educational Research, 65*(3), 107–112.

Shaw, D. C. (1949). A study of the relationships between Thurstone primary mental abilities and high school achievement. *Journal of Educational Psychology, 40*, 239–249.

Shaw, J. S. (1970). When Johnnie wants to fail. *Nation's Schools, 86*, 41–45.

Shaw, M. (1961a). Definition and identification of academic underachievers. In L. Miller (Ed.), *Guidance for underachievers with superior ability* (pp. 15–17). Washington, DC: U.S. Department of Mental Health, Education and Welfare.

Shaw, M. (1961b). Need achievement scales as predictors of academic success. *Journal of Educational Psychology, 52*(6), 282–285.

Shaw, M. C. (1964). Note on parent attitudes toward independence training and the academic achievement of their children. *Journal of Educational Psychology, 55*(6), 371–374.

Shaw, M. C., (1986). The prevention of learning and interpersonal problems. *Journal of Counseling and Development, 64*, 624–627.

Shaw, M. C., & Alves, G. J. (1963). The self-concept of bright academic underachievers: II. *Personnel & Guidance, 42*(4), 401–403.

Shaw, M. C., & Black, M. D. (1960). The reaction to frustration of bright high school under-achievers. *California Journal of Educational Research. 11*, 120–124.

Shaw, M. C., & Brown, D. J. (1957). Scholastic underachievement of bright college students. *Personnel & Guidance Journal, 36*, 195–199.

Shaw, M. C., & Dutton, B. E. (1962). The use of the Parent Attitude Research Inventory with the parents of bright academic underachievers. *Journal of Educational Psychology, 53*(5), 203–208.

Shaw, M. C., Edson, K., & Bell, H. M. (1960). The self-concept of bright underachieving high school students as revealed by an adjective check list. *Personnel & Guidance Journal, 39,* 193–196.

Shaw, M. C., & Grubb, J. (1958). Hostility and able high school underachievers. *Journal of Counseling Psychology, 5,* 263–266.

Shaw, M. C., & McCuen, J. T. (1960). The onset of academic underachievement in bright children. *Journal of Educational Psychology, 51,* 103–109.

Shaw, M. C., & White, D. L. (1965). The relationship between child-parent identification and academic underachievement. *Journal of Clinical Psychology, 21*(1), 10–13.

Sheldon, W., & Landsman, T. (1950). An investigation of non-directive group therapy with students in academic difficulty. *Journal of Consulting Psychology, 14,* 210–215.

Sher, E. O. (1974). The underachiever: A comparison of high and low achieving high IQ boys. *Dissertation Abstracts International, 34*(7-B), 3509–3510.

Sherman, M. (1945). *Intelligence and its deviations.* New York: Ronald Press.

Sherman, M., & Bell, E. (1951). The measurement of frustration: An experiment in group frustration. *Personality, 1,* 44–53.

Sherman, S. R., Zuckerman, D., & Sostek, A. B. (1975). The antiachiever: Rebel without a future. *School Counselor, 22*(5), 311–324.

Sherman, S. R., Zuckerman, D., & Sostek, A. B. (1979). The antiachiever: Rebel without a future. *Devereux Forum, 14*(1), 1–15.

Shore, M. F., & Lieman, A. (1965). Parental perception of the student as related to academic achievement in junior college. *Journal of Experimental Education, 33,* 391–394.

Shove, G. R. (1972). A test battery for the assessment of school learning difficulties, and its relationship to reflection-impulsivity in second and third grade boys. *Dissertation Abstracts International, 32*(9-A), 5049–5050.

Siegel, S. (1956). *Nonparametric statistics for the behavioral sciences.* New York: McGraw-Hill.

Silverman, H. J. (1974). Design and evaluation of a unit about measurement as a vehicle for changing attitude toward mathematics and self-concept of low achievers in the intermediate grades. *Dissertation Abstracts International, 34*(8-A, Pt. 1), 4717.

Silverman, H. W. (1969). The prediction of learning difficulties and personality trends in pre-school children. *Dissertation Abstracts, 29*(8-B), 3094–3095.

Silverman, M. (1976). The achievement motivation group: A counselor-directed approach. *Elementary School Guidance & Counseling, 11*(2), 100–106.

Silvern, S. B., & Brooks, D. M. (1980). Frustration as a factor in the height of low achievers' self-portraits. *50*(1), 225–226.

Simometti, N. (1968). Il problema dell'insuccesso scolastico [The problem of school failure]. *Difesa Sociale, 47*(4), 137–156.

Simons, R. H., & Bibb, J. (1974). Achievement motivation, text anxiety, and underachievement in the elementary school. *Journal of Educational Research, 67*(8), 366–369.

Simpson, R. L. (1970). Reading tests versus intelligence tests as predictors of high school graduation. *Psychology in the Schools, 7*(4), 363–365.

Simrall, D. (1947). Intelligence and the ability to learn. *Journal of Psychology, 23,* 27–43.

Sims, G. K., & Sims, J. M. (1973). Does face-to-face contact reduce counselee responsiveness with emotionally insecure youth? *Psychotherapy: Theory, Research & Practice, 10*(4), 348–351.

Sinha, N. C. (1972). Personality factors and scholastic achievement of school students. *Behaviorometric, 2*(1), 9–12.

Skeels, H. M., & Harms, I. (1948). Children with inferior social histories; their mental development in adoptive homes. *Journal of Genetic Psychology, 72,* 283–294.

Slavina, L. S. (1954). Specific features of the intellectual work of unsuccessful scholars. *SCR Psychological Bulletin, 8,* 1–11.

Sloggett, B. B., Gallimore, R., & Kubany, E. S. (1970). A comparative analysis of fantasy need achievement among high and low achieving male Hawaiian-Americans. *Journal of Cross-Cultural Psychology, 1*(1), 53–61.

Smail, B. (1985). An attempt to move mountains: The "girls into science and technology" (GIST) project. *Journal of Curriculum Studies, 17,* 351–354.

Small, L. (1979). *The briefer psychotherapies* (2nd ed.). New York: Brunner/Mazel.

Small, L. B. (1976). A comparison of an extended individualized reading instructional program with the regular reading instructional program and its effects upon reading skills of selected Black junior high school students who are underachieving in reading. *Dissertation Abstracts International, 37*(4-A), 1967.

Smith, C. P. (Ed.). (1969). *Achievement Related Motives in Children.* New York: Russell-Sage.

Smith, C. P., & Winterbottom, M. T. (1970). Personality characteristics of college students on academic probation. *Journal of Personality, 38*(3), 230.

Smith, H. C., & Dunbar, D. S. (1951). The personality and achievement of the classroom participant. *Journal of Educational Psychology, 42,* 65–84.

Smith, J. L. (1951). *Multiple-choice Rorschach responses of over and under achievers among college women.* Unpublished master's thesis, Catholic University of America, Washington, DC.

Smith, L. (1971). A 5-year follow-up study of high ability achieving and non-achieving college freshmen. *Journal of Educational Research, 64*(5), 220–222.

Smith, M. D., Coleman, J. M., Dokecki, P. R., & Davis, E. E. (1977). Recategorized WISC-R scores of learning disabled children. *Journal of Learning Disabilities, 10*(7), 48–54.

Smith, M. D., & Rogers, C. M. (1977). Item instability on the Piers-Harris Children's Self-Concept Scale for academic underachievers with high, middle, and low self-concepts: Implications for construct validity. *Educational & Psychological Measurements, 37*(2), 553–558.

Smith, M. D., Zingale, S. A., & Coleman, J. M. (1978). The influence of adult expectancy/child performance discrepancies upon children's self-concept. *American Educational Research Journal, 15,* 259–265.

Smith, S. L. (1972). The effectiveness of different reinforcement combinations on expectancy of success in achieving and underachieving elementary school boys. *Dissertation Abstracts International, 32*(8-B), 4907.

Smith, T. M. (1977). The facilitative effect of a modified contract instructional method on underachieving students. *Journal of Classroom Interaction, 13,* 44–47.

Smykal, A., Jr. (1962). A comparative investigation of home environmental variables related to the achieving and underachieving behavior of academically able high school students. *Dissertation Abstracts, 23*(1), 315.

Snider, J. G., & Drakeford, G. C. (1971). Intensity of meaning discrimination in academic achievers and underachievers. *Psychological Reports, 29*(3, Pt. 2), 1139–1145.

Snider, J. G., & Linton, T. E. (1964). The predictive value of the California Psychological Inventory in discriminating between the personality patterns of high school achievers and underachievers. *Ontario Journal of Educational Research, 6*(2), 107–115.

Snow, R. E. (1969). Unfinished pygmalion. *Contemporary Psychology, 14,* 197–199.

Snow, R. E. (1986). Individual differences and the design of educational programs. *American Psychologist, 41*(10), 1029–1039.

Soli, S., & Devine, V. T. (1976). Behavioral correlates of achievements: A look at high and low achievers. *Journal of Educational Psychology, 68*(3), 335–341.

Solursh, S. (1988). *The relationship between personality categorization and learning disabilities.* Unpublished honours thesis proposal, Department of Psychology, York University, Toronto, ON.

Sontakey, G. R. (1975). An experimental study of bright under-achievers. *Scientia Paedagogica Experimentalis, 12*(2), 231–247.

Southworth, R. S. (1966). A study of the effects of short-term group counseling on underachieving sixth grade students. *Dissertation Abstracts, 27*(5-A), 1241.

Specter, G. A. (1971). Underachieving high school boys' perceptions of their parents, friends, and educators. *Dissertation Abstracts International, 32*(6-B), 3653.

Speedie, S., et al. (1971). Evaluation of a battery of noncognitive variables as long-range predictors of academic achievement. *Proceedings of the American Psychological Association, 6*(Pt. 2), 517–518.

Spence, J. T. (1985). Achievement American style. *American Psychologist, 40*(12), 1285–1295.

Sperry, B., Staver, N., Reiner, B. S., & Ulrich, D. (1958). Renunciation and denial in learning difficulties. *American Journal of Orthopsychiatry, 28,* 98–111.

Spina, D. J., & Crealock, C. M. (1985). Identification of and programming for the gifted student and the gifted underachiever. *Canadian Journal for Exceptional Children, 2,* 8–13.

Spino, W. D. (1970). Semantic differential patterns of selected college freshmen as a basis for achievement differentiation. *Dissertation Abstracts International, 31*(1-A), 165.

Spionek, H., & Dyga, M. (1971). Kliniczna analiza związku niepowodzen szkolnych z tzw. nerwowości uczniow [Clinical analysis of the connection between school failure and so-called nervousness in pupils]. *Psychologia Wychowawcza, 14*(2), 178–182.

Spitz, R. A. (1972). Hospitalism. In S. I. Harrison, & J. F. McDermott, Jr. (Eds.). *Childhood psychopathology* (pp. 237–257). New York: International Universities Press.

Sprinthall, N. A. (1964). A comparison of values among teacher, academic underachievers, and achievers. *Journal of Experimental Education, 33*(2), 193–196.

Srivastava, A. K. (1976). Motivational variables and discrepant achievement patterns. *Psychologia: An International Journal of Psychology in the Orient, 19*(1), 40–46.

Srivastava, A. K. (1977). A study of inter-correlation between some variables found to be significantly related to underachievement. *Indian Journal of Behaviour, 1*(3), 26–28.

Stafford, K. P. (1978). The use of reinforcement differences on normal and underachieving children. *Dissertation Abstracts International, 38*(9-B), 4483.

Stainback, W. C., & Stainback, S. B. (1972). Effects of student to student tutoring on arithmetic achievement and personal social attitudes of low achieving tutees and high achieving tutors. *Education & Training of the Mentally Retarded, 7*(4), 169–172.

Staker, J. E. (1949). *A preliminary study of factors related to overachievement and underachievement.* Unpublished master's thesis, Illinois State University, Normal, IL.

Stalnaker, E. M. (1951). A study of several psychometric tests as a basis for guidance on the junior high school level. *Journal of Experimental Education, 20,* 41–66.

Standridge, C. G. (1968). The predictive value of nonintellectual factors and their influence on academic achievement. *Dissertation Abstracts, 29*(5-A), 1458.

Stangel, G. F. (1974). Intervention procedures in reading underachievement: The development of a teacher-school psychologist consultation model. *Dissertation Abstracts International, 34*(7-A), 3891.

Stanland, M. (1945). Educational achievements of parents and abilities of children. *Proc. Inst. Child Res. Clin. Woods Schs., 12,* 47–58.

Start, A., & Start, K. B. (1974). The relation between birth order and effort or conscientiousness among primary school children. *Research in Education, 12,* 1–8.

Steckel, M. L. (1930). Intelligence and birth order in family. *Journal of Social Psychology, 1,* 329–344.

Stedman, J., & Van Hevningen, R. (1982). Educational underachievement and epilepsy: A study of children from normal schools, admitted to a special hospital for epilepsy. *Early Child Development & Care, 9*(1), 65–82.

Stein, F. (1968). Consistency of cognitive, interest, and personality variables with academic mastery: A study of field-dependence-independence, verbal comprehension, self-perception, and vocational interest in relation to academic performance among male juniors attending an urban university. *Dissertation Abstracts, 29*(5-A), 1483–1484.

Steisel, I. M., & Cohen, B. D. (1951). The effects of two degrees of failure on level of aspiration and performance. *Journal of Abnormal and Social Psychology, 46,* 79–82.

Stendler, C. B. (1949). Building secure children in our schools. *Childhood Education, 25,* 216–220.

Stephens, G. (1949). Psychiatric problems in the educational sphere. *Understanding the Child, 18,* 13–14.

Stetter, D. (1971). Into the classroom with behavior modification. *School Counselor, 19*(2), 110–114.

Stevenson, H. C., & Fantuzzo, J. W. (1986). The generality and social validity of a competency-based self-control training intervention for underachieving students. *Journal of Applied Behavior Analysis, 19,* 269–276.

Stewart, M. (1985). Aggressive conduct disorder. *Aggressive Behavior, 11,* 323–331.

Stillwell, C., Harris, J. W., & Hall, R. V. (1972). Effects of provision for individual differences and teacher attention upon study behavior and assignments completed. *Child Study Journal, 2*(2), 75–81.

Stimpson, D. V., & Pedersen, D. M. (1970). Effects of a survival training experience upon evaluation of self and others for underachieving high school students. *Perceptual & Motor Skills, 31*(1), 337–338.

St. John, N. H., & Lewis, R. (1971). The influence of school racial context on academic achievement. *Social Problems, 19,* 68–79.

Stockard, J., & Wood, J. W. (1984). The myth of female underachievement: A reexamination of sex differences in academic underachievement. *American Educational Research Journal, 21*(4), 825–838.

Stoll, Lynn J. (1978). Teacher perceptions of reading practices in overachieving and under-achieving Florida elementary schools. *Dissertation Abstracts International, 38*(8-A), 4559.

Stone, P. A. (1972). Comparative effects of group encounter, group counseling and study skills instruction on academic performance of underachieving college students. *Dissertation Abstracts International, 33*(6-A), 2724–2725.

Stoner, W. G. (1957). Factors related to the underachievement of high school students. *Dissertation Abstracts, 17,* 96–97.

Strang, H. R. (1974). Changing disadvantaged children's learning tempos through automated techniques. *Journal of Genetic Psychology, 124*(1), 91–98.

Strauss, C. C., Lahey, B. B., & Jacobsen, R. H. (1982). The relationship of three measures of childhood depression to academic underachievement. *Journal of Applied Developmental Psychology, 3*(4), 375–380.

Strodbeck, F. (1958). Family interaction, values, and achievement. In D. McClelland, et al., *Talent and Society.* Princeton, NJ: Van Nostrand Reinhold.

Stromswold, S. A., & Wrenn, C. G. (1948). Counseling students toward scholastic adjustment. *Educational & Psychological Measurement, 8,* 57–63.

Su, C. (1976). The perceived parental attitudes of high-achieving and under-achieving junior high school students. *Bulletin of Education Psychology, 9,* 21–32.

Sugarman, B. (1967). Involvement in youth culture, academic achievement, and conformity in school. *British Journal of Sociology, 18,* 151–164.

Sullivan, H. S. (1954). *The collected works of Harry Stack Sullivan*. New York: Norton.

Sumner, F. C., & Johnson, E. (1949). Sex differences in levels of aspiration and in self-estimates of performance in a classroom situation. *Journal of Psychology, 27*, 483–490.

Sutherland, B. K. (1952). Case studies in educational failure during adolescence. *Journal of Consulting Psychology, 16*, 353–358.

Sutton, R. S. (1961). An analysis of factors related to educational achievement. *Journal of Genetic Psychology, 98*, 193–201.

Sutton-Smith, B. (1982). Birth order and sibling status effects. In M. E. Lamb & B. Sutton-Smith (Eds.), *Sibling relationships: Their nature and significance across the lifespan*. Hillsdale, NJ: Erlbaum.

Sutton-Smith, B., & Rosenberg, B. G. (1970). *The sibling*. New York: Holt, Rinehart, & Winston.

Swift, M., & Back, L. (1973). A method for aiding teachers of the troubled adolescent. *Adolescence, 8*(29), 1–16.

Swift, M. S., & Spivack, G. (1969). Clarifying the relationship between academic success and overt classroom behavior. *36*(2), 99–104.

Sylvester, E. (1949). Emotional aspects of learning. *Quarterly Journal of Child Behavior, 1*, 133–139.

Taber's Medical Cyclopedia (15th ed.). (1983). Philadelphia: F. A. Davis.

Talbot, M., & Henson, I. (1954). Pupils psychologically absent from school. *American Journal of Orthopsychiatry, 24*, 381–390.

Talmadge, M., Hayden, B. S., & Mordock, J. B. (1970). Evaluation: Requisite for administrative acceptance of school consultation. *Professional Psychology, 1*(3), 231–234.

Tamagini, J. E. (1969). A comparative study of achievement motivation in achieving and underachieving grade school boys. *Dissertation Abstracts, 29*(12-A), 4339.

Taylor, R. (1955). Personality traits and discrepant achievement: A review. *Journal of Counseling Psychology, 19*(3), 205.

Taylor, R. G., & Farquhar, W. W. (1966). The validity and reliability of the human trait inventory designed to measure under- and over-achievement. *Journal of Educational Research, 59*(5), 227–230.

Tefft, B. M. (1977). Underachieving high school students as mental health aides with maladapting primary grade children: The effect of a helper-helpee relationship on behavior, sociometric status, and self-concept. *Dissertation Abstracts International, 28*(9), 700–702.

Tefft, B. M., & Kloba, J. A. (1981). Underachieving high school students as mental health aides with maladapting primary-grade children. *American Journal of Community Psychology, 9*(3), 303–319.

Teicher, J. D. (1972). The alienated, older, isolated male adolescent. *American Journal of Psychotherapy, 26*(3), 401–407.

Teigland, J. J., Winkler, R. C., Munger, P. F., & Kranzler, G. D. (1966). Some concomitants of underachievement at the elementary school level. *Personnel & Guidance Journal, 44*(9), 950–955.

Tesser, A. (1980). Self-esteem maintenance in family dynamics. *Journal of Personality and Social Psychology, 39*, 77–91.

Thelen, M. H., & Harris, C. S. (1968). Personality of college underachievers who improve with group psychotherapy. *Personnel & Guidance Journal, 46*(6), 561–566.

Thiel, R., & Thiel, A. F. (1977). A structural analysis of family interaction patterns, and the underachieving gifted child: A three case exploratory study. *Gifted Child Quarterly, 21*(2), 267–275.

Thom, D. A., & Newell, N. (1945). Hazards of the high IQ. *Mental Hygiene, 29*, 61–77.

Thoma, M. (1964). Group psychotherapy with underachieving girls in a public high school. *Journal of Individual Psychology, 20*(1), 96–100.

Thomas, A., & Chess, S. (1968). *Temperament and behavior disorders*. New York: New York University Press.

Thomas, A., & Chess, S. (1977). *Temperament and development,* New York: Brunner/Mazel.

Thomas, A., & Chess, S. (1980). *The dynamics of psychological development*. New York: Brunner/Mazel.

Thomas, G. P. (1971). The identification of potential underachievers on the basis of color preference. *Dissertation Abstracts International, 31*(9-A), 4476–4477.

Thomas, N. L. (1974). The effects of a sensitivity-encounter group experience upon self-concept and school achievement in adolescent underachieving girls. *Dissertation Abstracts International, 35*(2-B), 1066–1067.

Thommes, M. J. (1970). Changes in values, perceptions, and academic performance of college freshmen underachievers in a remedial program. *Dissertation Abstracts International, 31*(5-B), 2969–2970.

Thompson, C. S. (1970). The effect of selected painting experiences on the self-concept, visual expression and academic achievement of third and fourth grade underachievers. *Dissertation Abstracts International, 31*(4-A), 1634–1635.

Thompson, G. N. (1945). Psychiatric factors influencing learning. *Journal of Nervous and Mental Disorders, 101*, 347–356.

Thompson, J. G., Griebstein, M. G., & Kuhlenschmidt, S. L. (1980). Effects of EMG biofeedback and relaxation training in the prevention of academic underachievement. *Journal of Counseling Psychology, 27*(2), 97–106.

Thompson, R. H., White, K. R., & Morgan, D. P. (1982). Teacher-student interaction patterns in classrooms with mainstreamed mildly handicapped students. *American Educational Research Journal, 19*(2), 220–236.

Thorndike, R. L. (1963). *The Concepts of Over- and Underachievement,* Columbia University Teacher's College, New York Bureau of Publications.

Thornton, S. M. (1975). An investigation of the attitudes of students, teachers and parents toward achievers and low achievers at the Grade 7 level. *Dissertation Abstracts International, 35*(7-A), 4265.

Tibbetts, J. R. (1955). The role of parent-child relationships in the achievement of high school pupils: a study of the family relationships associated with under-achievement and high achievement of high school pupils. *Dissertation Abstracts, 15*, 232.

Tilton, J. W. (1946). Unevenness of ability and brightness. *American Psychologist, 1*, 261.

Tilton, J. W. (1948). The definition of intelligence as ability to learn. *American Psychologist, 3*, 294–295.

Tilton, J. W. (1949). Intelligence test scores as indicative of ability to learn. *Educational & Psychological Measurement, 9*, 291–296.

Tirman, R. J. (1971). A scale for the clinical diagnosis of underachievement. *Dissertation Abstracts International, 31*(12-B), 7583.

Tobias, S., & Weissbrod, C. (1980). Anxiety and mathematics: An update. *Harvard Educational Review, 50*(1), 63–70.

Todd, F. J., Terrell, G., & Frank, C. E. (1962). Differences between normal and underachievers of superior ability. *Journal of Applied Psychology, 46*, 183–190.

Tolor, A. (1969). Incidence of underachievement at the high school level. *Journal of Educational Research, 63*, 63–65.

Tolor, A. (1970). An evaluation of a new approach in dealing with high school underachievement. *Journal of Learning Disabilities, 3*, 520–529.

Topol, P., & Reznikoff, M. (1979). Achievers and underachievers: A comparative study of fear of success, education and career goals, and conception of woman's role among high school senior girls. *Sex Roles, 5*(1), 85–92.

Torrance, E. P. (1980). Lessons about giftedness and creativity from a nation of 115 million overachievers. *Gifted Child Quarterly, 24,* 10–14.

Torrence, P. (1950). Effect of mental and educational retardation on personality development in children. *American Journal of Mental Deficiency, 55,* 208–212.

Travers, R. M. W. (1949). Significant research on the prediction of academic success. In W. T. Donahue, C. H. Coombs, & R. M. W. Travers (Eds.), *The measurement of student adjustment and achievement* (pp. 147–190). Ann Arbor, MI: University of Michigan Press.

Traxler, A. E. (1946). Evaluation of aptitude and achievement in a guidance program. *Educational and Psychological Assessment, 6,* 3–16.

Treadwell, V. (1975). Counselor education: Minority underachievers. *Journal of Non-white Concerns in Personnel and Guidance, 3,* 82–84.

Trotter, H. D. (1971). The effectiveness of group psychotherapy in the treatment of academic underachievement in college freshmen. *Dissertation Abstracts International, 32*(1-B), 573–574.

Troyer, M. E. (1948). How does marking on the basis of ability affect learning and interests? *American Psychologist, 3,* 297.

Troyna, B. (1984). Fact or artifact? The 'educational underachievement' of Black pupils. *British Journal of Sociology of Education, 5,* 153–166.

Turner, H. M. (1972). An experiment to alter "achievement motivation" in low-achieving male adolescents by teaching the game of chess. *Dissertation Abstracts International, 32*(10-B), 6040–6041.

Turner, J. H. (1972). Structural conditions of achievement among Whites and Blacks in the rural south. *Social Problems, 19,* 496–508.

Tuttle, H. S. (1946). Two kinds of learning. *Journal of Psychology, 22,* 267–277.

Tyler, R. W. (1948). Educability in the schools. *Elementary School Journal, 49,* 200–212.

Ulin, R. O. (1968). Ethnicity and school performance: An analysis of variables. *California Journal of Educational Research, 19*(4), 190–197.

Valine, W. J. (1974). Focused feedback with video tape as an aid in counseling underachieving college freshmen. *Small Group Behavior, 5*(2), 131–143.

Valine, W. J. (1976). A four-year follow-up study of underachieving college freshmen. *Journal of College Student Personnel, 17*(4), 309–312.

Valverde, L. A. (1984). Underachievement and underrepresentation of Hispanics in mathematics and mathematics-related careers. *Journal of Research in Mathematics Education, 15*(2), 123–133.

VandenBos, G. R. (1986). Psychotherapy research: A special issue. *American Psychologist, 41*(2), 111–112.

Vanderhoof, T. J. (1970). The effects of group counseling on low achieving students' perception of their college environment. *30*(10-A), 4237–4238.

Verniani, F. (1971). A comparison of selected child rearing activities used with achieving and nonachieving male school children. *Dissertation Abstracts International, 31*(9-A), 4895–4896.

Vernon, P. E. (1948). Changes in abilities from 14 to 20 years. *Advanc. Sci., 5,* 138.

Volberding, E. (1949). Characteristics of successful and unsuccessful eleven-year old pupils. *Elementary School Journal, 49,* 405–410.

von Klock, K. B. (1966). An investigation of group and individual counseling as remedial methods for working with junior-high-school underachieving boys. *Dissertation Abstracts, 27*(5-A), 1276–1277.

Vriend, J., & Dyer, W. W. (1973). Counseling the reluctant client. *Journal of Counseling Psychology, 20,* 240–246.

Vriend, T. J. (1969). High-performing inner-city adolescents assist low-performing peers in counseling groups. *Personnel & Guidance Journal, 47*(9), 897–904.

Wagman, M. (1964). Persistence in ability-achievement discrepancies and Kuder scores. *Personnel & Guidance Journal, 43*(3), 383–389.

Wagner, M. E., & Schubert, H. (1977). Sibship variables and the United States Presidency. *Journal of Individual Psychology, 33,* 78–85.

Wagner, M. E., Schubert, H., & Schubert, D. (1979). Sibship constellation effects on psychological development, creativity, and health. *Advances in Child Development and Behaviour, 14,* 57–148.

Walberg, H. J., & Anderson, G. J. (1968). Classroom climate and individual learning. *Journal of Educational Psychology, 59,* 414–419.

Walsh, A. (1956). *Self concepts of bright boys with learning difficulties.* New York: Teacher's College, Columbia University.

Walsh, B. R. (1975). On needing and giving help: The underachiever. *Independent School Bulletin, 34,* 31–32.

Walter, L. M., Marzolf, S. S. (1951). The relation of sex, age and school achievement to levels of aspiration. *Journal of Educational Psychology, 42,* 285–292.

Warburton, F. W. (1951). Relationship between intelligence and size of family. *Eugen. Rev., 43,* 36–37.

Warner, W. L. (1950). Réussite scolaire et classes sociales aux États-Unis [School success and social classes in the United States]. *Enfant, 3,* 405–410.

Washington, B. B. (1951). *Background factors and adjustment.* Washington, DC: Catholic University of America Press.

Wass, H. L. (1969). Relationships of social-psychological variables to school achievement for high and low achievers. *Dissertation Abstracts, 29*(8-A), 2578.

Waters, C. W. (1959). Construction and validation of a forced-choice over- and under-achievement scale. *Dissertation Abstracts, 20,* 2379.

Waters, C. W. (1964). Construction and validation of a forced-choice over- and under-achievement scale. *Educational & Psychological Measurement, 24*(4), 921–928.

Watley, D. J. (1966). Counselor confidence and accuracy of prognoses of success or failure. *Personnel & Guidance Journal, 45*(4), 342–348.

Wattenberg, W. W. (1948). Mobile children need help. *Educational Forum, 12,* 335–342.

Watts, D. B. (1966). A study of the social characteristics affecting certain over-achieving and under-achieving rural high school senior boys as compared to their urban counterparts. *Dissertation Abstracts International, 30*(7-A), 2735–2736.

Weber, C. O. (1946). Levels of aspiration. In P. L. Harriman, *Encyclopedia of Psychology* (pp. 45–46). New York Philosophical Library

Webster's deluxe unabridged dictionary (1983). New York: Dorset & Baber.

Webster's encyclopedia of dictionaries (1978). New York: Literary Press.

Wechsler, J. D. (1971). Improving the self-concepts of academic underachievers through maternal group counseling. *California Journal of Educational Research, 22*(3), 96–103.

Weider, A. (1973). The science teacher assays the underachiever. *Science Teacher, 40*(1), 19–21.

Weigand, G. (1953). Goal aspiration and academic success. *Personnel & Guidance Journal, 31,* 458–461.

Weigand, G. (1957). Adaptiveness and the role of parents in academic success. *Personnel & Guidance Journal, 35,* 518–522.

Weiner, B. (1968). Motivated forgetting and the study of repression. *Journal of Personality, 36*, 213–234.

Weiner, B. (1972). Attribution theory, achievement motivation, and the educational process. *Review of Educational Research, 42*, 203–215.

Weiner, B. (1976). An attributional approach to educational psychology. In L. Shulman (Ed.), *Review on Research in Education, 4* 179–209.

Weiner, B., Frieze, I., Kukla, A., Reed, L., Rest, S., & Rosenbaum, R. M. (1971). *Perceiving the causes of success and failure.* New York: General Learning Press.

Weiner, B., & Potepan, P. A. (1970). Personality characteristics and affective reactions toward exams of superior and failing college students. *Journal of Educational Psychology, 61*(2), 144–151.

Weiner, I. B. (1970). *Psychological disturbance in adolescence,* New York: Wiley.

Weiner, I. B. (1971). Psychodynamic aspects of learning disability: The passive-aggressive underachiever. *Journal of School Psychology, 9*(3), 246–251.

Weiss, P., Wertheimer, M., & Groesbeck, B. (1959). Achievement motivation, academic aptitude and college grades. *Educational & Psychological Measurement, 19*, 663–666.

Wells, F. L. (1950a). Psychometric patterns in adjustment problems at upper extremes of test "intelligence": Cases XXXIX-LVI, *Journal of Genetic Psychology, 76*, 3–37.

Wells, F. L. (1950b). College survivals and non-survivals at marginal test levels: Cases LVII-LXXXIV. *Journal of Genetic Psychology, 77*, 153–185.

Wells, H. M., & Bell, D. M. (1962). Binocular perceptual discriminations of authority and peer group figures among over, under and equal achievers. *Journal of Psychology, 54*(1), 113–120.

Wenger, M. A., Holzinger, K. J., & Harman, H. H. (1948). The estimation of pupil ability by three factorial solutions. *University of California Publications in Psychology, 5*(8), 1–252.

Werner, E. E. (1966). CPQ personality factors of talented and underachieving boys and girls in elementary school. *Journal of Clinical Psychology, 22*(4), 461–464.

Werner, R. S. (1972). Group counseling with underachievers in a community college. *Dissertation Abstracts International, 32*(7-A), 3708–3709.

West, C., & Anderson, T. (1976). The question of preponderant causation in teacher expectancy research. *Review in Educational Research, 46*, 613–630.

Westman, J. C., & Bennett, T. M. (1985). Learning impotence and the Peter Pan fantasy. *Child Psychiatry and Human Development, 15*(3), 153–166.

Wexler, F. (1969). The antiachiever: Dynamics and treatment of a special clinical problem. *Psychoanalytic Review, 56*(3), 461–466.

Wheelis, A. (1966). *The illusionless man.* New York: Harper & Row.

White, D. R. (1969). The selection and experimental study of poor readers in a reversal-nonreversal shift paradigm. *Dissertation Abstracts, 29*(10-B), 3926.

White, K. (1972). The effect of source of evaluation on the development of internal control among young boys. *Psychology in the Schools, 9*(1), 56–61.

Whiting, A. (1970). Independence concepts held by parents of successful and unsuccessful elementary school boys. *Dissertation Abstracts International, 31*(1-B), 387.

Whitmore, J. R. (1980). *Giftedness, conflict, and underachievement.* Boston: Allyn & Bacon.

Whitmore, J. R., (1986). Understanding a lack of motivation to excel. *Gifted Child Quarterly, 30*, 66–69.

Whittier, M. W. (1970). No flunking allowed. *College Management, 5*, 34–35.

Wicker, A. W. (1985). Getting out of our conceptual ruts: Strategies for expanding conceptual frameworks. *American Psychologist, 40*(10), 1094–1103.

Widlak, P. A. (1986). Family configuration, family interaction, and intellectual attainment. *Dissertation Abstracts International, 46,* 3504-A.

Wiegers, R. (1975). Cognitive mediation of achievement-related behavior. *Dissertation Abstracts International, 36*(6-B), 3132–3133.

Wigell, W. W., & Ohlsen, M. M. (1962). To what extent is affect a function of topic and referent in group counseling? *American Journal of Orthopsychiatry, 32*(4), 728–735.

Williams, J. (1947). *Educational attainment by economic characteristics and marital status.* Washington, DC: U.S. Government Printing Office.

Williams, T. D. (1969). Comparisons of college dropouts, returnees, and graduates on selected high school variables. *Dissertation Abstracts, 29*(9-A), 2972.

Williamson, E. (1936). The role of faculty counseling in scholastic motivation. *Journal of Applied Psychology, 20,* 324–366.

Willingham, W. W. (1964). The interpretation of relative achievement. *American Educational Research Journal, 1*(2), 101–112.

Willis, B. (1970). The influence of teacher expectation on teachers' classroom interaction with selected students. *Dissertation Abstracts International, 30,* 5072-A.

Willis, J., & Seymour, G. (1978). CPQ Validity: The relationship between children's personality questionnaire scores and teacher ratings. *Journal of Abnormal Child Psychology, 6,* 107–113.

Wills, I. H. (1969). The vulnerable child. *Academic Therapy, 5*(1), 63–65.

Wilson, J. A. (1959). Achievement, intelligence, age, and promotion characteristics of students scoring below the 10th percentile on the California Test of Personality. *Journal of Educational Research, 52,* 283–292.

Wilson, J. A. (1975). Over- and under-achievement in reading and mathematics. *Irish Journal of Education, 9*(1-2), 69–76.

Wilson, J. D. (1971). Predicting levels of first year university performance. *British Journal of Educational Psychology, 41*(2), 163–170.

Wilson, M. R., Jr., Soderquist, R., Zemke, R. L., & Swenson, W. M. (1967). Underachievement in college: Evaluation of the psychodynamics. *Psychiatry, 30*(2), 180–186.

Wilson, N. S. (1986). Counselor interventions with low-achieving and underachieving elementary, middle, and high school students: A review of the literature. *Journal of Counseling and Development, 64,* 628–634.

Wilson, R. C., & Morrow, W. R. (1962). School and career adjustment of bright high-achieving and underachieving high school boys. *Journal of Genetic Psychology, 101,* 91–103.

Winborn, B., & Schmidt, L. G. (1962). The effectiveness of short-term group counseling upon the academic achievement of potentially superior but underachieving college freshmen. *Journal of Educational Research, 55*(4), 169–173.

Winkelman, S. L. (1963). California psychological inventory profile patterns of underachievers, average achievers, and overachievers. *Dissertation Abstracts, 23*(8), 2988–2989.

Winkler, R. C., Teigland, J. J., Munger, P. F., & Kranzler, G. D. (1965). The effects of selected counseling and remedial techniques on underachieving elementary school students. *Journal of Counseling Psychology, 12*(4), 384–387.

Winnicott, D. W. (1951). *Collected papers.* London: Tavistock Publications.

Winnicott, D. W. (1957). *The child and the family.* London: Tavistock Publications.

Winthrope, S. (1988). *Underachieving personality styles in the workplace: Implications for management.* Unpublished doctoral proposal, Department of Psychology, York University, Toronto, ON.

Witherspoon, P., & Melberg, M. (1959). The relation between GPA and sectional scores on the Guilford-Zimmerman Temperament Survey. *Educational Psychology Measurement, 19,* 673–674.

Wittmaier, B. C. (1976). Low test anxiety as a potential indicator of underachievement. *Measurement & Evaluation in Guidance, 9*(3), 146–151.

Wittmer, J. (1969). The effects of counseling and tutoring on the attitudes and achievement of seventh grade underachievers. *School Counselor, 16,* 287–290.

Wittmer, J., & Ferinden, F. (1971). The effects of group counseling on the attitude and GPA of deprived Negro underachievers: With a profile of the counselor's activity. *Comparative Group Studies, 2*(1), 43–52.

Woerner, M. G., Pollack, M., Rogalski, C., Pollack, Y., & Klein, D. F. (1972). A comparison of the school records of personality disorders, schizophrenics, and their sibs. In M. Roff, N. Robins, & M. Pollack (Eds.), *Life History Research in Psychopathology* (Vol. 2, pp. 47–65). Minneapolis: University of Minnesota Press.

Wold, R. M. (Ed.). (1969). *Visual and perceptual aspects for the achieving and underachieving child.* Seattle, WA: Special Child Publications.

Wolfe, J. A., Fantuzzo, J., & Wolter, C. (1984). Student-administered group-oriented contingencies: A method of combining group-oriented contingencies and self-directed behavior to increase academic productivity. *Child & Family Behavior Therapy, 6*(3), 45–60.

Wolkon, G. H., & Levinger, G. (1965). Birth order and need for achievement. *Psychological Reports, 16,* 73–74.

Wolpe, J., & Lazarus, A. A. (1966). *Behavior therapy techniques: A guide to the treatment of neuroses.* London: Pergamon Press.

Wolpe, J., & Reyna, L. J. (Eds.). (1976). *Behavior therapy in psychiatric practice.* New York: Pergamon Press.

Wong, B. (1980). Activating the inactive learner. *Learning Disability Quarterly, 3,* 29–37.

Wood, R. (1984). Doubts about "underachievement," particularly as operationalized by Yule, Lansdown & Urbanowicz. *British Journal of Clinical Psychology, 23*(3), 231–232.

Woodrow, H. (1946). The ability to learn. *Psychological Review, 53,* 147–158.

Woodruff, A. D. (1949). Motivation theory and educational practice. *Journal of Educational Psychology, 40,* 33–40.

Wrightstone, J. W. (1948). Evaluating achievement. *Childhood Education, 24,* 253–259.

Wunderlich, R. C. (1974). Children and what they do. *Academic Therapy, 9*(6), 403–405.

Wyer, R. S., Jr. (1967). Behavioral correlates of academic achievement: Conformity under achievement- and affiliation-incentive conditions. *Journal of Personality & Social Psychology, 6*(3), 255–263.

Yabuki, S. (1971). [An ego-psychological approach to underachievement: Case studies on learning blocks as ego-defense]. *Japanese Journal of Educational Psychology, 19*(4), 210–220.

Yelvington, J. A. (1968). An exploratory study of the effects of interactions between cognitive abilities and instructional treatments upon attitudes, achievements, and retention. *Dissertation Abstracts, 29*(5-A), 1460–1461.

Ysseldyke, J. E., Algozzine, B., Shinn, M. R., & McGue, M. (1982). Similarities and differences between low achievers and students classified learning disabled. *Journal of Special Education, 16*(1), 73–85.

Yule, W. (1984). The operationalizing of "underachievement": Doubts dispelled. *British Journal of Clinical Psychology, 23*(3), 233–234.

Zajonc, R. B. (1983). Validating the confluence model. *Psychological Bulletin, 93,* 457–480.

Zajonc, R. B., & Bargh, J. (1980). The confluence model: Parameter estimation for six divergent data sets on family factors and intelligence. *Intelligence, 4,* 349–361.

Zajonc, R. B., Markus, H., & Markus, G. B. (1979). The birth order puzzle. *Journal of Personality and Social Psychology, 37,* 1325–1341.

Zani, L. P. (1969). Intensive vs. protracted counselor directed group counseling with under-achieving secondary school students. *Dissertation Abstracts International, 30*(5-A), 1834–1835.

Zeeman, R. D. (1978). Academic self-concept and school behavior in alienated secondary pupils. *Dissertation Abstracts International, 39*(3-A), 1452–1453.

Zeeman, R. D. (1982). Creating change in academic self-concept and school behavior in alienated school students. *School Psychology Review, 11*(4), 459–461.

Zeff, S. B. (1977). A humanistic approach to helping underachieving students. *Social Casework, 58,* 359–365.

Zerfoss, K. P. (1946). A note on the diagnosis and treatment of scholastic difficulties. *Educational and Psychological Measurement, 6,* 269–272.

Zilli, M. G. (1971). Reasons why the gifted adolescent underachieves and some implications of guidance and counseling to this problem. *Gifted Child Quarterly, 15*(4), 279–292.

Ziv, A., Rimon, J., & Doni, M. (1977). Parental perception and self-concept of gifted and average underachievers. *Perceptual & Motor Skills, 44*(2), 563–568.

Zuccone, C. F., & Amerikaner, M. (1986). Counseling gifted underachievers: A family systems approach. *Journal of Counseling and Development, 64,* 590–592.

Author Index

Note: Page numbers in italics indicate references.

Subject Index